Sir Herbert Baker

Sir Herbert Baker

Architect to the British Empire

JOHN STEWART

McFarland & Company, Inc., Publishers
Jefferson, North Carolina

This book has undergone peer review.

ISBN (print) 978-1-4766-8434-5
ISBN (ebook) 978-1-4766-4443-1

Library of Congress and British Library
cataloguing data are available

Library of Congress Control Number 2021050587

Front cover image: Sir Herbert Baker at the unveiling
of his memorial at Tyne Cot, France. Credit Michael Baker.

Printed in the United States of America

*McFarland & Company, Inc., Publishers
Box 611, Jefferson, North Carolina 28640
www.mcfarlandpub.com*

To my uncles Malcolm and Munro

Acknowledgments

Researching and writing this book has been a great pleasure, not least because of the enthusiastic help that I have received from a considerable number of people. First among these is Michael Baker, Sir Herbert's eldest grandson, who with his wife Caroline have hosted my many visits to their home in Bristol as I worked my way through their extensive family archive of letters and photographs. Michael has been my guide, adviser and regular decipherer of Sir Herbert's handwriting throughout the process. I'd also like to thank all other Bakers for their contributions.

I am also indebted to Doreen Greig and Michael Keath, both of whom have previously written of Sir Herbert's life and architecture during his years in South Africa. Doreen Greig's research and schedules of Baker buildings in particular have been invaluable, and also in South Africa I have had great help from Frank Gaylard and his enthusiastic team at artefacts.co.za.

I have also been assisted by both the archivists of the Royal Institute of British Architects who hold Baker's professional archive at the Victoria and Albert Museum and the incredibly helpful archivists of the Bank of England, as well as numerous Baker-building owners and occupiers who have allowed me access to the beautiful interiors of their buildings.

Finally, I'd like to once more thank my wife Sue for her constant encouragement and support, checking of births, deaths and marriages, passenger lists and newspaper articles, indexing, and her companionship on numerous building visits across the globe.

Table of Contents

Acknowledgments   vi

Preface   1

Introduction   2

  1. 1862–1892: "The Spirit of England"   5

  2. 1892–1896: "Land of Hope and Glory"   20

  3. 1897–1901: "Imperial March"   31

  4. 1901–1904: "The Light of Life"   51

  5. 1904–1909: "The Pipes of Pan"   65

  6. 1909–1912: "Civic Fanfare"   84

  7. 1912–1913: "The Crown of India"   103

  8. 1913–1915: "A Song of Union"   116

  9. 1915–1917: "A War Song"   137

10. 1917–1921: "For the Fallen"   152

11. 1921–1925: "Merchant Adventurers"   172

12. 1925–1931: "Pageant of Empire"   194

13. 1931–1946: "Through the Long Days"   217

Epilogue: "Fate's Discourtesy"   241

Chapter Notes   243

Bibliography   257

Index   259

Preface

This is the first full biography of the eminent British architect Sir Herbert Baker, 1862–1946. Sir Herbert Baker was not only one of the most successful and prolific architects of his generation, he also contributed more than any other architect to the celebration and proclamation of Imperial Britain throughout almost every part of its former empire in addition to numerous notable buildings in England, such as the rebuilding of the Bank of England, South Africa House, India House and Church House in London and Rhodes House in Oxford. He was an intimate friend of Cecil Rhodes, Jan Smuts, Rudyard Kipling and Lawrence of Arabia and lived and worked with "Milner's Kindergarten" in South Africa, a group of young men who included John Buchan, Lionel Curtis and Fabian Ware.

In India, he built New Delhi as an equal partner with Edwin Lutyens and, controversially, this book tells the tale of their famous dispute from Baker's perspective for the first time. The two architects also worked together for the Commonwealth War Graves Commission designing War Memorials throughout England, France and Belgium—Tyne Cot, the largest of all the First World War cemeteries, being designed by Baker. In his day, he was lauded; he was knighted in 1926, presented with the RIBA's Gold Medal in 1927 and buried in Westminster Abbey in 1946. He is still regarded as South Africa's leading architect but elsewhere his reputation has been undermined. I believe that Baker's work around the globe deserves to be drawn together and considered as a whole for the first time both architecturally and in his role as a leading contributor to the art of the former British Empire.

If Baker's friend Rudyard Kipling was the Poet Laureate to the Empire, then Baker was its Architect, and their contemporary Sir Edward Elgar its leading composer. Consequently, I have named each chapter of this book after one of Elgar's works, given in "*Italics.*"

1

Introduction

Every year, the Royal Institute of British Architects (RIBA) awards its Royal Gold Medal to an architect, of any nationality, who has made a truly outstanding contribution to the art of architecture. Their names are carved in stone in the entrance hall of the RIBA's headquarters building in Portland Place in London. It's an impressive list, starting with Charles Cockerell and including Frank Lloyd Wright, Sir Charles Barry, Alvar Aalto, Sir George Gilbert Scott, Le Corbusier, Richard Rogers, Alfred Waterhouse and, in the midst of this role call of the greatest architects of the 19th, 20th and 21st centuries, is one Sir Herbert Baker, who was awarded the medal at a banquet held in his honor on the 24th of June 1927. That London summer evening of celebration represented the pinnacle of both his career and his highly-valued professional reputation, which was soon to come under sustained attack.

His work is relatively little-known today and usually summed up, by those who have heard of him, as "the architect who demolished Soane's Bank of England." There is a vague recollection that he worked with, and fell out with, Sir Edwin Lutyens in New Delhi, but in some kind of a bumbling supporting role, which nevertheless allowed him to make a mistake which damaged the great Sir Edwin's design—"his Bakerloo"—as he wittily called it. The few portrayals of him make it clear that he lacked both Lutyens' natural brilliance as an architect and certainly his wit, with Baker often described as a dull "committee man." In South Africa, where he worked for many years, he is better known, principally as the architect of Cecil Rhodes' house in Cape Town—which today is hardly likely to further enhance his reputation. His work is inextricably linked to the British Empire and the subjugation of its native peoples and their cultures, and from our 21st-century post-colonial perspective, he (and almost all his peers) would be described as racist, sexist, anti–Semitic, homophobic and proudly xenophobic. And, as if all this were not bad enough, most of his architecture is Classical and thus held in contempt by what are now several generations of Modernists who have been trained to reject the past and to regard Classical architecture as a reactionary irrelevance. Sir Nikolaus Pevsner, that pioneering Modernist and one-time arbiter of British architectural taste, dismissed Baker as "naive and arrogant." He remains an unfashionable enigma.

But the more I delved and, more importantly, the more I studied his work, the more convinced I became that he was both an exceptional architect and, in the context of his age, a man of the highest integrity. More than that of any other architect, his work celebrated the British Empire, which he firmly believed to be a civilizing force for good in a violent and divided world. Far from being naive, he was a well-respected friend of many of the leading figures of his age including Cecil Rhodes, Rudyard Kipling, Jan Smuts,

John Buchan and Lawrence of Arabia and far from being arrogant, his architecture consistently shows a sympathy for its setting, his clients and the users of his buildings which many of his contemporaries often lacked. He is largely responsible for saving Soane's great encircling wall at the Bank of England, was an equal partner of Lutyens in New Delhi and, as to being responsible for an error there, was shamefully blamed by Lutyens for his own mistake.

His life story is fascinating and little known—his best architecture is outstanding (as his contemporaries recognized) and his reputation and contribution to British architecture is now long overdue for reassessment.

1

1862–1892

"The Spirit of England" (Op. 80)

Unusually, this tale starts and ends in the same place—a small, rather elegant, red-brick manor house called "Owletts" in the county of Kent in the southeast corner of England. Herbert Baker was born there on the 9th of June 1862 and died there, aged 81, on the 4th of February 1946. Unlike the earlier members of his family however, rather than being buried a little further up the hill in Cobham churchyard, Herbert, or Sir Herbert as he had by then become, was buried in the nave of Westminster Abbey—perhaps the greatest compliment that his beloved England could have paid him.

It was an honor that was well deserved, for the young boy who had been born and raised in the countryside of rural Kent had become one of the greatest and most prolific architects of his generation; a loyal and committed servant of imperial Britain; and whose buildings, more than those of any other architect, celebrated what he sincerely believed to be its benign, civilizing influence around the globe. The sheer quantity of his output is quite breath-taking—the Indian Parliament and government buildings in New Delhi, the South African government buildings in Pretoria, three cathedrals, numerous churches, several embassies, railway stations, offices and banks (including the rebuilding of the Bank of England in the City of London), university buildings, medical research facilities, schools, houses and war memorials throughout almost every country of what was then the British Empire. It was a career that, as a boy, he could hardly have dreamed of, that was achieved, as with so many successful people before and since in every field of human endeavor, through his determination, dedication to his craft and relentless hard work, rather than a natural brilliance. He lived by a set of fundamental beliefs that were developed during his childhood in Kent and which stayed with him throughout his long life.

Herbert was the fourth son of Thomas Henry Baker and Frances Georgiana Baker, one of twelve children—nine brothers and one sister—two further sisters having died when infants. Thomas Henry, like several of his forebears, was a local landowner, farmer and magistrate, and his family had lived at Owletts since its purchase by his great-great-grandfather in 1790 along with its surrounding farms. An inscription on one of its two great red brick chimneystacks suggests an initial construction date of 1683 while its richly-molded hall ceiling offers a completion date of 1684. These were prosperous times for landowners, and Herbert's mother was assisted in the running of the household by a staff of nine servants. As the family grew through the 1860s and '70s, the children moved into the upper floors of the house with the servants accommodated in a

"Owletts," the Kent home of Herbert Baker (author's collection).

newly-built wing to the rear. It was a comfortable and relatively wealthy upper-middle class household, which, while socially inferior to the Earls of Darnley who lived in nearby Cobham Hall, was socially superior to every other family in Cobham.

Within this lively, male-dominated environment, Herbert was an exceptionally quiet child. By his own admission he recalled that he "was very backward as a child, and I could not talk, my family records, until I was four years old."[1] What was then regarded as "backward," we would now describe as shy, quiet or introverted, and these were character traits which, though increasingly well concealed, he would exhibit throughout the rest of his life. But as he grew, and grew in confidence, he soon joined his brothers roaming freely through both their family estate and eventually the surrounding countryside and villages. It was an idyllic childhood and with no shortage of companions, one filled with sport—both cricket and football and, as they grew older, "shooting for the pot." Their father captained the village cricket team for whom they soon began to make appearances before becoming regulars every summer Saturday. He and his younger brother Alfred became inseparable and roamed by day and night.

Church on Sunday was obligatory for all the family and the servants, and young Herbert soon developed a strong Christian faith, valuing the quiet time for reflection which church offered every week, rather than resenting its intrusion into his weekend. But for Herbert in particular among the family, it was the countryside of Kent that held the greatest interest and attraction for, as he noted at length in his biography, the area around Cobham was steeped in the history of England. Watling Street, the ancient Roman road connecting the port of Dover on the coast with London, ran through the Bakers' estate, the Pilgrim's Way to Canterbury lay nearby, and he imagined "the eight black horses that carried the Black Prince on his last journey to his tomb in the choir in Canterbury Cathedral ... ambling through our woods."[2] Vikings, knights and Norman invaders had all passed this way en route from the coast to London, and Herbert's imagination was fired with tales of their adventures and "derring-do."

It was only natural that this fascination with the past should move to its relics—the ancient local buildings in the neighborhood—the 13th-century Cobham Church, the half-timbered cottages of the village and not least their cousins' 14th-century hall of Nurstead Court in the neighboring parish of Meopham. Soon sketching and brass-rubbing were added to his pastimes and Herbert began to develop a bond with the countryside of Kent that was sustained throughout his life, reappearing in his later work in flint walls, oak trusses, clay tiles and many other elements of the Kent vernacular. He quotes Ruskin in his biography—"In the children of noble races, trained in surrounding art ... here is an intense delight in the landscape of their country as *memorial*; a sense not taught to them, innate ... the obedience and the peace of ages having extended gradually the glory of revered ancestors also to the ancestral land."[3]

This enchantment with the past and its tales of chivalry and conquest would have been reinforced by his reading, both of history and fiction: the Knights of the Round Table, the Crusaders, Henry the Fifth at Agincourt, Drake and the Armada and Sir Walter Raleigh, bringing back news to Elizabeth the First of a new "Land of Promise" beyond the Atlantic Ocean. Like most of his Victorian adolescent contemporaries, Baker would have admired their nobility and codes of honor and been fascinated by their exploits, chivalry, weapons and heraldry. If this were not sufficient inspiration to spark his young imagination, there were also the more recent heroes of the British Empire—the soldiers and sailors who through their enterprise and bravery were slowly turning the world map red: Clive of India, James Wolfe in Quebec, Horatio Nelson, and the missionaries too (whom almost every contemporary Briton believed to be taking the Word of God to various heathen lands), especially Livingstone and Stanley, whose famous meeting in darkest Africa in November 1871 took place when young Herbert was just nine. Both he and several of his brothers would serve the mighty British Empire in an unshakable belief that, in their own way, they were helping to uplift the world.

Herbert and Alfred Baker (courtesy Michael Baker).

Initially, Herbert's schooling was erratic. It commenced

with "some terms in a dame's school in the old Elizabethan Restoration House, Rochester," followed by "some teaching at a vicarage two miles away"[4] which ill-prepared him for an unexpected entrance examination for Haileybury School[5] where his knowledge of the classics led to his failure and exclusion and a memory of "sitting all forlorn on my school box, which smelt of meat pies, at the station on my retreat homeward."[6] Fortunately, Tonbridge School, which was just 20 miles from Cobham, was less discerning and allowed both Herbert's admission and later, that of five of his younger brothers.

Tonbridge, founded in 1553, was then a minor public (that is, private) school with an emphasis more on developing good character than academic achievement. Like so many of the schools which catered for the middle and upper classes in late Victorian England, its aim was to produce "Christian gentlemen" and "good sports." Sport was seen as crucial in instilling values of fair play, discipline and the creation of an "esprit de corps" as well as developing the endurance and physical fitness required to equip the boys for service in the colonies. It was also no coincidence that Baker's headmaster at Tonbridge was the Rev. Dr. T. B. Rowe, who had been preceded and was succeeded by other "men of the cloth." Daily services in the school chapel further reinforced young Baker's interest in the mystery, history and symbolism of the church and he soon developed what was to be an unwavering Christian faith.

While he might have lacked the classical preparation sought by Haileybury, his childhood had prepared him perfectly for Tonbridge and despite his essentially quiet and thoughtful nature, fortunately, he excelled at sports, becoming captain of both the

Herbert (center) as Captain of Tonbridge School cricket team with Alfred behind, 1881 (courtesy Michael Baker).

school cricket and football teams. The photograph of him with his cricket team taken in 1881 shows a relaxed, calm, quietly confident leader—a role he assumed at Tonbridge and which he would later develop.[7] The achievement of this level of sporting success would have conferred upon him a quite extraordinary status within the school community, as Robert Graves recalled from his time at Charterhouse—"The 'bloods' (*members of the cricket and football elevens*) … were the ruling caste at Charterhouse; the eleventh man in the football eleven, though he might be a member of the under-fourth form, enjoyed far more prestige than the most brilliant scholar in the sixth."[8] The sincere regret with which his housemaster J. A. Babington wrote to his mother when Baker finally left Tonbridge emphasized the high regard in which he was held—"The boy who will succeed Herbert as Captain of the eleven & therefore as Leader in Games, is, I regret to say, not at all suited for so important a post. And it would have been a very great gain to the whole school if Herbert could have retained his present position for a time longer. I mention this as a proof how very sincerely we shall all lament his loss. Indeed, I do not think in the course of my whole school experience I have ever met a boy who bore his Athletic honors more modestly & more simply & more worthily in every way than Herbert has done."[9] Baker continued to either play cricket, run or ride, throughout his life both to maintain his fitness and increase his endurance, as he had been taught at school, with Juvenal's advice to his fellow Roman citizens, *Mens Sana in Corpore Sano*, remaining a guiding proverb.

Throughout most of his time at Tonbridge, he was particularly close to his science master Charles Whitmell, who took him on summer walking tours to Cornwall, the Welsh mountains, the Lake District and the Yorkshire fells, and it was Whitmell who first encouraged Baker's life-long interest in poetry (including his ability to quote at length from memory) with Wordsworth and the Lake Poets his enduring favorites.[10] It is said that he carried with him a small volume of Wordsworth at all times and, while this may be apocryphal, his love for both the Bard of the Lakes and for the beauty of the Lake District itself, where he often later holidayed and walked, was unquestionable. It was a wild and rugged landscape, in complete contrast to the fields and woods of Kent, but only emphasized for Baker the extraordinary variety and beauty of his beloved England. So, despite his quiet nature, we now have a young man who has the courage and strength of character to lead his school in the "manly" pursuits of cricket and football and also the sensitivity to lose himself in verse. By all accounts his childhood in Kent and education at Tonbridge had turned out what Odette Keun (a Dutch journalist who settled in England) described as the perfect Englishman—"Courtesy, kindness, obligingness, tolerance, moderation, self-control, fair play, a cheerful temper, pleasant manners, calmness, stoicism."[11]

By his final year at Tonbridge he had resolved to become an architect and he dropped his study of the classics to focus on mathematics and mechanics, which he thought would be more relevant. Reassured by his elder cousin Arthur Baker's success in establishing an architectural practice in London, his parents no doubt believed architecture to be a suitable career for a young man who had never excelled academically and whom they thought was good at drawing. And so at the age of 19, as his best friend and younger brother Alfred's thoughts turned to a career serving in the imperial army, Baker was articled to his elder cousin and commenced what was to be a long and rather dull architectural pupilage.

The study of architecture in Victorian Britain was very different from today's full-time university courses. It involved first being accepted for employment by a qualified architect, signing "articles" with them (effectively a contract of employment to cover the duration of their initial training of three to five years) and then supplementing the practical experience gained each day in the office with evening classes at a variety of schools of architecture. In London in the 1880s there were two principal options available for architectural training: the Architectural Association, which was founded as Britain's first dedicated school of architecture in 1847, and the Royal Academy founded in 1768 by Sir Joshua Reynolds. At the Royal Academy pupils attended lectures by academicians who also set design projects and publicly critiqued them, and thus the pupils could find themselves having their work reviewed by no less than Norman Shaw, Alfred Waterhouse or George Street. Baker attended both schools to ensure that his training covered all aspects of architectural practice as well as attending lectures at a number of the Guild Halls on practical matters of construction. One of his diaries from this period gives a flavor of this vagabond architectural education, referring to lectures on stained glass, building design, construction, history of architecture and photography at the Architectural Association, a lecture at Carpenters' Hall on timber, concrete and stonework, still-life classes at the Kensington Museum, visits with the Architectural Association to George and Peto's houses in Collingham Road and Street's Law Courts and his own purchase of Vitruvius.[12] The Royal Institute of British Architects had been formed in 1834 and granted its royal charter in 1837. In 1882, just after Baker had commenced his pupilage, it introduced a compulsory examination for admission to its ranks as an associate and this immediately became the focus for his studies.

The choice of his elder cousin's office for his pupilage must have been fairly straightforward, not least because the normal pupil's fee of £300 guineas was open to negotiation within the family, and by the 1880s Herbert's father's wealth had reduced considerably (as a result of both the cost of the private education of his many sons and the start of the great depression in British agriculture). Thus Herbert's "articles" were signed in September 1881 confirming a four-year pupilage with his elder cousin. While being far from one of the leading London architectural practices, Arthur had the considerable pedigree of having been articled to the great George Gilbert Scott, the leader of the Gothic Revival Movement, for whom he had worked for 14 years. He not only shared Scott's penchant for Gothic but also his habit of over-restoring existing churches with his efforts on the restoration of Gyffylliog Church in Wales, for example, being described as "wanton and senseless destruction."[13] Most of the practice's workload was ecclesiastical and did include a number of notable new Gothic Revival churches such as St. Lawrence in Northampton and St. Paul's in Kensington, London.

As with most office life, Baker soon settled into a familiar pattern—a full day's work in the office, initially tracing and copying but soon producing construction details and specifications, followed by evenings spent in lectures, sketching or working on various training assignments—a train to Cobham most weekends with cricket on Saturday and church on Sunday followed by walking, riding or sketching before the early train back up to London on Monday morning. Occasionally, weekends were spent on sketching trips throughout England and Wales with Baker carefully recording details of buildings wherever he traveled, much of which inspired his later work. He records in his biography that he later realized "what I missed by not going to a university, in the making of friends and in communion of youthful intelligence" but concludes that "there were compensations, however, in the early close apprenticeship to my profession, and the absence of the attraction of society, leaving undisturbed evenings spent in museums—I knew South Kensington Museum intimately."[14]

The year of 1884 brought a first trip to the European continent, spent sketching in Holland and Belgium before his appointment by Arthur as Clerk of Works for the construction of the new Church of St. Padern in Llanberis, North Wales. This involved Herbert supervising the building operations on-site on his cousin's behalf and appears to have provided the young pupil with both a wealth of practical experience as well as a welcome escape from office routine. Herbert, as we would now expect, made the most of his time in North Wales, exploring and sketching the lakes, mountains, churches, castles, gardens and local vernacular buildings and, with his elder cousin's aid, soon beginning

S. PADARN CHURCH. LLANBERIS. N.WALES.

Herbert's perspective drawing of St. Padarn Church, Llanberis, Wales (courtesy Michael Baker).

a measured survey of Plas Mawr, a large Elizabethan manor house designed by Robert Wynn (and built between 1576 and 1585) in the center of Conwy. Their efforts resulted in a modest publication in 1888, *Plas Mawr, Conwy, N. Wales*, in which Arthur kindly gave his younger cousin equal billing. More importantly for Herbert, Plas Mawr contained the seeds of many of his future domestic interiors, and its plain white plastered walls, mighty timber trusses and extensive heraldry would reappear in years to come in his own designs for houses around the globe. Though his pupilage was completed in September 1885, Herbert continued to work for his cousin until the summer of 1886, while actively seeking a new appointment to further develop his skills in the more creative atmosphere of one of London's leading practices.

Herbert was now 24—a tall, lean athletic figure, with five years of practical architectural experience—had progressed well in his studies, and if his various drawings from this period (including his very fine perspective of Llanberis Church of 1886) are considered, had become a very competent draftsman in both two and three dimensions. With the end of his time with Arthur near, he celebrated with his first tour of Italy along with several of his fellow students, which his diary captures beautifully—

> Train 10:50 to Milan with Cresswell, Woodthorpe, Taylor, Marks and Cruicks—Dover Calais, Basle, Lucerne, reached Milan 7:45—Hotel Bretagne poor—visited Duomo and various other churches—Verona-Hotel de Londres—expensive but good—to Venice—Hotel D'Angleterre—San Giorgio Maggiore—gondola to "San Redontore"—large, correct fine dome, undecorated and ugly—left for Florence to Sienna—Publico & Duomo—very much charmed with both—to Orvieto—to Rome—interior of St Peters with which I was much impressed—wet most days—Tivoli—the most beautiful place & spent very jolly time there—bought photos in evening—train to Naples—then on to Pisa that evening—went up Tower of Pisa with an American—to Lucca—only one in the Hotel—back to Florence—to Genoa (Palazzo Rosso) on to Pavia—to Certosa and to Lugano that evening—left Lugano for England via Basle—Calais to Cobham.[15]

This was very much a late Victorian rite of passage for any serious young architect, visiting and experiencing firsthand the key buildings of both medieval and Renaissance Italy, but it's interesting in Baker's case that among everything that he had seen, it was Tivoli, with both Hadrian's Villa and the great romantic terraced gardens of the Villa D'Este, which he noted as "the most beautiful place" and whose cascading terraces would later reappear in many of his own works. For most of his companions this tour was a once-in-a-lifetime opportunity, but for Baker it was a journey that would be repeated several times more, in very different circumstances.

His time with Arthur at 14 Warwick Gardens, Kensington, was over and on Monday the 18th of October 1886, he commenced work with one of the most illustrious practices in London—the partnership of Ernest George and Harold Peto at 14 Maddox Street, Mayfair. George and Peto were second only in reputation to the great Richard Norman Shaw (1831–1912) himself. In recognition of his architectural achievements, George was awarded the RIBA Gold Medal in 1896 (an honor his pupils Baker, Lutyens and Dawber would much later all receive). For Baker it was a move from a sleepy Gothic Revival backwater to the fast lane of Victorian architectural practice, and fortunately we have a record of the organization of the office—"Apart from the drawing office, the Maddox Street office consisted of a waiting room, a manager's office and two private rooms for the partners. The drawing office staff comprised, on average, six articled pupils and one or two paid assistants; the office manager dealt with the accounts and general administration and a number of clerks of works handled site supervision."[16] Baker joined as "an improver" but by 1887 had proved himself so invaluable to the partners that he was promoted to "leading assistant."

Harold Ainsworth Peto (1854–1933), the second of George's three consecutive partners in practice, was a gifted architect who went on to enjoy a very successful career as an outstanding garden designer, completing a number of significant late Victorian and Edwardian formal gardens ranging from the sumptuous Buscot Park in Oxfordshire (1904) to the Italianate Garnish Island in the South-West region of Ireland (1910), but it was George who represented the beating heart of the practice, with Peto's role, in contemporary parlance, being largely one of "business development."

Ernest George, like Baker, was a modest man, a fine watercolorist who spent his

Number 7 Collingham Gardens, 1888, by George and Peto (author's collection).

summers sketching and painting on the European continent, bringing back architectural ideas and details for inclusion in his work. As Jane Ridley, Lutyens' biographer (and great-granddaughter) recounted—"George's own room was oak-panelled in the Dutch style. George loved beautiful things, and antique dealers called regularly with Persian rugs, Delft plates and Japanese china. He furnished the windows with Flemish shutters and patterned them with panes of Dutch and German stained glass."[17] His buildings in the 1880s and '90s were a hybrid of Flemish architecture and the then-fashionable Queen Anne style with 1–18 Collingham Gardens (1881–4), which Baker had visited with his class from the Architectural Association, an excellent example. George borrowed freely from various Flanders merchants' houses and cloth halls to produce sumptuous town houses with Dutch gables and bands of horizontal windows contrasting with vertical bays in red brick with Portland stone or terracotta dressings. Osbert Lancaster, the cartoonist, sneeringly described the style as "Pont Street Dutch," but George's houses still make a rich and refreshing interlude in the orderly stuccoed streets of West London.[18] In his country houses, of which there were many vast piles, George adopted traditional English plans—the Elizabethan "H" and "E" plans with great Jacobean bay windows rising through several stories to picturesque gables (these features being later much imitated by all his pupils in their own work). His domestic interiors are of particular interest in the context of Baker's designs with their Dutch and Tudor influences evoked in richly carved and paneled woodwork which contrasted with complex, molded, stark white plaster ceilings. George's later public buildings included both Golders Green Crematorium (1905) and the Royal Academy of Music on the Marylebone Road (1911).

His design methodology appears to have been almost entirely picturesque as Margaret Richardson suggested—"He did not start working on a plan or section—but with a brilliant sepia perspective!"[19] At a time when many successful architects were either leaving many details of their domestic interiors to their assistants or even contractor decorators, George maintained tight design control of every element, regularly turning out full-size drawings of everything from door handles to covings or balustrades. As a result, his assistants, led by Baker, were required to support George in almost every other area of practice: in the preparation of presentation drawings, transforming George's sketches into construction drawings, managing the projects on a day-to-day basis and dealing with the building contractors. In the context of Baker's development as an architect it's therefore important to recognize that while this provided a truly excellent grounding in all professional matters it didn't involve George's leading assistant in designing any of the practice's buildings, a task over which George and his partners maintained total control. For an extremely competent introvert like Baker, it was in many ways an ideal role and one at which he excelled.

Despite this limitation, a place as an assistant in George and Peto's office was still a much-sought-after position, indeed such was the caliber of the practice's pupils and assistants that it was christened "the Eton of Architects' Offices," by Darcy Braddell, one of George's pupils, who went on to describe how assistants "were invited to cut their initials in their bench and inlay them with red sealing wax."[20] The list of talented assistants in addition to Baker is a long one and includes a number of important Arts and Crafts architects—Guy Dawber (1861–1938, who eventually took over George's practice), Robert Weir Schultz (1860–1951), Herbert Read (died 1935), John Bradshaw Gass (1855–1938), Ethel Mary Charles (1871–1962, the first woman to be elected as a member of the RIBA) and most significantly in terms of both this tale and his later outstanding achievements, the young Edwin Lutyens.

In addition to his considerable responsibilities in the office, Baker continued his architectural studies and now broadened them significantly by spending, in his own words, "evenings at the Bohemian discussions at the Art Workers Guild."[21] While his formal education was spent on practicalities and the classics and his daily work still dominated by historicism (albeit now of a "freer" kind), the guild offered Baker something much more radical and challenging. It had been formed by a number of pupils and assistants from Shaw's office in 1883 in the spirit of the great craft guilds of the Middle Ages. While its inspiration (like that of the earlier Pre-Raphaelite Brotherhood) may have been some imagined medieval age of chivalry and craftsmanship, its politics, which the conservative Baker would almost certainly have found rather extreme, were very much focused on social reform. Their principal concern, however, was the apparent decline of the artistic basis of architecture and the increasing separation of art and architecture. They believed that what was needed was a new "Guild of Artists" with architects, painters and sculptors among its members, with founding member William Lethaby stating, "The drifting apart of architecture, painting and sculpture is shown on the one hand in the trade decoration of our buildings, and on the other in the subject-painting and portrait-sculpture of our galleries. But any art-revival can only be on the lines of the unity of all the aesthetic arts."[22] At its first meeting it was settled that the group should consist of craftsmen, designers, architects and artists, all of whom should meet on an equal footing. Baker bought whole-heartedly into this concept of artistic unity and the role of artists and craftsmen in contributing to a collective architectural vision, and it was a principle which would be sustained throughout his long career.

The guild saw the separation of the arts running in parallel with the mechanization of construction to the exclusion of creative craftsmen—the very men whom they believed had in the past been capable of constructing the great Gothic cathedrals through collaboration and collective knowledge alone. Handicrafts and traditional techniques of construction therefore took on a new importance for the guild and its followers (even if it did condemn many workmen to spending days laboriously cutting floorboards by hand for example, rather than using modern machinery). There was an honesty and a romantic simplicity to both the guild's philosophy and soon to its early products, that appealed immediately to Baker, the countryman.[23]

When it came to social and political theory, their discussions were fueled by the writings of Pugin, Morris and Ruskin who were critical of the emerging industrial society and the standardized products of its manufacturing processes—its "dark satanic mills,"[24] which condemned workers to a city life of repetitive mindless drudgery rather than one of noble and dignified honest toil in the fresh air of the countryside (which, in reality, most had fled to escape the crushing poverty). For Baker, perhaps unsurprisingly, it was Ruskin's architectural theories rather than Morris's socialism which appear to have had the most impact. Ruskin believed that a truly Christian and humane architecture *must* be imperfect—what he called "Savage." For an impressionable young architectural student, Ruskin's dogmatism and easy-to-follow rules were naturally appealing. In *The Stones of Venice,* for example, he pronounced that artists should—"1. Never encourage the manufacture of any article not absolutely necessary, in the production of which *Invention* has no share. 2. Never demand an exact finish for its own sake, but only for some practical or noble end. 3. Never encourage imitation or copying of any kind, except for the sake of preserving record of great works."[25] As Peter Davey noted, these became "the rules of Ruskinian 'savageness' that for the next 50 years guided Arts and Crafts designers in everything they created from cathedrals to tea-pots."[26] In addition to the members of Shaw's office who had founded the guild, Baker also first met Reginald Blomfield there, and Blomfield described their biweekly gatherings at Barnard's Inn in Holborn—"Everyone smoked who wished to. The paper was read after which we adjourned for an interval in an adjoining room, for whiskies and sodas and other drinks, and then returned to the hall for discussion. These sometimes became vivacious!"[27]

A year after Baker had joined George and Peto another young pupil joined the firm, the 18-year-old Edwin Lutyens. These two young would-be architects could hardly have offered a greater contrast: Baker had completed a seven-year pupilage and was continuing with his studies towards associateship of the RIBA, while Lutyens had abandoned his architectural education at the South Kensington School of Art after just two years; Baker had attended public school, whereas Lutyens' education had been left largely to elder members of his family at home; Baker had been brought up in considerable comfort, while Lutyens' painter father had struggled to support his considerable brood; Baker was an athlete and a fine sportsman and enjoyed the company of his fellow men, while Lutyens had been a sickly child and was very much a loner; Baker was senior assistant, while Lutyens was the youngest member of the office and finally, Baker was very proud to have achieved his position at George and Peto, whereas Lutyens was desperately disappointed to have failed to secure a pupilage with his hero Norman Shaw. Despite these innumerable contrasts and a seven-year age gap, astonishingly, they soon struck up an unlikely friendship, with Baker later recalling—"I greatly enjoyed his company, his insight into some of the arcana of our art, and his wit and good stories," and though "he puzzled us at first … we soon found that he seemed to know by intuition some great truths of our art."[28] Christopher Hussey, Lutyens' biographer, astutely summed up their relationship—"From their earliest association Baker perceived and was deeply impressed by the quality of Lutyens as an architect," but "Baker entertained reservations too, for Lutyens' character. Serious and idealistic, he was amused but often shocked by his levity, though he might, on reflection, be disposed to agree with its aptness. A thoughtful reader, he had a memory as retentive for inspiring passages of literature as the other had for those of architecture. Lutyens mistrusted the trait, as confusing an architectural issue, no less instinctively than Baker mistrusted facetiousness as refusal to face a moral issue. Lutyens had the morality of an artist, which subordinates human to aesthetic values, and Baker the art of a moralist for whom the arts serve and illustrate virtues. Therein lay the excellences of each—and the limitations."[29]

They were to work together at George and Peto for only 18 months (Lutyens leaving in 1889 to undertake his first country house commission), but it was a relationship which would last their lifetimes, first turning from warm friendship to rivalry and eventually to bitterness over the next 60 years. Ernest George had a significant and incontrovertible influence on both men's early work which Baker later happily acknowledged, stating that what he had learned from him was "invaluable to me,"[30] whereas Lutyens' memory of his time at Maddox Street was that he "was sent at first to an architect whose name I forgot and was set to draw circles on oily paper. After two days I ran away."[31] Their differing recollections still speak volumes.

In September 1888, Baker toured Northern France visiting several chateaus in the Loire Valley, and a few weeks later we find him accompanied by Lutyens on a walking tour through Wales and Shropshire, with Baker sketching religiously as they went. Baker was both the better draftsman and sketch artist and Lutyens claimed to have no need to sketch, as one quick glance was sufficient for him to retain every detail of a building (a pronouncement that is somewhat undermined by the survival of 54 of his rather poor sketches from this period and a life-long habit of sketching on glass what he saw through it). They visited the ruins of Wenlock Abbey and Stokesay Castle with Lutyens later telling Baker that "all his timberwork … was based on what he saw at Stokesay."[32] Lutyens later recalled also visiting "the Wrekin which we climbed, and coming down ravenous we ate blackberries and I was sick, and thought that red fluid was my blood!"[33] The image of the tall athletic Baker striding up the Wrekin with the perspiring Lutyens stumbling in his wake would soon, however, be reversed.

In early 1889, following a number of minor commissions which Lutyens had carried out of his own accord during his pupilage, he was commissioned to design Crooksbury, a vacation home for Arthur Chapman, who had known Lutyens since his boyhood. And so, at the age of 19, with little architectural training or practical experience, Lutyens left George and Peto and established his own practice from his parents' house at 16 Onslow Square—an apparently reckless decision—but one that was nevertheless to begin a brilliant and astonishingly successful architectural career.

Lutyens' boldness must have deeply shocked Baker who after eight years of study and training still felt that he had much to learn. Shortly after Lutyens' departure, Baker entered the competition for the Royal Academy's Gold Medal, which if successful would have provided a year's study and further travel in Italy, but sadly his design for a city mansion was not selected. In November 1889, he sat and passed the examination for Associateship of the Royal Institute of British Architects finding himself "top of the list"[34] and the proud, if somewhat abashed, recipient of the Ashpital Prize for his year. His time in Maddox Street was drawing to a close, his long formal architectural education complete and so, with both he and his father now lacking the funds to purchase a partnership in a London firm, he returned to his native Kent to establish his own practice in the rather uninspiringly named town of Gravesend, just a few miles from Owletts.

There was to be no Crooksbury for Baker and almost all of his few first commissions appear to have been for the restoration of various Tudor timber houses in and around Gravesend. By now Lutyens (at 20) had been introduced to the great garden designer Gertrude Jekyll (then 46), who would be his mentor, both commissioning him to build Munstead Wood for her (completed 1896), further educating him in both the Surrey Vernacular and contemporary architecture (such as the work of Philip Webb whom Lutyens had been unaware of), and very helpfully introducing him to many of her friends and existing clients. Baker and Lutyens remained close throughout this period with Baker producing perspective drawings for several of Lutyens early commissions and being introduced himself to Jekyll, or "Bumps" as Lutyens had nicknamed her. As Baker later recalled of Lutyens and Jekyll—"This intimate friendship was, I think, the most valuable influence in his early career. She had a great personality and rare gifts; she was a skilled craftswoman and not only an expert gardener, a planter of flowers, but she had the painter's sense for their arrangement in colour harmonies. But her outstanding possession was the power to see, as a poet, the art and creation of home-making as a whole in relation to Life; the best simple English country life of her day, frugal yet rich in beauty and comfort; in the building and its furnishing and their homely craftsmanship; its garden uniting the house with surrounding nature; all in harmony and breathing the spirit of its creator."[35]

From his one-room, worryingly quiet office in Gravesend in 1891, even Baker's cousin Arthur's London practice must have then seemed to represent professional success and the road ahead must have looked long, hard and extremely uncertain. From a substantial role in central London in one of the best architectural practices in the country, he was now living at home once more and struggling to find work, never mind work of consequence as Lutyens already had. But his peaceful retirement to the countryside of Kent was not to last long. Fate was about to intervene in a most unexpected way that would completely transform his career and future life.

The discovery of diamonds in Griqualand in 1867 and the Witwatersrand gold rush of 1886 had led to a flood of emigrants to distant South Africa. In 1890, as Baker was setting up shop in Gravesend, his younger brother Lionel, then 20, had set off to seek his fortune in what was then the British Cape Colony on the very southern tip of the continent. The Cape had been of strategic importance as a staging post on the long sea journey from Europe to India for many centuries and indeed it was the Dutch East India Company who had established the first settlement which eventually became Cape Town in 1652. With the British dominance of India effectively established after the battle of Plassey in 1757, the British East India Company set their sights on the Cape as a key point on their trade route to England and thus Cape Town was taken by the British in 1795.[36] After a couple of switches of sovereignty in the interim, it was finally ceded to Britain with the Anglo-Dutch treaty of 1814, becoming the new capital of an expanding Cape Colony at which point most of the Dutch settlers undertook the "Great Trek" further north into Africa, where they formed their own republics. Rudyard Kipling visited Cape Town in 1891 and described it as "a sleepy, unkempt little place, where the *stoeps* of some of the older Dutch houses still jutted over the pavement. Occasionally cows strolled up the main streets which were full of coloured people."[37] By then the 18th-century Dutch town had largely fallen into decay and the few recent buildings such as the post office and brick Parliament house towered above the rest of the settlement from which tracks meandering off into the bush. The domestic accommodation ranged from brick or rendered one- or two-story houses, to larger apartments, complete with the verandas, fretwork, corrugated iron, bow and bay windows that were typical of almost any other minor colonial settlement of the British Empire at that time.

What soon attracted Lionel, the son of a Kent yeoman farmer, was not the gold (which was already transforming Johannesburg in the north into a settlement to rival Cape Town) but the potential for fruit farming. In the 1880s almost all the western Cape wine estates had been devastated by a phylloxera epidemic which had destroyed their vines. New vines, grafted onto disease-free American rootstock were soon planted but while they were getting established many of the farmers switched to growing fruit in the interim. Tales of how lucrative the Californian fruit industry had become, combined with the prospect of shipping fruit back to Europe in refrigerated vessels for the first time, created great excitement within the colony and Lionel was soon writing back to his father enthusiastically, as Baker himself later recounted—"The price of oranges was so much, we were told; a tree grows so many; a few thousand will make your fortune!" continuing, "My generous father, having already mortgaged his estate to the limit in order to send his nine sons to school, had nothing to spare. But squeeze out some money he did, though that last straw, added to the weight of losses in some bad farming years, compelled him to sell his estate with the exception of 25 acres of the homestead. It was an anxious decision for my parents to take. At their suggestion I agreed to go out to the Cape to report, and advise my brother about his plantation venture."[38] Herbert could hardly have refused—his parents were betting everything that they had on Lionel's success and all Herbert had to lose was a struggling Gravesend architectural practice.

He and Lionel were booked to sail in March 1892 and in February, just a few weeks before they departed, the first refrigerated shipment of peaches from South Africa arrived in perfect condition in London via the Union Castle Shipping Line. They sold for the extraordinary price of two shillings and thruppence each at Covent Garden market (at a time when a bank clerk's wages were 20 shillings a week).[39] Such news would have reassured the family that young Lionel was onto something and so the two brothers embarked on the *Norham Castle* at Southampton, bound for the Cape of Good Hope.

Herbert Baker in 1890 (courtesy Michael Baker).

Baker was well prepared for their adventure, he would soon be "30 years old and had reached some degree of maturity. His appearance was impressive and inspired confidence as he was exceptionally tall. Strongly built and athletic-looking; a rather small head made his figure seem larger than it was. His most striking feature was a pair of dark, deep-set eyes under imposing, bushy brows which, on occasion, revealed the penetrating mind which lay behind an honest and candid gaze."[40]

2

1892–1896

"Land of Hope and Glory" (Op. 39)

The South Africa that the *Norham Castle* was soon steaming towards was in the throes of dramatic colonial expansion—either bringing civilization to further tribes of barbarians or promoting the industrial-scale removal of most of their natural assets, depending largely on the date of one's viewpoint. There can be little doubt, however, that for the brothers, their quest was not entirely commercial but was also strongly tinged with the imperial idealism to which almost all serious young British men then subscribed wholeheartedly. Even Baker's architectural guiding star, aesthete John Ruskin, had preached in Oxford in 1870—"There is a destiny now possible to us, the highest ever set before a nation, to be accepted or refused. We are still undegenerate in race, a race mingled of the best northern blood. This is what England must either do or perish; she must found colonies as fast and as far as she is able, formed of her most energetic and worthiest men … their aim must be to advance the power of England by land and sea."[1] Sitting in Ruskin's audience in Oxford that day, no doubt listening particularly attentively, was a young Cecil Rhodes (1853–1902)—the man who would transform Baker's career from sleepy provincial practice to one of imperial glory.

By the time of the brothers' arrival at the Cape, Cecil Rhodes was already established as both the wealthiest and most powerful man in the entire continent. It was just a few months later in December of 1892, that Edward Linley Sambourne's famous cartoon depicting a pith-helmeted Rhodes bestriding Africa like some modern-day Colossus would first appear in *Punch* magazine.[2] Rhodes had been a sickly child and was sent by his parents to join his brother in South Africa when he was aged 17, where they hoped the climate would improve his health. At 18, in October 1871, he had left the Cape for the new diamond fields of Kimberley and within two decades his company, De Beers, had achieved almost total domination of the world's diamond market. He attended Oxford University (for which he developed a particular affection) intermittently during the 1870s and entered the Cape Parliament in 1880, being elected as prime minister in 1890, while his British South African Company effectively ruled the vast lands between the Limpopo River and Lake Tanganyika, which were soon to be officially named after him as Rhodesia (now modern day Zimbabwe).

Rhodes' extraordinary views were widely shared among his countrymen at the time and he proudly expounded, "We (*the British*) are the first race in the world, and that the more of the world we inhabit the better it is for the human race … just fancy those parts that are at present inhabited by the most despicable specimens of human beings, what an alteration there would be if they were brought under Anglo-Saxon influence.... If there be a God, I think that what he would like me to do is paint as much of the map of Africa British Red as possible."[3] Hard as it may be to understand looking back from the 21st century, but Rhodes and almost every one of his fellow Britons including Baker were utterly convinced, both that the British Empire's continuing expansion would bring further civilization, prosperity and Christianity to an even greater proportion of the world's population than the 25 percent that it already ruled at that time, and also that the British Empire would endure forever, like no other empire before it.[4] Already imbued with these imperial ideals through their upbringing and education, the Baker brothers were thus committed to both serve and prosper in their own colonial adventure.

Despite the drama of Cape Town's natural setting nestling under the great Table Mountain which jutted out dramatically into the South Atlantic Ocean, Herbert was far from captivated by this far-flung colonial outpost. For a young man who had lived and worked in the largest and wealthiest city in the world for many years, Herbert found Cape Town something of a shock, as he expressed in an early letter home to his younger (teacher) brother Percy—"The conditions are revolting to my London ideas."[5] On their arrival the brothers were able to make straight for Admiralty House in Simonstown where they were warmly welcomed by another elder cousin, Rear Admiral Nicholson, and his wife. It was here that they spent their first weeks on the Cape, overlooking False Bay where the British naval ships were anchored. As new arrivals they were entertained and introduced to the society of Cape Town and one evening, having been invited to dinner by Lewis Vintcent, a member of the Cape House of Assembly—to his utter astonishment—Herbert found himself seated directly opposite Cecil Rhodes. As he later recounted, "I sat entranced at their talk on South Africa and world affairs, but I said little or nothing, and went away much discomforted at having proved myself so unable to make the most of this golden opportunity." Fortunately for Baker, his fellow dinner guest Agnes Merriman was able to reassure him the following day that Rhodes had been interested enough to ask her more about "that silent young man."[6]

Two weeks after the Bakers' arrival, a further young English adventurer disembarked at Cape Town, concluding his long journey from California. His name was Harry Pickstone and he also had fruit farming on his mind as he arrived with both a knowledge of the latest cultivation techniques from the United States and a letter of introduction to Cecil Rhodes. Soon Pickstone, the Bakers and John Merriman were deep in conversation with Cecil Rhodes on the topic of fruit farming and fruit exports from the Cape. After several weeks' discussion and with Rhodes' encouragement, Pickstone, Lionel Baker and a further local Cape farmer entered into partnership and established their fruit farm near Stellenbosch. Herbert's mission was now technically complete but thanks to his new social contacts and relatively little local competition, he had found that he was already beginning to pick up architectural work and he started to wonder whether Cape Town might offer him a better prospect than sleepy Gravesend, at least in the short term. These early musings were captured in his letter home to Percy in June of 1892, some two months after his arrival—"Here we are in the Dark Continent & seems likely to remain—you will be glad to hear that I do not intend to give up my profession.... A man named Stent wants me to join him as partner.... I shall join him I think, but I am afraid there is not very much work to be done here, tho' there may be in a few years time ... of course most of my education will be thrown away, but I suppose I ought to stop if I can earn a living.... I may come home … took my first earnings today—£25 for the first month—hope it goes on. Feel happier now that I have earned my daily bread."[7]

Baker's first client in Cape Town was a member of Cecil Rhodes' cabinet, James Rose Innes, who commissioned a small addition to the reformatory in Tokai. Further projects trickled in—a small observatory for the roof of the government buildings in Pretoria, then the first buildings of Wynberg Boys' High School. On the back of these commissions, Baker established his first South African office in what must have been an astonishingly hot, little glazed turret on the flat roof of an old house at 43 St. George's Street, which had previously been used as an *uitkyk* or lookout for ships, from where he could both survey the ships arriving and departing in the bay below and also revel in the ever-changing moods and "almost religious feeling"[8] of the great Table Mountain above him. In October, he received his first new house commission, for a Mr. J. B. Moffat. Only a photograph survives of the house, which shows a rendered two-story detached villa with sliding sash windows—all in all a rather inoffensive seaside Queen Anne which would be more at home in Torquay than on its plot in the Cape Town suburb of Tokai.

This raises an important point, which needs to be kept in mind as we chart Baker's architectural development through the next few years, namely that, despite his considerable practical experience, he had next to no design experience beyond his student projects, and these early commissions in South Africa therefore represented the first real buildings that he had produced under his own name.[9] Unlike Lutyens, who appeared to have an inherent flair for architectural design, Baker's design experience up until 1892 was restricted almost entirely to matters of detail. He was an award-winning student, but only in his professional practice examination, and for a man who liked to listen more than talk, he now had to express himself in three dimensions in public for the first time and to begin to develop an architecture of his own, incorporating within it his already well-developed architectural theories and beliefs. In this context, it was hardly surprising that he initially fell back on tried and tested solutions, only slowly introducing innovation as his confidence as a designer began to grow. Fortunately, his workload quickly began to build, thus providing him with opportunities on which to experiment, but sadly, most of these, including Linkoping for a Dr. Smuts and a further detached Hopetown House for Alex Bell, were in the same unremarkable English suburban villa–style as Mr. Moffat's house.

In October, he provided brother Percy with a further progress report—

I am getting busy … my chief excitement lately is having begun cricket. I joined the Western Province Club … (*followed by a lengthy discussion of games, scores, pitch conditions etc.*)…. I have a few poor walks but have not yet succeeded in getting to the top of Table Mountain…. They seem to be doing very well at the farm so far…. I enjoyed the winter there and the duck shooting…. I am fairly busy now—I hope I can get some money out of them before I am quite reduced to starvation…. Boarding House terrible dull and dreary…. Poor form architectural work here with everything bad—not much pleasure to be got out of the work—so glad I did not go into partnership with that man—"Pecksniff"—he is a right blackguard I fancy and the biggest humbug that ever walked. I shall never get home till I get a partner or fail in business— the latter is the only chance and most likely.[10]

But fate, having already brought him to South Africa, was once more about to intervene in a way that would not only transform his immediate prospects and convince him to stay in the Cape, but even more significantly, offer him the potential to become one of the leading architects of his generation.

While traveling the countryside with Lionel to investigate fruit farming, he had become increasingly captivated by the natural beauty of the Cape landscape, as he had told Percy—"Everything is redeemed in my mind by the country, within an area no bigger than London itself there are mountains, forests, 2 seas, sand & wild coast & every kind of beauty"[11] as well as the graceful whitewashed Cape Dutch farmsteads that they had come across on the various fruit farms that they had visited. His confident sketches of many of the farmhouses survive—Steenberg, Watergat, Drakenstein, Roukoop, Rondebosch, Schoongezicht—with notes on window designs, decorations, materials, gable variations and colors. He admired their restrained palette of materials and their simple dignity "in the ordered layout of house, outbuildings, avenues, orchards and vineyards; beautiful in the simplicity of the architecture, white walls, solid teak or green-painted shuttered windows and doors, gracefully curved gables with softly modelled enrichments, and quiet 'moleskin' thatch."[12] The style was well established—long low houses with a single vertical accent at their center, where the decoration of a tall Dutch gable expressed the wealth of their owner with simple rectangular windows, with only the lower part shuttered, as can still be seen in Amsterdam today. His enthusiasm was understandable—this was the *savage* vernacular which the guild aspired to reproduce, and in this case, with a strong shot of the architecture of the Low Countries which he had seen at first hand on his travels and from which Ernest George, his former employer, had drawn so deeply for his own work. He studied the old homesteads and when occasionally his discussions with Rhodes strayed beyond fruit farming, they found that they shared a common concern that these old buildings were generally unappreciated and constantly under threat.

In Cape Town he had continued his normal regime of long, early-morning walks before the heat of the day both to maintain his fitness and to clear his head; it was on one of these that he met Rhodes and Hans Sauer returning from their early-morning ride on the Cape Flats. In Baker's own words—"He stopped and asked me to breakfast the next morning, as he wanted me, he said, to 'build his house.' This happy meeting and invitation determined my fortune."[13] "His house" was Groote Schuur (or The Grange as the local English referred to it)—a large farmhouse, previously owned by an early Dutch governor which Rhodes had been renting and planned to buy, and which he now wished to restore and extend. This was finally to be Baker's Crooksbury but with the added accelerant to his career that this, his first major domestic commission, was for no less than the prime minister of South Africa. It was to take his work on Groote Schuur, with a sympathetic client, to finally encourage Baker out of his shell and into his first experiment in Cape Dutch architecture.

In April 1893, he was able to update Percy on both his and his brother Lionel's affairs on the printed notepaper of his new office in South African Chambers—"The Pioneer Fruit Company has broken up—at least Pickstone has left—quarrelled with Van Reuen— the d---d fools…. I survey my jobs before breakfast 6 & after 5—can't leave the office much between, as I have no clerk. I shall have taken in nearly £400 in the first year … mountain climbing my chief amusement."[14]

Groote Schuur was soon purchased, and he was able to start work in earnest on its restoration and extension. Rhodes' attraction to the house and its surrounding estate was threefold—it lay to the south of the center of Cape Town in what was then largely open country from where he could easily walk or ride; it was rich in historical and cultural associations having originally been built in 1657 as a granary for the Dutch East India Company before its conversion to a residence; and, most significantly of all for Rhodes, from its rear garden he had an uninterrupted view of his beloved Table Mountain. It had been altered constantly throughout its long life, having already enjoyed a flat, thatched and pitched slate roof and pedimented gables as well as decorated Dutch gables at various times. Baker uncovered a sketch of 1838,[15] which depicted a stage of the house's previous existence which had probably only survived for around 10 years, but it was from this vision of a colonial Dutch villa under a thatched roof with a traditional covered *stoep* or veranda shading its entrance, that Baker was to take his cue.

Rhodes required a home for entertaining as his own lifestyle was famously spartan. As Baker himself recounted, his brief from Rhodes was minimal—"He explained to me his ideas, his 'thoughts,' as he called them, but gave no detailed instructions; he just trusted me"[16]—and then Rhodes departed for Matabeleland, where the First Matabele War was then underway.[17] (The next few years during which Groote Schuur was restored, extended and rebuilt was a period of intense activity for Rhodes, and he spent much of this period "up country" where his British South Africa Company was extending its land holdings by a combination of treaty and force.) Baker's efforts at this stage were largely focused on creating a small gentleman's residence within the confines of the existing structure, and indeed on its completion the original windows and *stoep* were still clearly discernable. Despite these constraints, Baker's plan is beautifully resolved with the *stoep* leading to a broad hallway off which anterooms lead to the dining room to the left and drawing room to the right. Directly ahead lies a hall, which spans across the ends of both main rooms, thus also enjoying the view of the mountain.

By September 1893, Baker had developed and completed his designs for the

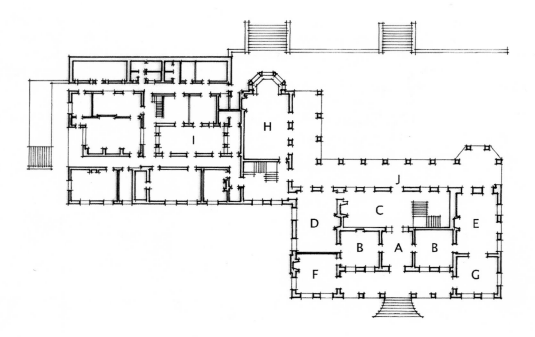

Groote Schuur ground floor plan. A Entrance Hall, B Ante Rooms, C Hall, D Dining Room, E Drawing Room, F Library, G Study, H Billiard Room, I Kitchens and Stores, J Stoep (author's drawing, based on Michael Keath plans).

restoration and invited tenders from contractors to carry out the work. Groote Schuur was to be no suburban villa but instead his first true Arts and Crafts design, with every detail resolved between architect and craftsmen, but finding skilled tradesmen who could work to the exacting standards that he had achieved with George and Peto in London was to prove almost impossible in Victorian Cape Town. As he later wrote, "The building crafts of the Colony were not of a high order. Cheap sea freights and scarcity of skilled labour encouraged the importation of everything ready-made from Europe."[18] "Accustomed by my home training to make details of all parts of the building for craftsmen to execute, I had never heard of this strange paper instrument (*an indent*) for importing everything all ready cast or machine made."[19]

Baker literally scoured the area for any type of craftsman who might help, as well as inviting tradesmen whom he had worked with in London to join him in South Africa. For example, George Ness, a metal worker, he found employed in an engineer's workshop at the docks, while Neil Black, a stonemason he came across, he encouraged to undertake every aspect of his trade from quarrying the stone to carving it to Baker's designs. He discovered clay on one of Rhodes' farms and instigated the construction of kilns there to produce both bricks and tiles for use in Groote Schuur. The scale of this challenge shouldn't be underestimated and was in stark contrast to Lutyens' early heavy reliance on the highly skilled Surrey craftsmen who covered his own early technical shortcomings in building Crooksbury and his other first houses.

Rhodes returned from Metabeleland in January (with resistance to the company's forces crushed, following the death of Lobengula the last king of the Ndebele people) to find the main part of the house completed. As Baker recalled, "I felt he was pleased, though characteristically he did not say so. His approval was inferred by his enthusiasm to go on with an extension to the building, the kitchens, billiard-room with his bedroom over it, and the long, deep, columned *stoep* at the back facing his beloved mountains."[20] His letter to brother Percy of the 3rd of June 1894 gives a further update on the state of his practice, his thoughts on the future and these early days of his relationship with Rhodes—"I am very busy and making money to spend at home some day I hope. But have to work for it—never less than 12 hours. 7–7. Rhodes is going strong, flushed with victory. He is pleased with what I have done and I get on pretty well with him—generally breakfast with him. He is generally considered a great Inapproachable. I dined there the other night & never realised before how entertaining he could be—told so many stories of the war & many little facts not generally known."[21] Baker, the great listener, was in his element.

He continued to pick up further work in the colony, and his appointment in late 1893 to design the new Church of St. Andrew in Newlands (a flourishing suburb of Cape Town near Groote Schuur) was to be the first of a string of ecclesiastical appointments. St. Andrew's offers further signs of Baker's growing confidence as a designer—perhaps as a result of his previous experience at Llanberis and his many restoration projects with his elder cousin Arthur, there is an assurance about this small church which hadn't been evident before. Equally importantly, and unlike his contemporary villas, it both truly reflects his Arts and Crafts beliefs for the first time and shows a thoughtful sensitivity to the extremes of the local climate. Built of dressed and coursed sandstone from the mountain above, it is designed in six buttressed bays with king-post timber trusses over. A simple arch divides the nave from the rectangular lower-roofed chancel beyond, whose altar is lit by three lancet windows, with stained glass by no less than the pre-Raphaelite artist

Sir Edward Burne Jones. Openings to the exterior are kept to a minimum with windows only in each alternate bay and yet, so strong is the Cape sunlight, that the interior has a rugged warmth while its massive walls and original thatched roof kept it naturally cool on all but the hottest days. This is Baker's first real piece of architecture in which he has started to express himself and it bears comparison with E. S. Prior's contemporary Bothenhampton Church in Dorset of 1887–89 or Lethaby's All Saints Brockhampton-by-Ross of 1902, which it precedes. His sources are the early English churches which he sketched as a boy and young man, such as St. Mary's at Reculver in Kent and the Chapel of St. Peter-on-the-Wall in Essex (one of the oldest churches in England), which he knew well. It is Gothic, stripped back to the bare essentials, but already with the quiet dignity that was to characterize his best work.

St. Andrews Church interior, Cape Town (courtesy Roddy Bray).

Construction had started on St. Andrew's in May 1894 and so, with Groote Schuur continuing, the year was spent with two substantial projects on-site, with the church finally being consecrated on the 30th of November. The year 1885 brought further house commissions and sadly, a return to the middle-of the-road roughcast suburban Queen Anne style of his first efforts, both for H. W. Struben in Witwatersrand and with a further commission from his first client, James Rose Innes, for a new house, Karatara, which was completed that year. By the end of the year his young practice had expanded with the appointment of his first two assistants, B. Bowley and J. C. Tully, the latter acting as Clerk of Works for Groote Schuur.

Just as Baker and his small practice were achieving some level of financial stability, he received news from his brother Ned (now a solicitor in Gravesend) that Baker's father had finally confided to him the true and shocking state of their parents' financial affairs. Herbert shared his thoughts once more with brother Percy—"What I have expected for many years has come at last—we all lived too extravagantly at home. I always knew it, but it was of no use remonstrating."[22] This was to be the start of a long and increasing drain on Herbert's hard-won finances as both he and his brother Ned sought to both support their parents financially and clear the substantial debts that had already been accrued. For Herbert, it was an immediate threat to his intended acquisition of a first home, the Grotto, which he had been on the verge of purchasing when he heard the news of his parent's pecuniary plight, but having carefully assessed his own financial situation he decided to proceed nevertheless, as he explained to Percy once more—"I have been sorely tempted & am going to do what you will say is a selfish thing. I have long coveted a beautiful little place—a house in a glen near the mountain with a beautiful garden—it is also near Rhodes new park.... I believe I shall buy it—but I can arrange to borrow most of the money so that I can send home enough I think. I think it is right as I lead a dog's life at present & want some gardening to give me exercise & it is good from a business point of view to have a place to ask friends to (*continued the following day*).... I have done the deed and am now a landed proprietor of 5 acres. ...goodness knows how I shall manage housekeeping but won't get forced into marriage if I can help it."[23] For Herbert, the purchase of the Grotto, within just three years of arriving in the Cape and funded entirely by the fruits of his fledgling practice, represented a huge achievement. His boarding days were over, he could now live in a little more comfort, finally entertain as a young professional man, and most importantly of all, be within a few minutes' walk of Rhodes and Groote Schuur. Indeed, it was through its proximity to what would shortly become Rhodes' home that their relationship was soon to develop from the mutual respect of client and architect into one of genuine friendship. With space to spare, he closed his office in Cape Town and transferred his small team to a ground-floor room in his new home.

While Baker was engaged in these personal matters, Rhodes maintained his own exhausting schedule, managing his financial empire, leading Cape politics and in the winter of 1894–95, even managing to fit in a tour of the classical sites of Europe as part of his continuing self-education. He was partnered on his tour by one of his closest friends, the charming and charismatic Scottish doctor, Leander Starr Jameson (who, it is said, inspired Kipling to write his poem "If").[24] After Rhodes returned from Europe, Herbert helpfully updated Percy—"I write in a state of nervous excitability—this Saturday night and I have been working 12 hours a day all thro' this week & many previous & what with worries from home & ordinary business & Rhodes return, I have been pretty

"The Grotto," Herbert Baker's first home in Cape Town, 1890s (courtesy Michael Baker).

well occupied mentally…. Rhodes has returned and is pleased with everything & is going ahead & has other schemes for the future—so I am all right."[25]

Unbeknown to their young architect, while touring Europe, Rhodes and Jameson had also been discussing how best to achieve their vision of a united South Africa that would span from the Cape Colony to Rhodesia. As noted before, with the transfer of the Cape Colony from the Dutch to the British in 1814, the introduction of English as the language of government and business and finally the abolition of slavery throughout the British Empire in 1833, the Dutch settlers had moved north to establish their own settlements which became the South African Republic (based in what the British referred to as the Transvaal) and the adjacent Orange Free State. Relative peace had then reigned between the British and the Dutch until the discovery of diamonds in 1867 which led to a huge influx of immigrants to the Transvaal, most of whom were British. Tensions grew, resulting in the First Boer War of 1880–1881, which was won by the Boers (the first occasion since the American Revolution that the British had been defeated and forced to sign a peace treaty on unfavorable terms).[26] A further gold rush of 1886 renewed tensions and these built during the early 1890s as the number of incomers (*uitlanders*) began to exceed the number of Boers in the Transvaal. The Boer government's response was to restrict the franchise for the *uitlanders* and to heavily tax both all the gold that was extracted and the dynamite which was used to extract it, thus further increasing the *uitlanders'* discontent. Rhodes' vision was to unite the Transvaal and the Orange Free State with the Cape Colony in a federation under British control, and in December 1895, Dr. Leander Starr Jameson became the unlikely leader of a raid into the Transvaal, which Rhodes (and secretly the British government) hoped would spark an uprising against the Boers. Unfortunately for Rhodes and even more unfortunately for Jameson, there was no uprising, the raid failed and Jameson was arrested and sent to London for trial, where, though found guilty and sentenced to 15 months in jail, he was lauded as a hero of the empire. For Rhodes, the Jameson Raid had been yet another bold gamble, but on this occasion one that he had lost and he too was to pay a heavy price. Baker was clearly following these events closely as his contemporary correspondence confirmed—"I expect there will be an impeachment of Rhodes like that of Warren Hastings—Members tell me that Rhodes is coming down to meet parliament but I doubt it. What terrible revelations those telegrams are...."[27] Despite denials and the withholding of incriminating correspondence between himself and Jameson, Rhodes was implicated in the planning, summoned to London to answer to the Colonial Secretary Joseph Chamberlain, and in 1896, subsequently forced to resign his position as both a director of the British South Africa Company and as prime minister of the Cape Colony. Lord Rosmead, who had been acting as high commissioner for Southern Africa and governor of the Cape Colony also resigned and was replaced by rising-star career diplomat Alfred Milner, who arrived in Cape Town in May 1887. Milner immediately appreciated that with the discovery of gold in the Transvaal, the balance of power had shifted from Cape Town to Johannesburg and as a consequence the Boers were now a very real threat to Britain's position in Southern Africa (never mind any further colonial aspirations for the conquest of the continent). While Rhodes maintained his wealth and commercial influence, the raid hugely damaged his reputation and the balance of political power in South Africa now shifted towards Milner, the new high commissioner.

Baker's work meanwhile continued on Groote Schuur, further domestic commissions trickled in to keep him and his new assistants busy, and that summer he was appointed as the Diocesan Architect for Cape Town, which immediately resulted in a further church commission from the diocese, for St. Barnabas in Tamboerskloof on the other side of Signal Hill from Central Cape Town and, even more significantly, he was party to early discussions regarding the possible construction of a new cathedral for the city. In May, the City Club, of which Baker was already a member, purchased a site for a new building on Queen Victoria Street in Cape Town and, in deference to their various architect members, initiated an architectural competition for their new clubhouse, which Baker was determined to win.

He decided that further assistance was required to cope with this growing workload and the next two staff whom he appointed both turned out to be his future partners. The first was 26-year-old Australian-born architect Franklin Kaye Kendall, who was to be at Baker's side for the next 20 years becoming first a junior partner a year later and then senior partner in 1906. Born in Melbourne, Kendall had been educated in London and had arrived in Cape Town earlier that year, working briefly for both of Baker's main local architectural competitors, John Parker and Sydney Stent (the "right blackguard" of Baker's earlier letter) before joining Baker in the Grotto where he quickly settled.

In the autumn of 1896, Baker contracted typhoid (one of the many deadly diseases to which everyone was exposed in the colonies) and was taken to the hospital in Cape Town. As he joked to his brother—"You have heard of my way of taking a holiday! I am just out from 9 weeks in bed & hospital.... I have chosen a very expensive form of amusement! Perhaps the long rest may do me good, but I might have got home in the time & for half the money it will cost me.... I have been shown a lot of kindness where

I didn't expect it."[28] While convalescing, he was visited by another young architect who had recently arrived in the Cape, Francis Edward Masey, who offered Baker his assistance during his illness and recovery. Masey, who was six months older than Baker, was an unusually talented young architect to be found seeking work in Cape Town in the 1890s. Born in London, he was the third son of architect Philip Masey, to whom he had been articled. During his time at the Royal Academy Schools he had won the Soane Medal, the Tite Prize and the Owen Jones Student Medal, all of which had funded European study tours. What brought this award-winning and well-traveled young architect to South Africa is unclear, but he had arrived earlier in the year on a three-year contract with the Cape Town Public Works Department, which he initially continued to work for while also assisting Baker. Kendall described him as "a very remarkable man, in some respects a bit of a genius," he "soon proved himself a very capable organiser with immense driving power, an artist to his fingertips with all the advantages and disadvantages of an imaginative brain."[29] By December, Baker was out of the hospital convalescing at the Grotto and the three new colleagues had begun working together for the first time on their competition entry for the City Club's new building, which Kendall recalled, involved long days and many late nights.

It was on one of these nights in the early hours of the 15th of December, that Baker's well-earned sleep was disturbed by the crackling sound of burning wood and, rushing outside his house, he saw the sky above Groote Schuur glowing red and shot with sparks, as he recalled, "The thatch once alight, the whole house was doomed; corrugated iron, which I had put under the thatch, was worse than useless."[30] Dawn showed the buildings almost completely gutted, with only the drawing room and the columns of the original *stoep* having survived. All Rhodes' possessions, including his papers, were lost in the fire. He was in Matabeleland when the fire took place and the news must have capped what had been a disastrous year for him. As he remarked at the time—"What with the Raid, rebellion, famine, rinderpest, and now my house burnt, I feel like Job, all but the boils."[31] Baker had been considering returning home to Kent to convalesce further but, "when Rhodes set me to work to rebuild it, I did not go home as intended, but stayed and gave my whole time to rebuild and furnish the house anew."[32] The reconstruction of Groote Schuur gave Baker the confidence to offer Masey a full-time position, so he resigned from the Public Works Department to join the growing team along with Baker's first articled pupil, Vernon Rees-Poole, in what by now was becoming a rather cramped office in the Grotto. Little did Baker realize that the appointment of these two trusted new assistants would prove to be the catalyst for the dramatic growth of his practice that would see it established as the leading firm of architects in South Africa within a decade.

3

1897–1901

"Imperial March" (Op. 32)

With Kendall and Masey on board, Baker was now able to spend more time seeking further work and extending his personal network of friends and clients in Cape Town. His elder cousin Rear Admiral Nicholson had provided him with initial introductions to the local British expatriate society and despite his naturally reserved nature, Baker had quickly developed a number of strong and beneficial relationships within this relatively limited group. As James Bryce noted in his contemporary *Impressions of South Africa*—"The upper stratum of that society, consisting of the well-to-do and best educated people, is naturally small, because the whole white population of the towns is small…. Cape Town, Kimberley, Bloemfontein, Johannesburg and Pretoria … are for social purposes almost one city. All the persons of consequence in these places know one another and follow one another's doings."[1] With his cousin's initial introductions and Rhodes' subsequent blessing, Baker was quickly and enthusiastically admitted to the inner sanctum of white South African society and, following his previous experience of trying to find work of substance in Gravesend, he was determined not to let this catch slip.

What his new friends saw in Baker was not a socialite, wit or brilliant dinner party conversationalist, or indeed even someone who was particularly comfortable in new company, but instead a serious, decent young man who enjoyed civilized, intelligent company, with them soon discovering that, below his often earnest and entirely respectable exterior, there lay an extraordinary energy and enthusiasm for life. Charles Wheeler, the sculptor, with whom Baker often worked later in his career, confirmed the same—"Though he enjoyed many friendships … he was not a good 'mixer.' He thought about his work during all his working hours, loved poetry and his garden…. Without being a prig, he liked the companionship of cultured people"[2] (and equally, often despaired of his forced travel companions). As they got to know him, they found a highly intelligent, thoughtful, interested and interesting man—a quietly articulate talker, an excellent writer and perhaps above all, a very good listener—they found that there was a depth to Baker and a warmth and sensitivity that defied the later caricature of him as a dull committee man.

Rhodes' selection of Baker as his architect, while being incredibly fortunate for Baker, was not by chance. Baker's genuine enthusiasm for the indigenous architecture of the Cape had struck a chord with Rhodes and as their relationship developed, Rhodes began to increasingly regard Baker as a man whom he could safely share his thoughts with and who might be able to help him repay the debt he felt he owed to South Africa

Herbert Baker, right, with friends at the Grotto (courtesy Michael Baker).

through some form of civic architectural legacy. Through Baker's work on Groote Schuur, Rhodes' intermittent occupation of it, and Baker's new role as neighbor, the two became increasingly close. Though a man of few words, to Baker Rhodes was an inspiring visionary. His aim was the

colonisation by British subjects of all lands where the means of livelihood are attainable by energy, labour and enterprise, and especially the occupation by British settlers of the entire Continent of Africa, the Holy Land, the Valley of the Euphrates, the Islands of Cyprus and Candia, the whole of South America, the Islands of the Pacific not heretofore possessed by Great Britain, the whole of the Malay Archipelago, the seaboard of China and Japan, the ultimate recovery of the United States of America as an integral part of the British Empire, the inauguration of a system of Colonial representation in the Imperial Parliament which may tend to weld together the disjointed members of the Empire and, finally, the foundation of so great a Power as to render wars impossible, and promote the best interests of humanity.[3]

As to the treatment of native populations within the empire, Rhodes regarded them simply as "savages" who should be treated "as children" and (while even in the 1880s and '90s, Rhodes had his detractors among Liberals in London), shocking as his views are to us now, they were commonly held among the British. John Buchan, another imperialist who shared these beliefs and who met Rhodes on several occasions said of him, "He impressed me greatly—the sense he gave one of huge but crippled power, the reedy voice and the banal words in which he tried to express ideas which represented for him a whole world of incoherent poetry. I did not know him well enough to like or dislike him, but I felt him as one feels the imminence of a thunderstorm."[4] Baker, likewise, had been immediately and utterly fascinated by this brooding lion of the British Empire, who despite appearances seemed to him to represent the very embodiment of the imperial spirit.

For someone of Baker's background and upbringing, his admiration of Rhodes was hardly surprising. What was more unusual was that Rhodes developed a similar interest in Baker, with Alpheus Williams, an American engineer and close friend of Rhodes confirming that Baker also "fascinated" Rhodes—"From the day he met him; the more he talked with him, the more that he saw that he too was a dreamer on a colossal scale. He recognized that he was just the man he was looking for, one who would be able to resuscitate all of the beauties of early Cape architecture which were sadly neglected."[5] These two serious, quiet men appear to have relatively quickly understood that they had much in common: both having lacked a university education with Rhodes having intermittently attended Oxford and Baker having gone straight from school to his pupilage and yet both had an insatiable appetite for personal intellectual development. Rhodes had no need for another acolyte to sit at his feet—he respected Baker and not just for his knowledge and appreciation of art and architecture, but also for his passion for literature and poetry and his ability to quote it at length. Rhodes admired Baker's intellect and his serious, quiet yet confident nature and envied his considerable ability to express himself and his ideas. Crucially, from Baker's education and Rhodes' travels, they both also understood the symbolic power of Western architecture to promote ideals, express values, connect cultures and acknowledge power.

After Baker's move to the Grotto, when Rhodes was around, they spent a considerable amount of time together as Baker recalled in his autobiography—"In the talks with him about his artistic ideals, which I had almost daily when he was in Cape Town, I gained some access to his inner mind which he was shy to reveal to others," and that "after discussions with Rhodes up to nearly the dinner hour, he would ask me to dine, I would scramble through the dark pine trees, dress, and rush back as the last of the mixed assembly of guests arrived."[6] Doreen Greig has suggested that Baker fell under Rhodes' spell— "Such was the power of Rhodes's personality and the strength of his 'thoughts' that he was more than a catalyst, he guided Baker's architectural thinking and disciplined his ideas so that, as many other men had done, he became another of Rhodes 'instruments' a medium through which the 'incoherent vision' of Rhodes's ideas could be given substance."[7] Certainly Baker's own much later biography of Rhodes, *Cecil Rhodes by His Architect*, verges on the idolatry, but wherever the balance lay between the two men, there is no doubt that like so many of Baker's other long and intimate friendships, it was based on a sincere mutual respect and his unquestionable discretion, and while this relationship with Rhodes (and many of Baker's other personal relationships) advanced his architectural career, there can be little doubt that had Baker been offered the opportunity to spend so much time with one of the leaders of imperial Britain such as Rhodes, without any potential architectural commissions, he would still have scrambled through the pine trees just as quickly.

While Baker's circle grew quickly in Cape Town, he also kept in regular touch with friends and family back in England including Edwin Lutyens with whom he maintained a very regular correspondence throughout his time in South Africa. In contrast to Baker, Lutyens had few friends; indeed Jane Ridley, Lutyens' great-granddaughter, goes so far as to suggest that beyond his client Edward Hudson (the founder and editor of *Country Life* magazine) and "wary of his colleagues' rivalry,"[8] Baker was in fact Lutyens only other male friend and further, that had it not been for Baker's removal from direct competition in South Africa, it is unlikely that even this relationship would have survived. Their many letters during Baker's time in Africa emphasize more than anything the differences between the two men and also the continuing respect that Baker, the elder and more experienced architect, had for the younger Lutyens' apparently innate architectural ability. Baker regularly sent drawings and photographs of his work to Lutyens who quite ruthlessly critiqued it, Lutyens' letter of 30th of March 1901 being a fine example—"I should like to have seen the outhouse connected with the main buildings … more simplicity … it is so easy to criticise…. I don't like the mantle shelf moulding … the cupboard hinges a little commonplace … the cupboard just a little too pinched … perhaps the frieze a bit narrower," and concluding, "it is so easy to criticise not realising the difficulties you have to contend with but the house is far and away better than the good average attempts in this country and would hold its own as A1 work anywhere … you can always say who De'll is this chap Lutyens?"[9] Yet Baker valued this criticism immensely as architecturally he was in many ways alone, attempting to express himself through his work for the first time and almost completely detached from the scene in London except for this contact with one of its rising stars. The truth is that from Baker's perspective too, the relationship would almost certainly not have survived such criticism had it been face-to-face and Baker's constant humility throughout most of this long correspondence was to badly mislead Lutyens as to the nature of any future collaboration between the two architects.

The other inevitable impact of Kendall and Masey joining Baker and eventually both becoming partners in his practice is that it began to obscure the authorship of the practice's architectural designs from this period onwards. It is tempting to assign much of their best work of the next few years to Masey, who came with an outstanding track record of award-winning design, but it is also clear from surviving correspondence that Baker always maintained his role as senior partner within the partnership, very much as he had been in his schooldays—as captain of the team. He rarely deferred to Masey even in matters of design, and indeed, any lingering doubts that it may have been Masey who led the practice on design matters from this point onwards are easily dispelled by the quality of Baker's own best work in South Africa, which occurred after Masey had later left the firm.[10] Frank Kendall later recalled that in the design of one of their office buildings in Cape Town, for example, "Masey did all the original drawings, but Baker 'took over' the elevations and improved them immensely."[11]

As if an omen, the first project which the three worked on together, Baker's competition entry for the City Club in Cape Town, was announced as the winner on the 15th of January 1897. Kendall wrote that their work together on the entry "was the turning point of the situation and the partnership between the three of us followed."[12] The design (which survives largely intact today as the City and Civil Service Club) has a few echoes of Baker's unsuccessful entry of 1886 for the Royal Academy's Gold Medal Travelling Scholarship "A Town Mansion" but here transformed in response to the local climate with the punched and modeled plane of rendered masonry fronted by a shaded first-floor veranda (today understandably but nevertheless regrettably now enclosed and air-conditioned) which also provided some relief from the South African sun for its entrance on the pavement below.

The City Club, Cape Town—Baker, Masey and Kendall's first joint effort (courtesy Lila Komnick).

The restraint of the slender, coupled Doric columns, which support the balcony and which are repeated at first-floor level where they support the roof of the veranda, gives way to a profusion of columns, keystones, egg-and-dart molding, metopes, tryglyphs, swags and scrolls above, which suggest an early entirely undisciplined and ill-informed joint stumble into Classicism by Baker and Masey. The interiors are typical Ernest George in dark-paneled wood below white-plastered ceilings. The building contract was signed in June 1897, and the new club building officially opened in December 1898.

Meanwhile, St. Barnabas was progressing slowly. Baker's first design, which he had completed the previous October, had been rejected on the grounds of cost. The final design, which was completed in October 1897, is a much-reduced affair, very much along the lines of St. Andrew's with the original side aisles, octagonal chancel and tower removed and the parish hall added to the side of a single central aisle. Despite the strictures imposed on him, Baker still managed a very creditable asymmetrical entrance by sliding the hall forward in plan to enclose a small space in front of the double sets of doors, below an inlaid cross and beckoning bell canopy above. Inside, the rubble walls here give way to brick, which is paneled at low level, thus losing much of the simplicity and warmth of the earlier St. Andrew's.

The reconstruction and extension of Groote Schuur continued with Rhodes now taking an increasing interest in the work. One of the only two letters which Rhodes ever wrote to Baker contained his instructions—"There should be no yellow wood but all teak" and "Keep beams in library and dining room and hall. The anteroom can be panelled. Do not alter anything. I do not want a Wimbledon Villa."[13] For an aspiring Arts and Crafts architect who sought restraint and simplicity, Rhodes must have seemed the perfect client. Baker also went on to relate that during the rebuilding, "though very considerate for the welfare, comfort and ease of his guests, he (*Rhodes*) gave no thought for his own comfort. At first he slept in a small room at the back, part of an old slave quarter, and we could only induce him to have a bedroom in the new wing of the house by persuading him, through abuse and chaff, that this outbuilding, as seen from his new back *stoep*, spoilt the view of the mountains. When this was removed we built the terraced garden up to some old stone pines, which we had discovered hidden in the jungle."[14] As Baker's health returned, he resumed his early morning rides and also began collecting furniture, metalwork and china to furnish the house from the old Cape farmsteads which he continued to visit and sketch.[15]

By the summer, Baker and his team were under real pressure with the City Club, Groote Schuur and St. Barnabas on-site and new commissions flooding in. Baker had agreed to act as executive architect for Sir Donald Currie, the chairman of the Castle Line Shipping Company, to oversee the construction of both a new hotel and an office building for the Castle Line in Cape Town which had been designed by the London firm of Dunn and Watson. He confided to Percy, "Although a lot of work is passing thro' my hands for much of it I am only consulting architect as a small fee and many probs. Churches chiefly don't pay at all."[16] Numerous further domestic commissions came in later in the year, some in assistance to the ailing elderly local architect Sydney Stent (who died in April of the following year) and several directly from Rhodes for workers' accommodation for his fruit farms in the Groot Drakenstein Valley, where Baker designed entire villages of simple whitewashed workers' cottages at both Boschendal and Languedoc, along with rough sandstone churches-cum-schoolhouses, complete with the gabled bell first used on St. Barnabas. Then, to add to this already almost overwhelming workload, the diocese instructed Baker to proceed with the design of a new cathedral for Cape Town.

Built as a small parish church in 1834, St. George's had become the city's cathedral in 1847 when its first bishop, Robert Gray (1809–1872), had been installed. Almost since his appointment, there were calls for a more suitable and substantial cathedral to be built, and by 1897 the diocesan synod had collected sufficient funds to request their architect to undertake the design of the new building. By the summer, his first design was complete and while it was Gothic in style, its planning had an irregular asymmetrical freedom which both echoed his Arts and Crafts sympathies and allowed his building to respond sensitively to its rather difficult urban site. Its fundamental planning changed little as his proposals developed over the next few years, with the tower, rather than marking the crossing of the nave and transept in true Gothic tradition, being attached almost as a campanile to the side of one aisle where it provided a secondary entrance with the main entrance positioned further down the same aisle, opening directly into the transept. This allowed the tower to close St. George's Street as the portico of the previous church had done and the main entrance to open off Wale Street, to which the nave ran parallel. As befitted a cathedral, the composition was completed with cloisters and a chapter house, on the axis of the transept behind the nave. As Baker explained in a later report to the diocese—"Whilst not overlooking the extreme beauty and essentially English character of this (central) position unless the tower be very large dimensions it would be necessary to have a comparatively narrow Nave and very large obstructive central piers. Both of these would be inconsistent with your expressed desire that the Altar should be visible as far as possible from all parts of the building."[17] The result is a remarkably well-resolved plan which responds equally well to the diocese's requirements and the site's considerable constraints and opportunities.

By the end of the year, Baker was utterly exhausted and ill once more, writing to the Archbishop of Cape Town that he was suffering "very indifferent health" and apologizing that he had "found it difficult to bestow on the design and drawings (*of the cathedral*) the time and care which such important work demands. For the last ten days I have been completely incapacitated … and … therefore been unable to finish the geometrical drawings or to colour the perspective as I intended."[18] Despite these omissions the revised design for the cathedral which he submitted to the diocese at the end of 1897 represented a considerable refinement of his first Gothic offering. The tower, in particular, now shorn of its steeple, had something of the stepped and battered effect of Henry Wilson's tower for St. Clement's in Bournemouth (1895) or indeed Charles Rennie Mackintosh's exactly contemporary Queens Cross Church of Scotland in Glasgow (1897), which itself was inspired by the 13th-century Church of All Saints in Merriott, Somerset.

It is often the fate of architects that their professional life is one of boom or bust and with Baker's fledgling practice already overloaded, 1897 concluded with his first commercial commission of new offices for the Guardian Assurance Company on Adderley Street in the center of Cape Town. By January 1898, the design was well developed: four stories and an attic with tall vertical bay windows below three Dutch gables, complete with miniature Venetian windows in each. With more than a nod to Shaw's New Zealand Chambers (1872), it was an elegant and more restrained design than the City Club and set a new architectural standard for Central Cape Town, although, as Doreen Greig put it so succinctly, in their office designs, Baker and Masey were generally "pioneers" in South Africa, rather than "innovators." While its design may not have been particularly

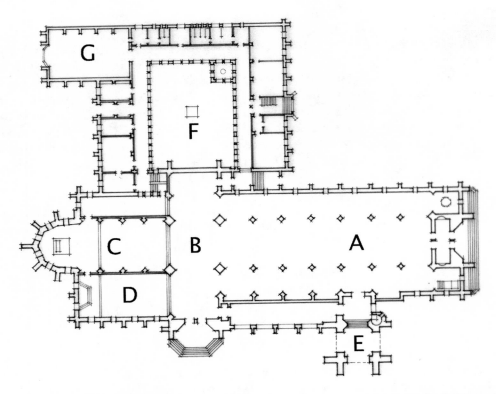

Cape Town Cathedral, ground floor plan. Key: A Nave, B Transept, C Choir, D Memorial Chapel, E Tower, F Cloister and Offices, G Chapter House (author's drawing, based on Michael Keath plans).

innovative, its construction certainly was, with "granite concrete" supplied by the Salt River Cement Works used throughout. (Sadly, it was demolished in 1955.) Two further church commissions were received from the diocese—St. Michael and All Angels in the suburb of Observatory and St. Philip's in Chapel Street in the suburb of Woodstock, both of which, while drawing on the designs of St. Andrew's and St. Barnabas, say more about the practice's almost overwhelming workload than they do of any real architectural development. This momentous year culminated suitably in the completion of Groote Schuur, with the final account signed on the 31st of December.

As Cecil Rhodes' home, Groote Schuur was to be the first of Baker's designs which would attract attention beyond South Africa, and although it has many qualities it has at least as many flaws; indeed Doreen Greig, in her book on Baker's South African architecture described it as "prejudiced from the beginning on nearly every count," the new and old looking "as if they have been shunted together and exist in a perpetually unhappy state of juxtaposition."[19] Certainly, the connection between the new and old blocks of accommodation is extraordinarily weak with just a single door in the corner of the dining room of the old block leading into the hall of the new. (See Figure 7, above.) The principal link however, is external, with the new back *stoep* wrapping across the back of the existing block and down the side of the new, thus directing the whole house, on the angle, to the view of Rhodes' beloved Table Mountain. The principal rooms are in the old block with the new providing (extremely remote) kitchen facilities around an external

The main entrance, Groote Schuur, with John Tweed's bronze relief over the door (courtesy Michael Baker).

court, as well as a new billiard room, and above, Rhodes' bedroom, again overlooking the mountain.

But it was the exterior which caused a stir. The home of the richest man in Africa was seen by many as a whitewashed colonial farmstead (complete with sweeping scrolled Dutch gables and twisted candy-cane chimney stacks) while architectural inconsistencies abounded—elegant rectangular Dutch windows with wooden shutters to their lower part sit below decorated arched and oval openings above; the bay to the billiard room and Rhodes' bedroom look particularly loosely attached; the specially-commissioned new bronze panel over the entrance too large for its gable and perhaps strangest of all, the simple sturdy Doric columns of the original entrance canopy replaced with Ionic. It appeared to many at the time that Baker was struggling with his reinvention of the Cape Dutch style but I'd suggest that his dilemma was one of symbolic representation rather than architectural form with Rhodes craving simplicity and yet Baker, despite his own architectural enthusiasms, feeling obliged to celebrate his client's status. The interior is very fine, very dark, very Jacobean and incredibly fussy in the style of Ernest George, so much so that one would not be surprised to step out from one of the rooms into a London street, rather than onto a *stoep* overlooking Table Mountain. It is only on the first floor where plain white plaster dominates, that the spaces come close to the "barbarity" of which Rhodes spoke—his own bedroom, with its humble single bed is utterly utilitarian. For Rhodes, his home was largely used for entertaining and having provided him with suitably austere personal quarters, he appears to have been delighted with Baker's public spaces. It brought his architect his first professional recognition, even though when published in England it was (quite correctly) compared unfavorably to Lutyens' exactly contemporary Orchards and Fulbrook. But let us not be too unkind to Baker—Lutyens was working in a long-established Surrey vernacular, while Baker was attempting to revive a regional style almost single-handedly. Baker also had no Gertrude Jekyll to guide him either in his studies of the local vernacular or in gardening and it was Baker who laid out the terraces at Groote Schuur and who would continue to design many of the gardens which accompanied his houses. Achieving the standards of craftsmanship that he expected was also an unrecognized effort with Kendall later recalling that he "had to fight tooth and nail for his art."[20]

At the start of 1899, Herbert was 37. Seven years after stepping off the boat onto African soil for the first time, professionally, he had arrived. In South Africa he was now well known as "Rhodes' Architect," his practice was soundly established, he had created a home for himself in the Grotto and, with the completion of Groote Schuur, his work was gaining recognition for the first time beyond the shores of the Cape. If 1898 had been a year of accelerating progress, 1899 was to represent a further change of gear. With Sydney Stent's death in April that year, Baker became the undisputed leader of Cape Town's architectural profession. Francis Masey was taken into partnership, Kendall appointed as senior assistant, the practice moved into large new offices in the Castle Line office building, which they had been supervising, and by the end of the year Baker had purchased a site for a new house of his own, overlooking the sea at Muizenberg. Fate had dealt him a good hand, but he was playing it well.

The year of 1899 opened with a further substantial commercial commission for new offices for the National Mutual Life of Australasia Company on Church Square in central Cape Town. Baker's beautiful colored drawings of the elevations of this building have survived and evoke an Edwardian elegance which would not have been amiss in central London at the time, but the most architecturally significant drawings are those which show the sections through the external walls.[21] These reveal the care that Baker had taken to respond to the harsh South African sun by the creation of an outer skin of arches and colonnades which both protected the actual external envelope of the building from direct sunlight and encouraged the creation of cooling breezes to flow around the exterior of the building. The windows themselves that sat within this sheltering external framework were a sophisticated combination of two arches—one small, which formed the window heads, and one large, which enclosed the opening windows with timber shutters to either side. In an age before air-conditioning this was a highly intelligent, low energy re-working of a typical Classical office block in response to an extreme climate. The project was first abandoned and then resurrected, with construction not finally being completed until 1904. Within the year, this commission was followed by his appointment as architect of offices for Wilson and Millar, a new department store on the ground floor in Adderley Street (next door to his office in the Castle Line building), office premises for George Findlay and Company further along the street and a new headquarters building for the South African Association (sadly lost), all of which conformed to a similar pattern established with the National Mutual Life of Australasia Company building with either deeply cut openings or screen walls below a colonnaded attic and steeply pitched roof. Further diocesan work also rolled in, with extensions to the Church of St. Saviour in Claremont, Cape Town, and a new non-denominational school in Burghersdorp; previous client H. W. Streuben commissioned a speculative design for 19 villas, while Rhodes continued to provide a flow of minor commissions for his various farms and estates. Amidst this deluge of new work, Baker found time for the pleasure of designing his own small villa above the beach at Muizenberg (on land bought from H. W. Streuben) which, though modest, was to be a model for many of his future houses in South Africa.

Baker himself can take up the tale—"I had discovered in my rides the exhilarating air on the sandhills and the shore, where the south-east trade wind concentrates round the Muizenberg headland. The wall and the columns of the broad *stoep* were white like the sands of Muizenberg; the roof was of grey cedar shingles. My adventure proved popular, and too many, alas! have followed it; and my lonely sandhills are now a fashionable seaside resort. My little house, which I called Sandhills, was built round a very small atrium, through the five foot opening of which we saw blue sky by day and the stars by night. The hall-livingroom was long, low, beam-ceiled with red Jarrahwood, had a continuous mullioned window which gave us a wide view through the white-columned *stoep* of the breaking surf."[22]

Sandhills is much more than simply a beachside Cape Dutch farmhouse, however. Despite the familiar *stoep* and double gables, as for the first time, Baker here achieved a

"Sandhills" on the left with Henry Baker on the sand, Muizenberg (courtesy Michael Baker).

synthesis of the traditional local vernacular (of which the guild would have wholeheart-edly approved) with the typology of the ancient Roman villa (which reflected an emerg-ing interest in Classicism). The atrium sits at the heart of the house providing covered circulation, daylight, fresh cooling air and as Baker noted, a view of the beautiful South African sky at night, but much more importantly architecturally, it has become the key organizational device of the entire composition and connects this humble seaside home with the ancient architecture of Greece and Rome. His new commercial buildings had already provided evidence of his growing interest in Classical architecture, and Sandhills, his own house, provided irrefutable confirmation. We know that (despite being anathema to most guild members) this interest had been developing for a few years with the success of his young practice allowing him to add both John Belcher and Mervyn Macartney's *Later Renaissance Architecture in England* and Reginald Blomfield's *History of Renais-sance Architecture in England* to his growing library. In this he was far from unique and indeed Masey's recent arrival from London may have further stimulated his interest, but for Baker crucially, this exploration of Classicism went way beyond matters of architec-tural style.

While Lutyens would later make a similar move, what attracted him was the aes-thetic perfection of Classicism, the subtlety of its geometry and the inherent artistic challenge of getting it right. For Baker, Classical architecture was much more import-ant symbolically, as it offered the potential to connect the mighty British Empire with those of ancient Rome and Greece. Equally importantly, Blomfield had identified the particularly English qualities of "modesty and restraint, purity and dignity" in his study of English Renaissance Architecture of the 17th and 18th centuries which also appealed directly to Baker, thus also linking Classical architecture with an idealized vision of the English character to which Baker wholeheartedly subscribed. Blomfield spoke of Sir Christopher Wren's architecture as having "a grace and sober misdemeanour … a quiet dignified charm … a sturdy masculine feeling,"[23] and he could equally have been describ-ing both Sandhills and its architect. Baker was a natural Classicist—his move towards its rigor, discipline and lofty ideals merely connected his upbringing, education and politics with his architecture in a new wholly-integrated vision. While it had been the Christian morality and fascination with the rural vernacular that had attracted Baker to the Arts and Crafts Movement, it was the potential offered by Classicism to celebrate the British Empire's power and "civilizing influence" that would soon supplant it in almost all his future work.

Rhodes himself had been continuing his own Classical architectural education, in the company of Dr. Jameson once more, with a further tour of the ancient world taking in Italy, Greece and Egypt, returning to Cape Town via England in July 1899 and within days of his return commissioning Baker to build a further house on his estate as a gift to the Currey family who had helped him and occasionally nursed him in his first two years in the diamond fields in Kimberley. Called Welgelen, this house exhibits a consider-able development of Baker's Cape Dutch style with dark-beamed living rooms, cool-tiled floors, plain gables and painted shutters—on this occasion with an asymmetrical plan, wrapped on two sides with a delightful vine-clad white-columned Tuscan Doric pergola from where the blue mountains could be seen through an old avenue of oak trees. This was almost immediately followed by a commission to restore the farmhouse at Nooitge-dacht near Stellenbosch, which had been purchased by Rhodes after the failure of Lionel Baker's ill-fated fruit farm there.

In September, Baker successfully applied for fellowship of the RIBA, his application supported by his old employer Ernest George, Henry Greaves (from the Cape Town Department of Public Works) and William Emerson, who was then the president of the RIBA. By October, the festering resentment between the British and the Boers that had led to the Jameson Raid had turned to war. The summer had been spent in fruitless negotiations in which Milner had demanded representation for the British settlers in the South African Republic and the Orange Free State. The Boers resisted, fearing, almost certainly correctly, that this would lead to the British settlers who were in the majority eventually ceding their territory to the British Empire. On the 11th of October after a series of ultimatums from both sides, Paul Kruger, the president of the South African Republic, boldly declared war on Great Britain. Rhodes, whose initiation of the Jameson Raid four years previously had done so much to stoke the dispute, immediately traveled north to Kimberley to ensure that his mines didn't fall into the hands of the Boers.[24] Consequently, he was soon besieged there by the Boer army (as were also the residents of Ladysmith and Mafeking, where the founder of the Boy Scouts, Baden Powell, was in command).[25]

In January, while Rhodes was holed up in Kimberley, Herbert gave brother Percy another update on his situation—"I have got my little house at the sea now and am living there—it suits me well, as I am tempted of the cool air to take exercise in swimming, walking and riding, which I should be too slack to do in the hot & relaxing inland air— and so I feel much stronger than ever before in the summer. I hope it will last. I have let the Grotto for 4 months for £25 per month furnished…. All these works are hanging on slender thread now, with Kimberley so closely invested. I am very nervous about it at present. Ruin or a fortune awaits us—as well as the country & the Empire … my great regret is that none of our family are fighting…."[26]

Kimberley was not relieved until the 15th of February 1900, shortly after which Rhodes traveled back to Cape Town. His enforced inactivity during the siege had inspired a long list of new commissions for Baker, and during a ride together on the first morning after his return he laid out his plans—a further house on his estate, which was to be used as a visiting artist's residence (the Woolsack), a new head office building in Cape Town for the British South Africa Company (the Rhodes Building) and a memorial to the British who had lost their lives in the Matabele war of 1893 (the Shangani Memorial). Baker had barely started work on these projects when at the beginning of March, he found a note in his sketchbook written by Rhodes—"I desire you to see Rome, Paestum, Agrigentum, Thebes and Athens. I am thinking of erecting a mausoleum to those who fell at Kimberley, a bath and a copy of Paestum. Your expenses will be paid and in case I undertake any of these thoughts you will receive the usual architect's fee of five per cent. C J Rhodes."[27] It was an extraordinarily generous gift to his architect and a token of what was now a close and valued friendship. A European grand tour with all expenses paid—Baker could hardly contain his excitement in his next letter to Percy—"I may possibly come home by next mail!! Tell no one in case I disappoint them, as there is many a slip! C.I.R. dear old fellow wants me to go to Egypt & Greece to see how his ideal heroes of old used to build…. I may be only 3 or 4 days at home…. What Excitement! (*Note added on the 8th*) Seen C.I.R. again & am coming with him on Norham, but I think it will be amusing to surprise Owletts!"[28] On the 18th of March 1900, they set sail together for England as Baker recalled—"I travelled home in the ship with him and sat at the same table, where he talked much of all these things (*the memorials, house and office building*). He stressed the duty imposed by wealth—*noblesse oblige*—of building beautiful homes where the owners could render gracious hospitality to the stranger and the less fortunate up-country miner, farmer, and pioneer. These houses, the Bath, and the monuments were conceived in pursuance of his 'doctrine of ransom'; by which he meant that those who despoiled the face of nature by extracting its wealth should render compensation by the creation of works of beauty and of use to humanity."[29] Whether *noblesse oblige*, a sense of guilt, or simply the wish to leave an architectural legacy that would live on after him, Baker was ready, pencil in hand, to give form to Rhodes' increasingly ambitious architectural visions.

After a few days at Owletts, which included a brief visit to see his cousins at Nurstead Court and with most of his time spent acquiring suitable new clothing for his travels, Baker caught the boat train to France and then continued by train to Brindisi in Italy, from where he caught a steamer to Cairo. Having already undertaken several tours of the ancient sites himself, Rhodes had largely dictated Baker's itinerary and having also provided generous funding, this allowed Baker to travel in a luxury to which he had previously been unaccustomed. He had also received strict instructions from his mother to keep her fully informed as to his progress with one of his first letters home to her coming from the Grand Continental Hotel in Cairo—"I have accomplished the journey from the Cape to Cairo all right; it is more than a third of the way round the earth, and I have just done a thousand miles more from here to Thebes and back. Yet I have enjoyed my visit immensely … the fascinating dress, customs and life of the people, the bright colour and work of the bazaars.… Thebes is beyond description wonderful: 6 or 7 huge well preserved temples and innumerable tombs with the colouring of the pictured walls as clear as when it was done 3 or 4000 years ago. The temperature was 110 at least in the shade.… I leave with no great regret for Athens tomorrow."[30] While Egypt and its temples on the Nile had clearly fascinated Baker, it was the Classical architecture of the two great all-conquering empires of Greece and Rome which Rhodes wished him to study in particular, and so he traveled on—"From Alexandria to Piraeus.… I dined at the Embassy last night and have been put on to the right people and am getting very great assistance in my work.… The scenery is very African, almost bare mountains with scrubby growth … yet … infinitely finer, with its beautifully placed buildings.… The beauty of the Acropolis is impossible to exaggerate, it is finer than the best I imagined."[31] Baker was clearly hugely impressed by the Acropolis—crucially—both in terms of the quality of the individual temples and the picturesque beauty of its dramatic hilltop site, confirming in his autobiography that he "rode round Athens, seeing the Acropolis from all distances."[32]

From Athens, another steamer took him across the Ionian Sea to Sicily, where he wrote from the Grand Hotel Des Palmes in Palermo—"I went yesterday for a pleasant trip to Segesta, an old Greek city deserted amongst the mountains on the West coast … interesting one more complete temple & theatre on bare mountain alone."[33] A further trip south to Agrigenta included both the Temple of Concord on its acropolis and the Tomb of Theron which he captured in a fine watercolor sketch (on which he later noted—"on which I based the Kimberley War Memorial") and then on east to the Greek and Roman ruins of Syracuse. From Palermo by sea once more to Naples, from where he visited Paestum, where the temples were again recorded in sketches and watercolors—"Paestum was very grand—3 nearly perfect Greek temples left alone in a marsh by the sea.… I heard of the fall of Pretoria at Paestum: appropriately as it was also my main objective"[34] and then north to Rome, where he had arranged to meet Percy. Together they toured the eternal city and concluded their visit with a trip out to Tivoli to see both Hadrian's Villa and the terraced gardens and fountains of the Villa D'Este which had so impressed him on his first visit as a young articled pupil. His tour completed, he crossed from Italy to Switzerland where his mother had traveled to join him for a few days' vacation with her son before his return to Cape Town.

In Baker's own words—"What I learnt on my travels, in Egypt, Greece, Italy and Sicily, which Rhodes liberality enabled me to enjoy in leisure and comfort—was of the greatest value to me both in what I built for him and to his memory and in all my after-work."[35] What Baker had seen, drawn and measured on his tour, would reappear in his future work again and again, not merely in the correct use of the orders and adherence to the laws of proportion of Classicism, but also in memories of the spaces, landscapes and climates that he had experienced; the shaded cortiles of the Roman palazzos with their cooling pools and fountains; the vast coffered dome of the Pantheon; the sculptures of Egypt under the baking African sun; the dramatic settings of the Greek and Roman tombs, amphitheaters and temples looking out over the Mediterranean, Ionian and Aegean seas; the terraces of the Villa D'Este cascading down the hillside in Tivoli; the composition of the Acropolis in Athens and the Capitoline Hill in Rome; the sheer scale, confidence and drama of it all and the contemplation of his own future opportunities to commemorate the British Empire in similar style. He returned to South Africa with the zeal of the converted, immersing himself in the design of Rhodes' memorials throughout his passage home. Finally arriving back at the Grotto after five months of traveling, Franklin Kendall helped him to unpack, later recalling that his luggage contained "a couple of boxes of architectural and historical books, which I helped him to sort and place on his shelves. With some curiosity I asked him when he expected to get time to read all these momentous tomes, to which he replied with a half guilty air—'Well you see, I have read them on my tour!'"[36]

After so long away and with so many commissions ongoing, there was to be no "easing himself back in." His workload immediately overwhelmed him and from around this time onwards as the practice continued to grow, he began to divide his commissions between the projects that he himself led and those which he would merely supervise, leaving most of the work to Masey. A contemporary, typed "List of Mr. Baker's Works" is among the documents held by the University of Cape Town Libraries and overwritten on this in Baker's own hand are his notes crediting authorship to either himself or Masey. What is striking is that the architectural quality of Baker's projects is so far above those of Masey. Masey, for example, is credited with the City Club and St. Philip's Church, which compare poorly with Baker's own Rhodes Building and St. Andrew's and so it would appear that, despite Masey's many prizes for design, by 1900 Baker was at the very least his equal.

First among Baker's chosen personal projects were always those for Rhodes, and almost immediately after his return he was able to finally present his ideas for further discussion with Rhodes. He personally produced beautiful renderings of the proposed Memorial Baths or "Nymphaeum" as they called it—it was to be "a temple sacred to the guardian goddess of the fountain," a "marble temple amidst pools of lilies and papyrus, like the 'Fountain Arethuse' at Syracuse" which he had recently visited.[37] Unfortunately, Rhodes was unable to convince his fellow directors of De Beers that they should fund the monument and so neither it, nor his imagined recreation of the temple at Paestum on Table Mountain, were ever to be built.

Baker's designs for Rhodes' two other monuments were, however, both constructed and are extremely important in the context of his life's work. The first—the Shangani Monument which Rhodes personally funded—was to commemorate the British South Africa Company's ill-fated "Shangani Patrol," who had been elevated to the status of martyrs of the empire. Vastly outnumbered, they had been slaughtered by Matabele warriors (who were, of course, simply defending their own lands from capture). Baker's design, which was finally erected in 1904, was to be the first of numerous memorial commissions which he was to carry out throughout his long career—a simple, stone sarcophagus, derived from the pedestal of Agrippa below the Propylaeum in Athens, complete with four bas-relief friezes by the Scots sculptor John Tweed once more, which are shaded by a crisp projecting cornice. There is a new and extreme Classical restraint here, which was to be repeated in his much larger Kimberley Honoured Dead Memorial, which was also dedicated in 1904.

The Kimberley Monument—Baker's first use of the elevated loggia (author's collection).

For Kimberley, Baker produced numerous perspective drawings, almost all of which were variations on the various Classical monuments which now he and Rhodes had seen, before a design was finally agreed upon based on the Tomb of Theron on Sicily but with the four-square columns freestanding above a solid base, such as in the Tomb of the Nereids in Turkey. The result was something of a triumph and almost certainly Baker's finest work to date. Like the Shangani Memorial, there was utter restraint, the most perfect proportions (including the correct use of entasis) resulting in a monument which glorified the heroic events with a solemn dignity. In discussing Lutyens' much later War Stone, Roderick Gradidge suggested that "it was Baker who, under Rhodes influence, had pioneered this form of abstract Classicism for war memorials. In 1904 he designed a dignified and Classical design to commemorate the defense of Kimberley outside that town. On a tall base of red sandstone stand 12 Doric columns in a square under a cornice. Engraved onto the base in simple Classical lettering are the names of the dead—there is nothing else."[38] For Rhodes, this was a fitting monument to the dramatic events of the siege, but for Baker, this tetrastyle portico which looked out from on high across the conquered lands of the empire, like the four caryatids of the Erechtheon surveying Athens, was to become something of *leitmotif* which would reappear again and again in his future work from Pretoria via New Delhi to Oxford and Cambridge. It became in many ways, his symbol of the empire, combining in a single architectural element its perceived superiority, dignity, power, civilizing influence and limitless vision.

His design for the new house for visiting poets and artists near Groote Schuur on Rhodes' estate fortunately also proceeded to construction. Called the Woolsack, it was built on a site chosen by Baker, Rhodes and Rudyard Kipling's wife Carrie in March 1900, and soon became a regular winter home for Kipling (then unofficial Poet Laureate to the Empire) and his family. Baker's own description covers all the basics—"The house was

The atrium of the Woolsack, Cape Town, Rudyard Kipling's winter home for many years, Groote Schuur (from *Architecture and Personalities*).

planned round a large columned atrium and a court paved with large red tiles on which stood tubs of blue hydrangeas. In the Roman manner the open colonnade is the way from room to room. I never heard complaints from the Kiplings that, against the gain of fresh air everywhere, had to be set off any discomfort of chills or cold dinners. The central atrium was indeed a delight in the soft climate of the coast; but one which I built in the hot Karoo was derisively called the 'Bakehouse'!"[39] While the language here is the same as Groote Schuur, there is a calmness and simplicity which Baker felt too modest for Rhodes' own house. Baker is here relaxed and confident and as Rhodes had told him "not to be mean," the craftsmanship throughout is excellent, even down to the carefully selected Dutch tiles that line a sunken bath. The Kiplings were entranced with it, and stayed in the house every year from its completion in 1900 until 1907. The family "would descend for five or six months from the peace of England, to the deeper peace of the 'Woolsack,' and live under the oak trees overhanging the patio, where mother squirrels taught their babies to climb, and in the stillness of hot afternoons the fall of an acorn was almost like a shot."[40]

The Rhodes Building, Cape Town (courtesy Lynda Marie Emel).

Baker had already briefly started work on the Rhodes Building before his departure for Europe and on his return began work in earnest on the design. Detailed drawings were complete by September and construction started in the spring of the next year, 1901. This proved to be a further variation on the use of an atrium to cool and light a building, but here used to serve a six-story office. The key to the building's organization starts at ground floor with a black-and-white-checkerboard paved courtyard in the center of which is a cooling fountain of red Verona marble topped with what was to become a much-used symbol by Baker—the Zimbabwe bird, the symbol of Rhodesia—which had already graced the staircases in Groote Schuur. As in his Cape Dutch houses, the courtyard was surrounded on three sides by a sheltering colonnade, but here with the fourth side being occupied by the elevator and stairs which were also lit from the court through all their levels. Records, stores and toilets take up the other internal spaces with the two exterior walls of this corner building providing light and air for the offices which overlook Baker's cathedral which was built diagonally opposite. The street corner is celebrated both in plan and section with two octagonal board rooms accommodated on the ground and first floors with a decorated first-floor bay continuing up into an elongated oriel window. Externally, the proportions are excellent, from the *piano rustico* of arched windows at street level, through the tall, shuttered office windows on the first, second and third floors, below a contrasting horizontal colonnaded top floor and the now inevitable Dutch gables with Venetian windows. In terms of his architectural development, the Rhodes Building shows his growing confidence in adapting the atrium to office use and his increased understanding of Classicism in the restraint of the granite detailing. It is a very accomplished city building with C. R. Ashbee, one of the leading architects of the Arts and Crafts Movement, who visited Cape Town in June 1903 expressing his delight with "the open court of the Barghello and the Palazzo Massimi applied to a place of business in such a dull humdrum, dawdly city as Cape Town," and also going so far as to say "I envy the architect of the Rhodes Building."[41] High praise indeed for a mere colonial architect.

What had at first been a trickle of new commissions a few years previously was now a flood. In addition to Rhodes' recent commissions and the continuing work on the cathedral, there was now also a restaurant in Stellenbosch; alterations to Government House and a staff cottage—The Retreat—in the grounds (which Lionel Curtis later described as "a perfect little house … equal to anything I have seen in the Arts and Crafts Exhibition")[42]; a house extension for wine-grower Louis Cloete; a new tower for the Church of Saint Paul; a manager's house for the Somerset West explosives works; two new houses—the rambling Madawaska and the Lilacs—complete with Italianate tower; a further commercial building for D. Isaccs and Company in central Cape Town and a further small church—the Memorial Church of St. John the Baptist in Mafeking. Baker's articled pupil Vernon Rees-Poole later recalled that there never seemed to be either enough hands or enough time to cope with the workload and it was only Baker's own driving energy that led them through it. As Rees-Poole continued—"Schemes were thought out and sketches produced in no time; like his walking, no one could keep pace with him. The only recreation he took was walking and horse riding on Muizenberg beach. One day, whilst galloping, his horse came down. Baker was thrown and broke his collarbone; he had to rest for a time, and that was the only short holiday I remember him taking."[43] In addition to this daily workload, both Baker and Masey also fulfilled what they saw as their professional obligations and were instrumental in the creation of the South African Society of

Architects, their activities soon leading to the constituting of the Cape Institute of Architects the following July in 1902. Lectures and meetings were organized, visits to construction sites and recently completed buildings undertaken and soon "Baker" and "Masey" prizes were being awarded to local students of architecture and engineering.

Meanwhile, a thousand miles to the north, the Boer War raged on. Early British embarrassments had been quickly reversed with the massive reinforcement of local forces by troops from around the empire, soon making it the largest fighting force that Britain had ever sent overseas. The outcome was inevitable. In conventional military terms, the war was won in late 1900 with the capture of Pretoria (of which Baker had heard while in Italy) and Britain had by then gained control of almost all of the former Boer territories. The Boers, however, did not surrender and commenced one of the first campaigns of guerrilla warfare, traveling quickly across the vast region that they knew so well, attacking British troops, convoys and the railways that transported them. The British were forced to change their tactics and as well as building a series of "blockhouses" throughout the region to protect their supply routes and creating their own "raiding columns" to counter the Boers, they also commenced a policy of "scorched earth" which was designed to remove any form of sustenance for the guerrillas. British troops swept the countryside, systematically destroying crops, burning homesteads and farms, poisoning wells and interning both Boer and African women, children and workers in concentration camps in which disease and starvation killed thousands.[44] It was now a war of attrition, which would drift on until May 1902, before the Boers were finally forced to accept peace terms.

For Baker and his architectural practice, ironically, the impact of the Boer War had been entirely positive, resulting in several of Rhodes' commissions as well as the Memorial Church at Mafeking, and in early 1901 he found himself presented with another potentially transformative opportunity. Alfred Milner, the High Commissioner for South Africa, anticipating the end of the war, was planning to move his headquarters from Cape Town to Johannesburg from where he could better manage the reconstruction of the Transvaal and its integration into the new British South Africa. In Baker's own words— "While guerrilla warfare went on like death-hunts between the two races—he invited me to go up there to aid in introducing a better and more permanent order of architecture. Building there in the past had been of a temporary and rather shoddy kind.... The houses and offices, built of cheap bricks and thin iron, bore a very impermanent look. But when the truth of Rhodes' saying, 'It is all one country now,' was realized, and men felt the sanctuary of the Pax Britannica, there was the opportunity for the architecture which establishes a nation. So with the prospect of abundant work I set forth once again on my adventures."[45]

4

1901–1904

"The Light of Life" (Op. 20)

One can only marvel at Baker's ambition, drive and self-confidence as he approached 40. Already established as the leading architect in Cape Town, with the Rhodes Building due to start on-site in April, construction of the Isaacs building just commenced, the Lilacs and Madawaska under construction, the Woolsack nearing completion and needing furnishing and while still personally working on the detailed design of the Kimberley Memorial plus numerous other minor commissions for Rhodes on his various estates, Baker immediately recognized the scale of this new opportunity and followed Milner to Johannesburg to further investigate the prospects.

Milner himself moved there at the beginning of March 1901, where author and politician John Buchan can take up the tale—Milner

was a solitary man; but his loneliness never made him aloof and chilly, and in his manner there was always a gentle, considerate courtesy. Milner's friends were his own (*Oxford*) college contemporaries and the young men whom he gathered around him. In those days we were a very young company, which Johannesburg, not unkindly, labelled the "Kindergarten." Our *doyen* was Patrick Duncan, who had been brought out from Somerset House to take charge of the Transvaal's finances. Milner himself and his personal staff lived in a red-brick villa, called Sunnyside, in the suburbs. His military secretary was Major William Lambton of the Coldstream Guards, and his aides-de-camp were Lord Brooke (afterwards Lord Warwick) and Lord Henry Seymour. Among the secretaries were Geoffrey Dawson, Lord Basil Blackwood, Hugh Wyndham and Gerard Craig Sellar. There was also a group who had special tasks assigned to them; it included Lionel Curtis, R H Brand, Lionel Hichens and Philip Kerr. Hugh Wyndham and I shared a staff cottage at the gate of Sunnyside, but most of my time was spent ranging the country from the Cape to the Limpopo. It was a pleasant and most varied company, wonderfully well agreed, for, having a great deal to do, we did not get in each other's way. Loyalty to Milner and his creed was a strong cement which endured long after our South African service ended, since the *Round Table* coterie in England continued the Kindergarten."[1]

These men—"this band of brothers … not merely able and enthusiastic lieutenants, but men with visions of their own of greatness and adventure"[2]—were to first become Baker's friends and later still, his clients; these new relationships, forged in Johannesburg, would survive throughout their lives as they all went on to serve the empire across the globe.[3] As Michael Keath noted, "If his friendship with Rhodes had made his success in Cape Town possible, his circle in Johannesburg would make it certain."[4]

Baker arrived later in March for the first of a series of lengthy visits throughout the latter part of 1901, which continued through 1902. Baker recalled later that he "felt at first rather restless and unsettled in the haphazardly developed mining town. But then there came to my rescue Lionel Curtis, a prime mover in all good ventures. On arriving in Cape Town he had seen and admired a little house (*The Retreat*) I had built for the Governor's staff in the Grounds of Government House. He came to see me and we made friends at once. I recognized that here was the man, another Edmund Garrett, with the personality and spirit I admired and sought as a comrade in the new quest."[5] Like most of the Kindergarten, Curtis was considerably younger than Baker—in his case 10 years—and as a result, he christened Baker "Grandpa," a name by which he became known by them all from the early days. A contemporary photograph of "The Kindergarten Group," in front of the hall chimney of Government House shows a strong athletic Baker with arms crossed, his back against the stone chimney breast, surrounded by the younger men.

Herbert Baker in 1903 (courtesy Michael Baker).

The first of the Kindergarten to arrive in Johannesburg was J. F. ("Peter") Perry, who enjoyed the title of Imperial Secretary to the High Commissioner. Like Curtis, and so many of the other members of the Kindergarten, he was a New College (Oxford) graduate. When Curtis arrived in Johannesburg in March with Milner, he boarded with Perry and his wife and Baker soon joined them on his increasingly frequent visits from Cape Town. Baker's letter home to his mother of May 1901 from Bloemfontein helpfully sets out his thoughts—"I have come up here at the request of the Administrator—Col Gould Adams, to advise him how to improve the house. It is gloomily gaudily decorated and wants the application of white paint & a bonfire. Owing to a depleted treasury there is little money to spend, but as things improve, I hope to make a better house of it.... I was lucky too in being here when Sir Alfred Milner stopped on his journey home." (*continued on May 7*) "I was so fit up in the high veld that I am half inclined to go to Johannesburg if I have a chance. ... Starting a new country w'd be interesting & it would be a chance to put a stamp on the Architecture of a new country. But we are looking ahead too much!"[6]

By December Baker's commitment had clearly grown. Curtis had "bought two acres of land on the edge of a virgin kopje (*small hill*) north of the town and of the mines; then there was nothing on it but a blockhouse and barbed wire. It overlooked a young plantation of firs and gum trees; and beyond, the summer green and winter gold of rolling grass-veld and away to the distant faint blue Magaliesberg Mountains, 'ramparts of a slaughter and peril' where the war still raged. We agreed that I should take over the land and build a house there in which he and I and other friends could live together. I willingly

The Kindergarten, back row: Lionel Curtis, Nel Hichens, Peter Perry, Hugh Wyndham, Herbert Baker, Geoffrey Dawson. Sitting: Lord Selbourne, Robert Brand, Patrick Duncan, Lady Selbourne, Lord Long, Richard Feetham. On floor: Philip Kerr, John Dove, Dougal Malcolm (courtesy Michael Baker).

took on the venture; and the Stonehouse, the first 'Moot-house,' grew out of the rocky ridge of the Koptje."[7] By early 1902 he was committed to a move to Johannesburg, leaving "with regret my dear little house at Muizenberg and comfortable quarters in the Castle Shipping Company's newly-built offices."[8]

Johannesburg was certainly in need of Baker's skills as Alfred Milner had quickly realized, having grown from a prospecting camp in 1884 to a sprawling corrugated iron township of almost 150,000 people by 1902 following the discovery of gold.[9] As in so many other colonial outposts, a grid plan had been established in 1886 which provided some structure to the nevertheless fairly chaotic urban environment. It was a long way from Cape Town—a full day's train journey—but for Baker, who still rode or ran each morning, its location on the Highveld (the broad grassy plateau that sweeps across the South African interior) would have offered a refreshing alternative to the warm winds, humidity and high temperatures of the Cape.

Encouragingly, within weeks of his arrival, Baker had already secured a number of commissions—almost all for new houses for the local "Randlords"—the men who had made a fortune from the diamond and gold mines. In those first months of 1902 he was working on new homes for John Dale Lace,[10] a gold-and-diamond magnate, for whom he designed Northwards, a vast Cape Dutch/Jacobean/Arts and Crafts mansion in local stone and render complete with double-height bay windows, arched loggias, Doric colonnades and a sumptuous interior that would have graced a later Hollywood mansion, plus in Baker's words, "a garden of herbaceous borders, water-pools, cypress hedges, and wide-spreading lawns"[11]; Inanda House for W. Wyberg, the Commissioner of Mines—a fine little white Cape Dutch lodge with twin gables either side of a Tuscan Doric *stoep*; for Sir George Farrar, the chairman of the East Rand Proprietary Mines Company,[12] he designed Bedford Court, a rather grander version of Inanda with the rendered Cape Dutch villa now raised on a local stone base and extended with flanking gabled wings and of course Stonehouse with Lionel Curtis, the design of which was completed by March. Baker found the construction skills in the Transvaal much as he had first encountered in the Cape with many of the interiors for these first houses largely made in the Cape and then sent upcountry. Once more, Baker was completely overwhelmed by the quantity of work that he had won and realized that he would have to build a new team in Johannesburg to help him to deliver this wave of new commissions. On the 12th of March therefore, he left Johannesburg bound for England to "obtain a good assistant to help."[13] His passage was booked from Cape Town and en route to his ship he visited Rhodes, who by now was gravely ill.

Rhodes himself had been in England the previous year—both to deal with business and political matters as usual, but also on this occasion to consult a London heart specialist. It was confirmed that his condition was now critical and he was advised to rest and set aside his many responsibilities for a time. As a result, "his plan was to occupy the rest of the year in the pleasures of travel. Acquiring an estate in Norfolk for his family heirs … touring Europe by motorcar, which was the newest craze of the rich, and winding up with a visit to Egypt"[14] prior to embarking at Southampton in January 1902 with Dr. Jameson for his return trip to Cape Town. During a rough passage he caught a severe cold and suffered a bad fall, thus arriving back in South Africa in a much worse condition than when he had left. As the winter months in Groote Schuur were invariably hot and airless, he asked to be taken to an old, then tin-roofed, cottage hard against the mountainside overlooking False Bay near Baker's seaside home at Muizenberg. Baker had offered him the fresher air of Sandhills, but he had declined and spent what were to be his last days on the cottage *stoep* overlooking the sea. James Rose Innes visited him there shortly before he died, finding him "mortally stricken and in sore need of spacious and airy surroundings, one of the most famous and wealthiest men in the British Empire."[15] Baker wrote of his visit in March—"I said my last farewell to him there in that humble cottage, and I shall all my life be haunted by the remembrance."[16] Rhodes died there in his single cast-iron bed on the 26th of March 1902, by which time Baker was back in England. It was uncanny that Milner should have opened a door, just as another was closing.

Little is known of Baker's relatively brief visit to England in 1902, but I think we can be certain that he visited both his family in Cobham, and his cousins, the Edmeades, at nearby Nurstead Court and almost certainly too, that he would have looked up his old friend, Ned Lutyens. He would certainly have been shocked at Lutyens' recent redecoration of his home and office at 29 Bloomsbury Square (Norman Shaw's old office) in which

Rhodes' cottage at Muizenberg where he died (courtesy Tom Tunstall).

the dining-room walls were now red and the drawing room jet black. Lutyens had married Emily Lytton in August 1897, the daughter of a former Viceroy of India and British ambassador to France, Robert Bulwer Lytton, and they already had two children, Barbara and Robert. This period was as close to domestic bliss as the Lutyens ever achieved and must have made Baker consider his own greater age and bachelorhood. Lutyens' reputation as an architect of sumptuous country houses was already assured. He had completed Munstead Wood, Fulbrook, Orchards, Goddards and the exquisite Deanery Garden for Edward Hudson, the founder of *Country Life*, who "was devoted to Lutyens and utterly convinced of his genius"[17] and who now published each of Lutyens' country houses in his magazine on their completion. His marriage had done Lutyens no harm either and during Baker's visit he would have been engaged on Knebworth for his mother-in-law Edith Lytton, Fishers Hill for his brother-in-law Gerald Balfour and Grey Walls for Alfred Lyttleton, who was married to another of the Balfour girls. Lutyens, at just 33, was already at the height of his creative powers with perhaps the most impressive of all his country houses, Marshcourt, nearing completion on-site. The two architects must have eyed each other once more with interest and a little envy—Baker well aware that Groote Schuur and the Woolsack were in a much lower architectural division than Deanery Garden and Marshcourt—while Lutyens was secretly impressed by Baker's larger practice, complete with a range of commercial, government and ecclesiastical commissions, the likes of which would elude him for many more years.

Baker's reason for being in London, however, was to find his new assistant—a potential partner for his ever-expanding practice—and he soon came across Ernest Willmott Sloper (1871–1916), who at the time was in a not particularly productive partnership with Ambrose Poynter. Bearing in mind the timescale, Baker must have very quickly and eloquently convinced him of the opportunities in South Africa as the two embarked together for Cape Town later in the month of April. The pair disembarked on the 7th of May and traveled up to Johannesburg the following week. With Sloper on board, Baker was finally able to establish an architectural office in Johannesburg, leaving Masey to take care of affairs in Cape Town with Kendall's assistance.

Rhodes' burial had already taken place by the time Baker returned from England, following something approaching a state funeral in Cape Town as the local *Gippsland Mercury* reported—"We have just emerged from a cloud of mourning and the last streamer has been taken down. For the past week the town has been smothered in black, each building trying to outdo the other, and I think it has seldom been the lot of any man to be mourned so sincerely ... all could not help feeling that the man who had made the country deserved all the honor and respect we could show his memory."[18] From Cape Town, where his body had lain in state for several days, his coffin was transported by train to Bulawayo, where "his grave is hewn, as he willed it, out of the solid granite on the top of a vast flat dome of rock and within its crowning circle of natural boulders, which he called 'the Temple.' The bronze slab bears no other words but his name and the dates of his birth and death."[19] Baker and Rhodes had visited the site together as it was to be the location of the Shangani Memorial. Rhodes' idea was for the memorial to be placed in the center of the circle of boulders on the hilltop but Baker had advised him to place it behind the circle with the stones acting as a "portico" to the monument. By the time of Baker's return, Rhodes was already entombed in his rock-cut grave in the center of the circle and it had been decided to move the monument further down the hill, where it was viewed from above, rather than below, as Baker originally intended.

In his will, Rhodes had left Groote Schuur, along with funds to maintain it, as the future residence of the prime minister of a united South Africa. His recently acquired British estates he left to his family. To his old college at Oxford, Oriel, he left £100,000, and the remainder of his fortune was to be used to fund Oxford University scholarships "to be awarded annually to students from Canada, the Australian colonies, New Zealand and South Africa, and to two students from each state of the USA. Rhodes explained that the purposes were not primarily academic, but to create men dedicated to the 'union of the English-speaking peoples throughout the world.' ... The scholars were to be chosen not merely for scholastic and literary ability, which counted for only four points out of ten, but qualities of manhood, ability at manly sports and moral force of character were to prevail."[20] Through his scholarships, Rhodes hoped that his vision of a federation of English-speaking states around the globe would finally be achieved. Inspired by Rhodes' generosity, Baker himself would soon establish an architectural scholarship at the British School in Rome for young South African architects.

By the time of Baker's return, thoughts had already turned to the provision of a fitting memorial to Rhodes and, when consulted, Baker "urged his passion for the site and views on the mountain-slopes above Groote Schuur. There he often rode and had placed a seat on which, looking northwards towards the hinterland, he would sit and dream his dreams.... I knew his vision of monumental architecture on this mountainside.... The 'incoherent poetry' of his vision was the desire to draw people up there in the hope that they would be inspired, as he was himself, by the mountain and the view; it was his instinctive feeling that landscapes seen against and through noble architecture humanized nature and added to their spiritual value."[21] A suitable spot at Devil's Peak on the mountainside was therefore selected and Baker commissioned to design the monument to his friend and benefactor.

Meanwhile back in Johannesburg, work had started on Stonehouse shortly before Baker's departure for England and, almost simultaneously, Lionel Curtis was appointed Colonial Secretary in Pretoria by Milner. Baker and Curtis agreed that rather than this being Curtis's house, in which Baker would stay while in Johannesburg, their roles would now be reversed and thus Baker bought the site from Curtis and continued to fund the construction on what was now to be his new home. Curtis soon found a site in Pretoria, for which Baker designed the White House—the clue is in the name—another low Cape Dutch villa, which is in some ways a more satisfying design than Baker's own Stonehouse. Rather than employing contrasting stone and white render as in his own home, there is a purity and consistency to Curtis's house, which is slightly compromised by the broader palette of materials in Johannesburg.

A steady flow of commissions continued throughout the summer with new clients practically lining up outside Baker's office door—Major Karri Davis, W. Pennant, Sir Percy Fitzpatrick, Raymond Schumacher, Lieutenant Colonel O'Brien—all of whom received variations on Baker's now ubiquitous "H" plan in stone or white render with a central axial sequence of entrance *stoep*, public rooms and veranda, flanked by bedrooms and service spaces and anchored by massive stone chimneys. Often built of stone hewn on their sites, these houses acknowledged the intense heat of the Transvaal summer with their deeply recessed *stoeps* casting welcome shadows and catching any breezes in the summer while also letting in the rays of the low winter sun. It was an incredibly successful formula and created popular comfortable homes with more than a whiff of Baker's own dignified restraint. Doreen Greig claimed that every detail of these houses and indeed of all his other projects was referred to Baker but this was simply impossible bearing in mind both the scale of the practice's workload and its division between Johannesburg and Cape Town. Instead, Baker developed this model for houses and a similar one for small churches for his assistants to follow with only the most significant projects receiving a high degree of his own attention. (This is in considerable contrast to Lutyens whose smaller workload and absence of partners allowed him to truly consider every detail.)

On the 31st of May 1902, the Peace Treaty of Vereeniging between the British and the Boers was signed, finally bringing the war to an end. The British were victorious but their "scorched earth" warfare had generated an (entirely understandable) hatred among the Boers. The chances of uniting the four colonies of the Cape, Natal, Transvaal and Orange River into a new South Africa seemed remote, and yet, within less than 10 years this would be peacefully achieved by a quite remarkable display of courage and trust by the leaders on both sides.

In July, Baker was appointed to design the new Government House in Pretoria. This was to provide both domestic and social accommodation for the governor of the Transvaal Colony. By August, Baker had presented his first proposals to Lord Milner and all was progressing well until the appointment of Sir Arthur and Lady Lawley in September, at which point matters moved backwards at increasing speed resulting in a change of location for the house in December, before an eventual start on-site was made in May 1903, after which work was suspended that August. How Baker and Sloper coped with their vast flock of clients and their ever-changing demands as well as knocking out designs and overseeing construction during this period is beyond comprehension, never mind Baker's ongoing responsibility for his Cape Town office which he continued to supervise through regular 2,000-mile round-trip train journeys.

Peace now brought Baker new clients from the enemy's camp. Samuel Marks, a close friend of Boer leader President Kruger and a participant on the Boer side in the peace talks, now wished to expand his mining and other interests south into Cape Town from his base in Pretoria. Baker designed a new house for him in Muizenberg (which was never constructed) but more significantly was commissioned late in 1902 to design a palatial new office for him in the city—the Marks Building—the name by which it is still known. From the design—the Edwardian Baroque that was so fashionable in London at the time, the lack of the rich modeling which Baker used to shade the interior spaces of his office buildings from the harsh South African sun, and the limited contemporary evidence, including Franklin Kendall's recollection that Masey "did the original design ... and Baker hardly touched it"[22]—I think we can conclude that this was carried out almost exclusively by Masey and his team in Cape Town. With their physical separation, Masey was beginning, quite naturally, to assert himself more and more in their practice's southern branch.

One Cape Town project, commissioned in 1902, which Baker kept total control over was a new house for mining magnate Abe Bailey who had been a close associate of Rhodes. Bailey had acquired the site above the cottage in which Rhodes had died, looking out over False Bay, where Baker had once hoped to build another seaside house for Rhodes—"Abe Bailey bought the site and built the house on Rhodes' terrace; there he entertained with the same broad-minded and generous hospitality as the man whose example he aspired to follow. And he followed his example, too, in bequeathing this house, *Rust en Vrede*, well called Rest and Peace, for the refreshment of those who have given good service to South Africa and the Empire. On the terrace we built a deep-arched and white-columned *stoep* so that the road below was hidden and nothing marred the view of the waves breaking on the rocks and the blue sea beyond.... On the rocks of the steep mountain-side behind the house a hanging garden was planted with flowers and creepers that like the salt sea-air."[23] It is a delightful and rather sumptuous house, sparkling white in the clean sea air and sunlight—basically Baker's "H" plan once more but extended here and there with Dutch gabled wings. The central hall, which opens onto a generous white, Doric-columned, vaulted loggia is paved in a pale green Cipollini marble and looks straight out to the shimmering waters of the bay which in turn are reflected in the vaults of the loggia. It is a simply stunning space—cool and graceful—with a sybaritic quality which would have been far too much for Rhodes. The entrance hall and stairs (though without the view) are equally fine in carved and paneled black African stinkwood, the only low point of the entire composition being the swooping lines of the arched entrance arcade which is incredibly thin and weak in three dimensions (a feature unfortunately repeated on several subsequent villas).

Like many successful architects before and since, Baker was now trying to juggle winning work, supervising construction, recruiting and managing an ever-larger team, maintaining client contact, fulfilling his professional obligations, continuing his own professional development, controlling the quality of work in two offices, designing the buildings, making sure that the business was generating profit rather than just turnover and in the case of one or two projects such as *Rust en Vrede*—even still furnishing clients' houses for them. In addition, since he had returned from London, he had been leading a nomadic existence between Johannesburg and Cape Town. He may have been envious

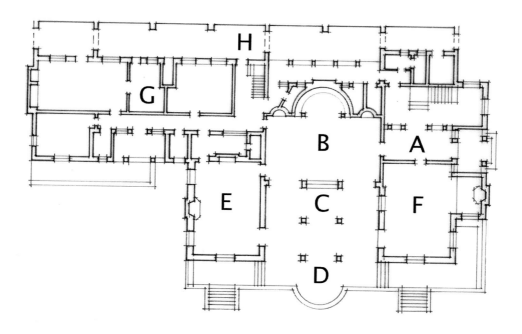

"Rust en Vrede" ground floor plan. Key: A Entrance Hall, B Hall, C Loggia, D Stoep, E Dining Room, F Billiard Room, G Kitchen and Servants, H Covered Way (author's drawing, based on Michael Keath plans).

of the domestic arrangements at 29 Bloomsbury Square, but how could he possibly find time for a family life in addition to all this? His visit to England in the spring of 1902 had allowed him to reflect on his own achievements but it had also made him realize that, at 40, if he was ever to marry and have children, the sands of time were now running somewhat faster.[24] While at Owletts, he had as usual visited his cousins at nearby Nurstead Court and with these thoughts in his mind, perhaps had looked upon the unmarried Edmeades girls in a new light.

His younger brother Charles, who was 30, was engaged to marry his cousin Mabel Edmeades, also 30, with a date set for October 1902, which would leave two Edmeades cousins unmarried. The elder of these, Mary, was 29, and the younger Florence 24, and while Mary was nearer to Herbert's age (albeit younger than his younger brother's fiancé) it was the livelier and more attractive Florence (who was some 16 years younger than Herbert) whom Baker began to envision as a potential bride. Having more or less restricted his choice to two women, Baker can hardly be blamed for choosing one rather than the other, but it was a bold and rather shocking choice nevertheless, considering the age gap (which unbeknownst to either party would condemn Mary to spinsterhood). We don't know what, if anything, was said at Nurstead that spring, but in September of 1902, we have a surviving letter from Baker to Florence, who is now addressed as "My fair correspondent"—"Two letters arrived here for me in one week…. The result however was a double radiance shed upon me, lightening my dull existence…. I am so horribly busy that I can't bolt home, as I should like to…. Love to all at Nurstead from their poor colonial cousin."[25] This was to be one of the first of a steady stream of letters between the two—apparently kept secret at Nurstead and also in Johannesburg, where Baker continued his apparently happy bachelor existence with the other members of the Kindergarten. Stonehouse was under construction, with everyone in Johannesburg viewing it as their soon to be completed moot-house, while Baker quietly had other ideas entirely. After great frustration with his builder, Baker's transient existence came to an end with the completion of his new home on the 16th of March 1903, and he was finally able to send for his furniture from the Grotto thus conclusively confirming Johannesburg as his future base.

Florence Edmeade, Baker's "Fair Correspondent" (courtesy Michael Baker).

Stonehouse is an unusual house and highly original. Baker himself refers to it as a "rock-built house,"[26] and it does stand like some mighty crag from which its interior spaces appear to have been carved. Its exterior character is strangely defensive, with its heavily-studded front door maintaining this effect, but once its outer defenses have been penetrated it reveals an exceptionally fine sequence of spaces which very successfully combine Baker's Arts and Crafts roots with his growing interest in Classicism. As he explained, "It was planned round a long-windowed hall with two-storeyed wings of small rooms on either side; and to the north, facing the kopje-terrace, the sun, and the distant view, there is an arched *stoep*, and forming the entrance to the south a white-columned atrium under and through which steps lead up from the front door in the rock wall below.... There, perched on high, 5,700 feet above the sea, we lived in pure air from all the winds that blew, and above the frosts of winter that settled in the plains below."[27] While the covered exterior spaces catch the breezes and enjoy the truly spectacular views, the interiors are restrained, simple and comfortable, with exposed beams on stone brackets above white-washed walls. It was therefore unsurprising that it was hugely appreciated by C. R. Ashbee during his visit in 1903—"I wipe out of my mind all the foolish preconceptions as to the ugliness or vulgarity of upstart Johannesburg, for I have today seen Baker's buildings, the red sandstone crag sites, the fir and cypress, and the rolling purple hills of the Rand. Baker's own house ... springing like a jewel castle from out of the rock, its arcades, and *stoeps*, its red shingle roof, the open court, the white columns and pergola with the circular garden below ... is one of the most exquisite pieces of architecture I have seen."[28] For those who have always looked at Baker's work through Nikolas Pevsner's eyes, such praise from such a highly respected source can come as something of a

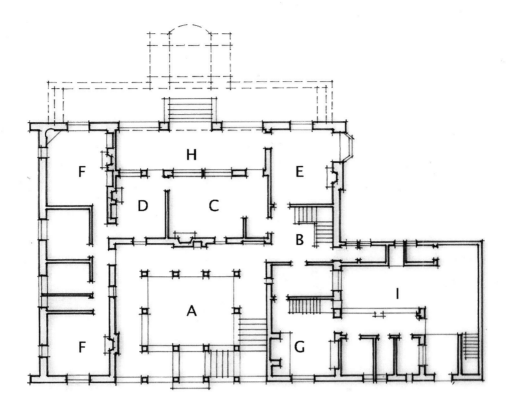

"Stonehouse" ground floor plan. Key: A Atrium, B Entrance Hall, C Hall, D Morning Room, E Dining Room, F Bedroom, G Kitchen, H Verandah, I Courtyard (author's drawing, based on Michael Keath plans).

shock. But it was to be the visitors to Stonehouse, rather than the quality of its architecture, that would have the most profound effect on Baker's architectural career.

It had always been agreed that Baker and Curtis would share the house but with so much accommodation available, Stonehouse soon became the home for those members of the Kindergarten who were posted to Johannesburg. These included "Nel Hichens, Feetham, and John Dove, all then engaged on municipal service. We all rode early, I after a gallop often to some house I was building, they perhaps to some distant inspection or settlement of a land question. Then after long office hours for all of us there were generally officials or visitors from the veld to dinner, often straining our domestic resources. Sometimes Geoffrey Dawson, Secretary to Lord Milner, Duncan, Brand, Kerr, and others joined us. Living with and being able to share the enthusiasm of these young men, for they were younger than I was—was a great enjoyment to me as well as an education in the broader issues of political and social affairs."[29] Thus Stonehouse placed Baker, along with Milner, at the very center of this group as one of its two elder members and as their host. Not only would almost every member later commission a house from Baker, but even more significantly, they would almost all progress to positions of considerable responsibility and influence across the empire, with the consequent rewards for their architect becoming even more substantial.

It was also in 1903, that Baker received what was to become known as Lutyens'

"Stonehouse," Johannesburg, showing the first-floor loggia above the studded main entrance door (courtesy Michael Baker).

"Palladio Letter," which signaled the start of Lutyens own conversion to Classicism—"In architecture, Palladio is the game!! It is so big—few appreciate it now, and it requires training to value and realise it ... it is a big game, a high game...."[30] It was also a game that Baker had been playing for some time with his own Kimberley Memorial (complete with inscription from Kipling) nearing completion (which Roderick Gradidge described as "clear and refined Classical architecture ... it is the most important precursor to his [*Lutyens*] own magnificent war memorials"[31]) and his early work on Rhodes Memorial already promising something even more elemental.

With the Cape Town office purring along nicely under Masey and with Sloper finding his feet in Johannesburg, Baker next turned his gaze to Bloemfontein, the former Boer capital of the Orange Free State. He had already had a number of discussions with Sir Henry Fuller Wilson who was Colonial Secretary to the Orange River Colony regarding both extensions to the government buildings and his own house and garden in Bloemfontein. By 1903, there was also the promise of substantial work for Grey College in Bloemfontein and when the extensions to the government buildings started on-site, he moved Franklin Kendall up to Bloemfontein from Cape Town to oversee construction and also took the opportunity of having his trusted senior assistant in town to establish a Bloemfontein office. Masey, meanwhile, was more than entertained in Cape Town with the Marks Building as well as a number of new commissions which included Swanbourne next to Baker's Sandhills at Muizenberg for Professor H. E. S. Freemantle in an identical Cape style and 'Koreela'h in Rosebank, Cape Town, another Torquay/Tokai variant for newspaper publisher J. A. Barraclough.

An integral element of Rhodes' vision had been not just that the British should control as much of the world as possible but also that areas brought under British control should be "settled" by encouraging the native British to relocate to the colonies thus exporting British culture and values as well as control and administration.[32] Milner shared this view and had both initiated the sponsorship of a settlement scheme in the conquered Orange Free State and also persuaded the Duke of Westminster (Lord Grosvenor), then one of the wealthiest men in the world (who had fought in the Boer War and acted as Milner's aide de camp), to buy over 20,000 acres of land east of Bloemfontein for the establishment of his own model settler estate. Lord Grosvenor had already experienced Baker's architecture first-hand, having also stayed in Baker's staff cottage in the grounds of Government House in Cape Town, and by 1903 the two were in discussion over the layout of the estate. The plan was to build a vacation home for the Duke—the Big House—along with outbuildings, stables, a dairy, another church/schoolhouse and a house for an agent, with the rest of the land being divided into farms. Each farm was to be provided with a house, a stable and a windmill to provide water, and they were to be "settled" by a combination of ex-soldiers and expatriates from Britain.

The Big House is an interesting design—another beautifully planned "H"-plan house with the enclosed space in front of the entrance designed as a garden court which led, through a small circular hall, to the public rooms and onto another very pleasant shaded Doric-columned *stoep* which enjoyed views out over the estate. The materials are typical of much of Baker's work in the Transvaal—squared buff local stone but here under an orange clay-tile roof—not a particularly attractive combination. The farm houses were smaller versions of Baker's "H" plan but, as Sloper reported to Baker as construction was nearing completion—"You approach them in general from such odd angles that the long symmetrical front loses half its value and it seems to me cannot have the adjuncts it cries out for."[33]

In June 1903, Baker turned 41, and though he gave no hint of his plans to any of his friends and colleagues, it would seem that he had already decided to embark on his next adventure. Sloper had proved to be a hit—"an excellent fellow with great character and distinction in his work."[34] He had also put down roots in Johannesburg, buying a site in Parktown where his own, very creditable, small Arts and Crafts house Endstead was then under construction. Consequently, late in 1903, having gained his confidence, Baker proposed to Masey that Sloper should be made a partner in their practice with responsibility for the Johannesburg office. A new deed of partnership was thus negotiated, agreed and signed in January 1904. The great tide of work which had followed Baker's arrival in Johannesburg was underway and Baker astutely sensed a slowing in the economy following the end of the war, which would mean that his partners would have sufficient work for the next year or so, without being overwhelmed by further new commissions. His business affairs were therefore well under control and he felt that he deserved and could now afford a few months in England to attend to other matters.

In late October he wrote to his fair correspondent, "Very slack in Johannesburg all millionaires hard up; so I hope to slip off home for a holiday in early spring—but there's many a slip! Cousinly love, Herbert,"[35] and then in November, "a line … to wish her and all the happy party at Nurstead a fat and jolly Christmas…. Poor men have to put up with a poor deal in colonising: don't you think so! Women ought to be made to colonise too!"[36]

On the 4th of December, he wrote to Masey confirming, "I selfishly want, after 11 years of incessant work here, to take things a little more easily."[37] He informed his partner that he planned a long vacation in England. On the 14th of January 1904 he left Johannesburg for Cape Town where he spent two weeks tying up loose ends before embarking for England at the end of the month, leaving a forwarding address of The Arts Club, Dover Street, London.

5

1904–1909

"The Pipes of Pan" (Op. 12)

From Southampton, Baker made straight for Owletts where he spent several weeks with his mother and now very frail father, visiting Nurstead regularly, before embarking on what would be his last vacation as a bachelor—to Rome and Venice once more. It would seem that of his friends in South Africa, only Lionel Curtis knew of his plans. He wrote to Baker ("Dear Grand Papa") in April concerned both that he, Hichens and Fleetham, were struggling to afford to run Stonehouse and that the estimate for his own new house had come out at £6,000 against his budget of £5,000. He continued, "Will you turn matters over in your mind and see what can be done.... It goes much against the grain to send you this worrying news but I thought it would be better to do so as the first item might conceivably affect your plans.... You have reached the time in life when a wife who understood your great language + magnificent eye would add greatly to your effectiveness + power of work ... the happiest alliances are not always those which were originally based on a passionate + overmastering affection.... Therefore should we hear that you were betrothed I think that for your sake all of us would be glad."[1]

On Baker's return from Italy, events moved quickly. Florence's father was hardly surprised that Herbert wished to marry one of his daughters but had no idea that it was the younger Florence and not Mary whom he had in mind. Nevertheless, he gave his approval and Baker proposed to Florence in early May during a walk in Ashen Bank Wood, writing to her shortly afterwards from Owletts—"I did not want to seem to rush you, and I want the poor Cape boys to be warned before they hear it from other sources. I have told the mother nearly all under secrecy. She seemed so pleased at the prospect—so come over and be nice to her, as you always are! ... I am so happy.... I have always been 'yours affectionately' but how much more I mean by it now."[2] While this was, by many measures, a marriage of convenience between two cousins, it is also clear from their correspondence prior to and after their marriage that it was not without romance and soon developed into a close, loving and supportive partnership for life.

Appropriate announcements were made and news of the engagement soon spread, being received with considerable surprise in most quarters. Lionel Curtis was among the first to write—"Dear Old Grandpapa, It was with a sense of unmixed pleasure that we all learnt of your engagement. Garrett is quite right. Colonists ought to marry if they can. True affection inevitably grows between two good people when there is no discrepancy of nature between them; it is for this reason that I am very glad to know that you have chosen as wife a woman whom you have known I suppose all your life,"[3] followed on the same day by a letter from Lionel Hichens, who had been taken completely by surprise—"My Dear Old Bear.... Perhaps it was not wholly a surprise because it was so entirely the right thing to do. Let us know the exact date of your return as I want to get a bag of confetti & pelt you at the station.... By the way the first news that any of us got was through *The Leader*. Is that what you call 'giving fair warning'? It is very sad to think our nice little family party is to be broken up.... May every happiness attend you in your married life."[4] Baker's brother Lionel, who had clearly harbored hopes of a marriage to Florence himself, had more mixed emotions—"My dear Bert, There would be no use in denying that your letter was a great shock, but all the same I congratulate you old chap from the bottom of my heart.... I had but little hope, seeing how utterly unworthy I was of winning such a brilliant woman.... You have done well and I wish you all good luck."[5]

With Baker's need to return to his business in South Africa becoming urgent, the date was set for Tuesday the 21st of June and the happy event took place at the 14th-century St. Mildred's Church, which stood just across the lane from Nurstead Court, where the reception was held. There was no time for a further holiday, and within days Florence was embarking with her new husband at Southampton for an unfamiliar life in a strange land 8,000 miles away, as so many colonial wives had done before her. Their honeymoon on board was interrupted by a cable on the 25th of July, informing Herbert that his father, having seen his son married, had died that day at Owletts.

Herbert and Florence's wedding party at Nurstead Court, 1904 (courtesy Michael Baker).

Baker had sent Sloper sketches of a number of minor alterations that he wished carried out to Stonehouse before his return, and one of these, the addition of a bay window overlooking the garden, Sloper paid for as a wedding present to the newlyweds. They arrived in Cape Town in late July and stayed at Sandhills while Baker caught up on business with Masey in Cape Town before traveling north, first to Bloemfontein, and then on to Johannesburg, arriving at Stonehouse on Saturday the 13th of August. Various wedding presents awaited them—a rather *risqué* warming pan from Masey and Kendall and a wooden tray from Lutyens. The Kindergarten was already scattering across South Africa at Milner's direction, and while Stonehouse still remained their meeting place when in Johannesburg, from now on it was to be first and foremost Herbert and Florence's marital home.

During Baker's seven-month absence in England, South Africa had seen the development of a post-war economic crisis, but as Baker had anticipated, his colleagues in Cape Town, Johannesburg and Bloemfontein had been kept hard at work delivering their many existing commissions and fortunately even winning a few of their own. In Cape Town, Masey had been fully occupied supervising the Marks Building on Parliament Street which was then under construction. At around twice the size of the earlier Rhodes Building, it was both the largest commercial project which the practice had ever undertaken and the largest and most prominent commission which Masey had ever overseen. This, combined with Baker's unavailability for advice, must have placed a huge strain on him. In Johannesburg, Sloper was similarly pressed with Roedean School having started on-site almost to the day that Baker had departed. Construction of the Duke of Westminster's house had commenced in February, and shortly after Kendall had come up from Bloemfontein to assist. Despite the worsening economy, Baker's Randlord clients continued with the construction of their new homes, and Northwards, perhaps the grandest of them all, was nearing completion. Lionel Curtis's White House was on-site at Muckleneuk, as was Sir George Farrar's Bedford Court, and three houses for judges James Rose Innes (Baker's first client in Cape Town), F. C. Dent and C. J. Mason were also under construction in Bryntiron, where a further justiciary commission had been picked up by Sloper for Mr. Justice Solomon. Sloper had also hooked Howard Pim as a new client during Baker's absence, finding a site for him on Gordon Hill Road (Timewell), and also designed a new home for Archdeacon Michael Furse (later Bishop of Pretoria), Bishopskop in Gale Road, Parktown. The designs which Sloper carried out in Baker's absence were all without exception variations on Baker's "H" plan with covered *stoeps*. Sloper had also continued his efforts to imbue their small church commissions with some dignity, and St. John the Divine in Randfontein, completed that year with its whitewashed walls under a corrugated iron roof, was a particularly good example of their small village churches, as was St. George's Church at Cullinan, also completed in 1904, this time with squared rubble walls below corrugated iron.

While in London, Baker had, as usual, been on the lookout for new assistants and had heard of a young architect from Kent, Frank Fleming, who had already gone out to Pretoria to help his sister establish an orphanage for Boer children. Baker wrote to him shortly after his return—"When I was in London, I was making enquiries about an assistant and gathered that you were in this country looking out for some position.... Since my arrival here, I do not see any immediate prospects of requiring an assistant with your qualifications but, at the same time, I should be very glad if you would, when you are next in Johannesburg, kindly call and see me or Mr Sloper."[6] Fortunately for Fleming, shortly after Baker's return, Drummond Chaplin would commission one of Baker's largest mansions, Marienhof, and the commission for Government House in Pretoria also suddenly spluttered back into life.

Baker had met a Mr. Birkenruth, a director of The Goldfields Company on board ship; Drummond Chaplin was the chairman of that company. Baker takes up the tale of his design of Marienhof in his autobiography—

> The site was on the farther end of the kopje (ridge) commanding the same view as my own
> house; but it touched the plantation below, so that young trees were already giving shade
> and breaking the long, horizontal distant view. The house was much like others that I have
> described, three-sided with a deep double-arcaded loggia between the projecting gable ends,
> somewhat Italian in design; but a wing, rather Gothic in feeling, ran out at the side, consist-
> ing in a high-roofed, bay-windowed living room. It has been criticized for the mixture of
> styles; but I think pedantically…. But the house did truly express the different characters of
> Drummond and Marguerite Chaplin: he calm, reserved, scholarly, magnanimous; she rest-
> less, insatiable, ever asking for the moon. The site favoured the design of a beautiful garden
> with terraces, water-pools, and a natural rock-garden in the lichened rocks on which the house
> stood.[7]

Baker was right in that his eclectic mixing of styles does not jar, despite the great Gothic bay window projecting from an Italianate/Cape Style villa, as its white render successfully unifies the whole. Less happy, and regrettably now becoming a signature feature, is the thin arched wall of the central loggia (first employed at *Rust en Vrede* and which Lutyens quite rightly condemned).

Sloper had received the instruction to proceed with the design of Government House shortly after Baker's arrival home, although the brief was still fluid with the

Baker's own perspective of "Marienhof" (courtesy Michael Baker).

suggestion that it should be built in various phases, as funds became available. With little option but to proceed on this basis, Baker and Sloper produced a new design which was colored to show three possible phases along with costings for each—red/£27,000, blue/£13,000 and yellow/£10,000 bringing the total cost to £50,000 excluding furnishing and landscaping the grounds, which had by then been extended to 138 acres. The brief and client requirements fluctuated constantly throughout the project with additional stables, a refrigeration plant and servants' hall being among a long list of additions, resulting in the final cost escalating to £94,000 which understandably raised official eyebrows. Despite rumors to the contrary, Baker was found to be entirely innocent of causing the cost overrun and was completely exonerated in the subsequent inquiry, which, helpfully for Baker, was chaired by Lionel Hitchens!

In terms of its design, it is a further variation of his "H"-plan format, arranged like Groote Schuur, in two blocks—principal and servant—with, in this case, the servant block slid forward to partly enclose an entrance garden court. The change of

Government House, Pretoria, under construction (courtesy Michael Baker).

site had moved the house to the very edge of the kopje, with just sufficient space for a terrace before a precipitous drop, which brought real drama to the sequence of spaces from entrance court, through the double-height main hall to a covered loggia and then the stunning view out across what was then a barren plain. Externally, it is white-gabled, Cape Dutch style, while internally, it is very much the English country house with paneled rooms, carved stone fireplaces and heavy beamed ceilings, for which Baker also designed much of the furniture. Along with the contemporary Marienhof, it represents perhaps the zenith of his Cape Style houses in what is now a well-developed language of white render, Dutch gables, wooden shutters, Tuscan Doric columns, atria, loggia, pergolas and terraces which perfectly served the lifestyle of his wealthy colonial patrons.

With these two new commissions, along with a further new house for lawyer Jacob De Villiers and a resultant growing confidence, Baker was able to write to Frank Fleming on the 12th of September—"Sloper and I ... have decided that we shall be very glad if you could see your way to come and help us in the office"[8] at a salary of £30 a month. Fleming was to prove another good appointment, becoming a partner in 1910 and an invaluable assistant to Baker just 10 years later in India. A larger office in Johannesburg was now required and on the 1st of December, Baker and his team moved into the Exploration buildings in Commissioner Street. Unfortunately, almost as soon as they had moved in, the economy took a significant lurch to the worse and Lutyens' letter from late in 1904 confirmed that Baker felt the outlook to be gloomy—"Your letter sounds a bit depressed—why!? ... I do think the position you have built up for yourself is splendid—far more than creditable! It is unique surely? Is there any other man who having left England has done so much for architecture & art in any other colony? ... You have had to create everything out of sand and biscuit tins. Yet you have not merely made a name in Africa but a name that has come back here.... You did have a chance of great achievement far greater than which we have any right to expect in this jack in office mediocre old country.... All good wishes to you both for the new year from both of us. & lots of work. Big work."[9]

An architect's life is almost entirely subject to the peaks and troughs of economic cycles and when heading into a trough, the drying up of new commissions is just one of the many challenges to be faced. Existing commissions are often canceled; enthusiastic clients suddenly have other priorities; builders become much more argumentative; staff become unsettled and fractious and clients tend to be much more reluctant to pay their architect, whether they are the representatives of government or a Randlord. Early in 1905, Baker was pursuing Douglas Pennant, Charles Anderson and Willhelm Dettlebach for unpaid fees for the design of their houses, all of whom had abandoned their projects as economic conditions had worsened. Even John Dale Lace, the multi-millionaire gold-and-diamond merchant, was starting to question the final costs of his luxurious Northwards. The viability of the new office in Bloemfontein was being questioned by Kendall, and with a hint of emerging tensions in his relationship with Masey he wrote to Baker—"In the event of my going back to Cape Town I really think that Masey and I should do much better if our respective work was more clearly defined—to avoid that very unsatisfactory 'overlapping' of duties which I am afraid has often been evident in the past."[10] Alfred Milner, now Viscount Milner, was suffering ill health and, having already declined several posts back in London, had informed Baker that he would soon be returning home. To add to his local problems, a further potential claim on his dwindling resources came from Owletts where following Baker's father's death earlier in the year, cousin Ned had reviewed the family finances and found the picture grim— "With regard to Owletts affairs—I have been staying there for a fortnight and have had several talks with the Mother. She is somewhat hurt at the suggestion that she is incompetent to manage her affairs. She points out—truly enough—that she has hither too not had a fair chance as the dear old Father let things get into such a mess, and never let her know how things stood financially."[11] Florence was struggling to cope with her first South African winter as temperatures in Johannesburg started to climb into the 90s and when finally Baker contracted the flu, they decided to spend a winter month in Muizenburg where the ocean air of Sandhills cooled their furrowed brows, thus establishing a pattern of annual breaks that would continue throughout their time in South Africa.

Baker's convalescence was spent working on his design for the Rhodes Memorial— his final homage to his friend and patron. He and Rhodes had variously discussed raising a monument, a Lion House (for which Baker had completed sketches in 1894) or a university on the Devil's Peak above Groote Schuur, and during their shared passage to England prior to Baker's grand tour, he had specifically instructed Baker to examine and record the temples of Segesta on Sicily on their mountainside sites overlooking the Mediterranean and also the carved lions at Thebes and those previously removed to the Louvre and British Museum, as it was these Egyptian examples which he believed to be most suitable for any monument on this African mountainside. With these clear ideas from beyond the grave, Baker had developed his design to a point where he could present it to the committee in Cape Town prior to his return to Johannesburg. His proposals were accepted without amendment and detailed drawings were requested against a budget of £20,000.

The Marks Building in Cape Town was finally completed and with Masey exhausted and with little further work to move on to, Baker agreed that he should return to England for a four-month vacation with Kendall taking over the Cape Town office and being made a partner in recognition of this increased responsibility. In Bloemfontein the detailed design on Grey College, their only commission there, had been taken from under their noses by the Public Works Department, who, short of work themselves, completed the project, with the tussle reported in the *Cape Times*—"For some reason or other the plans and drawings submitted by this firm failed (as is frequently the case with even the best firms) to meet with the approval of the Government, who have now given the work of preparing plans to their own Department."[12] This created yet another fee dispute for abortive work for Baker to resolve, with the college's initial offer of a settlement barely covering the firm's expenses.

By September, the situation was dire and to further add to his troubles, Baker's client Mrs. Chaplin, one of the most prominent members of Johannesburg society, for whom he had by then almost completed Marienhof, was giving him trouble, as he confided to Florence—"Balfour told me that Mrs D.C. is very angry with me…. It is awful ludicrous but she is letting gross lies about me which do a lot of harm to me & she is such an unreasoning lady that I can't reason with her. Its no use trying. Its … partly because I was angry when she abused Fleming…. I can't afford this as my connection and work hangs on too slender a thread."[13] The heady days of his first years in the Transvaal when his only concern had been how on earth his team would cope with their extraordinary workload were becoming a more and more distant memory, as the economic recession became a deepening depression.

Fortunately for Baker, he had both the birth of his first son, Henry, on the 3rd of July 1905, and the development of his design for the Rhodes Memorial to distract him.

He had shared his design with Kipling who was appalled, informing him that he thought it an "atrocious imposing monument"[14] but fortunately Baker valued Kipling's literary criticism more than his architectural and proceeded with his design of spartan simplicity, or even barbarity, of which he was confident Rhodes would have approved. After an early design which included a Roman tiled roof, Baker was now working on something much more radical. Frances Masey returned from England in August, having managed to include a Classical tour of his own during his absence, and proved a more perceptive and valued critic than Kipling as his rather interesting letter to Baker of August 28, 1905, confirmed—

> Dear Baker, Thank you … and for the consideration which you are prepared to give to my criticism from within on the design for the memorial … we should lean to a perfectly simple treatment of the Egyptian work rather than try to get our effect from features such as one finds in Greek and Roman architecture … working in accordance with Rhodes own ideas…. I cannot see what necessity there is for allowing people to walk on the top. Would it not vulgarise, and also desecrate it? … I enclose a sketch of the Propylaea which will illustrate what I have in mind…. In a case like this, one should not I think adopt a rule which would apply to any ordinary staircase, but make the steps steep … we can have a landing on each terrace to allow people to rest…. I feel I really have no business to raise this criticism.[15]

As Baker's final design confirms, Masey's respectful but pertinent comments, unlike Kipling's, were greatly appreciated.

Masey had been greeted shortly after his return from England in August with the positive news that their commission for the National Mutual Life Association of Australasia building in Cape Town had—against all the odds—been revived. They had started work on this with Baker leading back in 1899, with the project abandoned soon after. The design work had been largely completed but as the outstanding detailed design and construction drawings represented the largest proportion of their fee, this was welcome work for the team in Cape Town and Masey, after a well-earned rest, was able to move from the completion of the Marks Building to the start of construction of the National Mutual Life Association of Australasia building within the year. Baker had planned to visit him shortly after his return but had been delayed in Johannesburg both chasing an opportunity for a new school in Parktown and also defending his practice in a lawsuit brought by John Dale Lace in respect of the final account for Northwards. Fortunately, the arbitrator had found in Baker and the building contractor's favor, and he was able to press for payment of his fees.

Florence had already traveled south for her second South African winter and Baker now joined her at Sandhills. Beyond the National Mutual Life Association of Australasia building, there was little new work in the Cape Town office but then, as a result largely of his brother Lionel's efforts, Baker was commissioned by the farmers of Groote Drakenstein to design them a tiny church. Baker undertook the design work himself, resulting in a delightful little building whose whitewashed walls with smooth dressed stone openings are protected by an overhanging thatched roof which shelters a humble Romanesque interior. There was little work involved in detailed design and so construction started a few weeks later in November.

Shortly after this, the practice was blessed with the news that Sloper had won a competition for a new church in Arcadia, Pretoria. Fortunately, this and the church at Groote

The delightful Groote Drakenstein Church (courtesy Michael Baker).

Drakenstein were to be but the first two of a "second coming" of ecclesiastical projects. As Baker knew so well, the risks in architectural competitions were considerable and having been selected as winners in November, Baker found himself writing to the committee in December—"We fully understood from your previous letters and our meeting … we had been selected as the successful architects," and that in these circumstances it would be "unprofessional on our part to do any further work under the competition without being definitely appointed your architects."[16] Within weeks the matter was satisfactorily resolved but the experience can hardly have improved Baker's views of this extraordinary process in which architects submit free designs in the hope of their selection. Throughout these trials and tribulations in 1905, Baker had continued to refine his detailed design for the Rhodes Memorial and by December it was complete, approved by the committee and tenders were invited for its construction. At this stage, the final design of the temple building was settled, but it was to be reached by a comparatively modest three flights of steps. It was the death of Alfred Beit, the gold-and-diamond magnate, who had been another of Rhodes' close associates, whose bequest allowed Baker to now embark on something much more ambitious.

Its genesis is almost certainly either the Propylaea on the Acropolis in Athens (to which Masey had referred in their correspondence on the topic), or even more likely, the Pergamon Altar (a reconstruction of which had recently been completed in Berlin and much-publicized). In both cases, steps rise between terraces towards a temple gateway above with flanking colonnaded buildings stepping forward on either side. But Baker's version is more *savage* than either precedent, being instead a simple colonnade of verticals and horizontals, which gives it the "Egyptian treatment" to which Masey had also referred. Baker must have warmed to this suggested symbolic reference to Egypt as linking Cape Town to Cairo under unbroken British rule had always been part of Rhodes' vision. This parallel was then further reinforced by the introduction of the much-discussed lion sculptures, flanking each flight of steps as at the temple of Khons at Karnak in ancient Thebes, which Rhodes had specifically instructed Baker to examine. These connected the great Egyptian Empire and that of the British for whom by the end of the 19th century, the lion had become a symbol which was regularly incorporated in national statuary and heraldry, including the flag of Rhodes' own British South Africa Company. All this mattered immensely to Baker.

The two colonnades or loggias are themselves modest versions of Baker's earlier Kimberley Memorial (as are most of their details), and as noted before, this device was to reappear again and again in his work from this point onwards. Five great flights of steep steps lead up the hill to the colonnade with terraces between to pause and rest— the first flight divided by a massive plinth for statuary. Within the columns was to be a

The Rhodes Memorial, Cape Town, with Swan's lions and Watts's "Physical Energy" (courtesy Roddy Bray).

statue of Rhodes himself, which throughout the ascent would appear to be the focus of the entire construction, until having examined it, the visitor turns around and shares Rhodes' beloved view across the plain to the vast expanse of Africa below them. Baker had refined his design to a point of utter simplicity, with Doreen Greig suggesting, "The site … gave Baker a chance to demonstrate one of his greatest gifts as an architect, his ability to establish unity between a site and a building, also to exploit its dramatic possibilities by the skillful use of the most simple of architectural elements."[17] This was Rhodes' Segesta and Thebes but with more than a hint of Baker's beloved Villa d'Este, whose terraces cascade down a similarly steep hillside.

On the 15th of January 1906, Baker wrote to a young applicant—"I much regret that we have ourselves had to curtail the assistants in our office and that we see no prospect at present of making fresh additions to our staff."[18] Things were dire and it was the Transvaal which was hit hardest. In Cape Town, Masey had the design of the National Mutual Life Association of Australasia building to work on and had also been commissioned to undertake the design of a number of buildings for Dale College which the practice had been chasing for years, and in addition to this work, funds had finally been gathered to start the construction of the Cathedral of St. George that Baker had designed in 1897. The foundation stone had been laid with appropriate ceremony in 1901, but it had taken until late in 1904 for construction work to start on the foundations of the choir. Detailed design was now required for the superstructure which kept Baker personally entertained and provided further construction supervision work for Masey's team.

Meanwhile in Pretoria, Masey's half-brother Fred was now fully occupied on Government House on which construction had commenced; indeed, such was the scale of this project that assistants Joseph M. Solomon and Arthur J. Marshall were sent up from Cape Town to assist. These two became highly valued assistants throughout Baker's remaining years in South Africa before eventually establishing their own practice and (to Baker's horror) being commissioned for Rhodes' long-dreamed-of University of Cape Town project. Solomon had joined the practice in Cape Town as an articled junior, while Marshall, one of a number of Scots who worked for Baker throughout his career, went on to become Baker's chief assistant in 1909 and chief of staff in 1911, finishing his time with Baker with a stint in his London office in 1914.

So, it was in Johannesburg, where Baker was now based with his young family, that business was most challenging. Sloper, who like Baker, had been active in establishing the Transvaal Institute of Architects, was invited to represent them at the Seventh International Congress of Architects in London early in 1906 and, with little work to detain him, left for England in April. Baker was then unaware that his valued partner would never return to South Africa. Sloper appears to have made his decision in London, informing Baker by letter and formally relinquishing his share of their partnership in 1907. He adopted his middle name as his surname (as he had done before) and started his own practice as Ernest Willmott, occasionally assisting Baker on later English projects. Franklin Kendall was consequently now rewarded with a full partnership and Baker's practice restyled as Baker, Masey and Kendall Architects.

Baker was determined to generate further work in Johannesburg to sustain his family and his team in the Exploration buildings. There was a college chapel and a new church in Hilton Road in Natal, a house for Captain H. R. N. Bourne of the Colonial Secretary's Office in Pretoria, a possible new church hall in Florida, west of Johannesburg, a parsonage in Wakkerstroom, a church in tiny Christiania and the competition conditions

The nave of the Cathedral of St George, Cape Town (courtesy Luke Cabading).

were also requested for a new Transvaal Technical Institute (unsuccessful). By summer things were not going well on the Hilton Road projects, and Baker wrote to the Rev. H. Hammersley, thanking him for "informing me in advance of the decision of the Hilton Road Church Committee not to pay us for any designs for the completion of the church. As a matter of fact, I have already completed these…" and that in his view, "the committee were acting on the side of meanness."[19] But Baker, through his effective management of the building committee, soon had the project back on the rails and construction started later in the year. Baker's armory of tact, patience, tenacity, persuasion and diplomacy was much developed in these difficult times.

In October he left for the Cape, where he stayed until the end of November with much to occupy him, supervising construction of both the cathedral and the memorial, before returning to Johannesburg from where he made a number of trips to Pretoria, where Government House was nearing completion. In addition to designing the buildings, he had also either designed or sourced all the furniture and fittings once more, working closely with Lady Selbourne, the wife of the lieutenant governor, with whom Baker worked very happily, providing her with a dignified English country house interior many thousands of miles from her homeland. Not content with designing every element of the building, as Baker related, "With the Selbournes I enjoyed laying out the garden on the ridges and rocks and discussing with the expert gardeners and botanists the trees and plants that would best grow there and in the garden formed on the level ground above the kopje."[20] One of the most interesting features of the outdoor spaces was a sundial which Baker had designed, which showed the time in every major country of the empire. This was to be the first of a series of "Empire clocks" which Baker would design, often as a gift, for several of his future clients. Lord and Lady Selbourne moved in on the 1st of February 1907, after which Herbert and Florence became regular guests.

While Baker had been busy building a house for him, Lord Selbourne had been laying the foundations of a new South Africa in which the four British colonies of the Cape, Natal, Transvaal and Orange River would be united under a single government. Boer leader Louis Botha and his wartime ally Jan Smuts had already been successful in convincing the new Liberal British Prime Minister Campbell Bannerman to allow the former Boer states to become self-governing members of the empire—much to the disgust of many, including Milner, who thought it "sheer lunacy" to give South Africa back to the Boers. Selbourne, aided by several of the Kindergarten, soon developed the vision of a new country in which the British and Dutch could live together as equals into what came to be known as *The Selbourne Memorandum* (actually written largely by Lionel Curtis) which both set out the dangers of continuing with separate governance and promoted the advantages of moving towards a Union of South Africa. The first elections in the Transvaal were held on the 20th of February 1907 which resulted in Louis Botha being invited to form a government and thus becoming the first prime minister of the Transvaal on the 4th of March 1907 with Jan Smuts as his Colonial Secretary and Education Secretary. Botha and Selbourne's efforts would lead to a national convention in 1908 in which the four states were challenged to create a constitution for a new united South Africa.

For Baker, this intense political activity, while an interesting distraction, did nothing for the local economy and so, after discussions with Masey and Kendall, it was agreed to abandon their office in Exploration House in Johannesburg and to pull out of Bloemfontein at the earliest possible opportunity. Baker attended a meeting of the Rhodes Memorial Committee in Cape Town on the 2nd of February. It had been hoped that the plinth at the base of the monument would carry a bronze of George Frederic Watts' equestrian statue entitled "Physical Energy" which, in the artist's own words, was "a symbol of that restless physical impulse to seek the still unachieved in the domain of material things"[21] and as such was felt to represent Rhodes' pioneering spirit. It was claimed to be the largest sculpture ever cast in bronze in Britain and was exhibited in the courtyard at Burlington House for the Royal Academy Summer Exhibition in 1904, the year of Watts' death. This was now to be obtained and shipped to Cape Town, but there remained the sculpture of the lions and the Rhodes statue itself for the committee to now consider. At that

February meeting it was agreed that Baker was to be paid £150 for his return passage and expenses to travel to London to select and commission a sculptor for both.

Rudyard Kipling had spent his usual winter in the Woolsack, and he and Baker agreed to travel home together with their families. It was Florence's first trip home since her arrival as a new bride in the summer of 1904 and would be young Henry's first visit to England. They embarked at Cape Town on the SS *Kenilworth Castle* on the 3rd of April with Kipling much depressed about Botha's election and Baker not much better regarding the prospects for his practice.

On their arrival in London, Baker set to work to find a suitable sculptor for both the memorial lions and what was now to be a bust of Rhodes as the centerpiece of the monument. Let him take up the tale—"The type of lion that I had in mind was that of the Egyptian sphinx-lions…. My method of selection was to ask sculptors recommended to me to come to the galleries of the British Museum, and to judge of the appeal which the types I desired made to them. Some eminent artists failed to respond to the attractions of these noble symbolic creatures; but one, John Swan, R.A., understood and overflowed with enthusiastic admiration; and he was thereupon chosen."[22] By June Baker was able to report back to the committee that the lions "will cost about £5000 and we can spend that first and see what we have in hand."[23] Swan later traveled to South Africa to visit the memorial site and, in Baker's words once more—"He modelled the huge beast full-size on its granite pedestal, punching away on the clay with his strong arms and big hands. The plaster cast made from the clay model he took home, and from this the eight lions on the mountain-side were cast in bronze…. Swan also made the bronze head of Rhodes which gazes from its granite niche through the massive columns of the temple over the distant mountains towards the far north of Rhodes dreams."[24]

Baker's forwarding address was Owletts, where he received regular reports from Fleming on their various ongoing projects. He met Milner in London, now the chairman of the Rio Tinto Zinc Mining Company and a director of the Joint Stock Bank and, with his support, presented a lecture on his own work at the Mansion House in the heart of London's financial quarter—a considerable accolade for a colonial architect. Inevitably, he would have looked up his old friend Ned Lutyens, then deep in his competition entry for the new London County Council building on the Thames opposite the Houses of Parliament. Lutyens was desperate to break out of his country-house practice and move onto what he saw as "Big Work." Sadly, he lost the competition to the then almost unknown Ralph Knott, having spent most of the year on his design at his own expense. It was a bitter blow, which took him some time to recover from, both financially and emotionally. Baker must have shared his own concerns with Lutyens regarding the parlous state of the South African economy, and this visit home appears to have provoked his first thoughts of a return to England. The prospect of educating his young son and any further children in South Africa was also not to be contemplated, as he had already confirmed in a letter to his schoolmaster brother Percy a few years previously—"Schooling is very bad here—all decent boys go home."[25] In contrast to South Africa, the economy of Edwardian Britain was booming as the "Mother Country" enjoyed one last hurrah before the outbreak of the First World War. The sail back to Cape Town must have offered him considerable opportunity to contemplate where best his small family's future now lay.

The Bakers were back in South Africa by the end of August and arrived home at Stonehouse on the 11th of September. A new commission for a chapel at Michaelhouse School in the Balgowan Valley in Natal was one of the last received in the year. With a

Florence and Henry in the garden of "Stonehouse" in 1906 (courtesy Michael Baker).

reasonable budget, Baker led the design and had completed it by the end of December, submitting it along with his report to the governors on the 15th of January. With his significant involvement in the design, it represents both a fine religious building and a further useful gauge as to his continuing development as an artist with his early Gothic churches now almost entirely replaced by Romanesque. This move brought a further refinement to these relatively simple buildings and for the first time brought a new consistency to both his domestic and ecclesiastic architecture. There was something more of early Rome than early England in these later South African buildings, reflecting both his travels and the continuing development of his Classical language, which was now taking him from his earlier *savageness* to a cooler, and for Baker more natural, asceticism. His own description of the church from his report to the governors, confirms this thinking—"In anticipation of any criticism as to the absence of elaboration in the design, we would answer that beautiful architecture depends more on solid construction and good materials and workmanship, than on multiplication of detail. And in our opinion, this principle should be of the greatest educational value to South African boys, who too often have examples only of an opposite nature before their eyes."[26]

The year of 1908 started with a splutter of new commissions—26 miners' cottages and a small church in Cullinan for the Premier Mine Company for example—and Baker was working hard to generate further church work, even on occasion waiving his initial fees in an attempt to get the project moving. In April he was commissioned to design the Cathedral of St. Alban in Pretoria, which, despite its rather grand title, meant adding a new chancel to the existing brick-and-iron building until funds became available to carry out further work. (Baker only ever saw the completion of the chancel, sanctuary and a side chapel with the remainder being finally carried out in a modern style in 1957.) A further ecclesiastic commission for St. Boniface in Germiston, just east of Johannesburg, was received in the summer. Completed in 1910, this confirms Baker's switch to the Romanesque for church buildings and includes a fine square Italianate tower, built like the main body of the church in the local kopje stone. It is one of Baker's finest small churches with the strong sun and shadows of the highveld plateau giving it a distinctly Mediterranean feel. Another contemporary commission for the Church of St. Michael and All Angels in Sunnyside, Pretoria, on a site near the Governor's House, resulted in an almost identical and equally successful design.

By now Baker's relationship with Masey was showing signs of strain. The year hadn't started well for them with Masey having read a report of Baker's London lecture in *The Times,* in which he failed to get a mention, and complaining bitterly to his senior partner. Baker's initial response, namely that it was normal practice for the leader of any practice to take credit for the partnership's work and that the speech was "personal, not official"[27] cut little ice. Masey was now supervising the construction of Cape Town Cathedral, and their almost daily correspondence grew more and more fractious—on the 10th of January Baker wrote, "I shall be pleased at any letter that may be in the local paper and will write one if you like—but everyone at Cape Town knows,"[28] and on the 16th of January, "You did not understand I think, the point of my telegram."[29] They had started down a route from which there would be no turning back, eventually leading to the end of their partnership.

Baker had become more and more disillusioned with his lot in South Africa and was soon suggesting confidentially to Lutyens that he might return to England, where perhaps they could work together. Lutyens' private and confidential letter of May 1908 addresses the matter directly—

> The subject of your invasion of this old country. There is and must be plenty of room for good architects here. i.e., H. Baker ... & if you are really stopped in S.A. by depression. I don't see what else you can do.... Human nature prompts me to hope you won't come! & this remark is probably the instinct of self preservation which prompts me to pray you will stay out in Africa.... You would have a splendid chance: you have reputation and would start with all your experience in a clean slate.... For yourself—I should dearly love to have you home in England—my position is not so good! ... I should gladly lift you to my "well fortified heights" in a partnership. But I don't think when behind my works, they look either high or well fortified—I should not say this to any other man.... I could not say more to encourage you to come—but I do not know nor can I justly judge—what you stand to lose—but if Africa is 0—I should say come at once it can't be worse here.... If I had work enough for 2 I would make you an offer at once—but I haven't & I don't know how if you were willing—how a partnership could be effected.... I should dearly love working with you."[30]

The matter was the main subject of their correspondence throughout the summer, and by August Lutyens was confiding the bones of a partnership agreement to his wife, Emily—"I have written to Baker. I have never shown you his letter. The proposal is that on a joint income of £3000 he takes £1000 and I take £2000 and then as the income increases he takes 1500–2250, 2500–2750, 3000–3000, and then equal. He puts in a plea for £300 a year to start with as a living wage which is fair I think. He is coming home and then we can talk it over."[31] Discussions were clearly well advanced and the two architects both appeared committed to a new partnership together. As their letters are almost devoid of specific plans, beyond the commercial arrangement, it is interesting to speculate as to their motives.

As far as Baker was concerned, it was a fairly straightforward opportunity—a route back to England and new partnership with one of the leading British architects of his generation. For Lutyens, we can only surmise based on their correspondence of the previous 10 years that he anticipated leading design work with Baker running the business and relieving him of much of this pressure while also helping him to break out of his country-house typecasting and into the type of major public projects to which he now aspired. By 1908 this diversification had changed from being an aspiration to a necessity, as the recent, rather startling, falls in the London Stock Exchange had led several of his country-house clients to cancel or think again and this, combined with his failure in the London County Council Headquarters competition, had reinforced for him just how difficult such a move might be to achieve on his own.

The two architects had never worked together as equals, bound jointly and severally, as they would be for each other's actions as partners, their relationship to date having been based on 18 months together in Ernest George's office as pupil and senior assistant, several shared walking tours 20 years previously and their subsequent correspondence and occasional meetings in more recent years when Baker was in London. Baker was used to working in partnership, whereas Lutyens' brief partnership with E. Baynes Badcock had ended badly, but in 1908, they clearly both believed it could work as Baker wrote in typically literary style, "If beautiful Amelia really wants to marry Captain Dobbin."[32] As Christopher Hussey, Lutyens' biographer, suggested, "They were certainly drawn to one another by the qualities each felt himself to lack. To Lutyens, Baker was one of the 'big men'—tall, manly athletic, outwardly calm—that seem to have attracted him. The glamour of his friendship with Rhodes, and with the progressive young generation of administrators at the Cape, combined with his aloofness from professional competition in England to invest Herbert Baker's name with a high, slightly mysterious prestige."[33] When they finally did experience a partnership a few years later in New Delhi, their very different and now mature and equally strong characters were very quickly fully exposed to each other, and the grumbling started on both sides within months.

Jane Ridley suggests that Lutyens' "pipe dreams were dispelled by Emily, (*his wife*) who as usual had other ideas,"[34] but it seems more likely that the two architects' plans came to naught largely as a result of the South African economy finally starting to improve towards the end of 1908, thus saving Baker having to risk losing everything he had built there in the hope of an uncertain future in London. His second son Henry Allaire Edmeades Baker (known as Allaire) was born on the 12th of September, and his birth was followed shortly after by commissions for a new church and rectory in Benoni, south of Pretoria, a further rectory for St. George's near Stonehouse in Parktown, and finally and most significantly of all—a new Randlord house for Lionel Philips, the financier, mining magnate and politician and his socialite wife, Florence.

Baker's biography is entitled *Architecture and Personalities* for good reason, and Lionel Philips is yet another of the extraordinary range of characters for whom Baker built. Having started his career as a bookkeeper in London at the age of 14, he traveled to Kimberley on news of the discovery of diamonds and soon made and lost a fortune in partnership with Alfred Beit. He then befriended Rhodes and with his support established himself as the leader of the mining industry in Johannesburg becoming chairman of the Chamber of Mines in 1892. That year, Lionel and his wife decided to build, and it was Florence who selected a site on the ridge above the sprawling city—effectively thus establishing Parktown. Their house, Hohenheim, a rambling mansion in the style of Norman Shaw's Cragside (albeit under a corrugated iron roof), was designed by Frank Emley (or William Leck) and completed in 1894. From this base, Florence dominated Johannesburg society as effectively as her husband ran the mines. When his involvement in the planning of the Jameson Raid was revealed in 1896, he was tried and sentenced to death. After six months' imprisonment he was reprieved, fined and exiled to England, where he and Florence lived until the end of the Boer War when Alfred Beit persuaded them to return, at which point they both quickly re-established their previous positions in Johannesburg society.[35] Fortunately for Baker, Florence now required a new base in Parktown for her operations and the result would be his Villa Arcadia.

The year concluded with an approach from the general manager of the Central South African Railway Company, whose architectural competition for the design of a new railway station in Pretoria, had gone rather off the rails. The company was unable to select an architect from the entries which they had received, and with little architectural in-house expertise to guide them, the railway company secretary, fellow Kindergarten member Robert Brand, had suggested seeking Baker's advice.

Baker's advice to this potential new client was clear, that none of the entries had reached an acceptable architectural standard and by February 1909, Baker himself had opened negotiations with the company to undertake the work himself. Wary of criticism of unethical practice from the competition entrants, Baker sought and received approval from the Royal Institute of British Architects before proceeding further. Things were finally looking up.

Before the month was out, he was writing to Lutyens—"Dear dear Lutyens, the fates are intervening … though working with you where are summer and winter, flowers, spring, birds, and the prospect of being buried under a yew tree, all pull."[36] They would have to wait a few more years before these pen-pals would have their relationship truly tested. Herbert's brother Lionel's letter of 25th of February confirmed his decision to stay—"Hurrah! I was delighted to get your letter today saying you have given up the idea of going home to settle…. I am also very pleased to hear that your prospects are so much brighter."[37] Having languished in slow-moving pools for several years, Baker's career was accelerating into full flow once more and with this further rush of work his architecture would reach new heights.

By March, the station was almost in the bag as he wrote to Florence in Muizenburg—"There is still a little hitch about the station but I think all will come well…. I ought not to leave such a big thing—with so much more in prospect,"[38] and two days later, "A new job every day! How I long to come but how can I leave with all this work! There is a tide in the affairs of man, which taken at the flood leads on to fortune!!"[39]

The increase in workload, sadly, saw no corresponding improvement in Baker and Masey's relationship, and later that month Baker wrote to Masey—"I have been so overworked the last few weeks that I have found it impossible to draw up the promised final statement of the changes we propose," before concluding, "we have only to meet the circumstances at present existing which are that I have my office and chief sphere of interest in the Transvaal, and you your offices and sphere of interest in Cape Colony."[40] Frank Fleming was also to be made a junior partner, assisting Baker in Johannesburg, and the profits of the partnership were to be divided with Baker, the senior partner, receiving everything generated in Johannesburg as well as a third of the profits from Cape Town. The only element of this proposal agreed by Masey was that Fleming should become a junior partner and so the dispute rumbled on through 1909. While Masey had the Rhodes Memorial and the Cathedral to supervise on-site in Cape Town, it must have been startlingly clear to both men that all the action had once more moved upcountry and so Masey's thoughts turned to Rhodesia, north of the Transvaal, which seemed to offer him the prospect of both new work and a region in which Baker was not yet established.

For Baker, despite this on-going irritant, the next few years would represent the next great wave of his career, building on his work for Rhodes and Milner and establishing him, not just as the most prominent architect in South Africa, but also as one of the leading architects of the British Empire.

6

1909–1912
"Civic Fanfare"

The Villa Arcadia would occupy Baker and Mrs. Phillips for a number of years as the house continued to be extended and the gardens laid out on terrace after terrace below it. In Baker's own words, Florence Phillips "excelled in her large views and propelling enthusiasm for action. A little tactless and over-impulsive, she worked up such excessive steam that her engine frequently ran off the rails…. She had an April temperament; after a quarrel in the morning she would come to me in the afternoon in tearful repentance and all would be sunshine again."[1] The original house which Baker designed early in 1909 was one of his finest and represented another stride towards his mature Classicism. The plan was familiar with a principal block in which the main public rooms were arranged around a central sequence of porch, hall and *stoep* with bedrooms over, and a supporting block of kitchens, stores and servants' accommodation (as Baker had developed first at Groote Schuur). As at the Big House on the Westminster Estate, the servants' block also partly enclosed an entrance court. To the north, in lieu of one of his previous Tuscan Doric *stoeps*, Baker provided Mrs. Phillips with an elegant vaulted terrace enclosed by a beautifully proportioned Ionic colonnade. This supported a further terrace above at the first floor onto which the principal bedrooms open out allowing them to also enjoy the distant views out over the plain. With the exception of the hint of a curved gable over the front entrance, several candy-cane chimney stacks and the wooden shutters to the bedroom windows (an environmental necessity in pre-air-conditioned days), the entire composition is almost free of any Dutch influence and the Villa sits on its ridge like some pristine white Italian palazzo overlooking the Mediterranean, rather than the Highveld. It is confident, consistent and well-resolved architecture which celebrates its extraordinary site and like almost all of Baker's domestic work, provides a delightful series of interior spaces for the Phillips' to live and entertain in.

Dorothea Fairbridge, in her "Gardens of South Africa," described the view from the terrace just a few years later—"Seen through its columns the blue line of the Magaliesberg Mountains … and below me, falling sharply away from the *stoep* and melting into the blue green eucalyptus of the Sachenvald stretched a garden of exquisite charm…. Terrace after terrace lay below us, with flights of steps paved with the accommodating Transvaal sandstone…. Tall cypresses marked the line of the terrace, but in the Italian fashion and flanked by Italian oil jars."[2] Before the main house was completed and furnished, Baker was asked to add a library and music room, complete with pipe organ. He achieved

Baker's own perspective of the Villa Arcadia, Johannesburg (courtesy Michael Baker).

this by creating a delightful, single-story atrium courtyard between the main house and the new accommodation which served his client perfectly. For guests in the main house it provided a refreshing interlude in their stroll from dinner to their musical diversion but it could also be accessed directly from the entrance court thus allowing Mrs. Phillips to host musical events without the need to provide access via her own home, while for all the visitors regardless of their status, it proved to be a gracious sheltered court in which they could chat before and after recitals and enjoy a glimpse of the luxurious gardens below. Here Baker returned to his favored Tuscan Doric, but with coupled columns supporting timber beams, while an antique Venetian well-head in the center of the space reinforced the Mediterranean mood.

In March 1909, Baker started work on his design for Pretoria Railway Station. This was an extremely important building both in terms of Baker's career and his continuing architectural development. Not only was it his first significant civic building, but crucially, it was also of intense symbolic importance to Pretoria and actually—it's not stretching it too far to say—South Africa. For those who wanted to unite the new country, the railways were a key element in their plans to connect the four colonies, and it was in the Transvaal, whose capital was Pretoria, that the unionist movement was strongest. Since May of 1908, the National Convention had been meeting at rotating venues to discuss unification and the creation of a constitution for the new country. Each of the colonies was represented, with Baker's old friends John Merriman, Jacobus Sauer and Leander Starr Jameson representing the Cape of Good Hope, but it was the delegates of the Transvaal, led by the defeated Boer generals Louis Botha and Jan Smuts who, iron-ically, were in the driving seat. Botha was highly regarded both in the Transvaal and in England where he had attended the Imperial Conference in London in 1907 with Lord Selbourne introducing him to the King as "a born leader of men, a man of natural dignity of manner and reserve, who does not wear his heart on his sleeve and will not go enthus-ing with English Radicals."[3] Considering the bitterness of their recent war, it was quite extraordinary that the outcome of the convention was a set of proposals which were to treat both the Dutch and British as equals in the new country as a self-governing domin-ion of the British Empire (like Canada and Australia) with the monarch represented locally by the governor.

None of this would have been lost on Baker, with the unification of South Africa (including Rhodesia) having long been part of Rhodes' dream, and additionally, with many of his friends either involved as delegates or, in the case of several members of the Kindergarten including Brand and Curtis, in supporting the discussions and drafting res-olutions and the final proposals. The railway station was therefore to be a symbol of the new country—unified within the empire and representing the gift of human progress and civilization.

It was to be a Classical building but, unlike the Villa Arcadia, Baker was to draw on the well of English, rather than Italian Classicism, for inspiration. It was the architecture of Inigo Jones and Christopher Wren that Baker identified as the most appropriate lan-guage with which to represent this first symbol of the new country. But this new style was not coming easily to him—as his letters to Florence confirmed—"All say that if I do the station well, there's lots of work at Pretoria—so I must—but it is a very hard job—not like houses which I do so easily now—it is very difficult and I must work very hard at it." And later—"Still at it—on the Station—its coming slowly—Phillips has been in and has congratulated me on the Station—asked if you weren't pleased."[4] And in early April—"As usual worked late—did an enormous lot of work today—a new plan of station amongst other things. After dinner alone…. I retired to Studio to revise agreement on Station—a sleepy job—then now to bed—tired out."[5]

While many of the architectural elements of his design were familiar from his Cape Town office buildings—the rusticated base; the shuttered first-floor windows set within deep shading arches; the balconied venetian windows and the broad overhanging, shel-tering cornice—these were now mere details within a powerful overall composition that echoed Jones' Queen's House with its central first-floor colonnade, but here both twice the height and with Wren's double columns from St. Paul's, though here Ionic for colo-nial Pretoria rather than Corinthian for the capital of the empire. This rather grand com-position provided the backdrop to a new civic square and garden which concluded a long vista that stretches down what is now Paul Kruger Street from Church Square nearly a mile away with the axis terminated by a civic clock tower in the style of Wren, with its columns turned onto the diagonal, from where they project out across the vast space of the veld which the railways would soon connect.

The plan is his familiar "H" with a *porte cochere*, in lieu of a *stoep*, leading into a vaulted hall which cuts straight through the building to the platforms beyond. The interiors (though now much altered) were particularly fine with a clear hierarchy of materials from the marble of the first-class waiting rooms to paneling and tile for more utilitarian spaces. Throughout there is a cool restraint with the sun of the high veld con-trolled and manipulated to provide natural lighting both from the side and via a range

Pretoria Railway Station under construction (courtesy Michael Baker).

of rooflights throughout the building. There are a few inconsistencies—the curving side elevations are unusual, but work well, the local granite is a little dull and the detailing of the rusticated base a little too busy but, barring the plain wrong Gothic buttresses to the *porte cochere*, this is a very accomplished and impressive urban civic composition. It was a vast project for Baker's team in Johannesburg to undertake, and Edward Philip Solomon, who was then Minister of Public Works in Botha's Transvaal Government, was keen for the staff of his own department to assist. Brand came up with a compromise as Baker confirmed to Florence—"He'll suggest that I make the design & leave the carrying out—supervision to the Railway—if I can arrange suitable terms leaving me complete artistic control—I shall agree to this—it may save much friction and worry—and I shall be pleased"[6]

He made it to Sandhills just in time to spend Easter with his family and it was while he was still there, on the 11th of May, that the National Convention concluded their deliberations and published their proposals for the constitution and administrative arrangements for the new country. In addition to his role as Secretary to the Railways, Robert

Brand had also been acting as Secretary to the Transvaal delegation, and he later wrote of the convention, in his book *The Union of South Africa*,[7]—"All classes in South Africa, politicians and people alike, are sick and tired of disunion. They know the disasters which come from it, and they have experienced the calamities of war, and the leaders know it all better than anyone else. They met therefore, in the determination to have no more of it and to make one big effort for union, so that South Africa might henceforth live in peace."[8] "It is, therefore, no paradox to assert that out of war has come harmony."[9] The result of their deliberations was a new form of constitution, balancing power between the Crown, the South African Parliament and the provinces.

As Brand recalled, "The choice of a capital was bound to be a matter of extreme difficulty. There is nothing else which brings home so directly to the popular imagination the sacrifices which union entails," and "until the meeting of the convention the people of Cape Town had hardly conceived it possible that the capital should be elsewhere. ... But Pretoria has this great advantage, that it is central in position, while Cape Town is at the extreme end of the continent."[10] And also, "All that may be said with safety is that, whatever direction South Africa's development may take, Cape Town will never be at its centre of gravity.... Johannesburg itself, though it possessed many advantages, was out of the running. There is a general fear throughout South Africa of the influence of the mining industry."[11] A twin option was therefore proposed "bringing the government and the members of parliament into contact with two great centres"[12]... "and when the spoils were divided, the Supreme Court was given to Bloemfontein."[13] It was therefore agreed that, despite the administrative complexities, the new Parliament should meet in Cape Town and the government buildings should be located in Pretoria.

This was to be a new country in which both British and Dutch were treated as equals with English and Dutch both recognized as official languages and the problem of "the inferior races"[14] left for another day, acknowledged as being such a sensitive issue that attempts to reach agreement on it had the potential to disrupt the entire convention. The inclusion of Rhodesia within the union was also abandoned, with Brand stating, "The people of Rhodesia are said generally to be averse from the prospect."[15] The proposals agreed in the convention were ratified by the colonial parliaments and then taken to the British Parliament where, with notably few amendments, they were constituted within the South Africa Act, which was passed on the 20th of September 1909. It was an extraordinary outcome with the defeated Boers declaring their allegiance to the British Crown and the British colonialists agreeing to share power despite having won a war over their fellow citizens just a few years previously.

Baker returned to Johannesburg on the 12th of May, the day after the convention had concluded, with the prospect of new government buildings no doubt speeding his progress. As well as being well qualified, he was now also well connected for this significant new opportunity; Lord and Lady Selbourne, now good friends, occupied Baker's Government House in Pretoria; he was already working on the railway station for Edward Solomon, the Minister of Public Works, and the Kindergarten continued to be extremely well represented in the administration of the region. Baker had had much less contact with Botha and Smuts, but nevertheless if only through the Selbournes, he must have already met both. By the beginning of June, he was discussing his appointment for the government buildings with Edward Solomon. It was first proposed that the project should be managed by the Ministry of Works, with Baker as consultant architect but on the 3rd of June Baker wrote to Solomon—"Personally I would recommend the course now being adopted with the Station, with the difference that the PWD (*Public Works Department*) should take the place of the Railway Department in settling the several plans showing … arrangement and accommodation of the building."[16] Solomon concurred and Baker can take up the tale—"I was given a free hand in suggesting sites in and around the city. I explored the surrounding kopjes and selected two ideal sites overlooking the valley where Pretoria lies." The one to the south was large, flat and its buildings would be sunlit, but interestingly, Baker rejected this in favor of the much more dramatic and symbolic site to the north—

> The only possible site on it near the city was a narrow platform half way up, so that to avoid the cost of colossal retaining walls a large building here must be long and narrow, and its southward-facing main façade must be nearly always in shadow. There would be, moreover, no further ground for extensions on the platform.
>
> These were the disadvantages, but other features of the position had great attractions. While both sites had the dignity and nobility of a city set upon a hill, Meintjes Kop was nearer to the heart of the town, which it dominated as did the Acropolis the city of Athens…. And I was also much attracted by a natural concave depression in the rock platform such as the Greeks might have chosen for an open-air theatre…. So the vision came to me of two great blocks on the more level platform and connected round the top of the depression by a semi-circular colonnade overlooking an open theatre or place of assembly between the two great buildings.
>
> I went up there with Lady Selbourne, always a very wise councillor, and we climbed through the thorn bushes and over the rough rocks…. She admired and approved the site, stressing the value of its nearness to Government House as well as to the heart of Pretoria. These factors and the charm of the place determined my recommendation. I showed some rough sketches to General Smuts, and then he went with me to the site. He, with his quick insight and imagination, at once visualized the idea and its power to give dignity and beauty to the instrument of Government and the symbol of the Union. He and Botha thought, as Rhodes thought, in Christopher Wren's famous words—so apt that they bear repeating in full: "Architecture has its political Use: publick Buildings being the Ornament of a Country; it established a nation, draws People and Commerce; makes people love their native country, which Passion is the original of all great actions in the Commonwealth." General Smuts told me there and then to go ahead with my sketch plans.[17]

Baker's design was essentially a re-working of Wren's Greenwich Hospital in which symmetrical wings terminate in mighty domes, which in London frame the Queen's House by Inigo Jones beyond.

In his letter to General Botha at the end of June, Baker proposed that the buildings could be built in phases with one block of offices to meet immediate needs with the other and the colonnade added when funds were available, but Botha was in no mood to compromise, nor did he want any delay. The proposal to split the Parliament and administration was already under attack, and he had no wish to see the Union buildings being erected in Cape Town. Even at this early stage, Baker had also included a tall domed building above the Union buildings on the top of the ridge both terminating the axis and dominating the entire composition. (Again, Greenwich provides the model, with the observatory on the ridge above.) This was to be variously a Hall of Peace, a *heroon*, a shrine to all the races of South Africa or even at one point a Parliament chamber, and it was to remain as a key element within the overall composition (at one point served by a *via sacra* along the ridge) for several months further (and many years further in Baker's imagination) before finally being abandoned.

Baker explained the layout in which each wing

consists of offices required by the Ministers and Government Departments, and in the central connecting semi-circular buildings are the Library and Conference Room, each a circular domed room, and other rooms for common purposes. The main entrances to the blocks are from a road at lower basement level, where strong rooms were hewn from the rock; on a higher road at the back other entrances are at the ground floor storey; there are three storeys in all, apart from the vaults and strong rooms. In each block there are two open arcaded courts forming access and giving air to the interior rooms; there are no long dark passages there.... The great colonnade in front of the central range of common offices on the ground-floor level is approached up the broad steps and terraces on the amphitheatre.... Two tall dome-capped towers flank the amphitheatre. These are all reflected in the broad pools of water below.... The hill, which falls steeply from the building, is built up in terraces and great flights of steps with fountains below. The general planning of the terraces is reminiscent of the famed Villa d'Este garden at Tivoli.... Distinctive features of the upper floor, the 'piano nobile' of the building, are the columned 'temples'—they are hardly porticoes; loggias perhaps better describes them— leading out of the Ministers rooms [from where] Ministers can lift their eyes up to the surrounding hills and the vanishing distances and splendours of the high veld, from which they may gather inspiration and visions of greatness.[18]

It was a brilliant composition, which responded equally well to both the potential drama of the site and the challenge of symbolizing the two races, brought together in peace.

Throughout the development of his design for the Union buildings, he continued to share his thoughts with Lutyens who, as usual, was free with his criticisms—"I have written pages & notes & annotated but at this distance it seems almost impossible

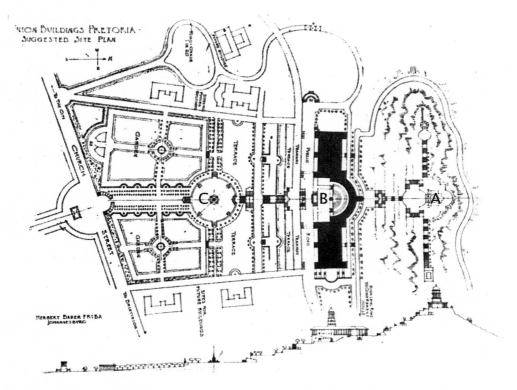

Union Buildings site plan. Key: A Temple of Peace, B Union Buildings, C Public Gardens (courtesy Michael Baker).

to make useful criticism…. I am rather fond of an entablature with the frieze omitted (*sketch included*) & the top member of the architrave becoming the lower member of the cornice … look at San Micheli's work. Wonderful. V. good. Can you get plans of the Verona palaces? They are splendid the placing of the courts & stairways & the detail etc. … what is nice is the fenestration of the wings … can you keep it…. I liked your big cornice … balustrade between the columns too high?"[19] In the midst of this activity, Baker was also trying to progress the railway station project, writing to the railway company on the 9th of June to seek authority to proceed with detailed design—"As I understand that both the Administration and the Department have approved the ⅛" scale sketch plans…. As soon as I receive formal instructions of the Administration, I will proceed with the contract drawings."[20] The company soon relented, detailed design was completed in August, a contractor selected, and construction started before the year was out. Baker had also won the work in Cape Town to adapt the Parliament of the Cape of Good Hope's buildings to serve the Parliament of South Africa, and Masey was looking after this work (amid much complaining about lack of resources and the need to pursue new opportunities in Rhodesia). Considering that Baker and his team were overwhelmed delivering construction design on the railway station and seeking additional staff in preparation for the detailed design of the Union buildings, he was understandably frustrated with his partner—"I should have thought that you and Kendall could have drawn it out, and saved the cost of assistants: it was all carefully measured up before if I remember right," and "I hope nothing will be left to disgrace the Union Parliament, and in relation to Rhodesia—'I do not see how you can do this work and go up there at the same time.'"[21] Despite offer and counteroffer, the two had failed to agree on the basis of a new partnership, and in the interim Baker had thus claimed the railway station and the Union buildings as his own. The end was now nigh.

Baker was also beginning to find out for the first time that with major public commissions come public controversy, professional jealousy and political interference, and there were soon calls for an architectural competition to be held for this most important of all South African commissions, rather than it being gifted to one architect by the prime minister of the Transvaal. Baker was well enough connected to ride the storm but the government felt that such was the noise, they would set up an advisory board to counsel them on the matter. Much to Baker's consternation, the board had only two members—Piercy Eagle, the architect to the Public Works Department (PWD) and Willem de Zwaan, one of Baker's local competitors in Pretoria. They reported in November, and unsurprisingly, strongly criticized Baker's design on the grounds of siting, extravagance and impracticality. Baker painstakingly countered their criticisms one by one, and Louis Botha approved Baker's design at a meeting of the Transvaal Cabinet Council on the 24th of November, which Baker had been invited to attend with "the whole scheme, in spite of the cost," being approved. As Baker continued in his autobiography—"General Botha asked me to do my utmost to complete the contract drawings for quantities and tenders in less time than I said I had thought possible; he said there were urgent reasons for his request. I shall always remember his penetrating look of trust and confidence; the explanation, I think of his magnetic influence which could not be resisted," and Baker goes on to report with justifiable pride—"The plans were completed and the foundations well and truly laid in *his* appointed time."[22]

As before in times of intense workload, Baker was exhausted and retreated to Abe Bailey's *Rust en Vrede* for a few days, from where fellow guest Richard Feetham was able to provide Florence with an update on his progress on the 1st of December—"The Bear is really picking up—is already decidedly better for sea air & sea baths. I had a delightful ride with him along the sands this morning ... not able as yet to run up the mountain!"[23] He was back in Pretoria for the opening of his Church of Saint Michael on the 9th of December, then back to Johannesburg in time for Christmas 1909. The festive period was spent with his family at Stonehouse, where he amused himself by reading Gilbert Murray's verse translations from the Greek of the Athenian dramas.

The contractual arrangements devised for the execution of the Union buildings were complex and while it would be easy to suggest that they had been "designed by committee," they simply reflected the practical realities of the available architectural and construction resources in Pretoria in 1910. Baker was to have overall responsibility for the design of the building; the Public Works Department directed by Secretary Charles Murray was responsible for the delivery of the project including the sourcing and specification of materials, and it was Murray's decision that the two wings and the central curved colonnade should be constructed by separate building contractors. As Murray later explained, "It was considered probable that no single Contractor could finance the whole.... In some ways we would have had less trouble if Meischke had got the whole, but there was an advantage in having two Contractors, especially as they were not on good terms and we were able to play one off against the other in questions of price."[24] To ensure that the project remained under tight control, Murray also decreed that only his team at the PWD would have any communication with the building contractors with the result that all Baker's instructions, drawings and specifications with the contractors had to be made via the PWD. The fact that this process resulted, not in chaos, but in the efficient construction of the buildings, was testament both to Baker and Murray's professionalism and the quality of the relationship which the two men enjoyed. Baker described Murray as "an official and engineer with the talents and imagination of the poets ... a hard-headed Aberdonian who, as an engineer, had had a hard struggle in the rough-and-tumble of a new country ... he was very suspicious, perhaps with some reason, of all professional gentry," and "might have proved a very difficult collaborator for an architect intent on the ideals of his art," but "he gave me his complete trust and showed a warm understanding of my ideals and endeavours."[25] On the 4th of April Meischke's tender was accepted for the wings and on the 17th of May that of Prentice and Mackie for the central colonnade. Baker had met Botha's timetable but it had been a Herculean effort which left him exhausted.

The year of 1910 started with a flurry of further commissions which would have been greeted with celebration just a few years previously, but with Baker's team flat out on the railway station and the Union buildings and with the Villa Arcadia now on-site, it was a challenge to cover them—extensions to Marienhof for Drummond Chaplin, a church at Creighton in Natal, instructions to proceed to construction on Blackroofs in Johannesburg (a new home for H. G. L. Panchaud, the Secretary of Witbank Colliery) and most significantly of all, one of Baker's grandest houses Glenshiel for Colonel William Dalrymple of which he wrote to Florence—"Hurrah! Old Dal. Wants me to build his house, on the kopje. £10,000 I hoped to get that ... up at 6:30 this morning and rode to Govt' House.... Poor Fleming awful over worked."[26]

In the midst of the Union buildings' detailed design, Baker had also finally parted company with Masey, who had left to seek his fortune in Rhodesia. Baker had made "a final proposal—That in return for renouncing all share here (*Johannesburg*) I give you three-quarter share of the work at Cape Town. In addition to this I will renounce all my

The Union Buildings under construction (courtesy Michael Baker).

share for 1909, or, if you think this is not liberal enough, I will renounce a part of the amount due to me in the past in your books, so that you can start afresh … on a new basis with a very small or no debt."[27] A very generous offer, but not enough to stop Masey from striking out on his own. Florence's letter from Muizenberg to her father of the 29th of May summed up the position—"Herbert is awfully glad that he came down as apart from the health question: he squared up one or two doubtful points in his Masey agreement & got it all signed & fixed up and said goodbye & he leaves for good on Tues. the 31st for Rhodesia where I don't think he'll get much work he will then go to America. Herbert is so fit after his sea bathing (twice a day) & quite cheeky & has to be suppressed, he has great larks with his boys & Allaire joins in the rough and tumble, as cheerily as Henry."[28] Baker had clearly resolved a long-term problem and the relief conveyed in Florence's letter spoke volumes. Franklin Kendall took over in Cape Town, with faithful Frank Fleming continuing to assist Baker in Johannesburg.

The 31st of May, the date of Masey's departure, was also the most significant date in the history of the new country with the Union of South Africa being established that same day. This meant considerable change for Baker, as Lord and Lady Selbourne departed to make way for Herbert Gladstone (the youngest son of the former British prime minister) in his new role as Governor-General of the Union of South Africa. His first act was to appoint Louis Botha, the leading Unionist, as his first prime minister of South Africa (with his main challenger having been Baker's friend John Merriman). Botha quickly appointed his first cabinet which included representatives of all the former colonies and with Jan Smuts as his Minister of Finance, Defense and Interior Affairs. Botha and Gladstone's aim was the continuing reconciliation of the two races and the integration of the former colonies, and they succeeded to a remarkable degree. Baker had lost close and influential friends in Lord and Lady Selbourne, but his current client Louis Botha was now the prime minister of a vast new country.

With the Villa Arcadia nearing completion in June, Florence Phillips' attention was increasingly being redirected to her other current project—a new art gallery for Johannesburg which would set the seal on her role as the queen of Johannesburg society. With her favored architect now overwhelmed with work, not to mention the already bitter local professional resentment at the award of both the station and the Union buildings to him, an architectural competition was arranged for the gallery building commission and Florence invited Sir Hugh Lane, "a foppishingly smart young art dealer"[29] from London, who was already advising her on possible acquisitions, to come to South Africa to assist her in judging the entries. Lane concluded that none of the architectural entries had reached an acceptable standard and, having already commissioned Edwin Lutyens to remodel his own house and garden in Cheyne Walk in Chelsea the previous year, suggested to Florence that he might be willing to design her gallery. Baker, sensitive to the growing criticism and already with more work than he and his team could cope with, immediately agreed, with what must have been a mixture of emotions ranging from pleasure at the prospect of soon seeing his old friend, to a certain unease about having Lutyens on his own patch. Lutyens received the telegraphed invitation from Lane while in Rome where he was supervising the construction of his British Pavilion for the 1911 International Exhibition and despite his own heavy workload agreed to come to Mrs. Phillips' rescue.

September brought the first elections for the new South African Parliament with Botha and Smuts' South African Party winning an easy majority and thus confirming Botha as prime minister. As decreed in Rhodes' will, this former Boer General now took up residence in Groote Schuur as the first democratically-elected prime minister of a United South Africa.

By early October, Baker was in Cape Town staying with Abe Bailey at *Rust en Vrede,* from where he confided to Florence—"F (*Fleming*) is seedy—overworking I think—not uncertainty as to his marriage I think. I feel a beast to be away & put it all on to him ... he is a devoted worker and I depend so much on him to get thro' this next crisis of my life. The next 9 months. Its awful to think of the work before me...."[30]

With Masey gone, Baker now sought further new opportunities for Kendall and his team in Cape Town. Much to his annoyance, the College Council of Rhodes University College, which Rhodes had endowed, had rejected his offer to design their principal new building in Cape Town and initiated a further architectural competition for its design. (For architects such as Baker and Lutyens who worked hard to develop extensive client networks, these competitions were becoming an increasing irritant.) He was deeply offended and thus utterly determined to win the commission, so, with Kendall and his team in Cape Town doing most of the work, Baker risked another competition entry. Their design, with its tall central clock tower and flanking wings was successful and several months later in February 1911, Baker was able to write to congratulate Kendall and offer bonuses from the prize money to all involved.

On the 26th of November, with suitable ceremony, the King's brother, the Duke of Connaught, laid the cornerstone of the Union buildings. While Baker was at the center of these celebrations of the commencement of his palatial government building, Edwin Lutyens was steaming towards him, lured by Mrs. Phillips' £1,000 retainer and designing Castle Drogo in his cabin as he sailed. Baker had warned both Lutyens and Hugh Lane that the introduction of an English interloper following the rejection of all the local architects' designs for the art gallery was likely to be controversial. Jane Ridley suggested in her biography of Lutyens that as "South Africa was Baker's territory ... before sailing Lutyens consulted Baker. Baker replied telling him not to come as there was no work. The letter was opened by Emily; by the time it arrived Lutyens was steaming towards the Cape."[31] Lutyens, however, was both well aware of Baker's heavy workload, having written to him earlier that year that he was "delighted to hear of work pouring in upon you,"[32] and also confirming in a later letter to Baker that he "did all you reasonably could (for my own sake) to stop my coming. I have only to publish your letter to me to show that your intentions were anything but selfish."[33] Baker certainly did have reservations about Lutyens' visit, but they were regarding Lutyens' character and the effect that his behavior might have on his own client relationships, rather than any fear of losing work.

Baker had actually gone to considerable lengths to organize Lutyens' trip, so that he could make the most of his time in South Africa, as Lutyens' biographer Christopher Hussey recounted—

> On arrival at Cape Town, December 7, Herbert Baker who had come especially to Johannesburg welcomed him with great warmth on board. Brer Ned and Brer Bear (as they came to address one another during these 10 hectic days) spent the first morning seeing Rudyard Kipling's house, Woolsack, the Rhodes Memorial, and the beginnings of Cape Town Cathedral—all of which were Baker's children; lunched with General Smuts, Sir Lionel Philips, and Dr Malan at Parliament House; then called on the Prime Minister and Mrs. Botha at his official residence Groote Schuur. We may, perhaps, at this point detect the first signs of an emotional excitement—whether owing to the climate, memories of the war, the impact of new and spectacular surroundings, the discussion of great projects with eminent personages, or the combination of these factors—which is the keynote of Lutyens' record of his tour. It may have gone slightly to his head.[34]

Lutyens stayed with Baker at Sandhills on his first night in South Africa before they both set off for Johannesburg by train the next day, where they were welcomed by Lady Phillips, Mrs. Baker, Hugh Lane and Baker's assistant Joseph Solomon at the Villa Arcadia where Lutyens was to stay. Having never traveled beyond Europe previously, Lutyens was fascinated by what he saw—

> The black people interest me enormously. Their faces, the soles of their feet and their white tongues and it is so odd to see them doing their work quite unconscious of my absorbed interest. My silly innocent jokes have a great success yet am warned by everyone (Baker) never to make one.... The town council etc. are all dead against Baker and they want to rope me in without Baker. This makes my position difficult—Baker is as good and generous as gold and I must be careful not to hurt him however advantageous to myself.... There is this villa decked land standing above a squalid town with here and there big buildings, a sort of Birmingham without its smoke.... Then beyond miles of chimneys belching black smoke and weird cat's cradle erections ... the mines, mines of gold, the very heart of the modern world, and beyond the veldt wasting for hundreds of miles.[35]

Within days of his arrival, Lutyens was commissioned to design the Rand Memorial in Johannesburg for which Lionel Phillips was patron, was discussing designing Johannesburg Cathedral with Baker, and soon set his sights on the Cape Town University commission as well.

Solomon, Baker's assistant, was utterly fascinated by both Lutyens and Lane (eventually deserting Baker for a position in Lutyens' London office) and Florence Baker appears to have shared his enthusiasm, at least initially, as she described the events of that December to her father—

We are trying hard to be cool and Christmassy but with a high thermometer & brilliant sun its as hard to realise as ever that plum puddings & mince-meat are made. We shall have Ned Lutyens over Christmas; so he will enjoy it as much, as the boys. Herbert is so happy with him & it is such a help & inspiration to get him here to discuss all details with & Mr L. has got the designing of the Art Gallery; the Rand Regiment Memorial & St Mary's Church with Herbert. They should all have been H's work but the jealousy is so fearful that that was impossible so it was best to get someone quite outside. H. will of course help him carry out the plans & they will do the church together. [The cathedral church at Johannesburg.] Mr Lutyens is a charming visitor & devoted to the boys & they to him…. Herbert was with Mr Lutyens most of the day & we dined twice at the Philips to meet him … tennis on Saturday Herbert played brilliantly and enjoyed it.[36]

But, as Baker had feared, many others were less enamored with Lutyens' famous wit as Jane Ridley recalled. Lutyens was rather shocked at witnessing Baker's achievements, and

he tried to outdo him and succeeded only in making a fool of himself. Mistaken with his balding head for the dull Governor-General Sir Herbert Gladstone, Ned alternately clowned and pontificated. He lectured the South Africans, Botha and Smuts, on how they should build in their own country, and he irritated Hugh Lane by playing the fool at gallery committee meetings. The talk of projects became giddier—a town plan, a university, a cathedral; his mind outran his pen, and letters home dissolved into incoherent scrawl…. The jokes never ceased. The Bishop of Cape Town [Baker's client for the cathedral] came to tea wearing an amethyst ring "as big as the tea cup he offered me. Of course I tried to take the ring and he nearly spilt the tea" while Mr and Mrs Pim, whom he met at dinner, were embarrassed to be asked "if there were any pimples."[37]

While Lutyens' wit is now generally treasured, in 1910 many of its recipients found it either shocking, offensive or both, and Lutyens left Baker with much smoothing of furrowed brows to be done after his departure.[38]

Lutyens and Lane boarded the train for Cape Town and their passage home on Boxing Day, and Baker must have waved them off with a sigh of relief. Lutyens' letter of thanks to Baker, which was written on the train, suggests he had been aware of how trying he had been—"I loved and do love the direct simplicity of your unwavering hospitality. Not a carping or ungenerous word, to me, who must by my very nature have tried you sorely…."[39] Baker had committed to assist Lutyens in guiding both the gallery and the Rand Memorial through the choppy waters of local resentment towards construction but Lutyens appears to have been largely unaware of the debt that he owed him in undertaking this role. On the contrary, on his return to England, he behaved (Baker later related) "with such a ruthless want of consideration for the wishes and instructions of his friends and clients that I wrote to him that his methods would make it difficult for me ever to collaborate with him."[40] It had been a sobering experience for "Brer Bear" which had left him licking his wounds, but it was to be nothing compared to the direct and professionally damaging attacks which Lutyens would one day subject him to.

While Baker had been engrossed in the design of the railway station and the government buildings in Pretoria, Francis Masey had been attempting to establish his own new practice in Rhodesia and by late 1910 had landed Salisbury's plum commission—its new cathedral. Baker's final offer of a revised partnership agreement with Masey of a year previously had proposed, in addition to a varied division of income, that Masey would have free rein to develop and deliver the practice's work in Rhodesia, but as far as Baker was concerned, with Masey's rejection of this proposal—the gloves were off. Consequently, in the spring of 1911, Baker, at the invitation of the cathedral committee, commenced discussions with them regarding the design of the cathedral. By May, he was writing to them thanking the "Committee for their kindness in requesting me to undertake this work. I should like to think over the matter a little before writing to you officially, and I ought also to explain the circumstances to Mr Masey before accepting the work."[41] As can be imagined, when Baker informed him, Masey was incandescent. Having moved to Salisbury largely to escape Baker and his extensive network, he had now not only been pursued, but as he saw it, robbed of his greatest prospect. Baker hardly needed the cathedral commission while Masey needed it desperately, but nevertheless, Baker cleared his appointment with the RIBA and Masey was advised that if he wished to pursue the issue that he must take action against the church committee and not Baker. In August, he commenced a lawsuit against the committee which was still to be heard when in early September, at the age of only 50, he died of pneumonia. It was a desperately sad end to a partnership which for so many years had been a close, supportive and creative one—initially poisoned—like so many architectural friendships before and since, by a dispute over credit for design work. Baker's design for the cathedral on which construction work didn't start until April 1913 was another Romanesque composition in grey granite with detached campanile and a concrete vaulted nave over semi-circular stone arches. Construction was abandoned with the outbreak of the First World War in 1914 with only the choir and sanctuary constructed; it was finally completed by others in 1950.

By the summer, one of his last great Johannesburg houses—Glenshiel—for Colonel William Dalrymple, was nearing completion. With his design of the Villa Arcadia, Baker had hinted that his move to Classicism might consistently include his domestic work as well as his public buildings, but in Glenshiel, as requested by his client, he produced his best South African Arts and Crafts house. Glenshiel is a delight in which Baker never puts a foot wrong. His textbook "H" plan is now developed into an Arts and Crafts butterfly plan (first developed by E. S. Prior and used by Lutyens on his earlier Papillon Hall) with his sequence of entrance, hall and *stoep* now enclosed by a formal dining room to one side and a grand staircase to the other, before the diagonal wings open out to the wonderful views from its site on the ridge. To the south is an exquisite two-story entrance porch (with more than a hint of Marshcourt) while to the north the *stoep* is here enclosed by three arches supported on elegant pairs of Tuscan Doric columns. From its sprocketed eaves to its tall brick chimneys, it is one of the "final hurrahs" of this remarkable architectural movement which was about to be almost entirely extinguished, along with the sons of many of its clients, by the horrors of the First World War.

It is tempting to imagine that at this point in his career Baker became more selective in his new commissions thus focusing his energy and imagination more directly on fewer more significant projects such as the railway station and the Union buildings, but this was never the case. Baker simply operated on a different business model from Lutyens and other sole partners, always working with carefully selected junior partners and senior assistants who could handle much of the day-to-day grind of the practice and who were quite capable of delivering much of the practice's workload in his style with minimal input from the senior partner. Despite the demands and responsibility of running this larger organization, it offered a number of benefits to Baker, not least the additional income that this approach generated. It was a more robust model which had seen him through the depression from 1903 to 1909 when his practice had proved quite capable of

"Glenshiel," Johannesburg, viewed from the garden (courtesy Michael Baker).

living off miners' cottages and one-room schools if required. It allowed him to concentrate his efforts on both winning new work and designing the practice's most important projects whether for Rhodes or the South African government, and while he shouldered the ultimate responsibility for every aspect of the practice, he was also able to consult his partners and draw on their experience when required. So, the numerous villas, the small churches, the extensions, alterations and cottages, no matter how modest, were always gratefully received and professionally delivered.

He had built a new life for himself with Florence and their children in Johannesburg, from where they could retreat in the heat of the South African winter to the cooling breezes of their beach house in Cape Town. He relaxed in his garden at Stonehouse where gardening itself had become a new and important pastime for him, and they had built their own tennis court there, regularly holding Saturday morning tennis parties. Florence had thrown herself enthusiastically and very successfully into the role of the architect's wife, hosting and visiting existing and potential clients and showing them around Herbert's completed and ongoing projects. Their letters suggest a successful, complementary, genuinely close and loving partnership which was probably considerably more than either had dared to hope for. For Herbert, it was a new and richer life; his most successful partnership, started at 42, at a time when he might have felt that a family life had passed him by. For Florence it was a happy marriage, a great adventure, an exciting contrast to life in rural Kent and a wealthier and much more pleasant lifestyle than most colonial wives enjoyed, although she did share with them their constant "thoughts of home." That summer of 1911, with their finances now restored, Florence was able to take the children to England for a holiday, staying at both Nurstead and Owletts, while Herbert was fully entertained in Pretoria with the station and the Union buildings, both of which were now under construction on-site. Little did they realize that their apparently idyllic life was about to be entirely disrupted by events then happening, not in Cape Town, Pretoria or Johannesburg, but across the Arabian Sea, in distant, ancient, mysterious, enchanting India.

On the 23rd of November 1910, just a few days before the foundation stone of the Union buildings had been laid by the Duke of Connaught, Lord Hardinge had been appointed as the new Governor-General and Viceroy of India. One of his first tasks was to arrange a durbar for the newly-crowned King George. The first durbar had been organized by an earlier Viceroy, Lord Lytton (Lutyens' father-in-law), and held in 1877, in the ancient Mughal capital of Delhi, where Lytton proclaimed Queen Victoria as Empress of India. In 1903 a further durbar was held in Delhi to proclaim her son Edward VII as Emperor of India and its superb organization and extended festivities, which saw almost all the Indian maharajas and princes gathered together for the first time to swear their allegiance to the crown, became known as "Curzon's durbar" after the then-Viceroy, Lord Curzon. Curzon's only regret was that the King himself had declined to attend and had been represented *in absentia* by his brother, the much-traveled Duke of Connaught. Hardinge was determined to outdo Curzon and not only successfully secured the attendance of the new King and Queen, but also further enhanced the occasion by using it to reveal what would become known as "the best kept secret in the history of India."

The British East India Company, from which Britain's Indian Empire had grown, had been first established in the trading port of Calcutta in Bengal on the northeast coast of India and as this colony grew to eventually encompass the entire sub-continent, the British had continued to govern from there. By the end of the 19th century its role as the capital of India began to be questioned as it was so remote from so much of the country and, with the opening of the Suez Canal, Bombay on the west coast had now overtaken it as the country's principal port. Despite these murmurings, the King's announcement at the durbar on the 12th of December 1911, came as a complete surprise—"We are pleased to announce to Our People that on the advice of Our Ministers tendered after consultation with Our Governor-General in Council, We have decided upon the transfer of the seat of the Government of India from Calcutta to the ancient Capital of Delhi."[42] At a stroke, the Moghul Empire's ancient Delhi had become an imperial capital once more. Just three days later, the King laid the foundation stone of what was to be a new capital city, and by early 1912 the race to design it was officially underway.

The Viceroy decided that a committee of experts should be formed to advise on the layout of the new city. John A. Brodie, the city engineer of Liverpool, was interviewed and quickly selected, followed soon after by Captain George Swinton, the chairman of the London County Council who was to chair the small committee, but finding a suitable architect with experience in town planning proved much more contentious. Lord Crewe, the recently appointed Secretary of State for India, was asked to propose a suitable third committee member to the Viceroy's Council, and there was certainly no shortage of candidates who thought themselves entirely capable.

The local government board had recommended Stanley Davenport Adshead, professor of civic design at the University of Liverpool, as the one architect in Britain who had made a systematic study of town planning. Patrick Geddes was consulted in his role as director of the Cities and Town Planning Exhibition of 1911 and suggested himself. The RIBA offered Henry Vaughan Lanchester, the architect of the recently completed civic quarter of Cardiff; John William Simpson who had recently acted as secretary general of the London Town Planning Conference in 1910 was considered, along with Edwin Lutyens who had the planning of the central square of Hampstead Garden Suburb to his credit. Leonard Stokes, Reginald Blomfield, Cecil Brewer and Robert Lorimer were also all in the mix, and Lord Crewe himself had suggested Raymond Unwin, the principal planner of Hampstead Garden Suburb.

The Viceroy professed no knowledge of Lutyens, but Crewe knew him from both Hampstead Garden Suburb and the committee for the Shakespeare's England Exhibition of that year, and with Lutyens' own impressive network in overdrive to secure him the appointment, Lord Crewe soon recommended him to the Viceroy along with Swinton and Brodie, but on the clear understanding that his appointment was for town planning and not the subsequent architecture. Lutyens had kept his friend Baker informed of progress at every turn and on the 29th of February 1912, could hardly contain his excitement—"I believe I am fixed up for Delhi.... As regards the buildings, who does it, they won't commit themselves. There will be more than one man can do.... Oh what fun if we could come together on it,"[43] and on the 15th of March he was able to write exultantly, "Delhi is all right!! I start on 27th March!!! It is a wonderful chance."[44] Baker congratulated him warmly—"My dear Conqueror of ¾ of the Universe ... full of the hugeness of my congratulations ... I wonder what you will do—whether you will drop the language and classical tradition and just go for surfaces—sun and shadow. It must not be Indian, nor English, nor Roman, but it must be Imperial.... On the day you sail you should feel like Alexander when he crossed the Hellespont to conquer Asia."[45] This is an interesting letter. As well as expressing his enthusiasm and pleasure at his friend's appointment, Baker's response also reflects his own thinking regarding an appropriate architecture of empire for the colonies and his perception of the parallels between the Roman, Greek and British empires and what he now understood as the challenge of designing imperial buildings for hot climates in strong sunlight. For Baker, Pretoria and New Delhi were akin to Paestum or Merida—outposts of a mighty empire whose architecture expressed a level of power and degree of sophistication which would fill its new subjects with shock and awe.

Baker wouldn't have been human had he not also suffered a pang of jealousy—surely he, more than any other contemporary architect, had shown how best to celebrate and express the benign might of the empire in the colonies? For Lutyens, Delhi was to be a godsend, not only providing him with the opportunity to design the palace which he had sketched and dreamed of for so long, in the shape of Government House (or the Viceroy's House as it was finally named), but it would also allow him to survive the imminent collapse of his country-house practice with the outbreak of the First World War. For Baker, it must have been a disappointment, but one wonders how he could possibly have responded to the opportunity bearing in mind his existing commitments and South African base.

The flow of new jobs in the Transvaal was continuing incessantly, including Byeways in the expanding suburb of Forest Town in Johannesburg for Robert A. Lehfeldt and Welgelegen Manor, Baker's last and finest Cape Dutch house, for the Mostert family in Balfour, southeast of Johannesburg. The Mostert's had originally owned Welgelegen in Rondebosch which Baker had already extended and remodeled for Cecil Rhodes, in fact Andries Mostert had attempted to buy back this former family home but had been outbid by Rhodes. He had moved north to the Transvaal where he had prospered as a building

The main building and encircling wings of "Welgelegen" (courtesy Welgelegen Manor).

and engineering contractor, and he now commissioned Baker to design the family's rather grand farmhouse there. The model was the original Welgelegen, and the result is a fascinating Cape Dutch house by the mature Herbert Baker. The main elevation is a traditional, white-rendered, symmetrical Cape farmhouse with central Dutch gable flanked by tall windows with shutters to their lower frames, but this is now framed by two encircling arcades of Tuscan Doric columns which each terminate in small pavilions with tall white chimneys. The southern elevation has a hint of the Arts and Crafts with its dormer windows and two great chimney stacks which rise up high above the roof to flank a central entrance and first-floor balcony. Internally, as expected, Baker has produced another delightful sequence of domestic spaces in which the family (and now guest-house visitors) are enveloped in either timber paneling or plain white plastered walls below fine timber beams or roof trusses. It is a very accomplished house which anticipates Port Lympne for Phillip Sassoon by almost a decade.

In Cape Town, Kendall was busy on St. Andrew's College where Baker had secured commissions for new classrooms, dormitories, offices and a new chapel, which with his return to a site in Cape Town, appears to have inspired a reversion to the Gothic of his early ecclesiastical work there. Two much more significant new commissions received in 1912 were for a new South African Institute of Medical Research in Johannesburg and a new building for the city's Union Club. Work on the cathedral continued at a snail's pace, but by the summer, the Rhodes Memorial was finally complete.

It was dedicated on the 5th of July 1912, without the presence of Prime Minister Botha; reconciliation between Dutch and British was one thing but celebrating Rhodes' life and work was still a step too far. For Baker, however, it was both a fitting tribute to his mentor and an exceptionally fine Classical monument which, as was his aim, would have looked entirely appropriate on a hillside overlooking the Mediterranean or the Aegean seas. Nestling "amidst oaks, pines, and protea trees that wave silver in the wind his temple-monument stands today."[46] At its center, Swan's bust of Rhodes, below which was carved an epitaph from Kipling—

Rhodes' "long view" from his memorial in Cape Town (courtesy Roddy Bray).

"The Immense and brooding spirit still,
Shall quicken and control,
Living he was the land, and dead,
His souls shall be her soul"[47]

On either side of the statue, two flanking colonnades of plain unfluted Doric columns look out to the distant land to the north, as Rhodes himself used to do, and the great cascade of steps flows down the mountainside, each flight guarded by Swan's mighty lions, until the great plinth at the base provides less of a full stop than a further springing-off point. On the plinth, Watt's statue of "Physical Energy" looks out to the north with its rider reining in his horse and shielding his eyes from the sun and fixing his sights on his distant goal, before setting off once more towards it. Roderick Gradidge, one of Lutyens' greatest admirers, compared it to Heathcote—Lutyens' first Classical composition—and found the memorial "a very much finer and more austere design." He described it as "an extremely tough Classical monument in granite; simple and undecorated, it bears little relationship to typical English architecture of 1900 and Lutyens was to do nothing like it until much later and, in fact, never anything quite so tough," going so far as to suggest, "no other English architect could have done it" or "came anywhere near to Baker in handling the orders in this stern yet elegant manner."[48] It is a fitting, powerful, entirely masculine and finely judged composition in which Baker did justice to both his friend and his art.

7

1912–1913

"The Crown of India" (Op. 66)

In Delhi, in the spring of 1912, Lutyens and the other members of the "Committee of Experts" were being transported around the city by elephant surveying possible sites, and opinions were already divided. The old city of Delhi lies on a plain, stretching between the River Jumna and a ridge from where the city can be overlooked. For the British, the Ridge held sacred memories which exercised a strong pull as a possible site for the new city. It was to the Ridge that the British had fled during the mutiny in May 1857 and it was from the Ridge that they had established artillery positions to lay siege to and retake the city from the rebels in September of that year. The Ridge was therefore strongly favored, but concerns were soon expressed that there was insufficient space to accommodate the entire new city there, while equally, the plain south of the existing city below the ridge was criticized as being poorly drained, malarial and unhealthy. Lanchester, who had managed to secure a role as a "temporary expert" proposed the integration of the new city with the old, but early estimates of the cost of the necessary demolitions and the compensation required concluded further discussion of this option. Having managed to get his foot in the door with his temporary commission, however, he then successfully extended its scope somewhat, staying on after the full committee members had returned to England and working directly with the Viceroy on city plans, much to Lutyens' intense annoyance and frustration. An early option of laying out the city on the plain with Government House above on the Ridge was soon also rejected with the Viceroy himself soon deciding that the entire city should lie below the Ridge with Government House raised slightly above its surroundings on Raisina Hill, which, though lower than the Ridge, still dominated the rest of the plain.

All of the committee's and Lanchester's city plans were dominated by Classical Beaux Arts or "City Beautiful" planning, with numerous elements of both George-Eugene Haussmann's Paris and French/American engineer Pierre Charles L'Enfant's Washington appearing again and again. Once the location of Government House was agreed upon and the decision made that it should face due east towards the river, rather than northeast towards the old city, a version of Washington, D.C., complete with its use of diagonals to produce radiating axial vistas, was soon developed. In lieu of the great axis which led from the Lincoln Memorial via the Reflecting Pool and the Washington Monument to the climax of the great dome of the U.S. Capitol, the final plan of New Delhi led from a monument to the King, along a new Processional Way flanked by reflecting pools, between symmetrical government offices (the Secretariat buildings) to the climax of a domed

Government House. Lutyens consistently denied the influence of Washington, but the evidence against him, including his own early sketches, is overwhelming.

While planning a new imperial city held a certain interest for Lutyens, his primary aim in Delhi was to secure the commission for the principal buildings. Despite the outstanding architectural quality of his country houses, he believed that he needed significant public commissions to achieve a place in the first division of British architects along with Wren, Jones and Shaw, thus preserving his reputation for posterity. His appointment to the committee had certainly placed him in pole position, and while in Delhi on his commission to plan the city, he had already taken the opportunity that spring to show the Viceroy (and importantly, his new ally, the Vicereine Lady Hardinge) sketches of his ideas for Government House, soon informing his wife Emily—"I think things are working out very well and I get my way and make my plans without disturbance and with right help etc. Lord Hardinge was very pleasant today and he has written to Lord Crewe that I should do Government House and the Great Place in front of it. The Secretariat buildings come in and would eventually form part of the scheme and I may get them too—if the competition bugbear don't frighten them."[1]

Lanchester, however, continued to be a painful and persistent thorn in Lutyens' side, and his suggestion to the Viceroy that all the buildings should be open to an architectural competition filled Lutyens with horror at the memory of nine wasted months on his unsuccessful entry for London County Hall. While Lutyens soon got both Lord and Lady Hardinge on board, Lord Crewe and others were less convinced, albeit less regarding his qualifications to design Government House than the process of his selection for such a prestigious public commission without any form of competition. Lutyens continued to keep Baker informed of progress throughout 1912, during which, in Hussey's words—"It became clear, indeed, that his pressing for Baker's collaboration varied in intensity in proportion to the imminence or recession of a competition for the official buildings."[2]

As with the architectural position on the Committee of Experts, there was no shortage of candidates for these plum architectural appointments—John Begg, the government of India's architect, when consulted, like Patrick Geddes before him, suggested himself; Sir Brumwell Thomas, the architect of Belfast City Hall, traveled to India to put his case and failed to even secure an interview with the Viceroy, while Sir Reginald Blomfield who was by then president of the RIBA was both a serious candidate in his own right and, unbeknownst to Baker, another potential collaborator for Lutyens. He recalled in his own biography—"One day I received a letter from Lutyens asking me if I would be his colleague in this work. I replied that I would and informed my friends that there was no need for any further action in the matter as it appeared to have settled itself," and thus, "I was deprived of the opportunity of work on a great scale and in the grand manner, which is the ambition of every architect worthy of his name."[3] As the weeks passed, Lutyens became ever more desperate but with Crewe advising everyone including the King and the Viceroy (who were now keen to appoint Lutyens) not to be hasty in their selection, by the autumn he had still not bagged his prey and the threat of a competition constantly hung over him like a dark and oppressive cloud. Opponents of Lutyens' appointment certainly had plenty of ammunition, as he was already regarded as an extravagant architect who worked only for the rich, and memories of his management of the pavilion for the British School in Rome on which tenders had come back at twice the estimate were still raw. Lionel Earle, who was private secretary to Lord Harcourt and who had been Lord

Crewe's private secretary until 1910, wrote to Lord Crewe stating, "I should not recommend him (*Lutyens*) to carry out the buildings did I not know that the Indian Government were able to chain him between elephants as regards finance."[4]

Meanwhile, back in South Africa, Pretoria Station was officially opened on the 2nd of September and with the station in use and the Union buildings now well on their way towards completion, combined with his vast South African portfolio, Baker himself was emerging as a serious contender for the government buildings in Delhi, and in the autumn of 1912, with Lutyens' apparent encouragement, he resolved to enter the fray. Suddenly, being regarded as "a colonial architect" had become an asset rather than a liability and he pressed his case as hard as possible through his own considerable network of contacts. Lord Milner was back in London and doing what he could. Sir James Meston (a friend, member of the Round Table and former adviser to the governments of the Cape Colony and the Transvaal) was now Secretary to the Finance Department of the government of India and proposed Baker directly to the Viceroy. He was supported by W. B. Gordon who was Secretary of the Indian Government Public Works Department (another member of the Round Table, whom Baker also knew from his time in the Cape Colony), and he in turn was supported by William Marris, who was Acting Secretary to the Home Government of India (who was another South African friend and yet another member of the Round Table). Baker sent Lutyens photographs of the Union buildings, and Lutyens shared these with the Viceroy as evidence of the capabilities of his potential collaborator (should he need one). Strangely, among all these heavyweight civil servants, it was to be a painter and one-time pupil of Norman Shaw, Reginald Barratt, who was a good friend of Lord Hardinge, who perhaps did Baker's cause most good by suggesting that the combination of Lutyens' and Baker's skills and experience was an ideal one. But it was to be Baker himself, who through a carefully crafted and brilliantly timed article in *The Times* which was published on the 3rd of October 1912, finally pushed himself into both public consciousness and serious consideration.

As Lutyens had earlier intimated, Hardinge, politically sensitive to local feelings, was committed to the new buildings all being constructed in some form of Indian style, preferably with traditional pointed Moghul arches, stone screens, minarets and bulbous domes as the now elderly architect and engineer Samuel Swinton Jacobs had achieved in his "Indo-Saracenic" buildings. This had become something of a public debate with Lutyens firmly positioned in the opposite Western Classical camp, famously telling his wife, "They want me to do Hindo. Hindon't I say."[5] It was into these dangerous waters that Baker's literary contribution entitled "The Problem of Style" was gently dropped. It had clearly been the subject of much careful drafting and indeed he was so pleased with the result that he later published it in full in his biography. This treatise, on an appropriate style of architecture for the new imperial capital of India, while timed to promote his own case, was heartfelt and genuinely reflected his own views and experiences of building for the empire in South Africa. He rather boldly rejected "The Indo-Saracenic Style" which he knew Hardinge then favored, suggesting, "While in this style we may have the means to express the charm and fascination of India, yet it has not the constructive and geometrical qualities necessary to embody the idea of law and order which has been produced out of chaos by the British Administration." What he offered in its place was "The English Classic Style" but adapted to the climate of "our Southern Dominions" and incorporating minor "Eastern Features" and drawing on "all that India has to give ... of subtlety and industry in craftsmanship."[6] It was something of a masterstroke and remains a fairly accurate description of the final architectural style adopted for New Delhi.

Lutyens was furious. He was both well aware that he was unable to compete with Baker in terms of literary architectural discourse and also strongly resented his potential junior partner possibly becoming the principal. He informed Baker a few days after its publication that he had "dined at the House of Commons on Tuesday night with Montague, there were about 50 there ... your letter to the Times is their chief complaint."[7] With others however, as Baker had intended, it had the desired effect. George Swinton, Lutyens' fellow Committee of Experts member now recommended Baker, both as an architect who already had major colonial and government building experience and as probably the only man with whom Lutyens could work, stating in a letter to Hardinge— "Here we have a man who *is* a successful architect and speaks not only like a poet, but like a statesman."[8] A few days later, this view was reinforced by Herbert, now Viscount Gladstone, the Governor-General of South Africa, who wrote from Baker's Government House in Pretoria to Lord Crewe that a joint appointment would represent the best possible outcome. By the end of the month *The Times* and *The Morning Post* were clamoring for Lutyens' and Baker's appointment.

Robert Grant Irving, in his excellent book on the building of New Delhi, *Indian Summer,* can take up the tale—"Lutyens meetings on October 26th with Sir Thomas Holderness, the new Permanent Under-Secretary at the India Office, was pivotal. Assuring Lutyens that it reflected no want of confidence in him, Holderness asked him if he would collaborate with Baker, as it would strengthen Lord Crewe's hands in dealing with inevitable criticism. Fully aware of the difficulties of obtaining the appointment for himself alone (as he frankly confessed to Swinton), Lutyens agreed at once and telegraphed Baker with alacrity." The answer came on the evening of October 29—"Willingly co-operate subject difficulties explained in my previous letter"[9]—namely that he would not collaborate as a junior partner. As Roderick Gradidge succinctly put it—"With some sharp footwork and getting in with the right people, Lutyens (not for nothing married to the daughter of a former Viceroy of India) ... managed to get the commission for the Imperial city of Delhi, not having built a single major public building.... It was obvious to everyone that it was essential that he had a collaborator and Baker, his old friend, was the obvious choice. In fact, in a fairer world Baker was the obvious choice as the principal architect, but although he had proved that he was capable of handling vast complex public commissions, he had merely worked in the colonies whereas Lutyens had built houses for all the right people, or their cousins, or their aunts."[10]

Back in Pretoria, the anticipation was intense, as Florence Baker confided to her father in her letter of November 4—"No more cables about Delhi. We are all excited & I do hope Herbert gets it on nice terms. We hear indirectly that there is a great force at work too get him there so we shall hear more I hope officially in two mails time we will cable if its immediate."[11] Baker had done all he could from Johannesburg and with the fish now finally hooked and heading towards the net, he decided to travel to London to make sure of his catch. On the 26th of November he took the train to Cape Town where he made arrangements for his absence with Kendall before embarking on the SS *Kenilworth Castle* for England on the 30th. His plan was to get to London as soon as possible, and if events allowed, to also take a short inspirational vacation in his beloved Rome before what, if he was successful, would almost inevitably be another intense period of work. As he sailed north from the Cape, Lutyens also set sail for India with Brodie and Swinton for the second visit of the Committee of Experts to continue with their city planning, and in Lutyens' case, to also further press his own case for the architectural commissions directly with the Viceroy.

As before with major decisions, such as when considering staying in or leaving South Africa, moving to Johannesburg or concluding his bachelorhood, Baker was carefully weighing up the situation. His long letter to his wife of the 8th of December while bound for England sets out his thoughts and many concerns—"I am much afraid that I may become a pawn a figurehead to keep Lutyens, while he has—as first in the field—all the best of the work leaving me the hot-work. I can't see—however much I think it over—that the job can be worked with only occasional visits. It must, to do justice to it, absorb all our energies for many years."[12] Even if Baker achieved the best possible option of an offer of appointment on equal terms with Lutyens, he remained far from sure that he could actually work with him, and while Crewe and Hardinge were now convinced that they made the perfect partnership, Baker had real reservations with the memory of Lutyens' behavior on his recent visit to Johannesburg still both fresh and troublesome. Baker was now 50, his professional position in South Africa was highly respected and unassailable, his now considerable level of income secure, his family life an extremely happy one and he and Florence enjoyed a considerable network of friendships throughout South Africa. On the other hand, if he could achieve an appointment to New Delhi on an equal footing with Lutyens and above all other British architects, it would be as Blomfield had written bitterly, an "opportunity of work on a great scale and in the grand manner, which is the ambition of every architect worthy of his name."[13] If given the opportunity, could he really resist?

While Herbert and Florence's parting was vexing for them both, it has provided us with a rich collection of, often daily, correspondence which gives a particularly valuable insight into Baker's thoughts as he worked towards his goal. Throughout these next few weeks he continued to be wracked with doubts as to whether he would accept the role in India if it were offered, how he would deliver it and from where, whether he could work with Lutyens and what would be the effect on his South African practice and his happy family life there. After being anchored off Portsmouth for a night unable to dock due to bad weather, he finally set foot on English soil on the 14th of December, taking a train from Southampton to London and then on to Cobham. The next day at Owletts, he wrote to Florence—"Hurrah—for your cable (*Florence had cabled to let Herbert know that she was expecting once more*)—I jumped out of my warm bed and danced with joy when I got it. I am delighted—dearest—more than I can say…. Well done Muizenberg—it was all that holiday. But I wish I were there with you to reprise!"[14] This was followed by an update on the 1st of December from London—"In such a whirl…. Lutyens office looking at plan of Delhi—very fine & learning all about his office & ways—I think mine are better!! Mrs Scott asked after my two beautiful boys![15] Very nice and is off to the S. Pole—via America, riding through Mexico!! Soon to meet her husband…. Then to Hampstead Garden City—very nice but disappointed with Lutyens work there—church especially … (lunch) then went to Chelsea Hospital…. Then to a sculptor who is doing work Ubs (*Union Buildings*) … found Curtis walked with him across the park … lunch with Astors…."[16] The remainder of the month was similarly split between business, lunches and dinners in London during which he took every opportunity to press his case as well as catching up with his family in Kent during fleeting breaks. Lutyens meanwhile, who was already in Delhi with the other experts, was still attempting to gain the agreement of the Viceroy to both the final siting of the new city and his own appointment for the buildings when the budding Indian Independence movement made a dramatic entry onto the scene.

To officially mark the move of the Indian government from Calcutta to Delhi, it was planned that the Viceroy and Vicereine should enter the ancient city of Delhi atop an elephant, in the style of their Mughal predecessors. Thus, as the parade made its way from the Red Fort by the River Jumna slowly up Chandni Chauk, the city's main thoroughfare, a bomb was thrown into the Viceroy's silver howda, where it exploded. Lutyens, following a subsequent interview with the Vicereine, gives an account of the event in a letter to his wife—

> She heard a report, not realizing it was a bomb, but felt as though the elephant was wrong or there was an earthquake. She looked at the Viceroy and saw his coat was torn and put her hand up to close the tear to tidy him when she realized that a large bit of meat (that is not her language) was sticking out of the Viceroy's uniform. She realized then what had happened. The Viceroy said someone has thrown a bomb—go on. She did not know how to stop the procession and thought Lord H. was probably mortally injured and another shock might hurt him again. She looked round for help and then saw only one man behind them and he was dead. So she said we cannot go on with a dead man in the Howdah and the procession must stop. H. said I suppose it must, stopped it and fainted…. The elephant behaved splendidly though slightly wounded—never ran off or showed fear. Jolly beasts elephants. I love 'em. The howdah, which I have seen, is an extraordinary sight—battered to pieces and soaked in blood.[17]

He added somewhat later, "Hardinge is tremendously pro–Indian and this is his reward."[18] Despite Hardinge's wish to act as if it was "business as usual," the effect of the attack was to bring the government of the country to a grinding halt and with the layout and design of the new city his personal project, Lutyens was left with little to do. What was even worse from his perspective was that when the Viceroy recovered he expressed a renewed interest in the northern site on the Ridge. This was anathema to Lutyens, whose variations on Paris and Washington required the flat plain below.

Baker heard the news of the outrage in London where he was now preparing for his vacation in Rome and possibly a journey to India, while also trying to secure a place for his eldest son Henry at Winchester College which had been recommended to him by that old boy, Lionel Hichens. While waiting to disembark at Southampton a few weeks earlier he had received a telegram out of the blue from Phillip Sassoon of the prominent and extremely wealthy Jewish Sassoon/Rothschild banking family whom he had arranged to meet, reporting after to Florence—"He wants me to design a small house on the hill over looking Romney Marsh & tho it will be difficult I think I will—I'll go down on Friday stay with him near Folkestone—see the site in the morning & he will motor me to Dover to catch the boat—I'll sketch the house on the train."[19]

Five days later, he was writing from his train waiting to depart from the Gare de Lyon in Paris—"Such a hurricane of a departure…. I met S. at Dover & we made plans over lunch … for a fairly large 'small house.' The house is to cost £8,000…. Funny little whipper snapper—Sassoon—Who the stage would represent—a nice feeble little son of a foreign baronet!" then continuing from Genoa—"I have just worked out Sassoon's house. It comes well I think. It is all to get the sun with *stoeps* not shading rooms yet facing south (*with sketch*)."[20] Three days later, he was writing from Rome—"Well here I am Florence, in the Eternal City! & I have had 2 very fine days…. Yesterday we walked round to many previous old friends—saw the new Brit' School—by Lutyens—only just a building."[21] Further sightseeing in Rome was followed by a further visit to Tivoli to see his touchstone the Villa d'Este and on Tuesday the 14th he traveled to nearby Frascati, returning late in the evening to find that a telegram awaited him—"The time has come! I got in late after 12 heavenly hours at Frascati—to find Lutyens cable. 'Viceroy has telegraphed here to see & arrange letters with Baker to cooperate adapting Western style to Indian sentiment to build Government House and other important buildings as Architectural advisers to Government of all Indians—come out as soon as he can & Holderness & Indian Office write confidential—asking me to accept & wire immediately—term etc. An Indian—Sir Swinton Jacob is to be collaborator on Indian local conditions & feeling etc. Toss up—heads I go & heads I don't!'"[22] On Thursday, the following day, he advised General Smuts of the offer on a confidential basis and sought his agreement to extend his leave while the Union buildings continued on-site. Smuts, by return, both gave his approval and advised that he accept the offer.

The next day, Friday, we find Herbert Baker waiting in the Council Room of the Indian Office back in London, apparently still undecided as to whether or not to accept the honor of the prospective appointment, from where he wrote to Florence—"I am sitting here in the Council Room with portraits of Warren Hastings dear face the 'Milner' of India—Cornwallis—Wellesley—Lawrence & other great heroes of Empire—and how can I refuse! They seem to call me where I am ordered—regardless of self & family & smaller interests (*and later*) Waited till 1:45 for Sir T Holderness. He was very nice and agreed to all my terms. Allows me to go for one month there and thinks I can work it all from S. Africa … 300 guin' for month + all expenses. I am to sail next Thurs' via Marseilles. He made it so easy that I c'd refuse if I wanted to & then Warren Hastings looked down at me in next room."[23] The deed was done; the imperial challenge accepted and Baker's and Lutyens' fates were now entwined.

The next few days before his departure for India were a maelstrom of activity of which the following extract from a very long letter to Florence offers just a hint—

Such a life since Friday when last wrote…. Sassoon's motor—to his site beyond Hythe overlooking Romney Marsh—very beautiful site…. Back to lunch at Sandgate—designing garden in motor … many letters including those to Winchester College! … The India Office & Sir T Holderness. The cable from the Viceroy arrived as I was there … found the Council had approved—but the Cape Gov't had still to know and approve. They had cabled Ld Gladstone … 3 boats and 4 trains between London and Delhi…. Then into Hudson of Country Life—talk about it all & Lutyens…. Arts Club late…. Blomfield president…. I found him great fun…. I Cd help thinking how odd it was—to meet the 20 old men I looked up to at the head of the profession—all my seniors—& I had in my pocket a commission to build the New Delhi!![24]

Four days later, he was writing from a train in "Italy once more. Just through the big Mt. Cenis tunnel for the third time in 3 week…. A letter from Lutyens arrived just as I left—He writes with a better sense of responsibility—(the blowing up of the Viceroy was good for him)—to show that life and politics outside architecture is not all a joke—and I think is tending more towards a style more in sympathy with my views…. The appointment is not public yet—Holderness said they were waiting to tell the King. I am glad I escaped quietly before the fuss."[25]

On board ship in the Red Sea, his doubts appear to have surfaced once more—"I have a big cabin and the decks of the Egypt are v. good—200 yds round = 9 times a mile…. I am rather depressed now—not feeling well—and going away from both my homes & the excitement being over the difficulties of the job rather overwhelm one…. I did too much during that last week—a great strain … & it is one reason why I hesitated about accepting—it will be continual I expect.... I worked hard all yesterday and finished my revised plan for the terraces at Un. Bdgs. And I shall send out all my remaining S.A. work & letters from Aden—as I did English work at Brindisi—then from Aden plunge into India. I have heaps of books & reports. Lutyens plan … it is only for 5 or 6 weeks India and then what joy."[26] As usual when afloat, Baker took the opportunity to work rather than socialize with his fellow passengers, most of whom he invariably found to be intellectually dull company. Despite already having all but completed the Union buildings which were directly comparable in scale and complexity to the Secretariat buildings in Delhi, he still appears to have felt relatively unprepared for the task. He was desperate to, as he saw it, "be prepared & up to Lutyens with his long start."[27]

Early on the 5th of February, the SS *Egypt* moored off Bombay and at 9 a.m. Edwin Lutyens set off in the Government House launch, through the choppy chaos of market boats, fishing boats and water taxis, across the bay towards the steamer, to greet Brer Baker and finally welcome him to India. His plan was to take Baker directly to Delhi by train, and the long journey proved to be an opportunity for Lutyens to brief him on the state of play, as Baker reported to Florence—"There seems to be delay in setting the site even—owing to Ld Hardinge's illness seems worse than people have admitted being much shaken in nerves and system I fear.... But we are to do Gov't House, the bigger buildings & Lutyens thinks Sir Swinton Jacob is a nice old thing & won't interfere much … only put in as a sop to the public and Indian feeling.... The day after tomorrow I shall go for my morning ride on an elephant."[28] Lutyens also confirmed, "The fight rages over Eastern v. Western," and Baker described once more in his letter the approach that he had first set out in his letter to *The Times*—"Lutyens & I agree as to how far we shall give in to Indian sentiment.... The solution is to build in accordance with the highest principles adapted to climate & conditions and bring in all we can of Indian skill that exists—not chaotically in Indian fashion & coherently & orderly.... Most of the modern buildings in Bombay are Gothic—& look so out of place.... I've talked to Lutyens until I am hoarse.... He is full of spirits and fun."[29]

After a few days in Delhi Baker was up to speed, as he confirmed to Florence—

Here I am and there's so much to write about that I wonder where to begin. But first I must lament over poor Scott's death[30]—how very tragic.... I have been here 4 days & am feeling better & happier after riding two mornings & a run on the sly tonight—in the dark lest the peaceful Indians should think me a madman! I feel all the better of it! … There is so much to do to catch up with the others & old buildings to see. I was very agreeably surprised with much of the old work.... I think we can introduce enough of it distilled in new compounds to appease the sentimentalists.... This is very confidential.... There is a great controversy raging here between the merits of the North and of the South site. The Commission are known to be reporting on the South and local feeling is much disliked and I think rightly. The North contains "The Ridge" famous in the Mutiny where our men held out so long & from which they attacked & took Delhi.... I would like to put Gov't House at the end of this ridge looking down the river—with the office Blgs half way down with an arched road under.... A sacred acropolis on the ridge.... It is not my job to give an opinion on the Town Planning or selection of site; but I feel this big point of view is not quite weighed enough. Lutyens fails here—showing his limitations. I admire his genius in work—but he looks upon it all as an abstract mathematical problem. He may be right but I don't trust his counsel in such matters."[31]

Lutyens' vision of the city was based on Washington and was thus essentially two-dimensional. For Baker, the Ridge drew him like a magnet, both offering a potential recreation of the dramatic siting of the Union buildings, raised high above the ancient city, and also as being one of the sacred sites of the mutiny and thus drenched in British blood. Baker was fixated by the idea of an acropolis, whose commanding presence above the city he saw as the perfect symbol of a dominant order, but he was also conscious of his role as architect and not town planner and at this stage conferred only with Lutyens, as Lutyens confirmed in a letter to his wife on the 18th of February—"Baker is at present very much pro–North and goes for the position on the Kopje as he calls the Ridge and does not yet realize as we do the conditions that govern the health and sanitation of this weird variable climate, but it is great fun and comfort having him. I don't think he treats architecture as seriously as I do."[32]

Baker's contributions were much appreciated by the members of the Viceroy's staff, among whom he was soon being described as "by far the best of the bunch. Quiet, businesslike and resourceful,"[33] while Lutyens was described that Indian winter by Edwin Montagu, the Secretary of State for India, as "posing as usual, cheerful and dangerous as ever.... He refuses to look at anything about him, he hates Indian architecture as much as ever, he likes straight, final roads and wants everything levelled ... he has absorbed nothing of the country.... He has, I fully believe, great genius; but, uncontrolled, he will produce a building or buildings intended to insult the aspirations of everything Indian."[34] For Baker, who had already completed numerous major public building projects, dealing with the Viceroy's senior team and members of the Indian Civil Service was normal practice, but it was soon quite clear to him that Lutyens, the country-house specialist, was completely out of his depth both in planning the city and in coping with officialdom. He had mused earlier that had Lutyens won the London County Hall competition it would have prepared him better for the bureaucratic rigors of New Delhi—"Perhaps the young genius would have been disciplined by working for

Edwin Lutyens (center) and Herbert Baker (right), surveying the site of New Delhi by elephant (courtesy Michael Baker).

sterner masters than his rich and indulgent private clients."[35] Lutyens, clearly struggling, instead focused on building a relationship with Lady Hardinge, his client's wife, through which to influence her husband, as he had so successfully done many times before, but unbeknownst to him "the arch, flirtatious letters he wrote to the Vicereine were printed by the Viceroy's private press and as official documents circulated among sniggering ICS officials."[36]

With so little resolved in relation to the siting of the city which would have allowed Baker to contribute to the design of its buildings, he was soon inevitably drawn into discussions regarding the city plan, firstly in relation to the layouts for the north site and soon, as all the reservations regarding the north site which had led to its previous rejection re-surfaced once more, in looking at the committee's preferred lower southern site. With Hardinge still largely unavailable for discussions, Baker, Lutyens and Swinton took time off to visit the Taj Mahal and the abandoned Moghul city of Fatehpur Sikri near Agra. Baker, unlike Lutyens, was utterly fascinated by this new culture, as he recalled in his biography—"I experienced to the full the delights of Indian travel; especially the old cities, fort-palaces, the stately tomb-domes and water gardens, temples, mosques, painted and sculptured caves … the sumptuous beauty of the Agra and Delhi-fort palaces…. Moghul gardens … enjoyed in my early rides," and the people too—"parties of Indians in their bright holiday attire in the garden of the Taj."[37]

This first short trip also provided time for Baker to consider his and his family's future, now that he had finally committed to his imperial quest, and on the 19th of February he wrote to Florence suggesting (as he knew she already favored) a permanent move from South Africa to England—

> Went to bed early and as a reward had a waking thought which you will like. It was to take a large house in the country—where I can work on Delhi! The alternatives are Johannesburg or London. The latter I like least—you couldn't be happy there—nor I—and I must get away from Lutyens—it is bad to be too much together—and from dining out which I want to avoid—so if it is to be England—it must be the country. This year is a crucial year for Delhi and it will be a big job but I shall do it best if I work in peace away from travelling and invitations and with my family. What fun we will have—the nice old home life back in England! And no separation even from Henry…. You would never be happy leaving him at school if we went to S. Africa … of course I may have to go for Union Buildings—not the opening—they can do that without me—but if they build the terraces…. Ask your friends about a house…. Ask the Kiplings…. I can afford it … so don't stick at price for a good thing. PS I picture you dancing round the room![38]

By the 20th, after his return to Delhi, he wrote to Florence once more—"Just received a number of letters—Your pleasure and pride in my appointment thrilled me & made me feel misty eyed! … Nothing more is settled…. I ride to the site early every morning. Work from 9:30—to 2—then in afternoon either work or see old buildings around the site. We went to Humayan's Tomb yesterday … you can ride for hours over deserted cities."[39] And in his letters over the next two days he added, "It is a wet morning so I can't ride…. I feel that I am already justifying my appointment. I feel that I can give a saner opinion on the vexed question of the site than Lutyens…. He has a very perfect plan on paper, which would be very magnificent wherever the ideal city is built…. Lutyens rather makes his facts suit his theories…. I am also strongly advocating a 'Sahib site' for the government as distinct from the rest of the town—on a raised plateau—a sort of via Sacra—a piazza Sacra…. I think the lifting up will impress the native mind…. I hope the boys like my cards…. I must get my self photographed on an elephant for them."[40] And, "I am still worrying over the vexed question of the site and feel Lutyens limitations—as a man not as an architect—to form a sound judgement."[41] By the end of the month, his confidence restored, the Viceroy made his decision and (having been finally warned off the Ridge by the King himself who regarded it as "sacred ground") he confirmed that the new city would be located on the southern site with Government House on Raisina Hill, as he had first suggested himself the previous November.

At this point, Baker intervened. He felt, symbolically, that to place Government House alone on Raisina Hill was inappropriate and suggested despotism rather than democracy and thus proposed that the Secretariats which were to house the Indian Civil Service—the true instrument of government in India—should also be raised up onto Raisina Hill where, as on the Acropolis, the Capitoline Hill in Rome or Darius the Great's "stupendous platform" at Persepolis (all of which Baker had visited), the most important buildings in the city would be clustered. This required moving Government House back from the edge of the hill to accommodate the Secretariat buildings, which would then form a gateway to it, with a ramp taking the processional way up from the Great Place onto Raisina Hill, arriving in a government court between the Secretariat buildings. By moving Government House back, the Secretariats thus took on a new prominence and their considerable mass obscured what would have been many of the direct views of Government House. It also meant that, while using the ramp up onto the hill, the long view of Government House along the axis of the Processional Way (or King's Way) would be temporarily obscured during the ascent onto the hill.

Lutyens and the other experts readily agreed to the proposal and it was presented to the Viceroy on the 26th of February who received it positively, but concerned that views of Government House would be blocked by the Secretariats, asked for time to consider it.

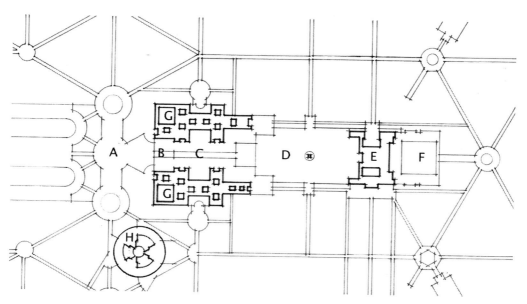

Layout of Raisina Hill. A The Great Place, B The Ramp, C Government Court, D Viceroy's Court, E Government House, F Viceroy's Gardens, G Secretariat, H Legislative Chamber (author's drawing).

The other matter to which the Viceroy returned on his recovery was that of architectural style. On this the two architects were now resolutely agreed and their shared mission was to deflect Hardinge from the use of the pointed Moghul arch. Permanent Secretary Sir Lionel Earle later recalled in his memoirs that Lutyens converted the Viceroy to the rounded arch with the quip, "Who designed the rainbow?" but, as usual, the reality was somewhat more prosaic and was the result of long discussions and various site visits to old Delhi by Hardinge and his architects. As Baker later recalled—"We went out to the Kutab with Lord Hardinge and explained the structural origin of the early examples of these four-centered arches; and compared them with the two-centered pointed voussoir arches of the Pathan tombs. He understood and very generously waived his opinion."[42] The architects were free at last to proceed with what Baker saw as an appropriate imperial Indian style and which Lutyens now believed would allow him to produce architecture on a par with that of his heroes.

After the next meeting of the Imperial Delhi Committee on the 4th of March, Baker was able to report back to Florence that he had had "a great day today. We met the Viceroy and he agreed to the alterations in the plan that I worked out and wanted. The raised site…. I am very pleased that I have got the Viceroy, as well as Lutyens, to my point of view. He agreed to many other points too which we wanted…. So I am much happier … settling details of agreement … £5000 a year for 7 years … not enough for such work … so I must argue for more…. We hope to visit Delhi once a year—14 of those long voyages!" (*next day*) "1½ again with the Viceroy and settled much. He has approved of all our suggestions and the agreement is ready."[43] The architects' original proposal of four separate Secretariat buildings had been revised to what the Viceroy thought would be a more efficient two and thus, following their meeting on the 11th of March, Lutyens was able to note on their site plan—"Seen and approved by H. Ex. March 11.13 with bigger Place in front."[44] They had their final meeting with the Viceroy on the 14th after which Baker wrote—"Such a day. Whirling on plans. 2 long Committees and interview with Viceroy & work again after as the Committee changed my conditions. But we made headway with agreement and plans & I hope it will come about that I leave next week via England as arranged…. It is so nice dealing with Gentlemen … 15th Hurrah! Settled today—all well and we can sail next Sat … the Viceroy asking me to go to London to see India Office and Sir S Jacobs."[45] It had been a resounding success for Baker and by the time he and Lutyens embarked in Bombay for England, he felt that he had more than earned his 10 guineas a day, having brought a broader perspective to the city planning, created the government acropolis, successfully deflected Hardinge from the Indo-Saracenic style and already established strong and useful client relationships which would pay dividends on his future visits.

He had also secured satisfactory terms for their future work, under which they would both receive 5 percent of the construction cost of all building work for which they were responsible (25 percent of which was to be paid on approval of their designs), £1,000 a year each for acting as advisers to the government on all architectural matters to do with the new city, first-class return steamship fares, first-class railway travel in India, a daily subsistence allowance and a fee of £5 a day each while away from home. With construction planned to carry on until 1920, it gave Baker a solid seven years of income on which he could now build a new practice in England.

As he mused on board ship, "Now with time for reflection I am glad I accepted Delhi. I feel I have been of some use. Lutyens could not be trusted alone—in spite of his brilliant ingenuity & designing power.... I think I have more influence with him than anyone else would but he is difficult to manage & we fight a good deal."[46] The two archi-

Edwin Lutyens, left, and Herbert Baker outside their shared office on Raisina Hill (courtesy Michael Baker).

tects worked together under an awning on the boat deck, with Baker later in the journey complaining, "I am so sick of his little jokes."[47]

Baker's stay in England was brief, arriving at Southampton on Monday the 7th of April and departing from there again on Saturday the 12th, during which time he confirmed to his wife that he had "had satisfactory interviews ... with Lord Crewe etc & got what he wanted."[48] The two architects parted as friends, little realizing that they had already sown the seeds of a dispute which would destroy their relationship and hugely damage Baker's professional reputation.

The week after they had sailed from Bombay, William Henry Nicholls, who had been appointed as architect adviser to the Viceroy's Imperial Delhi Committee, prepared a perspective sketch of Lutyens' Government House viewed from the base of the ramp which took the King's Way up onto Raisina Hill which showed quite clearly that all that would be seen of Government House from this point along the route would be the top of the dome. The sketch was shown to Lord Hardinge, who, having already expressed his concern that views of Government House would be partly blocked when he agreed to the architects' proposal to raise the Secretariats onto the hill, thought that this was both "perfectly obvious" and of "trivial importance."[49] Sadly, Edwin Lutyens, thought by many to be the greatest British architect of his generation, had completely missed it.

8

1913–1915

"A Song of Union"

While Baker was steaming toward home from India, Florence and the boys had once more escaped the heat of Johannesburg for the refreshing sea breezes of Cape Town, where she now longed to welcome her husband home, as she wrote to her father— "Won't he be glad to rest here for 6 months till October makes him take wing again poor old Bear Baloo he has undertaken a lot but it is so gratifying to feel that everyone realizes that even capital designing is not too big for him & that he will not fail! Oh! I am so proud!!"[1] Herbert disembarked at Cape Town on the 29th of April 1913. He had been away for five months during which time he had visited London and Rome twice and India for the first time. He returned with his appointment as one of the two principal architects for the construction of the new imperial city of Delhi secured and his position as one of the leaders of his profession much enhanced. Confident that he had made a positive contribution to the final resolution of the city plan, he now returned to his South African practice and the completion of perhaps his greatest architectural achievement—the Union buildings in Pretoria. Florence's letter to her father, of the following day, picks up our tale—

> Herbert returned to us safely yesterday morning & it is delightful to have him back. He looks very well I think & none the worst for 70 days of ship board. We are so busy picking up the threads of five months. Unfortunately, he had to dash off by the 8.40 train to the town! This morning and we know not when he will be back…. He is to interview Gen. Smuts at 11, Murray 11.30 Head of the Public Works Depart. Lunch Lady Phillips so we do not know when to expect him here. I wish he could have had one more day of peace with the boys. We three met him at the station at 10. Allaire was very quiet at first but soon became as cheeky and jolly as Henry. Five months is a long time at 4½ & they in half an hour had inveigled Herbert into their huge sand cave & buried him up to the neck in sand. I took a snap-shot of the architect of Delhi which I shall send you in great glee … it is lovely to have him back for even a precious five months tho' our future looks full of meetings and partings….[2]

Florence's excitement and pride at Herbert's appointment for New Delhi was undimmed and compensated to a degree for the dawning realization that his success would mean many months apart each year, for many years to come. For Herbert, the Secretariat buildings at New Delhi represented a huge and prestigious new commission, but he had by no means forgotten his existing clients with his first meeting after arriving home in South Africa being with General Smuts to reassure him that the completion of his Union buildings was now his principal focus. By early May he was on-site in Pretoria

116

Henry and Herbert on the beach at Muizenberg on Herbert's return from India (courtesy Michael Baker).

witnessing six months' worth of progress since his last visit. The buildings were all but complete now and he was personally able to oversee the completion of the terraces and amphitheater, the design of which he had been refining during his travels.[3]

The Union buildings were both the crowning achievement of Baker's career in South Africa and a fitting finale to this hugely important period in his life. Building by building since his arrival 20 years earlier, he had developed as an architect, improved his ability as a designer, encouraged local artists and craftsmen to assist him in his work, built a team of extremely capable assistants around him, provided professional leadership and training for the first time in the region and delivered an astonishing range and quantity of outstanding buildings while earning the universal respect of the local mine owners, industrialists and politicians of various camps. He had developed an architectural approach that was responsive to the extremes of the climate, sensitive to local vernacular traditions and, with his later public work in particular, expressive of the beliefs that he and his clients shared. For him, the Union buildings were in many ways a second Rhodes

Memorial—a celebration of the achievement of Rhodes' vision of a united South Africa under British rule—a symbol of both the might of the empire and its edifying influence. Painstakingly and fastidiously, inspired by what he had seen firsthand in Italy and Greece, he had moved from his original architectural roots in his cousin's Gothic, via the Arts and Crafts Movement towards the Classicism of the ancient Mediterranean empires, recognizing in it both its potency as an expression of power and its suitability for tempering the searing sun of the colonies, and in the Union buildings (with assistance from Jones, Wren and Lutyens) he produced his greatest design to date.

Its site, which he had selected, allowed this symbol of government to be raised above the city, dominating it visually and creating a higher plane for its leaders to occupy in the style of the Acropolis in Athens or the Capitoline Hill in Rome. For Baker the view out from this government *tabula rasa* was of equal importance, as it had been for Rhodes on Table Mountain, offering distant views, inspiration and thus encouragement for the leaders of the country to "take the long view." This was given expression in the great Ionic porticos or loggias to which ministers had direct access from their offices. The two wings of the building, each with their tower, express the two nations—British and Dutch—brought together in peace to form the new South Africa. They are identical, thus expressing their equality within the new country and now linked by the great curved colonnade enclosing the amphitheater, itself an ancient symbol of assembly and debate, that sits at the very heart of the complex.

Baker's original conception was that the wings and towers should frame a Peace Temple on the top of the ridge above, approached by a *via sacra* from below, but with the funding of the Union buildings proving quite controversial enough for the new country, this never progressed. Doreen Greig and others have suggested that this brings an unresolved duality to the complex and that it lacks a strong central feature but I'd suggest that,

The Union Buildings in Pretoria in the 1920s (courtesy Michael Baker).

intentionally or not, the two strong wings tied together by the colonnade and meeting place are actually a much more representative expression of the coming together of the races and also of the missing parliament chamber, which sits in Cape Town, a thousand miles to the south.

Baker's handling of the significant changes of level across the site is outstanding and, far from it compromising any aspect of the program, it is used again and again for either dramatic or symbolic effect (or simply practically, to avoid the cost of deep excavations for basements, stores or archives). So many of his buildings sit so naturally on difficult hillside sites that this great skill which he developed in South Africa goes almost entirely unnoticed, as the finished result, on which he worked incredibly hard, looks simply obvious. From the hillside, two routes parallel to the building provide upper ceremonial access directly to the colonnade and amphitheater and lower access to the offices via central entrances in each wing, which in turn lead directly into their central shaded courtyards. The curved two-story colonnade houses committee rooms, a library and two domed conference rooms and encloses the amphitheater, which drops away from this point towards the small domed rostrum from where an audience in the amphitheater can be addressed. From here two broad flights of steps lead to a further lower terrace which is traversed by a reflecting pool, then on again down central staircases to an avenue which forms part of the ceremonial route up the hillside, before further steps cascade down again to Government Avenue and then on once more to the terraces of the vast stepped gardens that connect with the city below and beyond. It is a masterclass in building on a hillside in the grand manner, as Baker had witnessed in Delphi, Agrigentum and Tivoli, with his exterior spaces here sharing the same dignified elegance as his particularly fine interiors.

The buildings themselves are a fine three-dimensional composition in which their strong horizontal emphasis is balanced by the verticals of chimneys, towers and columns with the continuous eaves line of the Roman-tiled roof uniting the whole. Gone is the rock-faced, square-coursed rubble of the railway station and so many of his Transvaal houses, finally replaced by exquisite dressed ashlar throughout. As Doreen Greig wrote—"The quality ... of the stonework is of the highest standard. The red sandstone of the arches, columns and walls of the Buildings, and the craftsmanship displayed in the working of the stone, the jointing of the walls and the semi-circular arched openings, their voussoirs and carved key-stones shows a perfection which Baker's work had not achieved before."[4] Indeed when one considers the grammatical errors of the railway station, produced just a matter of months before Baker started work on the design of the Union buildings, the consistent quality of their detailing is quite remarkable—elegant molded string courses and window surrounds, well-proportioned voussoirs, balconies and pediments and while the entablature is a development of the one used at the station, at Lutyens' suggestion, the frieze is omitted with the top member of the architrave becoming the lower member of the cornice. Now back on-site once more, Baker "waged unending warfare with the contractors on quarry marks on a plinth or dark streaks in an otherwise uniform red granite column in a central courtyard."[5]

Each block (both of which are angled back slightly to catch the setting sun) contains three floors of offices above stores and archives, arranged around three courtyards with these cool, central, external spaces in each block, which far from being utilitarian, are actually one of its principal delights. Drawing on his knowledge of the *cortiles* of the palazzos of Rome, Baker designed deep vaulted Tuscan arcades which both

The Union Buildings' sweeping colonnade and tower (courtesy Michael Baker).

shelter office workers from the African sun and provide cooling breezes for their surrounding offices, all of which thus enjoy through ventilation, while in their center, pools,
fountains and plants provide refreshing sights and sounds. The half-round arches of the
arcade are supported on double Tuscan Doric columns, which in a subtle move are parallel with the arcade on the upper floors and at right angles to it at ground level to suggest and encourage movement diagonally across the courtyards. These spaces represent
a brilliant synthesis of climatic control, architectural precedent and contemporary effi-
ciency. The central staircases are also derived from Mediterranean palazzos with sandstone Tuscan columns supporting whitewashed vaulting, making further cool, light and

airy shelters from the sun—the complex and challenging vaulted system of raking groining—resolved to perfection throughout.

The great loggias which terminate each wing of the offices are also subtly developed from their predecessors in Kimberly and on the Devil's Peak, no longer with regularly spaced Tuscan columns but here with fine Ionic capitals and arranged with great sensitivity. Baker described these as "columned 'temples'—they are hardly porticos; loggias perhaps better describes them—leading out of the Ministers' rooms, an idea which I repeated at the Secretariat at New Delhi."[6] The interiors are on a par with Baker's best, with the familiar Jacobean detailing that had already graced many of his grander Transvaal houses, Groote Schuur and Government House just along the ridge, being applied throughout with teak and stinkwood paneling and carved Tuscan columns typically giving way to cool, white-plastered ceilings between heavy timber beams. The furniture throughout was designed by Baker and locally made as was all the iron and brasswork—its beauty—a tribute to Baker's encouragement of fellow artists and craftsmen and his perseverance and progress since the day he first set foot in Africa.

The gardens, which were not completed until 1919, were both a key element of Baker's overall design for the site and a key factor in the entire complex's success and popularity. Baker "recommended the early planting of formal avenues of trees on either side of the tramline along the western boundary of the site and, on the hillside, a mass of dark pine trees to form a background on either side of the building" … while "the kopje was to

One of the Union Buildings' great loggias (courtesy Roddy Bray).

be reserved entirely for indigenous trees and shrubs such as aloes and cacti."[7] While the gardens continue to be much enjoyed today, the terraces and amphitheater which were designed to provide a meeting place between citizens and their elected representatives are all now closed to the public as a result of security fears, sadly, now making Baker's *tabula rasa* the territory of only the ruling elite.

The Union buildings were an extraordinary achievement both architecturally and in terms of project management with Baker, Charles Murray and their teams delivering the entire building complex on time and under budget in only four years from conception to completion. For Baker, he had managed to combine the cool Classicism of Wren's Greenwich Hospital with further lessons from the Greeks and Romans to create a powerful symbol of the new country as well as an efficient and effective administrative complex. For him it was an expression of the might of imperial Britain, while for his Boer clients, it confirmed the Dutch and British as equals in their new country and, most importantly, firmly anchored the administration of South Africa in the Transvaal. It was a triumphant success—in the words of the local *Transvaal Leader*—"An Inspiring Valhalla."[8]

While Baker had been focusing his energies on designing the Union buildings and securing the Secretariats in New Delhi, Fleming had been largely left to oversee the Medical Research Institute which was completed early in 1913, with Baker still in India. It represents another very interesting milestone in the development of Baker's architecture—another "Wrenaissance" design—here in white-painted rendered brickwork but with some very 20th-century technology below the surface. In terms of its plan, it

The Medical Research Institute, Johannesburg (courtesy Michael Baker).

is classic Baker—two wings, concluded with open loggias, enclosed first by a tree-lined courtyard encircled by a single story colonnade, through which we pass to a second courtyard enclosed on its three sides by two stories of accommodation arranged around another cooling fountain and pool. Continuing on axis, the visitor then passes below a high, circular-columned tower with a small dome (the finial of which has a skull with three serpents, emblems of Aesculapius, representing the efforts of science to control sickness) to a final third court beyond the tower which is fully enclosed as a very definite full-stop. Doreen Greig suggests Lutyens' whitewashed brick Nashdom in Buckingham-shire which had been completed a few years previously as a precedent, with some justifi-cation—the single story portico and shallow bays of the south elevation in both buildings are almost identical, but overall this is surely another variation on Greenwich. Interest-ingly, despite Classical appearances, the roof and floor slabs are of reinforced concrete, steel girders were used for the large spans and the dome, in which the water tanks are stored, is also of reinforced concrete. One wonders if this was either Fleming's influence or symptomatic of a lack of available resources in Johannesburg? It is another competent piece of Classical architecture, however, though rather bland in much of its detailing, and contains, as we now expect, a series of fine exterior and interior spaces. With the medi-cal research building complete and Baker back from India, Fleming took a well-deserved break in England himself, leaving at the end of May.

Fleming's major responsibility after his return was the new Union Club in Johan-nesburg, of which Baker had been a member since his arrival 10 years previously. The parallels between it and the Medical Institute are strong—this an Italianate city palazzo organized around another beautiful square, central cortile with pool enclosed by three floors of arcades of Doric and Ionic columns, very much as an exterior version of the entrance hall of Sir Charles Barry's Reform Club in Pall Mall. Once more we have a rein-forced concrete structure with a plastered brick exterior over a rusticated stone ground floor. One side of its corner site provides the main entrance centered on the courtyard with external *porte cochere* (since sadly swept away by road-widening) and the other has the president's room on axis on the first floor. The palazzo with open cortile was by now a highly successful organizational formula which Baker had first attempted with the Rhodes Building in Cape Town, perfected in Pretoria and would use again in New Delhi. It was to fully occupy Fleming throughout 1913 and further in 1914, on his own return from India.

From their letters earlier in the year, it was clear that the Bakers had already decided to return to England on a permanent basis early in 1913 and indeed Baker wrote that his acceptance of the Delhi commission "would mean forsaking a trust and allegiance to South Africa."[9] Not only did he now have the prestigious New Delhi appointment along with Lutyens, with whom he could confer in London, but he also had two sons aged 8 and 5 to be educated and, very possibly, as Florence was expecting once more, another boy on the way. The plan was that they would all travel to England with Herbert in October on the first leg of his return to New Delhi that year and that Florence and the boys would spend Christmas with the Edmeades at Nurstead Court, while Herbert and his assis-tants continued on to India. A new home in the country would have to be found, but with Lutyens offering Baker space in his India office at 7 Apple Tree Yard and accommodation at Nurstead and Owletts immediately available, these further arrangements could be put on hold for a time. Other issues could not however and while Baker oversaw the com-pletion of the Union buildings and his numerous other commissions, he also concluded arrangements for the future of his South African practice. The Cape Town and Johannesburg branches of Baker's practice had been run as separate financial entities for many years and in 1913, Baker formally split the partnership with two new practices being created—Baker and Fleming, based in Johannesburg and Baker and Kendall in Cape Town with Fleming being promoted to senior partner at the same time. Baker's further involvement in the Cape Town partnership was very limited and Kendall effectively operated on his own from October 1913, taking Scot James Morris into a new partnership, Baker, Kendall and Morris, in 1916, before Baker withdrew completely from this partnership in December 1918. Baker's relationship with Frank Fleming remained closer, although Baker and Fleming too was finally wound up in 1918 after which Fleming continued to practice on his own, eventually taking his architect-son Leonard into partnership in 1936.

On the 14th of August, Baker's third son, Alfred Patrick Edmeades Baker, was born and was baptized two days later by Baker's friend and client, Bishop Michael Furse, with Lutyens one of the godfathers *in absentia*. Baker had maintained his correspondence with Lutyens since their parting, continually offering wise counsel when Lutyens despaired, as in his letter of the 26th of September shortly before their departure—"My dear colleague.... You must realize the political standpoint in a political capital, or, if you don't, the reasonableness of politicians, our masters, in doing so. And you get your way best by doing so. That is the line of attack I think. Give them Indian sentiment where it does not conflict with grand principles, as the Government should do."[10] Baker's friend, Patrick Duncan, one of the Kindergarten who had been elected to the first South African Parliament, had decided to commit his future to the new country and so it was arranged that he and his wife Alice would rent both Stonehouse and Sandhills from the Bakers. Although Florence was soon recovered from the birth of her third child, their departure was delayed by Herbert having a bout of eczema and one last flood of new work for which further arrangements had to be made before they finally set sail for England and their new life in early October, on the SS *Kenilworth Castle,* once more. They traveled first class and it was arranged that Fleming would follow a week later and continue to New Delhi with Baker. Herbert had arrived two decades earlier with his younger brother to help him establish a fruit farm and now left at one of the happiest times of his life, as one of the most successful architects of his generation, with a loving wife and three young children, a considerable fortune and the prospect of even greater architectural and imperial glory to come.

Having had little opportunity to do so in South Africa, he worked on the development of his design for the Secretariat buildings throughout the voyage home. Their essential outlines had already been agreed upon in March as part of the city plan—two vast blocks of office accommodation, each almost a quarter of a mile long, to the north and south of the King's Way, acting as sentinels on the road of approach to the great finale of Lutyens' Government House. In effect these were another two "H"-plan buildings but with further wings extended to the east and west, with the eastern wings, below their high-domed towers, stepping forward to guard the entry to the sacred Government Court, while the western wings stepped back in deference to Government House beyond. As we have come to expect, Baker drew on elements of his previous buildings to inform his design with the Union buildings being the major source. As in Pretoria, the complex is organized around a series of courtyards which would once more provide cool oases and shady circulation routes protected by deep arcades from the even harsher Indian sun. The two Secretariat buildings, which are largely symmetrical, face each other

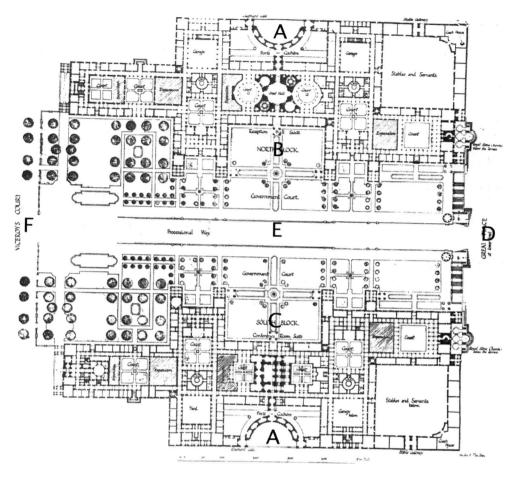

The Secretariats, ground floor plan. Key: A Main Entrance, B North Secretariat Block, C South Secretariat Block, D Great Place, E Processional Way, F Viceroy's Court (from *Architecture and Personalities*).

across Government Court, both enclosing it and providing a sense of calm and orderly government.

Both blocks are actually entered from the opposite side of the face they present to the court and it is in the entrance sequence, from their chattri-crowned *porte-cocheres* with carved-stone sentinel elephants a floor below the level of Government Court to the great domes which surmount them, that Baker extracted every ounce of drama from a relatively modest change of level. This is surely Baker at his best and on a par with anything which Lutyens achieved within Government House, with flight after flight of stairs carrying visitors onwards and upwards to the final climax of the first-floor reception hall in the south block and the entrance hall in the north. Baker's control of the spatial experience along these main routes into and through the building is outstanding, constantly contrasting light and dark, enclosure and release and richness with restraint, as he guides the visitor through the buildings, but it is his total control of every interior and exterior space which elevates the Secretariats to the level of great architecture—every corridor,

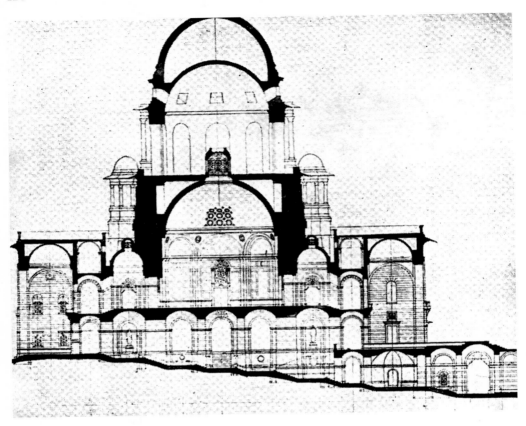

South Secretariat, cross section (from *Architecture and Personalities*).

antechamber or lobby provides a sense of dignity to the public service to which the buildings are dedicated and each is rich in views of adjacent courtyards, glimpses of levels below or above and all are flooded with natural light from various sources. Sadly, like so many of Baker's outstanding interiors, these extraordinary spaces are rarely seen or enjoyed by the public, or indeed fully appreciated by architects and historians.

By the time they berthed in Southampton on the 28th of October, Baker had only two weeks to prepare before leaving for India. While his family were welcomed home at Nurstead Court, Baker spent most of his time in London working with Lutyens at his India office at 7 Apple Tree Yard[11] where perspective artist William Walcott was briefed, based on sketches which Baker had completed on board ship and who Christopher Hussey, Lutyens' biographer confirmed, they supervised together.[12] Fellow architect Beresford Pite had lent Baker one of his assistants, Charles (Percival) Walgate, to assist with the drawings. Baker had several meetings with his solicitor Balfour, considering drafts of the agreement with Lutyens, attending numerous meetings at the India Office while also managing to fit in a site visit to Port Lympne on the 4th of November followed by dinner with Rudyard Kipling that evening.

The financial arrangement that was negotiated and agreed upon between the two architects saw their 5 percent fee divided equally between them, with a pooling of all expenses into a common pot. This was then to be divided equally between Baker and Lutyens and set against their fee income. It was understood that Baker's expenses were likely to be higher than Lutyens (not least because Lutyens paid his staff so poorly) and so this arrangement was devised to ensure equal profits from the commission for both architects. Following lengthy consultations with their solicitors, the agreement was signed by both Baker and Lutyens on the 11th of November. On the 12th, the next day, Baker was at Owletts to see his mother before sailing for India, where he received a telegram from his solicitor at 4:30 p.m., informing him that Lutyens' solicitor, Francis Smith, now wished to vary the agreement on Lutyens' request. Baker was absolutely furious that little more than 24 hours after signing their contract, as Jane Ridley observed—"Lutyens had gone back on his word … breaking the gentleman's code and confirming Baker's worst fears…. Baker now saw him as an arrogant bounder."[13]

The next morning, Baker left early for London for a hurried consultation with his solicitor prior to catching the boat train at Victoria Station. The two architects met on the station platform where Baker publicly vented his wrath upon Lutyens. George Swinton, who was due to travel with them, was so shocked that he warned the Viceroy of their "serious row"[14] and Baker remained so angry that he refused to talk to Lutyens for the next four days of their shared journey. His diary entry for the 18th of November reads, "Discussed Agreement all day Lutyens."[15] This resulted in a revised apportionment of expenses. It was a minor financial victory for Lutyens, but for Baker it was a bitter taste of things to come and he now felt bound to a man he could no longer trust.[16] His letter to Florence from near Suez, confirmed his disappointment—"As I cabled I feel both fitter and happier having had it out with L. It all seems right now but his past conduct is so inexplicable and if there is always to be such difficulty over any business, one can't look forward to 5 or 6 years of it with much comfort that relations are friendly now. Fleming is pleased with your letter. He is a comfort. I remain very bearish with other people."[17]

The SS *Egypt* docked in Bombay on the 28th of November, from where the group set off by train for Delhi. Their task on their previous visit earlier in the year had been to reach agreement on the site for the new city; it was now to gain approval for their building designs and confirm the precise relationship between them on Raisina Hill. Before they had left in March, both architects had presented their outline designs for the buildings and even at that stage, Hardinge had informed Lutyens that his design for Government House must be dramatically reduced in scale. Rather than make the reductions requested, Lutyens had appealed to the King to intervene on his behalf with the Viceroy, but to no avail and, having thus merely further damaged his relationship with Hardinge, he had spent much of the summer grappling with this task. On the 16th of December, as Baker wrote to Florence, they had their first formal meeting with the Viceroy and committee—

It was all favourable on the whole. He wanted my buildings further apart, which is reasonable…. Then after discussing points of the Town layout he came to the question of the cost of Gov't House & he said sternly and emphatically that he will not spend more than the sum allowed. This was a bomb shell to Lutyens who thought he would get his own way & he is very dejected about it. I try to get him to see reason & reduce—but he is awfully difficult. He won't surrender. I was faced with the same difficulty—saw it ahead—and Fleming & I have been working night and day to modify the plans & cost—and we have now succeeded—and are all right. I think all will come right because I think the Viceroy spoke so sternly deliberately to frighten him & does not mean to cut it down quite so much as he said … he has been too spoilt in always getting his way and he can't now—having come up against something bigger & stronger than he has been accustomed to. I hope it will do him good—and make things easier for me—he is so egotistical—illogical & self willed—that collaboration is a continual difficulty and requires a great deal of patience…. The Viceroy and Vicereine came & talked about it—but I can't give my partner away—so it is very difficult indeed.[18]

Lutyens' letters home to Emily were equally critical of Baker—"I don't think Baker really cares so long as he makes his pile & pleases the powers that be,"[19] he wrote at the end of December. But it was Lutyens who remained with the problem and, having first, quite astonishingly, proposed that Government House be completed as he had designed it but as a shell, without fittings, any services or furniture, he finally accepted that he had no option but to reduce the scale of his design once more, and thus commenced the task, depressed, alone and now also afflicted with dysentery.

The Bakers' letters over Christmas, while still covering events in Delhi, were dominated by Florence's search for a house to lease in Kent, near Owletts, Nurstead Court and a mainline station to London, with Baker also suggesting that Florence now purchase a car and hire a chauffeur—"Indulgent husband!"[20] With encouragement from the Viceroy, who wished them to see as much native architecture as possible, after Christmas, Baker and Lutyens set off for several days in Varanasi, where they stayed in the palace of the maharaja, with a stop en route at Lucknow, where Baker viewed the ruins of the Residency, another of the famous scenes of the mutiny where the largest number of Victoria Crosses ever awarded in one day had been won in its second relief, in November 1857. From Varanasi, they traveled out to Sarnath, where they saw the Asoka pillar and its famous lion capital (which was to later become the emblem of independent India). Baker found their tour both interesting and valuable and on his return to Delhi was delighted to find Phillip Kerr, another member of the Kindergarten (and by then editor of *The Round Table*), visiting and he was thus able to combine a few more "social days" in Kerr's company with his continuing work. On the 14th of January he reported—"L (*Lutyens*) is realizing inevitable—and working prodigiously at new plan—poor fellow it is hard to have to do it. The Com't won't consider it at all nor any scheme officially—until his is complete—I don't know how long the delay will be,"[21] and by the 18th, "A long day with the Viceroy…. I have several talks with him—he finds me rather saner & more reasonable than my colleague."[22]

By the end of the month, with Lutyens still wrestling day and night with the redesign of Government House, Hardinge relented, and the committee continued its considerations of the overall layout of Raisina Hill, by the end of the month confirming the layout in terms of the distance between the Secretariat buildings, the distance between the Secretariat buildings and Government House, and the maximum gradient for the ramp which took the King's Way up from the lower Great Place to the upper Government Court between Baker's Secretariat buildings. Lutyens was actively involved in these discussions which effectively confirmed that all that would be seen of Government House from the base of the ramp was its dome (as Nicholls and Hardinge had already discussed the previous spring). Lutyens appears to have been the only party involved who had failed to grasp this point. For Baker, the temporary loss of view of Government House was of little matter as his conception was that both the Secretariats and Government House should occupy a "sacred" higher plane and it was only when one had ascended to its Olympian heights that the imperial buildings could be fully appreciated in all their awesome glory. Jane Ridley, Lutyens great-granddaughter, has suggested that Baker "was perhaps guilty of bad faith in not discussing it," but she had to finally conclude, "The point was so basic that Lutyens should have seen for himself."[23] Lutyens' biographer Hussey also seeks to excuse his error stating that he was "ill, tired, dispirited and preoccupied,"[24] but neither can deny that to miss it was a schoolboy error and thus all the more embarrassing for Lutyens, when the scales finally fell from his eyes.

Despite their differences (and private criticisms of each other), Baker and Lutyens continued to work together in their shared office on Raisina Hill. Baker's letters home were full of plans for the future and of his faithful partner Fleming—"So sad at my hinting I shall not go back."[25] With Lutyens much recovered, he and Baker embarked on another tour in the company of Malcolm Hailey the president of the Viceroy's Committee and Hugh Keeling the Chief Engineer, which provided another opportunity for the architects to get to know these key members of the Viceroy's team. This tour of "Rajputana" included Bikaner, Ajmer, Jodhpur, Chitor, Jaipur, Amber and Udaipur during which they were entertained by nawabs and maharajas in their palaces, with Baker frantically sketching and making notes of everything he saw, quite fascinated by the dramatic siting, history and romance of the palaces and forts. Lutyens, as usual, was scathing, in a letter to his wife describing the maharaja of Bikaner's new palace—"The new palace the Viceroy admires so much would from an architectural point of view disgrace Putney Hill.... After breakfast we motored to the old fort. A large barbaric pile.... Some of it too awful for words—no gollywog could better it!"[26]

They were back in early February with Keeling's engineers having priced Lutyens revised plans during their travels and Baker writing—"Today I learn that these again exceed—and I can't think what will happen—whether we can get right—or whether we have to chuck it or are chucked—Lord knows when we shall leave now—I am very much worried about it.... Fleming will leave in three weeks time—That will be another blow." And later that day, he confirmed that Lady Hardinge had visited them following receipt of a letter from Lutyens complaining of his treatment and trying "to force more money out of the Viceroy.... This letter upset the Hardinge's very much.... They say that the Viceroy is awfully upset ... and is very angry with Lutyens.... Mrs Benson [Evelyn Benson, friend

View of the ramp up to Government Court from the Great Place (courtesy Lensmatter).

From left: Herbert Baker, Malcolm Hailey, and Hugh Keeling on tour in India (courtesy Michael Baker).

of Lady Hardinge] is a great friend of Lutyens but is angry with him now & agrees with what I think of him: a spoilt child—very clever—and amusing—but impossible in business or in a position of trust…. I took Lutyens for a walk afterwards and lectured him but he is so egotistical and can't see that he can do wrong and I seem to make no impression on him…. The Engineers & Committee will report on his new plans in a few days & then we shall know the worst."[27]

By the 5th of March Baker was writing—"It looks now as if Lutyens plans will not be approved this visit and that he will go home in the same position as last year—a year wasted. Mine I hope will go on. He is not a bit ashamed as I should be!"[28] What was even more frustrating for Baker than the lack of progress was that, as Lutyens amended his designs for Government House, he demanded that Baker amend his completed designs for the Secretariats in response to his changes—"He threatens to take the Gov't to alter my plans—whereas he is all alone to blame—and wanting to force me into the trouble—disloyalty—I don't much mind that but one can't give over full thoughts to the work with such continual irritation—and it worries me into illness—and I often think it wl'd be best to resign than go on with such heartbreaking conditions. I must try to be loyal to him and so can tell no one."[29]

Baker's frustration however, was nothing to the Viceroy's. He was under intense pressure to proceed to construction as criticism of the principle of the move from Calcutta (led by former Viceroy Lord Curzon) remained strong and was now being joined by those who balked at the expense of the new imperial city. He had confided in Baker on New Year's Day 1914 that "delay would be fatal."[30] From the design work already completed he was now aware that he would not be able to deliver the city for his much publicized budget of four million pounds and even worse, that the latest estimates from Keeling and his team suggested a likely cost of six million pounds, assuming that Lutyens got Government House back under his budget of half a million. All this, of course, was lost on Lutyens, who continued to complain bitterly that his budget was simply insufficient to allow him to produce something "fitting," with an increasingly frustrated Baker additionally complaining that "outside his work he has no reverence for anything. Religion. Politics. Empire all are a farce to show off his own wit."[31]

On the 8th, Keeling confirmed that Lutyens' reductions had finally brought Government House within budget, and on the following day the Viceroy and the committee approved his design in principle but requested various further revisions including lowering the vast dome over Government House's Durbar Hall. Baker was delighted and now longed for home. But the Viceroy, determined to start construction and having lost his trust in Lutyens, informed the architects that they must now be party to a formal agreement stating that the overall dimensions agreed upon for the buildings and their inter-relationship on the hill would not be varied. Thus, on the 17th of March, shortly before their much-delayed departure, both Baker and Lutyens signed a contract to this effect. Hussey suggested that Lutyens' signature on this document which confirmed the essential elements of the final design of Raisina Hill including the ramp was some minor bureaucratic oversight on Lutyens' behalf, whereas in reality, it was the solemn conclusion to a frustrating winter in India for all involved. Having secured this guarantee from his architects, Hardinge instructed excavations to commence immediately.

Baker and Lutyens traveled home on the SS *Macedonia*, embarking on the 21st in the company of Lady Hardinge at whose table they dined, much to the relief of Baker, who could thus avoid the other passengers. He was at his most "bearish"—still upset by events in Delhi and dreading his next five winters with Lutyens. He had worries too about his new life in England, staying at Owletts with the family until they found their new home, establishing another office, finding new staff and missing Fleming's steadfast support and company. He badly needed a base in England from where he could work as he had no wish to spend any more time with Lutyens than he had to, despite there still being space at Apple Tree Yard. There was a mountain of work to do on the Secretariats with only the scale plans agreed and all detailed design and construction drawings still ahead. It was a daunting prospect. Unbeknownst to the architects, their fellow traveling companion, Lady Hardinge, was returning to London for medical consultation. Her "seediness" was soon diagnosed as cancer and she died, tragically, on the operating table just a few months later on the 11th of June, aged just 46. She had been Lutyens' last potential ally in Delhi.

Baker returned to Owletts, which by then must have been bursting at its seams, with Florence and the boys, his brother Ned and his family, his mother and unmarried sister Bea all now in occupation. He couldn't work there and despite his wish to have a new home with space for his office in the country, he had no immediate option but to rent office space in London where he could build a Delhi team. He offered a job to Charles Walgate from Beresford Pite's office, who had briefly assisted him the previous year, who accepted, and leased 27 Eaton Place where they set up shop. Walgate, then only 28, was to prove an able and valuable assistant to Baker throughout the Delhi years—a talented architect, he had recently completed his studies at the Royal College of Art under Pite's professorship and Delhi represented a considerable opportunity for him. Walgate later recalled, "We soon had a staff of about 10 … and though I was among the younger I found myself in charge, exchange of all information, and buffer to guard HB (to all his intimates) from the daily worries of a hastily assembled staff."[32] In addition to Charles

Walgate, Baker's young team also included Walter Sykes George, another of Pite's students who would soon become Baker's resident architect in New Delhi, and Alexander Thomson Scott, who would much later become Baker's final partner. They were all soon working night and day with two vast buildings to take from sketch design to construction detail. Baker's diary entries for most of the days of that last long glorious summer, during which the clouds of war gathered overhead, simply read "office all day."

As both he and Lutyens completed drawings, they were shipped to the Imperial Delhi Committee for comment and approval, including in June a signed plan by Lutyens which would return to haunt him for many years to come. Its reference was "C.E.-221-9, series II" and it showed the layout of the Government and Viceroy's Courts, with the ramp as finally constructed, rising at 22 degrees and terminating opposite the start of Baker's first great loggia, thus blocking his dome from continual view along the King's Way. Yet he still remained oblivious to this point. Walcott's perspectives of New Delhi stole the show at the Royal Academy Summer Exhibition, when it opened in June with four of the drawings of Government House, including "No.1823. Government House, Delhi, as seen between the Secretariats"[33] attributed to Lutyens, and three of the Secretariats, to Baker.

Later that month on the 28th of June, Gavrilo Princip, a Bosnian Serb, pushed through a crowd in Sarajevo towards the car of Archduke Franz Ferdinand, heir to the Austro-Hungarian throne, and shot him and his wife, killing them both and setting in motion a series of events which would plunge the world into war. Tensions had been growing for decades as Germany became an increasingly effective competitor for Great Britain and eyed its vast empire enviously. Domination of the seas was the key to Britain's success, allowing it to trade around the globe from every outpost of its far-flung colonies, and the previous two decades had seen a naval arms race between the two nations. The Balkans, lying between mighty Russia, Austro-Hungary and the fracturing Ottoman Empire, was regarded as "the powder keg of Europe" and so it proved when Princip fired his shots. Austria declared war on Serbia, to whom Russia was allied. Serbia was also allied to Austro-Hungary. Russia was also allied to Britain and France while Austro-Hungary was allied to Germany. July saw a month of frantic diplomatic maneuvering—the July Crisis—but to no avail. At the end of that month, the dominoes began to fall: both Russia and Germany mobilized for war, with Germany declaring war on Russia on the 1st of August; France mobilized in defense of Russia on the 2nd; on the 3rd Germany declared war on France and entered Belgium en route to attack France; Belgium invoked the Treaty of London of 1839 which obliged Britain to defend it and so on the 4th of August Britain declared war on Germany. By the end of September, Japan had entered the war on the side of the British and French and the following month the Ottoman Empire entered in support of Germany and Austro-Hungary. No one during that glorious English summer of 1914 could have dreamed that the greatest empire that the world had ever seen had reached its zenith, that Britain's declaration of war on Germany would mark the start of its long decline, and that with it, a way of life would disappear forever.

Lutyens' country-house practice evaporated almost overnight when a stock-market panic followed the diplomatic crisis, three of his clients canceling their projects on one morning in late July. The future of the new imperial city in Delhi was soon also under threat and with it, Baker's new life in England. Work on Sassoon's house continued, along with a trickle of profits from Johannesburg, but that would not sustain the Baker clan for long. Pressure mounted on Lord Hardinge and would be sustained throughout what remained of his term as Viceroy with the long-standing critics of the move from Calcutta, led by Curzon, seeing their chance and taking the opportunity to attack. Hardinge countered however during the first months of the war, successfully arguing that to cancel the new city was tantamount to abandoning India, and he soon gained the King's (unusually resolute) support. From his summer residence in Simla in the foothills of the Himalayas, he instructed the Delhi committee to spend ahead of budget to accelerate construction, and late in 1914 the workforce briefly peaked on-site at an astonishing 29,000—a level which would never again be achieved during the entire period of the city's construction. Despite the Indian Civil Service's efforts however, the war soon began to take its toll, material costs escalated, freight rates increased and soon manpower had to be redirected to the war effort, all of which started a series of delays which would dog the construction of the new city for years to come.

The omens for their winter in India were not good. In September, Lutyens' wife had informed him, "If our love is to continue it can only be on my side by a severance of our physical Relationship,"[34] to which Lutyens had responded that he was so upset that he could not "do anything I feel ill and depressed," and continuing, "The thought of India so hopelessly far and alone for months without a friend, in a world of Bakers, makes me sick."[35] The Lutyens had been drifting apart for a number of years as Emily "sought after truth" with her theosophist friends and fought for "Votes for Women," much to Lutyens' embarrassment, but nevertheless, her letter was a stunning blow and added to his financial woes brought on by the war. One can well imagine that Baker boarded ship with equally little enthusiasm, at the prospect of several months in Lutyens' company.

Their relationship on board was strained from the start as Baker immediately proposed a "moratorium" on Delhi work until they reached India, much to Lutyens' annoyance, but fortunately for both architects, they had socially, and for Baker intellectually, acceptable companions on board, at least as far as Cairo. Lutyens had secured a commission for William Nicholson, the painter, to paint an official portrait of the Viceroy, Lord Hardinge, and he joined them both on board. He later categorized Lutyens' unending stream of puns and jokes during their passage as being like an architect's fee—only 7½ percent good. Baker found solace in the company of three young men—"The Three Musketeers"—who were traveling to Cairo to join Thomas Edward Lawrence (of Arabia) in the military intelligence unit there—George Ambrose Lloyd, Aubrey Herbert[36] and Leonard Woolley. While Baker discussed archaeology and politics with the three, Lutyens played chess "fast and furious" with George Lloyd and wrote nonsense verses. Aubrey Herbert thought Lutyens "a divine imp, sillier than anything I have ever dreamt of, quite futile and occasionally brilliant."[37]

On their arrival in Delhi they were informed that 22-year-old Edward Hardinge, the Viceroy's son, had died from wounds while serving as a lieutenant with the 15th (The King's) Hussars in France just the previous week. For Hardinge, still mourning the death of his wife in June, it was a further devastating blow. The Imperial Delhi Committee carried on without his involvement under Sir Malcolm Hailey's presidency meeting twice a week, invariably with both architects present and much to Lutyens' frustration. He complained that Baker "had the committee in his pocket," knowing he lacked Baker's ability to forge effective relationships with his fellow men or match his eloquence or experience in the management of such meetings, whereas Baker, far from being contemptuous of the committee, admired and respected many of its members, in particular Hailey, whom he described as an "active and courageous leader, with a wide knowledge of India and a sympathetic understanding of the architects in their endeavor to express her spirit in their buildings. He had the saving sense of humor characteristic of the Indian Civil Servant which helps to carry them through the perplexities and pathos of India…. They were red-letter days when he was able to accompany me on my usually lonely early-morning rides watching the progress of the developing city."[38]

Baker had lost all trust in his partner from the moment that Lutyens had gone back on their agreement during the previous winter, and the following spring, which was the first time since that they had actually worked together, Lutyens' behavior only added to his concerns and frustrations. For Lutyens, Baker had also proved to be a great disappointment. After their years of correspondence in which he had mercilessly criticized Baker's work without rebuke, he must have anticipated a willing acolyte and instead had found an equally strong personality who was in so many ways professionally much more capable. Their differences became more and more accentuated in India, where they were thrown together day after day unable to resolve matters between them and increasingly having to rely on the committee for adjudication. They both constantly complained to their wives about the other with Lutyens stating, "Baker has not been any help architecturally and I have to fight him and the world to get anything done thoroughly to what I believe is right. It all seems right with words but when words become deeds they all go wooly and sloppy and nothing matters so long as people don't know and if you can't describe a thing it is a thing that doesn't matter—a gallery I can't play at,"[39] and, "He is very selfish too. It is a bore. He has great, good qualities and can be very charming and is to those in his own interest. I don't mind that if he didn't put it before the work…. I miss Lady Hardinge's help and influence enormously. This is all private."[40] Meanwhile Baker was confiding in Florence that, after Lutyens' behavior over their agreement the previous winter, it took all his Christian charity to work with him at all. At least on this visit Baker had with him his new senior assistant Charles Walgate and also Walter George, who would remain in Delhi as Baker's representative for the next few years. These two young men were given an astonishing level of responsibility considering that Walgate was only 29 and George only 34 at this time, and both deserve considerable credit for their contribution.

While the architects continued to develop their building designs, the committee raised and discussed an astonishing range of issues required for the creation of the new city, from the planning of staff houses through sewage and sanitation to the smallest details on Raisina Hill. The foundation stones of the city had been laid by the King and Queen on the site of the durbar in 1911, but rather embarrassingly, the city was now rising elsewhere, and so it was agreed that the stones should be moved to Raisina Hill and accommodated there with due deference. After considerable debate it was decided that two chambers should be created below stone chattris[41] within the great sandstone eastern rampart of the Secretariats, one on either side for the King and Queen, and that to deflect any criticism they should be renamed the Commemorative Stones. Each chamber was to have a fountain—a symbolic spring—from which the vast water gardens on either side of the King's Way would be fed before flowing into the River Jumna and eventually out to sea to join Britannia's waves. It was an idea which combined Lutyens' wit with Baker's love of symbolism and probably drew on both, but once agreed by the committee, it was one for which both claimed authorship (and there are few issues which can divide architects more strongly than claiming credit for a brilliant piece of design). It was but one small example of just how much more could have been achieved in Delhi had they combined their skills in a close collaboration, rather than constantly bickering.

On the 3rd of January, Lord Hardinge and his young daughter Diamond visited the architects at their office, of which Baker wrote to Florence—

> Ld. Hardinge motored himself over with Diamond his daughter aged 16—it was sad meeting him after the double loss—but we at once plunged into the plans.... We had a satisfactory meeting with the Committee.... We dined with the Viceroy on Sunday & I talked to him most of the evening.... The V.R. was very interesting & frank about things.... Today another committee—we are doing much more this year. And I carried my point about the prematurely born Foundation Stones of the King, Queen laid at the Durbar—They can be relaid in the new building ... enshrined as commemorative stones—and I am making a shrine for each with water bubbling out from under a black marble inscribed stone—which will here after be worshipped as sacred. I thought they might not agree, but I carried it today—so we have done a lot in a week![42]

While the angle of the ramp in the King's Way had been discussed and agreed upon the previous winter, there were still concerns among the committee members that the slope should not be too steep for future processions which would include both mounted troops and horses and carriages, and so in January, a series of further experiments were carried out in which the architects, the Viceroy and members of his committee were driven in a carriage up lengths of ramps of varying inclines from 20 degrees to 25, after which all involved agreed that the ramp from the Great Place to Government Court should be constructed at 22½ degrees. Far from Lutyens being ill or overworked at this time, he wrote to his wife on the 14th of January that he was "very relaxed here," and, "it is much better fun and time goes quick,"[43] and yet again, despite riding up and down an incline of 22½ degrees, he still failed to grasp the impact that the ramp would have on the approach to his Government House.

By February, Hardinge was back in the saddle full-time and cracking the whip. The architects were under pressure once more as the Viceroy wanted to ensure that the engineers and contractors had sufficient detailed design work completed to allow them to continue with excavations and foundations without delay after the architects returned to England at the end of March. Lutyens protested, with considerable justification, that it was difficult to confirm exactly what was required in the lower levels of a building until the upper levels had been designed. Lutyens also complained about the standard of local craftsmanship, but Baker, who had dealt with equally severe conditions previously in South Africa, did what he could to help Hailey and the contractor, recommending foremen for key trades and arranging for Mr. W. B. Cairns, Baker's leading stonemason from Pretoria, to move to India and thus establish the mighty Delhi stoneyard in July 1915.

In the midst of all this Delhi work, Baker had also managed to pick up a commission for a house in Simla for judge Sir George Rivers Lowndes—The Yarrows—which he described as "a pleasant diversion."[44] By the 11th of March, Baker was flagging, as he confessed to Florence—"Oh dear! 2 weeks more of Lutyens. He is such an awful brute to work with—but alas!—3 weeks on board with him! I have got to despise him so—such arrogance and egotism. I often wonder how I shall live through 6 more years of it. And my only job left! I like the place & the people we have to work with but it is awful to have such a colleague—however it has to be gone through with!! Excuse this howl. I was trying to help him, to prevent him writing rude personal things in a report to the

"The Yarrows" in Simla, India (courtesy Michael Baker).

committee—he writes so badly—he was insolent & we have just had a row! But I shall forget it tomorrow!"[45]

At the end of March, the architects set off for Bombay and the steamer home once
more, but there was to be no happy working together under an awning on the top deck
of the boat this year. It was a gloomy voyage with both recognizing that with the war and
progress being so slow on-site, their marriage of inconvenience must inevitably now last
even longer.

9

1915–1917
"A War Song" (Op. 5)

The England that Baker returned to in the spring of 1915 was a very different place from the pre-war days of the previous year. Thoughts of a quick skirmish and it "all being over by Christmas" were long gone and the Allies and the Germans had established themselves on a "western front" in a line of trenches which ran from the Channel to the French-Swiss border; this was to be their battleground for the next three and a half years. The spring had seen the start of what was to be an Allied offensive which occupied most of 1915, but despite the British and French enjoying a three to one superiority over the Germans, they achieved little. By the summer 86,000 of the original 100,000-strong British Expeditionary force who had traveled to France in 1914 were either killed, wounded or missing in action. Following the disastrous Gallipoli campaign which had been designed to open up an eastern front and a chronic shortage of shells on the western front, Asquith, the Liberal Prime Minister, had been forced to form a new coalition government bringing both Lord Crewe and Lord Curzon into his cabinet. Month by month as the conflict dragged on the wealth and youth of Britain's great empire was poured into fighting the war, and month by month its status as an invincible superpower, inexorably, unnoticed, slowly ebbed away.

For Baker, his life slipped into an old familiar pattern from his days as Ernest George's assistant of weekdays in London and weekends in Kent. He and his team in Eaton Place were fully occupied with the Secretariats and in any case, there was little new work to chase. Sassoon's house Belclaire at Port Lympne was nearing completion with Sassoon now visiting it en route to and from France, where he was serving as private secretary to Field Marshall Haig. He kept up a regular correspondence with Baker from France with a constant stream of ideas and complaints—"As regards the big room decoration I will confess to you that I am not at all pleased with it. It is much too heavy and dark.... Couldn't you utilize it in Delhi?"[1] The house was completed that year and then followed by a string of further commissions around the estate for farm buildings, the restoration of cottages, extensions to the house and eventually a swimming pool, before Sassoon's request for a Moroccan courtyard in the center of Baker's house finally led to a parting of the ways and the arrival of society architect Phillip Tilden at Port Lympne.

The house that Baker designed was a curious mix of Cape Dutch and English Arts and Crafts that shouldn't really have worked, but did. Two red-brick wings, capped with Dutch gables (which in England take on a rather Jacobean feel), enclosed a south-facing terrace which was then further extended and protected by curved single-story wings.

Sassoon's "Belclaire," Port Lympmne, Kent, from the great lawn (author's collection).

From here, double flights of steps descend to a great lawn with a pool enclosed by hedges, with further flights continuing down into the lower woods. From the terrace, Sassoon's guests, who over the years included everyone from the Prince of Wales to Charlie Chaplin, looked out across Romney Marsh to the sea and beyond, on clear days, to the cliffs of France. It was Baker at his best on a steeply sloping site that many others might have struggled with but which he now knew simply offered greater opportunities for drama and enchantment.

That summer, the war arrived in London, as Herbert reported to Florence—"In the thick of it last night as they dropped a bomb … or incendiary in the Garden … it sent a flame 10 ft high on the lawn!"[2] Herbert survived however, and on Saturday the 14th of August the Bakers left together for a three-week summer vacation by the sea in Llanbedrog in North Wales. A few weeks before his dreaded departure for Delhi his mood was briefly lifted when he found out that Florence was expecting once more. Lutyens meanwhile had his own troubles to contend with as he was in Rome where his building for the British School was over budget, as he confided to his wife—"War with three committees, one in Rome two in England make the British School so difficult and everyone seems X with me! … I have given them £1500 worth of fees at least, so my journey is heavy hearted and little by little the committee … just spoils the building…. I hate it and can't do anything without sympathy and encouragement…. Some troop trains are in front of us I expect as the train is very late. I hope I do not miss the connection."[3] Despite the return of part of his fee, the building was soon abandoned with only the front range completed. In October he was on the continent once more en route to India via Spain, spending a week of luxury at the Palacia de Liria in Madrid from where he searched the surrounding countryside for a site for a country house for the Duke of Peneranda in the Duke's chauffeur-driven Rolls-Royce. From Madrid he traveled to Gibraltar where he met Baker and from there they sailed together to Cairo on the next leg of their journey to Delhi.

As the ships to Bombay from Cairo were now reduced to a weekly service because of the hostilities, they spent several days there staying with the new British High Commissioner, Sir Henry McMahon, whom they knew from Delhi where he had served previously, thus giving Baker an opportunity to show Lutyens some of the architecture of ancient Egypt. Lutyens was resolutely unimpressed with the works of the Pharaohs—"Great God-fearing children playing with huge toy bricks and telling their stories in picture words with no adjectives…."[4] The final leg of their passage through the canal and the Red Sea was spent with Baker quietly reading books on Indian history and religion, much to Lutyens' frustration.

Baker had been unwell on the crossing but by the 31st was able to write, "I am practically well & got back most of my strength,"[5] and by early January he was back in the architects' office working on symbols for the decoration of the Secretariats, to Lutyens' disgust, as he informed his wife—"Baker's very busy making out emblems for India, the Provinces and indeed all Dependencies, Crown Colonies etc. of the British Empire…. I maintain that an architect should always design in three dimensions, it is his job…. Architecture should begin where literature leaves off, each depending on the other."[6] Fortunately for Baker, Hardinge shared his interest in heraldry and was keen to discuss and approve such details. He was now very conscious that his term as Viceroy would conclude that March, and the selection of his successor was the subject of considerable discussion both in London and in Delhi with an announcement anticipated at any time with Baker noting, "Some guess L'd Chelmsford—I hope it is L'd Derby."[7] He was desperately disappointed at the prospect of losing Hardinge as he had developed an increasingly close and effective relationship with him, the two often spending time together discussing politics, Indian affairs, possible conscription, Round Table articles and details of the Secretariats—"It is nice getting him to myself to discuss my fads!" It was now clear that with the impact of the war—"There will be little money spent on the buildings for many years. Keeling says he expects to be up to the first platform level where he ought to have been now in 18 months time & so Delhi will take me most of my working lifetime!" but the next day he was able to report positive progress in the same letter—"Saw the V.R. & got his approval of my scheme for decorating the King and Queen's chambers, where the stones are. My estimate for the whole building came out right and the V.R. said he 'congratulated me warmly' upon it. Lutyens has not got his through & I think they are nervous about it. The V.R. has no trust in him on this subject."[8]

His health still poor, Baker recommenced his early morning rides but felt exhausted and without his usual energy and found his work "dreary." His letters home, while including sketches of what he had seen for his boys, were also dominated by thoughts of future domestic arrangements and an eventual return to Owletts. By the 16th, he had finally moved into his own rented house in Delhi and was working on details of a cottage for Sassoon, as a break from Indian work, when he confirmed, "The new Viceroy is announced—L'd Chelmsford … a nice, sensible gentlemanly person but not of commanding ability I'd say…. The Committee tomorrow is about L's plans for staff houses—which—as usual—work out double the price allowed! There will be a row again…. He thinks he can cajole every one into accepting his estimates—but he can't…. My estimates are all right—it is novel for me to be the economical architect!"[9] A few days later Lutyens was complaining to Emily—"Baker curiously tiresome and numb as to what lines and levels are right and what not in landscape and other gardening work,"[10] which turned out to be rather an ironic statement when just a week later he visited the site to discover for the first time that the portico of Government House would be entirely obscured by the ramp up onto Raisina Hill as he complained in his illustrated letter home of the 29th— "I am having difficulty with Baker. You remember the perspective showing the secretariats with Government House beyond. Well I find he has designed his levels so that you will never see Government House at all! From the Great Place. You will just see the top of the dome! He is so obstinate and quotes the Acropolis in Athens, which is in no way parallel.... I have now put a protest in to him in writing and he will be angry and I shall have to carry it further. His perspectives [exhibited under Lutyens' name at the Summer Exhibition] are imaginary and it is too naughty to mislead like that."[11]

And so, with Lutyens finally confronted by the physical construction of the ramp, he realized for the first time what everyone else involved in the project had understood for the last two years and his battle—"his Bakerloo"—to amend the design of Government Court to accommodate a better view of Government House began. Lutyens had no intention whatsoever of admitting his mistake and instead sought to both justify it through a series of excuses and to blame Baker for his error. Even Hussey, Lutyens' biographer, explained Lutyens' failure to understand what every other architect and layman involved in the project had realized, as a minor bureaucratic oversight, suggesting "Lutyens had, in a moment of aberration, put himself technically in the wrong."[12] The truth was that Lutyens had completely failed to grasp the impact that moving the Secretariats onto the hill would have on the continuous view of Government House from the Processional Way. His mental model of Imperial Delhi was almost entirely two-dimensional—a long axis, with Government House on a hill as its conclusion, like the Capitol in Washington, but this was not what the two architects had eventually, jointly, proposed to the Viceroy, then quoting the entirely relevant Capitoline Hill in Rome and Acropolis in Athens in doing so.[13] Further, Walcott's perspective, which Lutyens now claimed had misled him, had been produced for public consumption to explain the architects' vision, not to explore it, and even Lutyens' daughter Mary later confirmed that "Walcot had drawn this from an imaginary point thirty feet above ground."[14]

From Baker's perspective, this was just the latest in what had already become a long series of increasingly bitter disagreements with Lutyens. He returned his "protest in writing" to him with handwritten comments and concluded with a note, "It is silly writing formal letters to me. I have explained my point of view so often to you." Lutyens had written—"We assured the Viceroy that the graded approach from the Great Place would not interfere with the view down the main avenue from the Portico of Government House." To which Baker responded—"I have no recollection of this." Lutyens—"The question did not become practical until last year when the level of the Great Place was determined." Baker—"It was settled then with your help. You approved of the grade then." Lutyens— "These were useful data to acquire and essential to any design and it did not necessitate a design—as it at present stands." Baker—"The grade was definitely settled by the Committee for this processional way." And so on, Lutyens setting out what would be a series of arguments to excuse himself and blame Baker, with Baker responding coolly and factually to each point.[15]

With Baker having responded, he thought fully, to Lutyens' concerns, he left for a few days in Lucknow where an Indian, Cambridge-educated Nihal Singh, wished Baker to design a house for him. His next letter to Florence is dominated by a discussion of domestic arrangements in England and his only mention of Lutyens is a hope for "a lot of rest after 5 months with E.L.L.!"[16] By the 30th, he was in Simla where he enjoyed the company, the views of the Himalayas, the cool air and plenty of exercise, both riding and walking.

Back in Delhi, Lutyens raised the issue by a letter to the committee on the 10th of February. It was discussed at the meeting on the following day, and its president Sir Malcolm Hailey invited both architects to make their case in writing, on receipt of which the committee would make a final decision. Lutyens proposed that in lieu of the short ramp previously agreed, the entire length of Government Court should be excavated to provide a continuous view of Government House. The sides of the ramp could either be grassed or stepped and communication problems between the two Secretariat buildings could be addressed by underground linking corridors with elevators in each building, if necessary. Baker reminded the committee that the concept for Raisina Hill (which the architects had jointly presented) had been that of a raised sacred place along the lines of the Capitoline in Rome or the Acropolis in Athens and in both these precedents the crowning buildings were partly obscured during the upward progress towards them and, far from being detrimental, the partial screening provided a sense of drama once the upper level was finally reached. He likened Lutyens' proposed amendment to a "railway cutting" which would destroy the sacred aura of Government Court, make communications between the two Secretariat blocks extremely difficult and further delay the project. A further point was made to the committee by Hugh Keeling the chief engineer who confirmed that you "can only obtain a view of the base of the columns of Gov't House if the grade is cut back to within 160 feet of the Jaipur Column."[17] In other words, not only would the ramp have to bisect the entire length of Government Court, but it would also have had to continue into the Court of Government House itself to achieve Lutyens' stated aim.

The architects' representations were discussed at the 101st meeting of the Imperial Delhi Committee on the 20th of February with the minutes of the meeting recording that they regarded Lutyens' proposal as a "matter of great importance," as it involved "a departure from the plans at present accepted by the Committee, on which the work so far in progress is based," and confirmed, "The Committee have submitted the history of the case to a careful examination with a view to discovering some ground for the contention of Mr. Lutyens that there has been a departure from the original intention." They believed the perspectives to have been produced "in order to elucidate for the lay mind the general view which would be obtained of the central group of buildings," and found, "It is sufficiently clear that the grade and general picture which would result from the scheme were agreed on by the Architects of the Central buildings and definitely approved of by the Committee by the end of the cold weather of 1913–14. This is placed beyond doubt by the fact that as early as June 1914 Mr. Lutyens filed a plan (C.E. 221/9 series II) in which he shows the gradient terminating east of point A. The grade has formed the basis of all work subsequently executed. The Committee feel that it is established that there has been no departure from the original proposals of the Architects," and concluded, "In short, without discussing the artistic merits of the alternative picture, the Committee feel that the expenditure which would be considerable would produce a result involving serious material and administrative disadvantages, and cannot be justified."[18]

Baker was satisfied that the matter had been concluded, allowing him to proceed with his design without revision, as he wrote to Florence shortly after—"The argument with L. I told you about—has been settled in my favour by the Committee. That is a relief.

L. says he will take it to the Sec. of State! But at that I only laughed!"[19] As far as Lutyens was concerned, the matter was far from resolved and he took it up directly with Lord Hardinge who had authority to overrule the committee. This resulted in a lunch appointment on the 10th of March at which Lutyens was given short shrift by the Viceroy who informed him that he strongly supported the committee's decision, but he foolishly offered Lutyens the option of raising the matter again with his successor, Lord Chelmsford. In a note to Malcolm Hailey following the meeting, he was much more resolute, suggesting that Lutyens concerns were "patent to everybody two years ago," that his new proposal would resemble "a glorified railway cutting," be "extremely inconvenient" and that, in his view, Lutyens raising the issue at this point was "little short of a scandal."[20] A few days later, the Viceroy invited Baker to lunch telling him he that was "very angry" at Lutyens' proposed changes to the design of Raisina Hill, that he had been "a thorn in his side from the beginning," was utterly irresponsible when it came to cost, and he laughed as he told Baker that Lutyens had said, "I am accustomed to have my opinion always taken! ... He told me L. had offered to pay for alterations. He asked if I thought L. would resign. I said no! emphatically." The Viceroy further asked Baker, "as a sensible man," to "reason with him & get him to drop the matter," during the passage home, as "his whole attitude of grousing and disloyalty and wild talk when he does not get his way in everything is doing everyone harm and more especially himself." It was from this point that Hardinge started to refer to Lutyens in his conversations simply as "the spoilt child."[21]

Lutyens knew he had blundered, whether too busy trying to bring Government House within budget, tired, ill or simply careless, but from his perspective (and it was initially almost entirely from his perspective) he believed that his greatest work, his long-imagined palace, was going to be hopelessly compromised and that it was all Baker's fault. As Lady Sackville, one of his greatest supporters, would later bemoan, Lutyens lived in constant "fear of being criticised if he does the slightest thing wrong architecturally."[22] Lutyens had no friends in Delhi with whom to press his case: his long friendship with Baker hadn't survived their second visit; his great ally, Lady Hardinge, was no more; he had offended, annoyed or frustrated almost everyone else who was involved in the project; he had no previous experience of dealing with officialdom and, as he had naïvely told the Viceroy, he simply wasn't used to not getting his own way. He was alone and his only hope now appeared to be that the new Viceroy, Lord Chelmsford, would reverse the committee and Hardinge's decision.

Baker regarded the incident as merely the latest of Lutyens' outbursts and had no idea that it would develop into a long, painful and damaging saga. Shortly before departing, he confided (rather smugly) to Malcolm Hailey—"Whether the 'Acropolis' idea of our original conception was right or wrong, now that it is there, it appears to me inconceivably unwise to cut the raised court in two by a continuous deep cutting, or to cut it away in endless or useless steps.... I should be leaving so happily otherwise. My secretarial estimates, Keeling tells me, are quite satisfactory and he seems as satisfied as I am with George, my representative whom I leave behind, and his capacity for the work, so I have no anxieties as to my own work."[23]

The two architects boarded the SS *Caledonia* at Bombay on Monday the 20th of March, barely on speaking terms and determined to avoid each other if at all possible throughout the journey home. Unfortunately for Baker, he had acquiesced to the Viceroy's request that he should attempt to resolve the matter with Lutyens while on board and so on the first Sunday of the trip (no doubt hoping for divine intervention), he broached the subject once more as his diary entry confirmed—"I found him quite impossible to talk to. I told him I would not talk unless he kept temperate. I told him what the Viceroy had asked me to say to him—that disloyalty to master & decisions was harmful to the lot & to himself and asked him to try & see the better side of people & their point of view. I think it had a little effect tho' it was impossible to keep him to the point. He said he would resign and tell the King."[24] Most of the remainder of their journey was spent with both architects writing letters to Lord Chelmsford, the new Viceroy who had commenced his term on the 4th of April, with Lutyens regretting that absorption in his profession had prevented him from realizing the rules that control bureaucratic methods and Baker now citing Rajput citadels as well as Roman and Athenian architectural precedents.

As their spat over the length of a ramp began to develop into a paper chase, the rather more serious matter of the real war in France and Belgium was developing into the industrialized slaughter of a generation of young men. Baker constantly kept in touch with events with Florence regularly sending him *The Times* while he was in India, and the news can't have helped his mood. His own sea crossings were now by no means risk free with the P&O steamer *Persia* on which Baker had traveled having been sunk by the Germans just a few months previously with the loss of many passengers. To add to British imperial concerns that Easter, an armed insurrection had erupted in Dublin led by Irish Republicans who were demanding their independence from the empire, the Home Rule League was established in India (with the enthusiastic and active support of Emily Lutyens) and Baker's friend General Smuts was then engaged in suppressing the Maritz rebellion in South Africa. The empire was creaking at the seams and, while young men traveled from across the globe to fight with the British in France, many sought independence as their reward. Certainly, in India there was a growing sentiment that the Raj's days were numbered and it soon became obvious that the new Viceroy Lord Chelmsford was much more interested in assuaging these increasing demands for political reform than in the detailed design of the new imperial capital.

Soon after his return to England, Baker and his family moved out of Owletts, Florence having finally found a suitable house for them to rent in Kent, Hartley Manor, which was close to Owletts, Nurstead and a mainline station to London. On the 26th of June, their daughter Ann was born, finally giving Herbert the Barbara (Lutyens' daughter) he had longed for. His 12-month lease on Eaton Place was nearly up and so during that summer of 1916 he and his team moved to 14 Barton Street in Westminster, which he leased from Westminster School and which would become his professional home for the remainder of his career. There was still a vast amount of detailed design required for the Secretariats, and Baker also spent much of that summer working on his designs for the staff quarters or "the bungalows" as he referred to them. Designs were required for every class of civil servant, and he personally spent a considerable amount of time on this task, producing a wide variety of options including complex hexagonal and butterfly plans. Despite the effort that he (and Lutyens) expended on the design of the staff houses, in the end the budget for them was so significantly reduced that most were designed by members of the government of India (under the leadership of Robert T. Russell, their chief architect). The exceptions were Lutyens' houses and stables within the Viceregal estate and six houses on King George's Avenue (now Rajaji Marg) and one on Akbar Road, by Baker (which was christened, once more, "Baker's Oven"—this time by Lutyens). Baker's "bungalows" were actually two-story, unlike most of Lutyens', and similar in design to his house in Simla. Like so many of their predecessors, they were organized around a central social space, entered on one side and then opening onto a veranda overlooking the garden on the other.

Meanwhile, the two architects' bickering continued, before the matter was apparently concluded once and for all on the 13th of May with Lord Chelmsford's decision, which was conveyed via telegrams to Baker and Lutyens—"GOVERNMENT INDIA HAS ISSUED OFFICIAL ORDERS DIRECTION COMMITTEE TO RETAIN INCLINED PLANE AT GRADIENT ONE IN TWENTY TWO ALREADY DECIDED ON."[25] This was followed up by a letter from Sir Claude Hill from Simla, trusting that as Lutyens "knew that his arguments had received the fullest possible consideration, he would treat the matter as closed."[26] Hill could hardly have expected it to still be rumbling on when he retired from his post in 1921.

There were few new opportunities for architects in wartime England and with most young men either volunteering or being called up for active service, resources were thin on the ground for those with work. Baker was constantly worried that Walgate would be called up and much relieved when his senior assistant was declared unfit for military service. The scale of their task in carrying out the detailed design and delivering all the drawings required for Delhi was simply awesome. The entire building was drawn in plan, section and elevation at half an inch to a foot (1:20 approx.) with many of the drawings being 6-, 8- or even 10-feet long. Over the next 10 years every element of the building would be designed and drawn in detail with full-size drawings provided for every column fluting, capital, soffit, panel, bracket, balcony, string course, voussoir, keyblock, molding and corbel. The drawings were almost all completed in London and then shipped to India where Keeling's engineers would inspect them, compare what was proposed to their cost estimates and only then authorize them to be released for construction, with much of Baker's resident architects' time being taken up with the management of this process. It would have been a herculean task had the Secretariats been constructed in London, never mind on the other side of the globe.

Lutyens was facing similar pressures on Government House but he had also caught wind of what might just be his next big opportunity, hearing that the Bank of England was considering an architectural competition for the redevelopment of their buildings on Threadneedle Street. On the 14th of July, he wrote to the governor, Lord Cunliffe, asking if there was any chance of him being allowed to see him. Though he wouldn't recommend the process, he had obtained a copy of the RIBA's *Guidelines for Architectural Competitions* which he'd be happy to pass on, then going on to state, "I have also had the temerity to make a rough thumb nail sketch for a possible bank building for your delectation, and to prompt discussion!"[27] Unfortunately for Lutyens, the governor had no intention of personally interviewing architects, no matter how eminent, and so Lutyens was forced to send the competition rules to him 10 days later along with a note criticizing the competition process in general and with particularly bitter reference to the London County Hall competition. The bank continued to favor a competition, however, and opened a correspondence directly with Ernest Newton, then president of the RIBA who, like most RIBA presidents, was keen to ensure that as many members of his profession were involved in giving their designs away for free as possible.

Baker and Lutyens met several times that summer when absolutely necessary, to confer on Delhi details, before Baker left for Woolacombe in North Devon with his family for three weeks' vacation at the end of August. Far from accepting the decisions of the Imperial Delhi Committee and two Viceroys, Lutyens meanwhile was continuing to press his case unsuccessfully with the new Secretary of State for India, Austen Chamberlain, who held the party line, before finally appealing directly to Queen Mary herself, who, when told of the catastrophe of the ramp and the appalling reductions which Lutyens had been forced to make to Government House, arranged for an audience with the King so that Lutyens could bring the royal couple up to date with the terrible events in India. And so on the 4th of November, Lutyens, armed with plans, perspectives and photographs, attended Buckingham Palace where he not only shocked the King and Queen by the changes that had been wrought to his original plans of Government House which he had first shown them at Balmoral in 1912 but also raised the issue of the ramp and the impact that it had on views of Government House.

The King was outraged, but with all real power resting in his government, he was unable to take any direct action. When those involved with the project heard of the meeting and of what were now the King's concerns, they were quick to counter Lutyens' scheming. Hardinge, who was now Permanent Under-Secretary of State at the Foreign Office, immediately advised the royal couple as to the facts of the case (which was reinforced most strongly by Austen Chamberlain briefing the King's Private Secretary Lord Stamfordham) and arranged for Herbert Baker to meet Queen Mary to hear Baker's view of events, after which Queen Mary reproached Hardinge for having appointed Lutyens in the first place! Lutyens was running out of options.

In late November the two partners set off for India once more on what had become a dangerous wartime passage. At Port Said, they took on board the surviving passengers from the SS *City of Birmingham* which had been sunk by a German submarine, and Baker later confirmed that they too had been chased and shelled and returned fire. He continued to keep in touch with political events at home and learned on the 14th both that Asquith's government had fallen, having failed to achieve a breakthrough on the Western front, and even more pertinently for Baker, that the new Prime Minister David Lloyd George had immediately formed a War Cabinet of five men, including Lord Milner, as he wrote from Aden—"I am so elated beyond words at Milner's appointment to the War Council. That is a sign of L.G.s courage & sense. One has the highest hopes now of finishing the war & of the future of England & the Empire afterwards—Hurrah! Hurrah! Hurrah!" While Lloyd George and his War Cabinet would achieve victory, sadly for very many young men from across the empire, it would not be for another two more years (during which time Milner was further promoted to Minister of War). Back down to earth, Baker reported, "L. nicer mannered when the dangers are menacing, has given place to the old unpleasantness, I hoped he had been humbled a bit & so I fear a bad time ahead. His estimates I heard parts from George at Port Said are for the bungalows double! So there will be trouble and I get the brunt of it and there will be no fees I fear … there are worse troubles in the world than these of mine." He continued the letter when he reached Bombay and added the following, rather interesting footnote to his letter—"If I write anything especial about my work. I think you should keep it. There may be interest in all these matters & controversies some day. I expect L. writes very fully his point of view and in most cases my letters to you will be my only record—I don't care for myself— but I should like my sons, when they read about the New Delhi in the future & anything that may be written to know my point of view."[28]

This visit marked a significant change in Baker's attitude to Lutyens. Previously, though incredibly aggravated by his behavior he had literally laughed off his threats, but after witnessing his persistence including his involvement of the King and Queen, Baker began to feel that having committed to a future in England, his reputation was now vulnerable to Lutyens' unjustified and increasingly spiteful attacks. As everyone in Delhi had already found, there was no reasoning with him and it was becoming increasingly clear that he would go to any lengths to achieve his goal—this was not to be a game of cricket or football, nor would it be governed by any gentlemanly set of rules—he was dealing, not with a sportsman, but with someone whom he now regarded as a knave.

By Christmas Eve they were in Delhi, where Baker received several telegrams bringing news of his mother's death. He wrote to Florence—"Well dearest, my lovely Christmas Day has turned to a very sad one. I went to early service in Delhi—the Mutiny Church (St. James')—and when I got back I saw three cables for me—They brought the sad news all together. It was a shock to me. I left her, dear soul, so well I thought, and I remember thinking that she would live for many years.... I am glad now I saw so much of her during my last few weeks & days and saw her so happy—so as to leave a beautiful memory of the end," and continuing on the 27th to Florence, "Last night during the time of the funeral ... I slipped out ... and wandered in the beautiful cold starlight & pictured the sad scene with the sun setting on the short day in mid winter.... This is the first week abroad for 24 years that I have not written to the dear old soul! Much love to you dear & all the boys & sweet Ann, Herbert."[29] He would receive his last letter from his mother a few days later on the 7th of January.

Soon his thoughts were turning to Owletts and he reiterated his earlier concerns that he could not let it go out of the family. He believed that though he must "keep my promise & offer it to my elder brothers, I don't see how either of them could manage it at all—much less permanently & satisfactorily and so it must come upon us," concluding that although the cost of repairs and alterations would be high, they will save their current rent and thus, "I hope you will readily agree that it is best."[30] The extended Baker family would soon concur that only Herbert and Florence could afford to take the house on and, having been sustaining it financially already for some time, that it should pass to them without further payment. By the end of the new year, Florence was settled in her new home.

That winter in Delhi established a pattern which would run through the next few years. Construction of the new city had slowed to a snail's pace with labor on-site at only a third of pre-war levels, and both architects realized that the project program and thus their joint sentence would inevitably be further extended. Design work proceeded on both the detail of the buildings on Raisina and those beyond in the wider new city with regular meetings of the committee to review proposals and estimates. Lutyens and Baker now disagreed on almost everything, and the committee meetings became weekly battles in their own personal war of attrition.

Lutyens, now that he could speak to them directly, lost no time in attempting to get Lord and Lady Chelmsford on side in his battle for the amendment of the ramp (despite Lord Chelmsford having already confirmed his opposition to any alteration), and on the first occasion he was invited to dine with them, he told Emily, "I had a long talk with them both after dinner—alone. I told them about the King's visit and all K. and Q. had said. The only difficulty is money,"[31] and of one of their early Committee meetings he wrote, "Yesterday we had the committee meeting to settle the bungalows. Mine came out, as I expected, as they rightly should, too high. Baker's horrors came out too high but possible.... I have a really jolly scheme. Baker has no scheme—just slap dash cocky olley anyhow orum."[32] Baker meanwhile informed Florence that he had complained to Malcolm

Hailey—"My Chief of Committee about L. & his disloyalty … as he announced his intention of 'kicking up a row in London' over some of my work, given to me because he had failed on it! I thought I should see Hailey. I told him all I had put up with in London & with the Queen—the difficulty of being loyal to my master and colleague! I found him sympathetic—in fact he much resented L.'s disloyalty to him & the Indian Gov't. But there is no one here quite strong enough to give him a good dressing down as L'd Hardinge did. Of course it is all very bad for my reputation in London."[33] It was now open warfare and it continued in their shared office on Raisina Hill where Lutyens and his assistants ate their meals at one end of a shared refectory table while Baker and his team took up their position at the other, with Lutyens and Baker staring at each other down the board.

By March, as usual, he couldn't wait to get home, but in view of his experiences in the Mediterranean on his outward journey he wrote on the 19th, "I have been very business like to put my house in order before embarking on perilous seas!"[34] and explained that he had written his will leaving everything to Florence and expressing his wishes that she give gifts to the servants and gardeners at Owletts and to his housekeeper in London and that his share of their South African practice should be given to his partner Frank Fleming. With his conscience clear, he set sail for England on the SS *Medina* on the 27th. Enemy action, however, had become the least of his worries. His professional reputation was now under sustained attack and with his practice based on one single (albeit very large) commission, he was now seriously concerned that he was taking direct hits from Lutyens' constant and increasingly public criticism of him. His family life was happy, his domestic and professional arrangements were resolved, but it seemed that he would now have to live never knowing when Lutyens' next torpedo would be launched.

By April 1917, Baker and Lutyens were home and would not return to India again until late in 1919. Britain had a war to fight and while Chelmsford, his council and the India office were all committed to the project continuing, work on-site was reduced to an absolute minimum to reduce expenditure to a level which would merely prevent the most skilled craftsmen leaving and save the completed work from deterioration. As the war dragged on and Britain's wealth and power seeped away, Raisina Hill in 1917 and 1918 must have looked more like the ruins of yet another former conqueror's capital rather than the foundations of a future imperial city.

For Baker, Lutyens, and the other members of their profession, there appeared to be little new work to be won while the country was focused on war, but then from the heart of the conflict came an unexpected opportunity for both architects. Fabian Ware (whom Baker knew from South Africa where he had been one of the Kindergarten) had, since his return to England, been both appointed and fired as the editor of *The Morning Post* newspaper, founded his own paper which soon failed and been found a job in the Rio Tinto Zinc Mining Corporation by Lord Milner, its chairman. When war broke out, he immediately attempted to enlist to fight, but at 45 his offer was rejected as he was deemed too old. Again, through Milner's influence, he was given command of a Red Cross mobile ambulance unit in northern France, its objective being to search for British wounded and missing soldiers and to transport them back to the British lines, but he and his unit also became increasingly involved with burying the dead. Ware was struck that there appeared to be no system in operation to mark and record the rapidly accelerating number of graves. With his and others' encouragement, the Red Cross agreed to fund the provision of wooden crosses with durable inscriptions to mark the graves, and in March 1915 his work in leading this process was formally recognized with the creation of the Graves

Registration Commission. The War Office in London became aware of Ware and his work, and in October 1915 it was agreed that they should take over responsibility for the commission and he be given the rank of major to give him greater authority in France. He immediately commenced discussions with the French and Belgian authorities, which led to their governments passing bills allowing the British Ministry of War to acquire land in France and Belgium for cemeteries, with the land being given by the French and Belgian governments to Britain in perpetuity and with the British government being responsible for the cemeteries' maintenance as *sepulture perpetuelle*.

The first cemeteries which were created were simply rows of wooden crosses and no sooner were they completed than what was at first a trickle soon became a regular stream of grieving relatives of the fallen to visit the graves. With future ownership of the cemeteries secured, thoughts turned to both their maintenance and the question of permanent memorials, and so the Imperial War Graves Commission (IWGC) was created on the 21st of May 1917, with the Secretary of State for War Lord Derby as its first chairman and Fabian Ware as its first vice-chairman and chief executive. Not only did Ware have the challenge of recording the graves, developing an appropriate and consistent treatment for the cemeteries and establishing an effective maintenance organization, but he soon faced demands from well-connected families who wished the bodies of their sons to be brought home to Britain for burial. It required all his skills of diplomacy and sheer determination to achieve an agreement that all men and officers who had been killed would be permanently buried as close to where they had fallen as possible, and controversially, that their graves should all be marked in a consistent style with no regard to rank, as equal comrades in arms and death.

When it came to considering the design of the permanent cemeteries and memorials, Ware consulted widely in London before inviting Charles Aitken, the director of the Tate Gallery, Baker and Lutyens, his deputy, Lieutenant-Colonel Arthur Messer (an architect and member of the IWGC's staff) and Arthur Hill from the Royal Botanic Gardens to accompany him to France where they could advise him on matters of design. Baker, not surprisingly, was both very interested in the opportunity and equally reluctant to enter into another association with Lutyens, realizing "from experience at Delhi that there would be a conflict inherent in our different natures and outlook," and thus responded to Ware's invitation that "while it would not be wise to attempt any close collaboration in design," he "would willingly serve as an independent architect with Lutyens on the Commission."[35] On the 19th of July, the working party set sail for wartime France, from where Baker takes up the tale in his letters to Florence—"Here I am. Somewhere in France, in the chateau of our Headquarters, (*near Hesdin*) with lights burning and no blinds or curtains and with no sound of guns, all perfectly peaceful! … We were met at Boulogne by Gen'l Ware and after a welcome lunch got into motors and went to a cemetery Vimereau (*Wimereux*) along the coast from Boulogne and then to Estaples (*Étaples*) where we spent some time amongst the distressing graves…. Tomorrow will be more real and exciting as we go nearer to the historic and tragic scenes of last year and this spring that we know so well by name. I am thrilled at the thought of it. I never thought I should see them…. I think I can write about it all as it is not connected with any military events of today."[36]

Although this first letter from France conveys only Baker's very first impressions of the battlefields, it also speaks volumes of Baker's and the majority of his British contemporaries' attitude towards the war. He was "distressed" by the mass graves at Étaples, which even in 1917 made it one of the largest First World War burial grounds, but this emotion was almost overwhelmed by his excited anticipation at visiting the scenes of British and imperial heroism. For Baker, these young men had died for a noble cause, like crusaders or Arthurian knights before them, and while he knew from the loss of friends' sons just how bitter each of these blows was for the family involved, he believed that their deaths brought honor upon them nevertheless. Interestingly, Lutyens' attitude was entirely different from Baker's. While he joked constantly and often inappropriately as usual, soon earning himself the nickname of "The War Baby," privately he was deeply moved by the evidence of the carnage, writing to Emily about "the obliteration of all human endeavour and achievement."[37]

Over the next few days, the party traveled by car from 9:00 a.m. to 7:00 p.m. to witness both the battlefields and the temporary cemeteries with their hundreds, often thousands, of simple wooden crosses as Baker wrote on the 11th—"We saw several cemeteries, one or two nice ones in orchards or near woods which can easily be made very attractive in a reverent way. Then to the historic fields: Pozieres High Wood, Butte de Waldencourt and later to Tiepval (*Thiepval*) all on the hills, now utter desolation. Of most of the villages there are no signs whatever.... At Tiepval there is a bigger mound which was the chateau with its basements. The famous butte is just a heap of chalk. Of other villages there are the splintered rafters of roof sticking up in places but no wall standing and no tree living, just splendid stumps.... To even Hills—the Kew expert—amazement and the shell holes ... are now covered with charlock, poppies and other plants."[38] On the 12th—"The rule now is that only very plain temporary wooden crosses are allowed, until we decide what is to be done. So Mrs Madge can't have hers. I am pressing for something very simple here where the body is and encourage relatives to concentrate their efforts on the tablet in the home church or village where the spirit will be. They will but seldom if ever come here, but will for generations be inspired by that in their own country.... One can faintly hear the guns here, just as in Kent no louder." To this letter he added the following advice to Florence, confirming that, as a result of the war, his finances were becoming as stretched as Lutyens'—"I said go slow financially in a card, because I was reckoning up in my bank book and found I had only enough to pay bills and income tax. I must get some capital from S. A., as no money will come in from my English jobs until after the war, if I have any, and Delhi is pretty dry now."[39]

Baker found the Somme fields "thrilling & realistic & sad & very interesting. I realise now what we were up against there and what heroism triumphed there. I wanted to see where the S Africans got their honour, but we cd'nt go actually in to the Wood (*Delville*) and perhaps it was as well we did not.... A town we went to 3 days ago was shelled the next day and bombed two nights running.... The multitude of graves and plans of graves counted by the 1,000s, is very depressing at times, which L's unsympathetic flippancy doesn't relieve! But they are all nice men here who are working on the job."[40] By the 12th, the party was now meeting as a committee to discuss initial ideas and to formulate an appropriate and consistent approach to the design of the permanent cemeteries. On the 14th, they agreed upon a number of recommendations, including that there should be "four types of cemetery ... those for which a monumental effect was required (such as High Wood, the scene of fierce fighting on the Somme); the special base, garden or forest cemeteries such as Étaples; town cemeteries (where a cloister might be appropriate); and village cemeteries (which, depending on size, could either have a cross or Calvary, a shelter building or a chapel and caretaker's cottage as appropriate). The Working Party also agreed that each grave should be individually marked and that there should be no private crosses or memorials in the cemeteries … the cemetery boundary should be marked with a wall … with the top parallel to the horizon … and it was held to be important that both the appointed architect and the landscape architect should jointly inspect all the cemetery sites."[41] These recommendations, with minor variations, were soon approved by the War Graves Commission and formed the strategy for all future work. When it came to the design of the monuments in the cemeteries, Baker and Lutyens locked horns immediately.

Two months before the working party set off for France, Lutyens had written to Fabian Ware proposing the idea of the War Stone—"On platforms made of not less than three steps the upper and the lower steps of a width twice that of the centre step: to give due dignity: place one great stone of fine proportion 12 feet long set fair and finely wrot … facing the West and facing the men who lie looking ever eastward towards the enemy."[42] It was a brilliantly simple conception, elegant, radical, and at a stroke removed all issues of multiple religions from the battlefield commemorations. As Lutyens also noted, this long, low slab would sit perfectly within and echo the flat landscape of northern France and Belgium. Ware was immediately attracted to the idea. For Baker and Charles Aitken, the idea that any symbol other than the Christian cross which in wooden form already crisscrossed the temporary cemeteries should be used was inconceivable. Baker saw Lutyens' proposal as so typical of the man whose interests beyond form and space were largely unformed. Baker proposed a simple stone churchyard cross and soon developed this idea into an even deeper symbol with the addition of Henry the Navigator's ship which took the crusaders to battle surmounting it, with its stone shaft being pentagonal to represent the five dominions of the empire. He produced a number of further variations for non-Christians including an Ashoka Pillar for the Indian dead and a Star of David for the Jewish. As to Lutyens' War Stone, Charles Aitken felt that "a large monolithic altar in all graveyards, irrespective of size and character would be a mistake, as it would be out of scale and character in many of the small rural graveyards. Even in the larger cemeteries, altars would be somewhat useless. I am of the opinion that the adoption of some form of churchyard cross would express better the spirit of the war and its use would be more harmonious with the surroundings in France."[43] While Baker and Lutyens' relationship was already soured, their differences on this occasion related to their fundamentally different approaches to architecture which Lutyens saw largely in terms of form, space and materials and Baker saw equally as a vehicle for symbolic meaning. New battle lines were thus quickly established.

On his return to England, Baker found to his horror that Lutyens, having produced his own note of his audience with the King and Queen the previous November, had submitted it to the rather quaintly entitled *Home Advisory Committee on the Furnishing and Decoration of Government House, Delhi* with a view to the committee overturning the Viceroy's decision and amending the ramp. Having been established two years previously with a remit to advise on the interiors of Government House (rather than leaving the matter to successive Viceroys and Vicereines), it had not in fact met until prompted (rather suspiciously) by Queen Mary in early 1917. In July 1917, Lord Crewe, its chairman, read out Lutyens' account of his royal audience including the King's criticism of the inclined way. Both Sir Thomas Holderness and Lord Hardinge, who fortunately for Baker were now both committee members, advised that the matter had already received due and careful consideration, but nevertheless, after considerable debate, the committee resolved to consider the matter once more inviting both Lutyens and Baker to personally testify, before finally resolving several months later that while they felt the present scheme regrettable, they could not accept the now heavy cost of remedying it. Throughout this further painful process for Baker, Hardinge constantly reassured him that as far as Lutyens' proposals were concerned, "any changes which would involve fresh expenditure cannot be contemplated."[44] To Baker's credit, while he could have fallen back entirely on the argument over the cost and delay that would be caused by Lutyens' proposals, he continued to doggedly refer in each arbitration to the original architectural concept for Raisina Hill which Lutyens and he had jointly presented to Lord Hardinge.

Their fresh dispute over the design of the cemetery war memorials rumbled on through the summer and autumn with both architects busily lobbying for their alternative proposals. Lutyens was on stronger ground here, not only with Ware on board and unusually his wife (who enlisted her ex-Viceroy father's support), but also now actively promoting a positive proposal, rather than a costly revision. In an attempt to break the deadlock, Lutyens proposed to Ware that he should dismiss the "genius committee. Then you settle on the big stone—and get us all to work again on another footing with the big stone settled."[45] Ware resisted until November, when he finally moved to replace Charles Aitken, Baker's principal ally, with Sir Frederick Kenyon, the director of the British Museum, whom Ware knew would support the War Stone. Kenyon pulled together the work of the committee and its architects into a comprehensive report which he submitted to the commission in January 1918, confirming everything that had been agreed in France the previous year and endorsing the idea of the War Stone. As a sop to Baker and his many supporters (including the Archbishop of Canterbury), Kenyon also proposed that each cemetery should contain a cross as a symbol of Christian faith. Lutyens had won, was ecstatic, and having savored victory was no doubt further encouraged to continue his campaign on the ramp.

Despite the slowing of construction in India, detailed design work on Imperial Delhi continued both in Barton Street and Apple Tree Yard, though both teams were now much reduced. Sassoon's telegram to Baker, received before he had even set foot back on English soil, must have raised his hopes of a possible country-house practice in England, but these were now long gone and, unknown to both Baker and Lutyens, would never return. Herbert and Florence had taken possession of Owletts, which was to be their home for the remainder of their lives, but beyond some redecoration there was no money for the alterations which Herbert wished to carry out. With no visit to India that winter, next to no new work, a war raging with the final outcome still far from certain, and money tight, Baker would only have been human had his thoughts not drifted off to the warmth of the rolling high veld, the firm sands and crystal-clear waters of Muizenburg, and his successful and highly profitable practice there.

10

1917–1921

"For the Fallen" (Op. 80)

The new year didn't start well for Baker with Lutyens' knighthood confirmed in the Honours List when it was published on the 1st of January. While Lutyens received "a very nice letter from Baker,"[1] and Baker would have fully believed that his architectural achievements entirely merited the award, it represented a further strengthening of Lutyens' status and influence in England which might bear upon Indian matters. Lutyens was already also an Associate of the Royal Academy and had proved that he could mobilize an extraordinary network of influential contacts when required as the discussions over the War Stone had proved. Baker had won another round of the battle of the Processional Way but each fresh bout created further sympathy for Lutyens' position and despite his innocence, Baker was being continually presented as one of two protagonists. It was damaging, debilitating and the thought of still being joined in partnership with Lutyens for many more years was deeply depressing.

By early 1918, Fabian Ware's thoughts had developed into a clear plan of action and despite his Kindergarten relationship with Baker, it was Lutyens with whom he was in greatest sympathy, at one point giving Lutyens hope (as he had first had in Delhi) that he might get everything for himself—"Just had a pleasant talk with Gen. Ware. His idea is that I am made top dog to carry it all out!!! Employing Baker etc!"[2] But this was not to be and, much to Lutyens' disappointment, Ware gave Kenyon overall responsibility for design. On the 5th of March, Baker, Lutyens and Lutyens' jilted bridesmaid from Delhi, Sir Reginald Blomfield, were formally appointed as Kenyon's three equal principal architects at a salary of £400 per year (raised to £600 in 1919). Their role was to act as consultants on the design of the cemeteries, and Kenyon proposed that they should be supported by the commission's own full-time employed junior architects, who were to be paid a salary of £500 per year and who were to be largely based in St. Omer in northern France. In addition, standard fees were also paid to the architects for the design of specific memorials at 4 percent of construction costs. Over the next few years, these two groups of architects became known as the PAs and the AIFs (Architects in France) with all the AIFs who were finally selected having seen active service themselves.[3] Their number included Gordon Leith, who had joined Baker from the Public Works Department (PWD) in Pretoria to work on the Union buildings and whom in this work Baker found to be the ablest of those who were assigned to him. Three experimental cemeteries were commissioned and, as the sites had been divided on a geographical basis between the PAs, Blomfield designed them all in accordance with the principles already

152

established. It was at this time that he also designed his stone cross with hexagonal shaft and bronze sword attached, which was used in all the future cemeteries along with the War Stone.

While these initial projects proceeded in France, both Baker and Lutyens worked on their designs for the headstones—all of which were rejected—with the final design being the output of a special committee which Ware had created in response to the controversy surrounding the issue as a result of the commission's earlier decision that there should be "equality in death" and the "subordination of individual choice"—as Kipling, by then the commission's literary advisor, put it—the wealthy should not be allowed to "proclaim their grief above other people's grief."[4] The final version of the headstone, including Kipling's wording, was not approved until 1920. For Baker there was little more to do. No further cemeteries would be designed until the conclusion of Blomfield's experiments and these were not completed until 1920.

The war was entering its final stage. In March, Germany signed a peace treaty with Bolshevik Russia allowing them to concentrate their efforts on the western front where they launched a major offensive which aimed to secure victory before the impending involvement of American troops. The United States had declared war on Germany the previous year and assisted with supplies and raw materials but it was not until the summer of 1918 that their American Expeditionary Force joined the conflict, with decisive effect. By October, Germany requested an armistice which was duly signed at 11:00 a.m. on the 11th of November. The war was over and Baker and his fellow Britons rejoiced at another heroic victory for their empire, though few realized then that the human and financial cost of victory had made it something of a Pyrrhic one. The Russian Empire had fallen with its royal family murdered that July; the Austro-Hungarian Empire had been dissolved; the Ottoman Empire was crushed and the mighty British Empire was exhausted.

Indians, who had loyally fought for their mother country, now expected to be rewarded with at least self-government or preferably independence. Lord Chelmsford and the Secretary of State for India, Edwin Montagu, had presented a report to the cabinet that summer proposing a series of reforms which would eventually be enshrined in the Government of India Act of 1919. Under its direction, the franchise was extended, significant powers were devolved to elected provincial councils and a new central legislature was established comprising two chambers—the Council of State and the Indian Legislative Assembly, both of which remained under the authority of the Viceroy. The proposals both appalled British Conservatives and disappointed Indian Nationalists in equal measure, but the long, and for Britain, debilitating process of transferring imperial power to the people of India had commenced.

For Baker, like most Britons, the war had been shocking in terms of the human cost but it had also been an opportunity to celebrate heroism and bravery. Of all the British heroes of the Great War there was one above all others who had captured the imagination of the nation with his exploits in leading the Arabs to victory against the Turks—the legendary Lawrence of Arabia. It was on the evening of Sunday the 17th of November that Baker first met Lawrence at dinner, after the evening service in the chapel of New College Oxford, and his letter to Florence of the following day conveys his excitement—

I doubt if you read some time ago that it was a Colonel Lawrence an archaeologist who lead the Arab forces in Arabia & Palestine. He apparently alone did it—went over there from Egypt & had much influence with the Arabs that he attracted 40,000 and led them up thro' the desert & so you know, kept cutting the line and harassing the Turks. I sat next to him tonight & he is a mere boy … fresh face & wonderful blue eyes … its difficult to get him to talk as he prefers to talk of archaeology his hobby … & I loved that too … his military exploits are most romantic. The Turks and Germans feared him so that they put a £20,000 on his head…. He gave wonderful descriptions of blowing up Turkish trains & then cutting the line near Damascus…. They w'd make him King of Arabia if he could—they worship him but he is going back to archaeology—a mere boy, think of it! To have made a Kingdom!"[5]

Here was a real-life hero for Baker—brave, apparently modest, wanting no reward for his astonishing military achievements and having served his country, happy to return to the study of archaeology—a true Corinthian. Extraordinarily, despite the significant age gap, Baker and Lawrence became good friends and within a few years could be found strolling the streets of London together in the quiet dusk as they discussed archaeology and architecture, with Lawrence, whose fame had by then grown immense, avoiding recognition while in the company of the rather distinguished older man.

A few days later Baker was finally able to report a new commission—"A man Davis rang me up & said he'd bought a nice place & wanted to do a lot to it & me to do it … fat & prosperous & wealthy and what house do you think it is—Chilham Castle! Nice having jobs in Kent & it will pay!"[6] His new client was Sir Edmund Davis, an early friend of Rhodes, mining magnate and art collector. It was not only a timely commission financially for Baker, but also one that he took great pleasure in, restoring one of Kent's great historic houses for a client for whom money was little object. The largely 17th-century Jacobean house was a most unusual one: reputed to have been designed by Indigo Jones, it was built as a hexagon around a courtyard with the south side removed. While much of Baker's painstaking work at Chilham was restoration, he also improved the circulation around the house, installed modern services, added a marble swimming pool and replaced twin Gothic entrance lodges with two well-proportioned Jacobean versions. The Chilham Castle commission was followed by one for Drummond Chaplin, his client for Marienhof in Johannesburg, who was retiring to the Cape and thus required another new home. This was to be Noordhoek, Baker's last house in South Africa and something of a Classical finale in white render with a tall Ionic loggia below a flat balustraded roof.

By the end of November, Baker was back in France with Ware, Blomfield and Lutyens, touring his prospective cemetery sites. It was to be a fairly depressing trip—"Disappointing gloomy day. The motor came 2 hrs late, so didn't start till 11 and only saw 2 cemeteries. I got back late 7.30, missing way and getting into all sorts of awful shell-destroyed roads and then learning that I was invited to dine with the C-in-C (*Sir Douglas Haig*) : 15 miles off and too late to go. Sassoon asked me and on the phone afterwards said he and the C-in-C were all alone. What awful luck to miss it! … I saw Neuve Chapel, awful desolation and being flat marshy country and winter, I suppose it looked worse than the Somme…. We saw the big German cemetery at Sailley sur Lys, near 10,000 graves where we smashed them so!"[7] Baker, like most of his contemporaries, took great pride in the acts of heroism that had emerged from the slaughter. Today, when we think of the Great War, we tend to think Seigfried Sassoon, but even after its conclusion, Baker and most of his contemporaries still thought Rupert Brooke.

At home, most of Baker's new commissions were for war memorials, and throughout the next decade he designed a total of 24 memorials for schools, counties, cities, towns and villages throughout England as well as numerous private family tombs and plaques for village churches around the country. His inspiration in all these works was the Kentish churchyard, whose flint walls, simple stone crosses and sturdy oak lych-gates would reappear again and again in almost all his designs, and it was only in the largest cemeteries and national memorials that he allowed himself anything approaching the monumental. His contribution ranged from modest stone crosses with octagonal shafts on octagonal bases on which the names of the dead were carved, such as those near his home at Cobham and Meopham (which were completed in 1921), to the larger stone crosses, such as the County of Kent memorial in Canterbury (1921) or the Rochester memorial (1922), which both included a stepped base to the plinth, or the very fine Hampshire and the Isle of Wight memorial in Winchester (1921) which was placed in front of the main entrance to Winchester Cathedral, where it is framed by the great west window and from which he laid out a new avenue of yew trees which lead off into the historic city.

Several of his village memorials were endowed by wealthy local families who had lost a son in the war. These included the exceptionally fine lychgate to St. Faith's Church in Overbury, Worcestershire, which was unveiled on the 12th of September 1921. Perhaps the most poignant for Baker and another of his finest was the Blackmoor War Memorial Cloister in Hampshire, which was unveiled in 1920. This was commissioned by his friends from Johannesburg, Lord and Lady Selborne, in memory of their second son, Captain Robert Palmer, who had been killed in Mesopotamia in January 1916. Here a rustic timber-framed cloister encloses a garden, which opens to the village and in which is placed a stone cross on the octagonal base on which are again carved the names of all those from the village who lost their lives.

But it was to be school memorials which provided Baker with his most significant English commissions. His two eldest sons were both now at Winchester College, and he started discussions with their headmaster Montague Rendall about a war memorial as early as October 1915 with the idea of a new school hall emerging as the first proposal. Like most of the public schools, the losses amongst their former pupils were shocking. Almost all former public schoolboys who enlisted had had experience in their school corps and were thus invariably commissioned as officers, with most required to lead their men "over the top" armed only with a whistle and a service revolver. At Winchester, the number of boys on the school roll at that time was around 450 and the school's losses, including both former pupils and staff, totaled 513. Old Wykehamists (as their former pupils were known) alone secured four Victoria Crosses during the war. The plans were discussed in November 1917 during an old boys' dinner, attended by the headmaster and 70 old Wykehamists given leave from duty, at Salon Godbert in Amiens, France, behind the British lines. Seven generals and twelve colonels graced the dinner, as well as three young subalterns whose names would sadly appear on the memorial that they discussed that night.

Baker soon developed a close relationship with "Monty" Rendall and the two became lifelong friends. Sad as his subject was, he recalled, "The years I spent over my work upon the Winchester College War Memorial, both in the designing and building of it, were among the happiest in my life."[8] He relished the company, while "working at Winchester amid all that is best in England was a glorious experience to me; its venerable buildings; its romance and traditions; King Arthur, the Round Table and Camelot; King Alfred; the cathedral; Wykeham and the first English public school, and its youthful manhood, inspired by the learning of the past with ideals and adventures for the future."[9] When fundraising for the hall faltered, Baker, whose preference had always been for a memorial space rather than a functional building, proposed the construction of a new cloister for the school.

Its site was carefully chosen so that it would form a daily route for the majority of the boys who lived outside the school, leading from the South African War Memorial gateway where they entered the school grounds into the main precincts of the school, itself thus forming what Baker described as a *Via Sacra*, "where they, and all who through the

The tranquility of the Winchester College War Memorial cloister (author's collection).

ages enter here, lift their hats in reverence to those who died for their country." Let Baker describe his design—"The walls are faced with roughly knapped flints with bond-stones in the manner of old Winchester walls.... The bond-stones are blazoned with heraldry and symbols representing the battle-fields of the war; those in the semi-circular ashlar-domed corners have the arms of the Dominions and symbols of their associated colonies and the provinces of India. Large slabs of Derbyshire marble-stone are inscribed with the names of the Fallen, with escutcheons of the Allied Nations above."[10] The cloister is a tranquil triumph with perfectly-proportioned double Portland stone Doric columns supporting ashlar half-round arches, from which fine crown-post oak trusses spring to form its vaults. The memorial cross in the center of the courtyard is by Alfred Turner, Gertrude Jekyll designed the garden and the school art master, Reginald Gleadowe, designed an inscription in Lombardic style lettering which runs in a continuous band around the interior of the cloister, concluding, "IN PEACE OR IN WAR BEAR THYSELF EVER AS CHRIST'S SOLDIER, GENTLE IN ALL THINGS, VALIANT IN ACTION, STEADFAST IN ADVERSITY," with the word PEACE positioned centrally, on axis. It is quintessential Baker—drawing on what seems to be almost every period of English architectural history and somehow successfully managing to combine ancient flint church walls, medieval oak trusses, Wren's ashlar Naval College, Gothic buttresses and a Purbeck stone slate roof into a single integrated composition which on its completion felt as if it had already been part of the college for several hundred years. The foundation stone was laid in July 1922, and it was dedicated on the 31st of May 1924 in the presence of the Duke of Connaught, who 14 years previously had lain the foundation stone of the Union buildings in Pretoria. Its design was lauded on completion, and it remains one of the few works of Baker's in England which still attracts consistently positive comments today.

Baker was invited to design a memorial for Eton, but his proposals were rejected by the building committee on the grounds of cost. In his own words—"The same fate befell a somewhat similar scheme which I proposed for my old school, Tonbridge." But he built at Harrow, an institution which intrigued him. "When I paid my first visit to Harrow and drove up to the Headmaster's House, I felt I had come to the wrong place, so little did the scattered and heterogeneous buildings suggest a great school. So it was essential, I thought, that the design should take a form which would link together these buildings and give them an appearance of unity. A misshapen boarding-house occupied the ground between the Old School and the sacred Mill ... the Chapel and the Speech Room. This house the Committee generously agreed to pull down."[11] As Baker suggested, his design brought what was then some much-needed dignity to the setting for the war memorial. This vaulted space, which was dedicated to the 642 old Harrovians who had lost their lives, is focused on a stone tomb, as in Overbury. The building is in red brick, flint and Portland stone and very much in keeping with the old schoolhouse, its principal flourish reserved for its great Jacobean bay windows. The foundation stone was laid by the Archbishop of Canterbury, himself a former pupil, in 1921, the shrine dedicated in July 1926 and the buildings finally completed in 1932.

What few now realize is Baker's success in creating order from the chaos with which he was presented on that first visit. The narrow site for his building would challenge any architect, with a three-story drop from back to front between two existing roads and a further story change of level along its length. On this meager roadside scrap, Baker managed to create a small court in front of the memorial building from which double stairs rise to the Old School building above, thus providing a formal entrance to the school

Baker's new entrance court and the Harrow School War Memorial (author's collection).

for the first time. The memorial loggia opens off this court and on entering the building, the route rises in a series of graceful flights of steps to a further new first-floor courtyard beyond which serves as the entrance to William Burges's speech room above. From front to back, Baker placed internal double stairs to the rear of the building as part retaining structure, which rise and turn to serve the principal rooms which overlook the street below. It is a brilliantly successful solution to the most difficult of sloping sites, and the peaceful repose with which Baker's building sits above his new court, as at Winchester—looking as if it had been an integral part of the school for several centuries—is the ultimate testament to his skill.

There were many other monuments and memorials which were discussed: a memorial library for New College, Oxford, a memorial for the Royal Artillery facing Hyde Park

Corner on the rear of Buckingham Palace's garden, a Combined Forces memorial as a semi-circular colonnade facing Buckingham Palace and enclosing the Queen Victoria Memorial and the one which was perhaps closest to his heart, the addition of a circular cloister to the Chapter House of Westminster Abbey entered opposite the state entrance to the House of Lords, to provide space for the ever-increasing number of commemorative monuments and plaques to which the war had added. It was an idea that Baker continued to promote for many years without success. But it was to be Lutyens who, with his Cenotaph—a masterpiece of restraint and Greek proportion—which was unveiled at 11:00 a.m. on the 11th of November 1920, would not only produce the centerpiece of national mourning, but with its completion, would also achieve that rare event for any architect, of gaining recognition from the general public for his work.

London was returning to some kind of new normality. On the 2nd of February 1919, Baker was finally elected to the Athenaeum Club in Pall Mall following a long-standing proposal by none other than his old friend Edwin Lutyens, made back in 1914—how things had changed.[12] After his return from South Africa, Baker had also been elected to the famous Kent cricket club, the Band of Brothers, which was then, and for many years after, led by Lord George Harris. Harris was also the treasurer of the Marylebone Cricket Club, and this resulted in Baker being appointed as their architect. His first commission was to design a memorial to W. C. Grace, one of England's greatest cricketers who had died in 1915. As the memorial was to be funded by public subscription it was agreed that it should therefore be on public view, and the idea of new main gates to Lord's Cricket Ground in Marylebone was soon proposed and agreed upon. Baker's design, which was completed in 1922, has survived much redevelopment of the ground and includes flanking Portland stone walls with cast-iron gates which bear the symbols of cricket—a red ball, surrounded by the golden rays of the sun. In 1922, Baker was invited to submit designs for new stands, and these, the first cantilevered stands at Lord's, were completed in phases between test matches between 1924 and 1926. As the minutes of the MCC record, dealing with the committee was a particularly excruciating process which tested even Baker's skills of tenacity and diplomacy to the absolute limit. Despite this, on the completion of the stand he presented the club with a weathervane depicting "Old Father Time" which, though Baker's stand is now long gone, is famous throughout the cricketing world and still looks down on Lord's today.

With new work to occupy them, several of Baker's pre-war team were returning from active service. One of this group, who would soon establish himself as leading assistant, was Alexander Scott, then 31. He had studied at the Glasgow School of Architecture and following two years as an assistant to Alexander Nisbet Paterson in Glasgow and a tour of Italy had joined the office of fellow Scot James Miller in London, from where he moved on to Thomas Mawson's office before joining Baker in Eaton Place prior to the war. Scott immediately took over as lead assistant on Delhi in Barton Street on his return and would travel out with Baker on many of his further visits to India. To make space for his growing staff numbers, Baker took on the lease of 2 Smith Square just around the corner in Westminster. He knew the house well as Geoffrey Barton (editor of *The Times*) had lived there for a number of years. Following Barton's marriage in June, Baker moved in and "many were the happy gatherings with my friends over our simple meals served by my devoted Scottish housekeeper, Mrs Donnat."[13] From this point on, Barton Street became the office with occasional visitors staying in Baker's old flat on the top floors from time to time, and he also offered Smith Square to friends when overseas.

The Bakers on holiday. From left: Alfred, Allaire, Sylvia, Herbert, Ann and Henry (courtesy Michael Baker).

After a month's vacation with his family in August, Baker's thoughts turned to India once more. With the war over, annual winter visits were to be resumed. Baker knew that Lutyens was sailing in November and so left in late October to avoid a shared passage, arriving in Bombay on the 4th of November, shortly before Lutyens sailed from Southampton. By late the next day Baker was in Delhi, and he spent the next few days inspecting the little progress on construction that had been achieved since his last visit and discussing plans and estimates with Keeling. As a result of Lord Chelmsford's reforms, a new central legislature was to be created and this was now to comprise three, rather than the original two, chambers—the Council of State, the Indian Legislative Assembly and to appease the local maharajas, a new Council of Princes. Initial thoughts that these new institutions could be accommodated within Government House or the Secretariats were soon rejected, and it was agreed that a new legislative chamber (or Council House as it was later called, with typical English understatement) was required. This in turn created a significant architectural problem as the critics of Lutyens' Beaux Arts plan such as Patrick Geddes had earlier identified, namely that it was extremely difficult for such a formal plan to respond to changed requirements such as the need for a major new government building within the central area.

The Secretariats under construction (courtesy Michael Baker).

A number of sites were considered but there were really very few practical options and it was therefore quickly decided that it should occupy the triangular space to the side of the Processional Way below Baker's northern Secretariat, terminating the long diagonal axis from old Delhi and the new Connaught Place and thus linking the new native legislature with the ancient city. In the context of the New Delhi plan however, the phrase "a monstrous carbuncle on the face of an old friend" immediately springs to mind and despite later suggestions from Lutyens and others that a balancing public building such as law courts could be sited on the other side of the Processional Way, nothing was ever carried out.

Lutyens arrived in Bombay in late November[14] and within days of his arrival in Delhi it became clear to Baker that despite his efforts to discuss business in a civilized manner,

Lutyens wouldn't play ball, with Baker recording in his diary—"I told him I welcome such friendly discussion & they w'd be much more frequent if he would not be so rude—as he was quite unprovoked the second day after his arrival."[15] By the end of the month, things were no better as he confided to Florence—"Oh such a dreary Saturday. Working away till 5.0 ... I would not mind if I had a sympathetic companion—but it is always an atmosphere deprecation & veiled sneer at my work & which is hard to thrive in."[16] It was clearly going to be a cold and frosty winter and, as it turned out, the unhappiest period of Baker's time in India. Prior to Lutyens' arrival, Baker had been given the commission to design the new legislative chamber, having been the unanimous choice of the Viceroy's committee, and his design work was already well under way. In compensation, Lutyens was to design the Indian War Memorial which was to be built on the main axis of the Processional Way between the Great Place and its conclusion in Princes' Place.

Baker's response to the triangular site and need for three chambers was a three-winged building with each wing containing chambers of varying shapes (square Senate, semi-circular Council Chamber and octagonal Council of Princes) linked to a central circular great hall under a high dome which symbolized the participants' shared responsibility for the government of India. Contained by the wings were single-story colonnades terminated by octagonal chattris in similar style to the *porte cocheres* of his Secretariats, which in turn provided three entrances to the building, each responding to one of the three axial routes of approach. As one would now expect of a mature Baker design, it was beautifully resolved in plan, responded well to its site and would have been an appropriate symbol for the newly-reformed Indian Legislature. It adopted a similar language to the Secretariats and Government House with lower red and upper buff stone under a dominating dome, but despite these many strengths, it lacked both the drama and the imperial grandeur of the buildings on the hill above.

Shortly before Christmas, Baker presented his initial design to the committee and it was immediately criticized by Lutyens. Embittered by his failure to have the design of the Processional Way amended, emboldened by his victory over the War Stone and with his public popularity enhanced by the Cenotaph, he had clearly now decided to go on the offensive. Baker had never before had his position undermined with a client in this way and was quite unprepared for Lutyens' attack. Lutyens proposed to the committee that instead of Baker's three-winged building, the legislative chamber should instead be circular in plan providing a stronger termination to the diagonal axis from the old city. Baker, shaken, was asked to consider both options as well as accommodating further increases in accommodation, with Lutyens' proposal gaining some immediate support in the meeting. For Baker, such a simple geometric shape was anathema: gone would be the symbolism of the three chambers, which his design so clearly expressed; gone would be any view of the central great hall's dome and gone would be the connections between the architectural language of the Secretariats and the legislative chamber. He quickly realized too that placing the building's circulation around the outside of a drum was an incredibly inefficient use of space which would create a half-mile long corridor around the building, much of which would be rarely used. It made no sense to Baker and he saw it immediately as yet another triumph of geometry over practicality and symbolism (or *sentiment*, as he would have put it).

He dutifully developed both options as instructed, but when it came to the next committee meeting on the 10th of January, to his horror, he found that it was Lutyens' vast wheel that gained the most support. Lutyens was jubilant as he wrote to Lady Emily—"I said what I thought and in the end I got my points, the site and the shape of the building. I insisted on his designing the new buildings to mask the faults of secretariats he is building now, and I went for his shape, and for one that filled the site he didn't like, but I won the day I am glad to say."[17] For Baker, it was nothing short of a disaster as he now faced the prospect of spending the next few years developing and then overseeing the construction of a design he thought entirely irrational and unsuitable, thus putting a "very severe strain ... on me and my band of able helpers."[18] While he continued to develop the proposal, he also made no secret of his view that it was a mistake that would be regretted in the future. In a final attempt to convince the committee before it was too late, he submitted a report outlining the many weaknesses of the circular plan. On the 31st of January he spent hours discussing his position with his friend Sir William Marris, as he recorded in his diary—"I discussed the Leg. Ch plans openly with him. He relieved my mind on the rightness of my feelings as to the danger of geometry over ruling sentiment & expression in the design."[19] Marris, at least, understood and shared his reservations, describing the circular plan as "a little fantastic & undignified—like elephants dancing,"[20] and like Baker, believed that it reflected neither the purpose of the building nor any constitutional principle.

Baker's report was considered at the committee meeting on the 6th of February and, despite a minority of members expressing similar concerns to Baker's, it was rejected, although Sir Claude Hill (as usual when a controversial decision was required) did confirm that the final decision rested with the Viceroy. On the 10th, Hill phoned Baker to let him know that the Viceroy had agreed to proceed with Lutyens' circular plan. On the 20th Baker saw the Viceroy, as his diary recorded—"He said members of Cabinet had raised matter of plans not liking circular building—I discussed it on lines of my report— but did not say definitely if I wanted the matter reopened. I was to see him again."[21] The following day, they met again and in appropriately sporting fashion and complete contrast to Lutyens' utterly determined approach, Baker stated his case—"I told him my opinion that I had been given 'out' & it was for him as Umpire to reopen the question— on my report. I said there were obvious expediency in not reopening. Later he said the matter was settled ... having no support on Committee or Council it was thought inexpedient to reopen the question & cause long delay. I hardly feel fortified to forcing the matter to such an issue."[22]

Baker was deeply disturbed by the predicament he now found himself in. For the first time, the Viceroy and the majority of his committee had sided with Lutyens. Lord Hardinge was gone and even his key allies, Keeling and Hill, who he had previously been able to rely on, had backed Lutyens. His relationship with Lutyens had deteriorated from friendship to hostility, and worst of all, it now appeared that it was to be an open and very public hostility which could only undermine his professional position and reputation. When struggling with a committee or defending his work in South Africa he did so alone and robustly but then he hadn't faced an equally distinguished architect across the table who was constantly undermining him. He resolved to make a further attempt to discuss the issue directly with Lutyens.

On the 23rd of February he "tried to talk about it to Lutyens in evening but quite unprovoked he was so rude to me & even Viceroy that I found it impossible and useless."[23] Lutyens' reaction can only have increased his concerns. Snubbed at his first attempt, he buried himself in work while mulling over alternative approaches.

His revised design for the circular legislative chamber building was very much a development of his own first winged design, but now contained within Lutyens' great perimeter ring which formed a continuous corridor around the entire building, enclosed on the ground floor and open within a colonnade above at the first floor. As Baker had anticipated and explained at length in his report, far from providing the majority of circulation space for the building, the circular corridors on each floor were in addition to the circulation spaces that ringed the legislative chambers and linked to the retained central great hall. The three chambers were now all recast in a similar horseshoe plan but varied in size and treatment in response to their differing requirements, with raking seating at ground level, first-floor galleries and arched clerestory windows above. Externally, three single-story *porte cocheres* provided modest entrances to this vast complex and addressed the three diagonal avenues that served the building.

Given the enormous scale of work required to produce the design of the building, Baker had cabled his assistants Alexander Scott and Herbert J. Manchip and asked them to join him in Delhi. Curiously, the day after their arrival, Baker had the most astonishing discussion with Lutyens which he recorded as a rather garbled note in his diary, apparently offering to "consider the question of reconsidering Process' way questions."[24] As he had already declared himself "out" with the Viceroy, it seems unlikely that he would now bargain the ramp against the circular legislative chamber and it can therefore only be construed that this was another, rather desperate, olive branch, offered in an attempt to repair their relationship and save his reputation from further potential attacks. The following day he refers to "Thinking out Process. Way question" in his diary, and adds, equally tantalizingly, "Told L. I did not feel justified in raising the question of Process. Way."[25] It appears that while he would neither promote Lutyens' proposed changes nor necessarily support them, he had offered to no longer oppose them on artistic grounds. After everything that Lutyens had already put him through, it was either a hugely generous and suitably Christian offer of good faith or, more likely, a rather desperate attempt at damage limitation. With Baker unwilling to raise the matter and Lutyens having already received Chelmsford's "final" decision, no further action was immediately taken by either architect. It is not surprising that Lutyens wrote to Emily—"I am much happier about Delhi this year,"[26] and no doubt thoughts of the imminent arrival of another Viceroy who might look favorably on amending the ramp the following year added to his general good humor.

On Baker's return to London and his office on Barton Street, he found that he had a new lodger "living above the shop." Following his meeting with T. E. Lawrence at New College, they had corresponded regularly, Baker continuing to be fascinated by this real-life imperial hero and Lawrence equally interested in the famous architect whom he instinctively felt he could trust. Lawrence had hoped that out of the bartering at the Paris Peace Conference there might emerge the Arab state that he and King Faisal had fought for, but by 1920, these dreams were dashed as the French and British carved up the Middle Eastern territorial spoils between them and after an unsuccessful attempt to defend Damascus from the French, Faisal himself had been driven into exile, leaving Lawrence deeply depressed that their heroic efforts had in the end come to naught. He had wanted to write an account of the Arab campaign for some time and when his growing fame led to the offer of a research fellowship at All Souls College in Oxford with £200 a year, which would allow him to concentrate on his book, he accepted it. Even in Oxford however, he was hounded by the press, and in December 1919 while changing trains at Reading Station, his manuscript was stolen, obliging him to start the entire book again. Lionel Curtis, who was a fellow of All Souls, informed Baker of Lawrence's plight and Baker offered Lawrence his old flat on Barton Street if he wished to use it. He guaranteed that his staff would be sworn to secrecy and Lawrence would be free to come and go as he pleased. So, in February 1920, as Baker later wrote, "He found a haven of peace in the attic of my office in quiet secluded Barton Street."[27]

After Lawrence's death in 1935, Baker presented a paper, as one of his friends, to a symposium held in his memory[28] which provides an insight into the unusual relationship between the then 58-year-old architect and the 32-year-old leader of the Arab Revolt—

> He refused all service and comfort, food, fire or hot water; he ate and bathed when he happened to go out.... He worked time-less and sometimes round the sun; and once, he said, for two days without food or sleep, writing at his best, until he became delirious. He wrote most of the "*Seven Pillars of Wisdom*" there. He usually slept by day and worked by night; in airman's clothes in winter cold.... On summer evenings we would tramp the traffic-free London streets, talking of our likes or dislikes of buildings old and new; returning to a late supper; or alone he would wander in the shadow of the night.... He could not be induced to tell of his adventures in the War, except in his kindness to my young son; or as a bait to draw out the adventures of others.... When I took him to see the brasses of Cobham Church, with which I was familiar, I was surprised to find that he knew, for instance, all about the number, place and condition of the beautiful early type with the inlaid Lombardic lettering ... he had something of the divine discontent of the artist, never satisfied with his work.... I felt I would have followed him, had I been younger, in any adventurous quest.

Charles Wheeler's autobiography provides a further insight into Lawrence's time in Barton Street—

> The small room in which he wrote and slept above Baker's office was littered with books. He was constantly sent new books for comment or review. He told me that one day he found it practically impossible to get into bed, so he filled his knapsack with the most recent novels and made nocturnal visits to Canons' houses in Westminster Abbey Close to deposit those volumes which he thought most suitable in the most appropriate letter-boxes.... His presence at No 14, Barton Street was kept a secret from the general public. But one morning the telephone bell rang and a voice announced: "Is Colonel Lawrence there—I am George Bernard Shaw." The duteous office boy slapped down the receiver with "Tell that to the Marines." Ten minutes later a loud knocking on the door heralded G.B.S. in person.[29]

He stayed and wrote for over a year, until shortly before he joined the RAF, during which time Baker got to know a little of his complex and troubled character. They continued to write and meet regularly throughout what remained of Lawrence's life and in one of his letters to Baker in 1925, he recalled his time above the busy drawing office—"I'll always remember Barton Street, as the best—and freest place I ever lived in: and I'm most grateful to you for having let me live in it after my odd fashion. If my Arabian book is any good the merit of providing a workshop for it is yours. If its no good then I've misapplied a part of your workshop. Its good of you to offer me its continued use : and I wish I'd evacuated it properly. All my things are yet there I'm afraid...."[30] There is a certain irony that the greatest architectural servant of the British Empire should have his office marked with a blue plaque which records only that "Lawrence of Arabia lived here."

Baker needed the lift of Lawrence's presence as his winter in India had taken its toll. In addition to the Viceroy and his committee siding with Lutyens and his own confusion over the ramp, he now had to develop a vast design for the legislative chambers which he thought absurd. To add to his anguish, he had had another fall from his horse during his

last days in Delhi and on his return to Barton Street immediately received the resignation of his chief assistant Charles Walgate, who was leaving for South Africa. His rever-
sal of fortune had been swift and painful, and it was Alex Scott who picked up the reins.
Although he had started working for Baker in 1913, Scott had been on active service from
1914 to 1918, so they had only worked together for 18 months, but Baker had already recognized his abilities and was now grateful for his support. He was quickly promoted to
chief assistant in Walgate's place, eventually becoming Baker's partner in 1929. That summer of 1920, Baker and Scott organized the Indian work together, thus providing Baker
with the chance to now focus on the work for the IWGC and their other memorials.

Blomfield's first war cemeteries had been completed to public acclaim, and so with
a few modifications and the conclusion of the debate regarding the design of the headstones, work on both the cemeteries and the memorials now proceeded apace. The cemeteries were the first priority as many families were now visiting France and Belgium to
view their loved ones' graves only to find Ware's fading wooden crosses within roughly
fenced burial grounds. In total, Baker was responsible for the construction of 112 cemeteries and seven memorials to the missing, with the overwhelming majority of the cemeteries carried out by AIFs under his supervision. Baker had actually been one of the first
to identify the need to commemorate "the unidentified dead" and had raised the issue
with Ware as far back as July 1917. Unidentified bodies in cemeteries were to be buried under a headstone bearing the inscription "Known unto God" but almost half of all
the empire's soldiers killed in the conflict—over half a million soldiers—were "missing"
rather than unknown. The commission agreed that memorials should be erected to them
bearing their names as near as possible to where they fell.

Baker personally designed the cemeteries and memorials at Tyne Cot (the largest
of all the First World War cemeteries with almost 12,000 graves), Caterpillar Valley, Cite
Bonjean, Delville Wood, Dud Corner, Neuve Chappelle and V. C. Corner. The cemeteries varied in layout but almost all were symmetrical with a War Stone, a Cross of Sacrifice
and an entrance building or gateway placed in varying relationships to each other largely
depending on the terrain. Baker's memorials, with the exception of his later memorial
to the Indian Army at Neuve Chapelle, were all in similar Kentish churchyard style, in
complete contrast to his memorials in South Africa. At Kimberley and Devil's Peak, Baker's designs were monuments to the dead, but they were also symbols of Britain's imperial might, designed to overawe their native viewers with the power and sophistication of
their conquerors. In his First World War memorials, Baker's aim was entirely different.
He believed his task in France "was to beautify the hallowed resting-places of our Dead;
and, even when they slept on hard-won battle-ground, to glorify the victory rather than
the sacrifices seemed to savour of that undue pride which the Greeks called *hubris*....
An English churchyard was always the idea in my thoughts ... its trees and gardens surrounded by stone walls with an arched gateway and chapel, perhaps, and covered cloister walks. This sentiment seemed better to express the British feeling for their honoured
Dead than the intellectual Grand Manner."[31] While sincere, and sensitive to the feelings
of many of the families who had lost their loved ones, unfortunately, achieving the intimacy of a village churchyard was almost impossible when the graves were numbered in
the thousands.

At Tyne Cot, Baker designed both the cemetery and the memorial "on the muddy
ridge of stricken Passchendaele ... called Tynecot by Northumberland regiments.... It
was laid out around the graves of those buried on the field of battle near the biggest of

many blockhouses. I was told that the King, when he was there, said that this block-house should remain … a pyramid of stepped stone was built above it, leaving a small square of the concrete exposed in the stonework…. On the pyramid we set up on high the War Cross; thus from the higher ground at the back of the cemetery the cross can be seen from across the historic battlefields."[32] Like most of Baker's memorials, it takes the form of a long wall, here semi-circular in knapped flint on a plinth of dressed stone and capped with two courses of stone slates. Set into the face of the wall are stone panels inscribed with the names of the missing. It is pierced on axis by a finely judged Doric colonnade and terminated by stone open-arched domed pavilions with a carved sheltering angel topping each. As in all the cemeteries, the architecture is complemented by carefully selected planting and while lacking the intimacy of an English churchyard, he successfully achieved an extraordinary air of tranquility, even at the scale of Tyne Cot. It was finally unveiled on the 20th of June 1927.

After Tyne Cot, the largest is Dud Corner at Loos, commemorating men missing at the battles of Loos and Bethune. Unlike Tyne Cot and most of his other cemeteries, here the memorial walls carrying the name panels form the enclosing side walls of the entire cemetery terminating in blank Doric pavilions engraved with the name of the cemetery on either side of the roadside entrance. At the far end he designed two pairs of domed pavilions, surmounted by carved crowns, each pair linked by a colonnade behind which are semi-circular open courts, the walls of which also carry further name panels. In the center of the rear boundary a third semi-circular wall encloses the Cross of Sacrifice and drops down to provide a release from the enclosure and a long view across the plain on which the battles took place. The entire structure is in cream ashlar with the walls topped in slate once more. The memorials at V. C. Corner, Fromelles and at Caterpillar Valley, Longueval, are on a much smaller scale. In both cemeteries one boundary wall supports stone panels on which are inscribed the names, and Baker placed a small pavilion at each end of the wall to provide shelter. Unfortunately, the mix of ashlar, undressed stone and

Baker's perspective of Tyne Cot Cemetery (courtesy Michael Baker).

slate as well as their detailing is overly complex and much less successful. The smallest of his memorials, also to New Zealand troops, is in Cite Bonjean Cemetery in Armentieres where 47 names are simply inscribed on a panel in the boundary wall.

At Delville Wood, Baker had already designed the cemetery when in 1920 the South African government purchased the woods (then just blackened stumps) to create a national memorial on the site of the most costly engagement which the South African Brigade had fought on the western front. Of the 3,150 men who defended the woods, only 768 survived. Baker was their natural choice as architect, and he rewarded them with one of his best memorials: an elegant and extremely dignified design in just flint and ashlar with his architecture combining with a (now mature) replanted oak avenue to provide a place of tranquility, reflection and commemoration. The central archway is "crowned with a flat dome on which is set a bronze group of two men in the pride of youth holding hands in comradeship above a warhorse."[33] These symbolize the Dutch and English races once more, who so soon after their own conflict, fought together against a common enemy of their shared sovereign. It was unveiled by Mrs. Annie Botha, widow of Louis, amidst a dramatic thunderstorm on the 10th of October 1926.

The South African War Memorial, Delville Wood, France (author's collection).

Baker later recalled that among "the many little cemeteries designed by me and built by our happy band of architects and engineers, and planted and cared for by our skilled and devoted gardeners and botanists, I remember with the greater pleasure some rustic scenes near small French farms and villages, and in the flat lowlands near the Rue du Bois. Some were partly surrounded by wide stretches of water; and one especially dear to me was Le Trou Aide Post, on the site of an old grange, within a four-square moat where lilies and yellow iris grew in its clear water overhung by weeping willows which chequered with shade its smooth grass banks."[34] One can sense Baker's relief to be working with a "happy band" of architects and engineers who respected him, his abilities and experience. It was a world away from Delhi. Where there had been war, there was now peace—a peace that Baker longed for in the rest of his professional life. But for Lutyens, his campaign was far from over.

For Lutyens, Baker's offer to drop his opposition to his proposed changes to Government Court represented a further opportunity to revive his proposals. Unusually, he had avoided immediately rushing into combat, realizing that pursuing the matter directly with the Viceroy while in India was unlikely to succeed where he had already failed before, so he had bided his time until his return to England where he approached Sir Claude Hill who had now returned from India and been appointed to the Home Advisory Committee in London. Hill, when hearing of Baker's change of stance, was convinced by Lutyens that this new circumstance merited reporting to the committee, where the reopening of the debate could at least be considered. Emboldened once more, Lutyens even informed a correspondent of *The Times* that the design of the ramp was about to be "corrected."

The two architects engaged in a prolonged ping-pong of letters throughout the correspondingly cool summer of 1920. Baker, exasperated, at the end of May wrote, "The more we meet and talk about the job the better, but for heavens sake do not let us start file making."[35] To which Lutyens responded the following day, "If you find you are unable to meet my principle of plan as regards Delhi I shall & it will be with great regret know that the chance of our working together is impossible—so we had better & shall in future as in the past keep our respective & allotted spheres of design."[36] In June, Baker knocked the ball back stating, "Surely you cant mean what you imply in your letter that, because the point of the Government Court has been decided against you by the Government, and that I do not think it right to take the initiative of reopening it, you will refuse to work together in future on Delhi? Just think it over—is not it rather a childish attitude to say that because you cant always get your own way, you wont 'play' any more. I have given way to you in nine cases out of ten when we have differed and raised no criticism in many more."[37] Lutyens was unmoved.

With construction on-site in Delhi still hardly recovered from the war, to Baker's relief, it was agreed that there was no need for the architects to arrive for their winter visit before January 1921. Baker was able to spend Christmas at Owletts before leaving for India on the 6th of January, arriving in Delhi on the 23rd. When he surveyed the building site the next day he was appalled by the lack of progress since his last visit. The original program for the construction of the Secretariats and Government House anticipated completion in 1917 with final accounts closed in 1918. What Baker saw in January 1921 was that, while the Processional Way had been largely completed and planted and the Great Place below the Secretariats was almost complete, his Secretariats were only two-fifths constructed, Government House a third built and the bungalows three-fifths.[38]

What was even worse was that work on the principal buildings had now all but stopped with only the residences progressing at any meaningful pace. Baker and his team had been working on the design of the legislative chamber for almost a year and yet even the foundation stone was not due to be laid until the following month. Discussions with Keeling revealed that wage and material inflation created by the war had continued to increase, coupled with the need to fund the new legislative chamber which had not originally been planned. Keeling even floated the idea of retaining the red sandstone lower floors of the state buildings but completing the upper levels in rendered brick rather than stone, which, apart from radically altering their designs, would require the architects to completely re-detail the upper floors of their buildings. For Baker, Delhi had transmogrified from a glittering prize to a recurring nightmare in which he returned to India each winter to achieve less and less and suffer more and more.

One of Baker's Chattris at the base of "The Ramp" (author's collection).

As if all this wasn't bad enough, the slowing of the pace of construction was now so severe that his shared fee with Lutyens would no longer be sufficient to cover their costs and if they continued to service the projects, it would soon be at their own expense. Far from helping, Lutyens had just commissioned and paid for a new model of his proposed revisions to the ramp from their shared account which he refused to even let Baker see. Baker broached the subject of fees with Keeling, even suggesting he would have to stop work if the matter could not be quickly resolved and Keeling advised him to write formally to the committee, setting out his case and stressing its urgency.

Baker eventually persuaded Lutyens to sign a joint letter to the committee which he had drafted, which sought additional fee payments to cover both the prolongation of their appointment and the extra work instructed including the massive legislative chamber building. The committee's response was unusually swift on this occasion as Baker reported to his wife in his letter of the 22nd of February—"The Gov't of India have very arbitrarily refused, to sanction our claim for war losses.... I mean to fight it here before I go—Lutyens is no use in such things & would not mind seeing me ruined—I think I deserve it for not blindly following the heavensent genius."[39] From Baker's perspective, while previously thinking that Delhi couldn't get any worse, he now faced losing an estimated £4,000 as well as his professional reputation and, he must have occasionally thought, his sanity. As with all Delhi matters, this proved to be but the first round of a long and further debilitating series of claims, negotiations and multiple approvals before the request for additional fees was finally resolved.

Baker finally saw Lutyens' model of the revised ramp for the first time when Lutyens presented it at the New Capital Committee meeting on the 3rd of March and its presentation was merely noted by the committee. In a last attempt to win Lord Chelmsford's approval before his departure, Lutyens wrote him a long and detailed plea on the 6th followed up by a similar letter to Lady Chelmsford a few days later, but to no avail. The Earl of Reading was to take up his new appointment as Viceroy on the 2nd of April and, unbeknownst to the architects, awaiting him on his desk among many more important matters was the report from Edwin Montagu setting out the Home Advisory Committee's views on the ramp for his consideration.

Baker's last weeks in Delhi were spent in something close to desperation as his letters home expressed—"Ending the day in despair again. Keeling been in suggesting radical alterations in the plan of the Sect's which if accepted would mean tearing up the whole set & starting again—This I would not do and would rather chuck the job altogether ... it is all monstrous."[40] With little further to be achieved, Baker set sail for England on the 19th of March relieved to be leaving both Lutyens and Delhi behind him. His ship docked at Aden on the way home, where he "found a letter from Cecil Lubbock, whom I had only once met before, asking me to see him on my return. My surprise was great."[41] At one of the lowest points in his professional career, Baker had landed the rebuilding of the Bank of England.

11

1921–1925

"Merchant Adventurers"

The bank had been considering the redevelopment of their site in the city for some time. Their existing buildings had been constructed over the preceding two hundred years and no longer served their needs or symbolized an institution whose status as the world's leading bank was now under challenge. The Federal Reserve Bank of New York had recently opened for business in their brand-new state-of-the-art building on Liberty Street in November 1914. In comparison, the stately single-story banking halls of the Bank of England, which were now becoming dwarfed by their surrounding buildings, looked and felt like a throwback to the 18th century. The Federal Reserve Bank's new building thus appeared to look confidently to the future, while the Bank of England's staterooms and cloistered courtyards merely celebrated a glorious past.

Most of the bank's development during the mid- and later 19th century had been focused on building regional branches (including Sir Charles Cockerell's exceptionally fine banks in Manchester, Liverpool, Bristol and Plymouth), while the bank's staff and resources in London had quadrupled from one to over four thousand during this period and were scattered around the city in various offices. By the start of the First World War, the Court of Directors who oversaw the bank's activities had decided that a new London Headquarters building was now a necessity, both to allow them to compete effectively with the upstart Americans and to express their own confidence in their future global role and status.

By the end of the war, the fact that the bank was considering rebuilding had been common knowledge in architectural circles for some time (of which Lutyens had got wind). In November 1916 the bank created a building committee which included the governor, then Lord Cunliffe, his deputy and four further members of the Court of Directors including Charles Lubbock. In January 1917 they asked the RIBA to recommend names of prominent architects to participate in a limited competition. By now, our friend Sir Reginald Blomfield had succeeded Newton as president of the RIBA, and he advised both that they should appoint a technical assessor (modestly offering his own services at 2 guineas per hour), and also that the competition should be delayed, "as so many architects were involved in war work."

Little progress was made during the war years, and it was only when Montagu Norman took over as governor of the bank in 1920 that momentum very quickly built. Norman, who without precedent remained at the helm for the next 24 years throughout the rebuilding of the bank, had a clear vision of what he required. He was "determined to

Robert Taylor's "Court Room" in the Bank of England (courtesy the Bank of England Archive).

return the City and the Bank to its pre–1914 glory days, when the City stood at the centre of global finance and the Bank of England's prestige, power and independence were a function of its control over gold-backed sterling."[1] Though from an old Bank of England family, he also represented a new generation of directors who were differentiated from their predecessors by "their degree of cultivation ... university educated, collectors and connoisseurs, and fully capable of grasping the symbolic import of the Bank of England's architecture."[2] In May 1920, he replaced the previous rebuilding committee of eight with a new committee of three—Cecil Lubbock, member of the Court of Directors since 1909 as chair, along with George Booth and Alan Garrett Anderson. It was these three who soon selected Baker as their architect.

But first, before considering an appointment or competition, they wished to clarify their own thoughts. To assist them they appointed Aberdonian Francis William Troup

(1859–1941) who had established his own practice in London and by 1920 had already completed the remodeling of the old St. Luke's Hospital for the bank as their printing works and provided a very large new office for them in Blackfriars House (1913–17). Troup was invited to explore and advise on the strategic options for the redevelopment of the institution and to investigate how much accommodation could be provided on their Threadneedle Street site, and specifically, whether or not all the bank's London staff could be brought together there. By early 1921 he had produced four studies complete with models. Of these, three saw the demolition of everything within Soane's perimeter wall with five-story blocks arising immediately behind the wall and central sections rising to eight stories high while one retained many of Soane and Taylor's perimeter banking halls but with higher central blocks and windows punched through the perimeter wall at street level. All four retained the historic Garden Court and also responded to the historic rights of light enjoyed by the surrounding buildings which required that any building elements over five-stories tall should be set back from the site's boundary.

On the 3rd of March 1921, Charles Lubbock was able to provide a full and considered report to the Court of Directors which proposed a way forward, concluding, "We have suggested that the existing exterior walls, that is to say, the existing exterior elevation, should, if possible, be retained. We recognise that this suggestion imposes limitations upon our new building and that it might be preferable, from the point of view of architectural design, that the site should be entirely cleared for the new building. We do not feel competent to make a definite recommendation on this point without expert advice, and we ask the Court to authorise our selection of an architect of outstanding reputation, who should be asked to report and advise us upon this question on terms which would be without prejudice to any subsequent step that the Court may decide to take."[3] The minutes of the Court of Director's meeting recorded, "The Court approved a Report from the Committee authorizing the selection of an Architect with whom they could discuss and elaborate plans, and to assist in deciding whether the new building should retain the existing walls or be built on a cleared site."[4]

Lubbock had considered an architectural competition but concluded that he had no wish for a jury of architects to force an architect upon the bank and further that any outline designs provided in a competition could be no more than indicative, requiring the selected architect and the bank to more or less start again together, after the architect's selection. (Here, both Lutyens and Baker would, for once, have strongly agreed.) As he had advised the directors, Lubbock wanted an outstanding architect to advise them and in that context the three principal architects already selected by the Imperial War Graves Commission were the front runners, with Baker and Lutyens' profile, thanks to Delhi, placing them ahead of Blomfield, and so Lubbock sounded out clients who had worked with them both.

Neither Baker nor Lutyens had then designed a bank, and so neither had either direct experience nor apparently many contacts in the city. (Lutyens' regular future banking client Reginald McKenna, who was married to one of the Jekylls, had become chairman of the Midland Bank in 1919 but would not employ Lutyens to design a bank for him until 1926.) On this occasion, it was to be Baker's network of increasingly influential friends, rather than Lutyens' family connections, which almost certainly gained him the appointment.

Robert Brand, who had already helped steer Pretoria Station and the Union buildings in Baker's direction in South Africa, was now the managing director of Lazard Brothers and on the board of both the North British Insurance Company and Lloyds Bank. Brand's fellow director at Lazards, Sir Robert Kindersley, was a member of the bank's Court of Directors. Lord Selbourne, Baker's friend and client for Government House in Pretoria, was also then a director of Lloyds while both Brand and Baker's closest friend from his Johannesburg days, Lionel Hichens, was a member of the Political Economy Club along with Cecil Lubbock. Lubbock would certainly have been reassured that Baker could be trusted for the bank whereas Lutyens' reputation was already established in London as being that of a willful and intellectually lightweight architectural genius. (Jane Ridley suggesting, "They wanted an architect not a court jester.")[5] As Daniel M. Abramson explained in his excellent book, *Building the Bank of England: Money: Architecture: Society: 1694–1942*, Baker was not just the most professionally capable, but equally importantly, he was the most socially compatible. He was, to quote Abramson, "A gentleman in the same mould as the Bank of England Directors, like Lubbock the classical scholar, and Booth the connoisseur of the arts. Architect and client understood each other socially and culturally, important supplements to Baker's professional abilities." Indeed, "Baker was perhaps the most rational choice of architect the Bank of England had made in two hundred years. Baker gained the commission on reputation and merit, not through extensive prior connection to the Bank directorate, like Taylor, Soane or Cockerell. Nor did Baker's selection raise questions of adequate training, experience and social standing…. Baker's experience in the planning and design of prestigious monumental public office buildings exactly suited the programme for the rebuilding of the Bank of England."[6] Thus Charles Lubbock wrote to Baker who was then in India, inquiring as to whether or not he was "prepared to advise the Bank on the question," whether the "existing exterior elevation of the Bank should be preserved … even at the sacrifice of some convenience? …or (on the other hand) ought the site to be cleared to make way for an entirely new building?"[7] Baker was, indeed, prepared to advise them.

He had returned to Owletts on the 3rd of March and on the 14th met Francis Troup in the morning to review his work before his first meeting with the Rebuilding Committee that afternoon. The following day he was shown around the existing building for the first time. What he found was a rabbit warren of courts and banking halls which had grown up piecemeal as the bank's needs had grown and as they had acquired more and more of their present site between the main entrance on Threadneedle Street and Lothbury Street to its north. It had expanded exponentially from what was originally a small private bank established to act as banker to the government on the 1st of April 1694, and in 1734 it had moved to its present site when George Sampson was appointed as their first architect. He had provided a series of Classical palazzos for the bank, which stepped back northwards from Threadneedle Street with courtyards separating a series of bank buildings. From these first buildings (completely lost by 18th- and 19th-century reconstruction and expansion), the bank's subsequent architects had responded to its growing and changing needs. It was only during Sir John Soane's tenure that the northern part of the site had been finally acquired thus allowing him to wrap the entire complex in a two-story high blank decorated stone wall which had come to represent the public image of the bank for the next 100 years.

The majority of what Baker saw on his visit was the work of Soane who had been architect to the bank between 1788 and 1833. Baker immediately acknowledged the quality of Soane's work and from that first visit throughout his work on the bank resolved to save or reinstate as much of it as he possibly could while also producing a new bank building which was fit for the 20th century. What is generally regarded as Soane's model of toplit vaulted banking halls was actually developed by Soane's predecessor Robert Taylor. Taylor's Three Per Cent Transfer Office of 1765–68 contains almost every element for which Soane is held to be famous at the Bank of England, including a lath and plaster–domed ceiling pierced with three circular drum rooflights surrounded by a further toplit colonnade, thus first converting one of the bank's then traditional open-air courtyards into an interior space. Within his first 10 years as the bank's architect, Soane replaced Taylor's fine Broker's Exchange Rotunda, Bank Stock Office and Four Per Cent Office, all of which were rebuilt in a style for which Taylor's Reduced Annuities Office forms a clear and original precedent.

As Soane's great exterior wall to the bank (which Cockerell had raised to provide a patrol rampart during his term of office) was windowless, most of the interior spaces were toplit or served by clerestory lighting with a series of elegant courtyards (particularly Soane's fine Lothbury Court) providing the only side-lighting within the complex. At the heart of these internal and external spaces was the historic Garden or Cemetery Court (which had been used for several burials) which continued to give this now great bank something of the character of a Georgian town house rather than a major financial institution. It was chaotic, picturesque, very English, extraordinarily beautiful in places and entirely unsuitable for modern banking. Though there were many contemporary voices who were sad at the loss of so many architecturally important spaces, there were few who proposed that this large and incredibly valuable site in the very center of London's financial district should be abandoned by the bank and Soane's work saved in its entirety for posterity; indeed it was anticipated by almost every commentator (including the contemporary trustees of the Soane Museum) that the site must be redeveloped by the bank once more, as Soane had done before.

From that first visit in April 1921, Baker was convinced, not just that Soane's external walls should be retained but also that as many of the existing interior spaces should be saved as well, and his in many ways unenviable task was to attempt to accommodate the bank's needs while doing so. For Baker, as usual, it was not simply an architectural issue. Montagu Norman wanted a new building which looked forward, but for Baker, it was equally important that the new building complex should look back as well, to celebrate and reinforce the bank's great heritage and history as an institution which stretched back to the 17th-century goldsmiths of London and their early promissory notes. For Baker, the comprehensive redevelopment of the site would not just be unpopular, he believed it would also be entirely inappropriate. Francis Troup was retained as an adviser by the bank after Baker's appointment in 1921 and spent the summer providing Baker with background information and measured drawings from which to work.

For Lutyens, it was a summer of very mixed emotions. Both architects were informed by letter on the 16th of June that the new Viceroy the Earl of Reading had considered Montagu's report on the Processional Way and decided, to Baker's relief, that "the Government of India … have come to the conclusion that the matter cannot be reopened and that the decision previously arrived at must be reaffirmed."[8] This was followed shortly after by the RIBA's presentation to Lutyens of their highest accolade, their Gold Medal for Architecture, the public popularity of the Cenotaph proving to any doubters that the award was overdue. At the presentation dinner, Lutyens was so overcome by emotion that he was unable to complete his speech and burst into tears. That was to be his reaction too when he heard the news of Baker's appointment for the Bank of England. Lady Sackville, his then client and confidante, reported that he had been unable to eat and that she had "seldom seen him so upset and white and yet he was very brave and we hardly talked about it."[9]

By July, Baker had completed his report and sent it to Charles Lubbock on the 6th, along with a supporting letter from his old Art Worker's Guild friend, William Lethaby. Baker set out his brief and went on to make his recommendations:

"The opinion, with the request for which you have honoured me, has for its reference, I understand, the following three-fold values:

1. The maximum efficient accommodation obtainable on the site.
2. The retention of the old buildings, more especially of the external walls, considered from the point of view of architecture, of historical and sentimental association, and the sense and reality of protection from the dangers and noise of the public streets.
3. An ultimate building of architectural dignity worthy to give expression to the pre-eminence of the Bank of England."

And continuing,

> It will be, I think, unnecessary for me to add my advocacy to the widely acknowledged importance from the points of view of archaeology, architecture and historical association of the retention of as much of the old building as may be possible without too much sacrifice of the other vital considerations involved. We must and can rightly assume the highest value of the old building considered both as Sir John Soane's famous masterpiece and as the historical Bank of England, but in any architectural appreciation of the architect's work, emphasis must be laid on the fact that his genius is especially distinguished in this building by his varied and ingenious treatment of domical sky-lighted construction, instances of which occur in nearly all the rooms and corridors of the Bank. They give an exceptional sense to its architecture of dignity and fitness to the purpose of the Bank. True respect can therefore be paid to the architect and his work, as well as to the historical associations of the Bank, as much by the preservation of these domical rooms as of the facades.

This is particularly significant, as the bank had previously only suggested considering the retention of Soane's wall. Baker went on to advise that there will be those who may call for the entire building to be preserved, just as there are those who propose its entire demolition to make way for a new building. He acknowledged its location "as the fount and source of the financial life of the city" and suggested that while retaining the wall will satisfy the majority, it should not be pierced, as Troup had suggested, but instead the bank should wherever possible retain Soane's toplit spaces behind it. He considers the need to set back any higher new building to respond to adjacent owners' "rights of light," suggesting this would substantiate the retention of the low domical rooms directly behind the wall and also highlighted the very real risk to the bank that any comprehensive redevelopment of the site would offer the Corporation of the City of London the opportunity to widen the surrounding streets and thus further reduce the site available to the bank. He acknowledged that if his strategy were adopted, it would inevitably mean the loss of the old Cemetery Court but concluded that it would, in any case, lose most of its current charm when surrounded by eight-story offices. He proposed instead a new, larger court, which would provide both light and air to the new higher central spaces. Taylor's surviving court rooms, which couldn't be retained in their present position, should be moved to a central position within the plan and given a new status as the conclusion to the central axis from the main entrance. A second circular court in which vans could turn with a covered porch for receiving bullion should be created with several of the old rooms rebuilt around it. Soane's famous Lothbury Court would be lost but his rotunda saved. He proposed to link the old and new "in one common façade" at the main entrance and concluded, "By the preservation and incorporation in the new building of the old external wall, of the banking halls behind it and of many other old rooms of Sir John Soane's building, should go far to meet the reasonable conservative sentiment of the public, and would enable your Court, while not ignoring its obligation as Trustees of a precious national heirloom, to develop on its traditional site a new bank which would be sufficiently large and efficiently planned to fulfil the new duties imposed upon it by the war; which without any necessary conflict of style, might record in its architecture for future generations the Bank's historical periods of growth during the two great wars of England's history and which might contain the elements of architectural dignity commensurate with the Bank's position and destiny in the City and the Empire."[10] To which Lethaby in his supporting letter added, "In regard to the exterior I am of the opinion that the present front would make a fine lower storey to any sympathetic superstructure and again I wish to speak of its valuable and historical character."[11] It was a bold, and in the circumstances, architecturally sensitive proposal which took the retention of Soane's work far beyond the expectations of the bank and it was thus received with some surprise by the rebuilding committee. Nevertheless, Lubbock instructed Baker to proceed to develop his outline plans and sections to support a formal proposal to the Court of Directors.

Any regrets at leaving South Africa or worries about the impact of Lutyens' criticisms upon his reputation must have now finally been assuaged. If he could convert his advisory role to the bank into a full commission for the design and execution of its rebuilding, combined with his completed Union buildings in Pretoria and his Secretariats and legislative chamber in Delhi, it would be he rather than Lutyens who would be seen by many of his peers as the leader of his generation of British architects. Baker had come to Lubbock highly recommended but as they worked together through the autumn and winter of 1921, he gained Lubbock's respect both as a man and as a valued, thoughtful and rational architectural adviser. Lubbock was impressed by Baker's grasp of the project in all its complexities, his sensitivity to both the existing architecture and the culture and traditions of the bank, and his ability to work confidently at this scale and to build effective relationships with the three committee members and the other staff of the bank whom he consulted. By the end of the year, Lubbock was convinced that they had found the right man to take the project forward.

In June Baker visited France once more, accompanied for the first time by Florence, who was just as affected by the mass graves as Baker had been in 1917. While visiting Baker's Tincourt New British Cemetery near Peronne, Florence came across a Mrs. Warren who had traveled from England to visit the grave of her son Albert who had died fighting on the Somme. As Baker recalled, the "poor woman" was "shivering in the cold rain. For two years she had saved her mites to visit the grave of her son; and instinctively she turned to my wife for sympathy and comfort," and so, "I urged that there should be in all cemeteries, even the smallest, some little building, both as a shelter from the weather and a resting-place for thought and prayer."[12] With funds once more now available thanks to his work for the bank, from this point onward, Baker took Florence or one of his sons with him on most of his visits to France.

In early October the rebuilding committee reported to the Court of Directors out-lining Baker's advice on the retention of both Soane's wall and banking halls along with an outline design by Baker and their own commentary. In addition to retaining many of the existing banking halls, Baker also proposed continuing the pattern of toplit banking halls around most of the circumference of the site behind the screen wall with the higher blocks set back except over the main entrance, where a new higher-level portico stepped forward over Soane's original. The original Cemetery Court was lost, but replaced with a large new Garden Court while Soane's Tivoli Corner (inspired by the Temple of Vesta in Tivoli), which he had originally planned as a second public entrance to the bank, was cast as an entrance once more and now led to a new domed toplit internal circular court. It was a beautifully resolved and very elegant plan, which combined the existing with the new in a single seamless composition. The Court of Directors was extremely surprised by the proposed retention of so much of the original building, with several opposed to even the retention of Soane's wall which they believed constrained future options and failed to provide the new image for the bank which they believed to be one of the main purposes

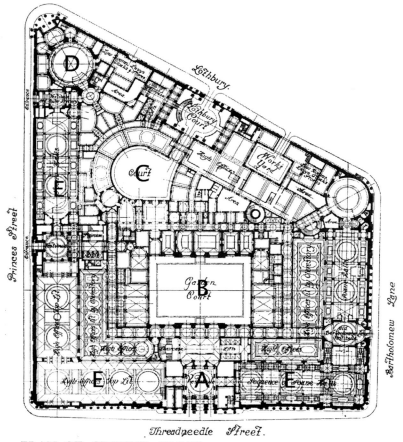

PLAN OF GROUND FLOOR

Ground floor plan of the Bank of England. Key: A Main Entrance, B Garden Court, C Bullion Court, D Tivoli Corner, E Banking Halls (from *Architecture and Personalities*).

of their proposed investment. No conclusions were reached at the meeting and at the end of October, the rebuilding committee asked Baker for further information on the option of a full demolition.

On the 12th of December 1921, Baker presented his second report to the rebuilding committee which considered full demolition, as requested. He acknowledged that demolition and the construction of an entirely modern building would certainly fulfill the bank's functional requirements but suggested that a modern office building would be entirely inappropriate for such a venerable institution and would lose any association with the bank's unique history. He again warned that the demolition of Soane's wall would provide an opportunity for the City of London Corporation to widen the pavements of both Threadneedle Street and Princes Street thus reducing the available site area and reminded the directors that any new building would have to step back before it could rise higher than a few stories due to the surrounding properties' rights of light. He explained that, bearing these issues in mind, any new building would in all likelihood take the same form as his existing proposals which managed to retain much of the original. He acknowledged the advantages to an architect of a clear site and free hand to design but concluded, "In the partial self-suppression which would be imposed by the retention of portions of the existing building, the architect would not only mete out some measure of justice to his great predecessor and to a monument of the past history of the nation, but with the help of his patrons might achieve the distinction of crystallising in one great work of art the spirit both of the past and the present."[13] He acknowledged that his initial scheme fell somewhat short of the capacity required to accommodate all the bank's employees on the site and that a new building could achieve this and so, with considerable regret, offered a new plan which sacrificed Soane's rotunda to allow him to increase the overall accommodation thus fulfilling his brief without the wholesale demolition proposed. It was, like his earlier letter to *The Times* on the subject of an appropriate architectural style for Imperial Delhi, a finely judged, entirely rational and extremely persuasive narrative. His report was conveyed to the Court of Directors where his well-reasoned case proved impossible to withstand and thus he saved much of Soane and Taylor's work from the destruction proposed by several of the directors of the bank and the partial destruction of Soane's walls (including his Tivoli Corner) proposed by the Corporation of London. He deserves to be lauded for that achievement.

On Monday the 10th of January Charles Lubbock advised him that the Court of Directors had approved his proposal and that he should proceed to prepare drawings for release to the press. The bank representatives themselves were only too well aware of the controversy that their plans were likely to generate and while their course was now set, they wished to minimize opposition by being as transparent as possible as to what was proposed, explaining their rationale, and seeking the widest achievable public and professional support for their strategy before any of the necessary demolitions commenced. It was a much happier and confident Herbert Baker who, accompanied by Florence for the first time, caught the train for Marseilles and India on Wednesday the 12th, now suitably fortified for a further few months of Lutyens.

That visit of early 1922 proved to be something of a watershed in many ways. Both architects, having spent Christmas at home, were now accompanied by their wives. Baker, as Lutyens had done the previous year, now took a new house (5 Hastings Road) where Florence would join him again on several occasions. For Herbert it proved to be a satisfactory retreat from the office which he still shared with Lutyens. There was yet another new Viceroy, Lord Reading, whom Baker had yet to meet, but who it was said regarded the entire Imperial Delhi project as a waste of public money. The new Indian Legislative Assembly had started to meet, thus providing a further source of criticism as to the cost of the new capital, and within weeks they had already suggested that the construction of Baker's legislative chamber should be halted and resumed with three local Indian architects designing each of the chambers. The first month of the Bakers' visit that year was overwhelmed by preparations for a visit of the heir to the imperial throne, the Prince of Wales (later briefly Edward VIII) that February. Demands for Indian independence were growing louder and louder to such an extent that prior to the prince's visit to Calcutta, over 10,000 arrests were made and the "prince arrived to an unprecedented level of policing, with armored cars patrolling the side streets and a cordon around the entire city."[14] Some activities were unchanging however, and construction continued at a snail's pace with Baker musing that with the foundations of the legislative chamber now commenced it would soon catch up with the construction of the Secretariats (it actually overtook them) and of course, there was always Lutyens' pursuit of the amendment of the ramp.

With the establishment of the New Capital Committee the previous year, many of the issues which had previously been taken to the committee for discussion were now delegated to Keeling the chief engineer, whom Baker now referred to in his letters home as "our leader." Keeling had been tasked by Lord Reading to find savings, and at their first meeting in February he informed Baker that the towers of his Secretariat buildings were to be omitted and that he should prepare himself for further cost-cutting. It was grim news to pass on to Scott when he arrived a few days later. The Prince of Wales visit to view the buildings was an equally depressing affair. Baker recorded in his diary that "he showed little imagination or interest in the design"[15] and at the end of the visit the prince concluded that the entire project was a waste of money and ought to be stopped. Lutyens found the prince to be "nervous and bored, certainly self-conscious," and his presentation of the model of Government House was greeted with the prince's only comment of "Good God!"[16]

In the context of this financial environment, only someone with Lutyens' combination of dogged determination and political naivety would have considered raising the issue of the ramp once more, but despite already having received Lord Reading's decision in writing the previous summer, he scheduled a further discussion for the New Capital Committee meeting on the 3rd of March. Keeling allowed Lutyens to put his case once more and present the model which he had had made to show his proposed revisions before revealing that his team had produced a revised cost estimate for carrying out Lutyens' alterations in the sum of £166,650. (The entire budget for Government House was £500,000.) It was a staggering additional cost for a project on which their client was already seeking savings, and Baker knew that finally, at long last, after almost 10 years of frustration, the game was up. Despite Keeling's estimate, Lutyens' letters show that, astonishingly, he still maintained a lingering hope that Lord Reading would agree to his revisions, but his mood—so triumphant in the last two winters—was now one of utter despair in which he contemplated resignation, rather than as he saw it, having his professional reputation ruined. Lady Emily, now in Madras, gave him blunt advice regarding his proposed resignation—"You have made one big blunder and you *must* pay for it. Be a man and stand up to your own mistake. You are perfectly right to make your protest and do everything you can to get the matter altered but when once you are beaten take it like a man."[17] Lutyens now finally accepted that he had lost, but resolved rather than "taking it like a man" to do everything in his power to ensure that it would be Baker who "*must* pay for it," immediately breaking off all communications, which proved to be just the start of a five-year-long sulk.

For Baker, it wasn't a victory, but merely the conclusion of Lutyens' campaign to have their design amended. The Processional Way was largely constructed and Government Court had been saved, but he still had no agreement on additional fees, he was being required to make drastic changes to his own designs, the legislative chamber was under attack and his relationship with Lutyens was at its worst. A few days after the committee meeting his own diary recorded, "Talk with George about resignation."[18] But neither architect resigned. By the time of Baker's departure at the end of the month his towers were saved, Keeling was making optimistic noises regarding his fee claim and he had been instructed to complete the detailed design required for the legislative chamber with all haste. After a brief tour of Agra and Lahore with Florence, they sailed from Bombay on the 25th of March.

While he had been away, Cecil Lubbock had consulted the RIBA regarding Baker's approach to the redesign of the bank and also sought their views as to the possible direct appointment of an architect without competition. The president, now Paul Waterhouse, responded that Baker and the bank were "on the right lines and that he had previously formed the opinion that if ever the Bank was rebuilt it would be right to retain the outside walls and offices and build up from within."[19] He also informed Lubbock that he saw no reason why the bank should not now appoint Baker directly. On the 15th of June, the Court of Directors approved Baker's outline design and agreed that their proposals should be given the widest possible publicity, and to cap an incredibly positive month, on the following day, he (and Lutyens) received a letter from Keeling enclosing a further letter from Alexander Brebner, Under Secretary to the Government of India, in which Brebner stated, "I am directed to inform you that, at the request of Sir Edwin Lutyens the question referred to above (*Revision of Processional Way*) has again been examined by the Government of India. As a result of this examination it was decided, not to reopen the question, but to reaffirm the decision previously made against any modification of the accepted design."[20]

A few days later, Baker extended an olive branch to Lutyens (though now from a position of considerable strength)—"It was so stupid; you wouldn't speak to me on the voyage home … we have got to get through together—cant we talk over lunch one day—here if you will come—or at the club … lets do that at all events, there's a good Lutyens that once was."[21] To which Lutyens responded with a largely delusional diatribe listing Baker's offences, opening with—"I used to count on you as one of my best friends, and a man I held in great affection, but I cannot help feeling that a great deal of my work in Delhi has been wasted and spoilt because I trusted to your loyal co-operation; and that this trust has been misplaced" and going on to blame Baker for rejecting his original city plan on the plain, ignoring his protests against raising the central buildings onto Raisina Hill, causing much of his extra work in reducing the size of Government House to pay for the cost of building on the hill, and concluding with, "It can never be 'glad confident morning again.'"[22] To which Baker responded (with a now I think excusable smugness)—"I am very distressed that in your letter of the 4th July you should have reopened the controversy which should now after this final decision of the Government of India be looked upon as closed and loyally accepted by both of us … if, as you say, there has been a 'colossal artistic blunder,' it is one for which you must share the responsibility … the rest of your letter is in my opinion full of mis-representations…. Do I pray you cease flogging a dead horse, so that nothing may prevent us concentrating our full energies on the vital interests of our work together at Delhi, which has suffered by this controversy."[23] Lutyens concluded their exchange of letters on the 20th—"I see no hope or usefulness in continuing this correspondence, nor why we need meet at lunch, I am sorry our views are incompatible.... The Government admit they know nothing about architectural design and like kittens when their eyes open the question will open automatically—so that's that."[24] Baker had now done all that could be reasonably expected of a partner and Christian gentleman and thus accepted Lutyens' silence.

On the 25th of July, Baker's plans for the rebuilding of the bank were published widely in all the daily newspapers, the architectural press and various other journals including *Country Life* and the *London Illustrated News*. The proposed changes to a much-loved institution, as the directors had correctly anticipated, caused considerable debate over the next few months in the form of editorials and much reader correspondence. The general consensus was voiced by the conservative *Daily Telegraph*, who pronounced, "The Bank as designed is finished. The dead hand ought not to stand in the way of the fulfilment of modern needs.... The directors are not dealing with a prairie site; but with the particular area of land that is most coveted in all London, and the ideal of what might be knocks hardly against the severely practical matter of what is ... and none need envy them their grave responsibility."[25] *The Spectator* concurred:

> It may be taken as settled that the Bank is in urgent need of greatly increased and more conveniently arranged accommodation and that further decentralization is impracticable.... To the layman Soane's designs seem to impress a certain meagre "sadness" and, being largely carried out in plaster, his London interiors are admittedly not very festive-looking in their usually dingy condition. Certainly no work by so interesting an architect should be lightly destroyed, and the Bank authorities have instructed their architects, Mr Baker and Mr Troup, to preserve whatever of the present remarkable and historic labyrinth may be found compatible with a radical rebuilding. That surely is as far as it is reasonable for the governors to go, and those who protest that the instructions should limit the architects to doing the best that they can without disturbing Soane's work would seem to have lost all sense of proportion.[26]

While, as might be expected, *The Daily News* was more direct—"It is typical of British public method that this Bank, this family affair that is also the citadel of world finance, should in actual fact consist of a rabbit warren of small halls and offices no more than one storey in height, incorporating an old private house and a small burial ground, and encircled by a pompous architectural wall in an antiquarian style, having no relation whatever to the rooms behind it."[27]

Country Life magazine, which generally took Lutyens' part on architectural matters as a result of his close relationship with their founder Edward Hudson (and who several years later would insist that the entire building should have been preserved as a national monument), both commended the directors in having the courtesy to publish their proposals and were extremely positive in their initial coverage—noting that while "nothing could exceed the ingenuity and dignity of these domical-vaulted and top-lighted spaces. The great Rotunda is less successful," and concluding, "The claims of Taylor, of Soane, of history and sentiment are met with sympathetic skill."[28] Only *The Sphere* proposed that the building should be retained untouched while *The Builder* favored total reconstruction. Perhaps more importantly, the contemporary architectural journals were consistently positive regarding Baker's design, including *The Architect*, which was fulsome in its praise for Baker's design noting that he had:

produced order out of chaos, and that in a manner which shows the most careful consideration of the means by which the chief features of the work of Soane can be preserved and amalgamated in a structure which gives the Bank of England the additional accommodation it needs.... Where possible, Soane's work is retained and the model of the toplit banking hall, already established by Taylor prior to Soane's involvement is developed in a series of elegant halls which now form a series of domed offices which surround the higher central section.... Plus the new garden court, which despite suggestions that it is dark and dingy, is a delightful, elegant, well-lit space.... The official statement regarding the scheme which we publish leaves little ground for criticism, except that the authorities have shown themselves, if anything, over-cautious in their desire to retain Sir John Soane's work unaltered. We say this because, with all its merits, the Bank of England is not a great architectural masterpiece.... We must congratulate Mr Baker in his avoidance of the pitfalls with which such a task as his is beset, and we are glad to be able to unhesitatingly endorse the general lines on which he has suggested solving a most difficult problem. If he is entrusted—as we hope he will be—with the actual work, we hope he will not allow himself to be too much fettered by a desire to design in accordance with the precedents set by Soane. For nothing which Sir John Soane ever did convinces us that he could have produced so admirable a scheme as that prepared by Mr Baker; and while, for economy and other reasons, it is wholly right to retain much of the existing work, we may be quite sure that the architect who has designed the Secretariats at Delhi and the great South African Parliament House could erect on the site of the Bank a finer building than Sir John Soane ever dreamt of.[29]

Writing a month later, *The Architects' Journal* noted, "The great architectural question of the moment that is exciting layman and architect alike is the proposed alteration to the Bank," describing "the present plan" as "a veritable rabbit warren," and allotting "the critics of the proposals ... into three camps:

1. Those who would do away with the present building entirely.
2. Those who accept the proposals put forward in their entirety.
3. Those who agree with the retention of the outer walls of the present building, but do not consider that the treatment of the new interior blocks is the best solution of an admittedly difficult site."[30]

Importantly for Baker and the bank, the trustees of the Soane Museum, in a letter to *The Times*, accepted that "however much one may regret the disappearance of much of Soane's design of the interior, the need for increased accommodation for the business of the Bank is probably beyond dispute."[31]

By August, the bank could conclude that their architectural adviser's sensitivity to their existing historical and architectural heritage had served them well and that the launch of their inevitably controversial proposals could not have gone much better. Beyond *The Sphere* (which rather ironically for Baker was targeted at British citizens living in the colonies), the principal architectural criticism was and remained Baker's new portico over Soane's original entrance. The other aspect of the huge publicity that the launch of the new design had generated was an unexpected interest in the architect of the proposals which brought a rather startled Herbert Baker blinking into a limelight until then solely occupied by the architect of the Cenotaph. *The Daily Mail* had introduced him as "a tall slender man of 50, lean-faced, rather ascetic-looking, with the scholar's air of abstraction—that is Herbert Baker FRIBA."[32]

After the publication of the plans, the Corporation of London had sent a deputation to the bank to request that they be amended to allow for the widening of the roads and pavements on Threadneedle and Prince's streets, to reduce congestion. Baker and

Lubbock met them and explained that the bank wished to retain Soane's wall in its entirety and would be very reluctant to give up any part of their site which as it stood could only just house all their staff once the redevelopment was completed. The corporation warned the bank that they had the power to compulsorily purchase the land but (having already sought legal advice), the bank informed the corporation that if they wished to proceed to compulsorily purchase the land that they would have to compensate the bank at market value. As the bank's site was then probably the most expensive piece of real estate in Britain, the corporation withdrew their threat and the bank agreed as a concession to consider providing a public route through the Tivoli Corner to ease congestion on the pavements.

The trustees of the Soane Museum proved more difficult to shake off. Baker invited them and the museum's curator, Arthur Bolton, to visit his office to see the drawings and models and to discuss the issues, but they consistently declined to become directly involved in the process. Arthur Bolton in particular refused to engage in any way, simply taking the narrow view that all Soane's work should be preserved, and he consistently decried its destruction. Reginald Blomfield, Paul Waterhouse and Aston Webb, who were Soane trustees, "simply hated the portico" as it was in their opinions alien to the horizontality of Soane's design and they also hoped to preserve more of the interiors. For Baker, the portico was a fundamental and symbolically important element of the new bank which unified the old and the new, and he was already personally committed to saving as much of Soane's (and Taylor's) work as practically possible. Their correspondence would be sustained for over a decade through the entire rebuilding process with Arthur Bolton resolutely opposing every minor alteration of Soane's work.

With Keeling's agreement, Baker had arranged to visit Delhi earlier that winter so that he and Florence could get back in time for a family Christmas at Owletts. They left London on the 5th of October, catching the SS *China* from Marseilles the following day, and arriving in Bombay on the 20th and Delhi on the 21st. Baker's diary records that he "went straight to Lutyens but he w'd not talk to me,"[33] and now emboldened by the bank commission and the resolution of the ramp in his favor, he sought out Keeling and demanded a new and separate appointment from Lutyens (which Keeling later refused), but it was to be the bank which was to continue to occupy his thoughts while in India after he received disturbing correspondence from Lubbock on his design.

Baker's proposed new portico above the entrance was taking a lot of flak in architectural circles (led by the Soane trustees), and Lubbock proved sensitive to the criticism. Unbeknownst to Baker, he had shared his concerns with fellow rebuilding committee member George Booth in October—"As you know, Baker is in India; I do not expect him back until the beginning of the New Year." The portico "is a question which we shall have to face seriously as soon as we get together again."[34] In his letter to Baker, he shared his unease for the first time—"Naturally, it would be with great diffidence that I should put forward views of my own on architectural matters; but when I find that my own feelings are echoed and confirmed by a growing body of instructed opinion, I could hardly advise my colleagues to refrain from asking you for suggestions of alternative methods of treating the problem."[35] With his self-belief now fully restored, and without Lutyens in the opposite corner, Baker responded as he would have done to criticism of his work in South Africa—"I remain in spite of much thought, unshaken in my faith that some such feature will best link the two planes or facades of the building together, so as to give the necessary sense of unity of architectural and historical expression that when we get really to work on the design one will naturally, without prejudice to first conceptions, explore all avenues to success on this all vital problem."[36] From Baker's perspective it was a symbol of the new bank and, in sharing a plane with the existing wall, the ultimate expression of his strategy of combining the existing and the new elements of the building in a single unified composition which acknowledged both the bank's history and its continuing prospects.

The Bakers left Delhi on the 6th of December and, after a few days in Bombay, arrived back at Owletts on Christmas Eve. Herbert was back in the office in January where in the midst of all his work on Delhi and the bank, he also received his first English church commission for St. Andrew's in Great Ilford, Essex, for which he produced a very fine variation on his later South African Romanesque style, in red brick inside and out, with the finely-crafted exposed-brick interior being one of his most successful ecclesiastical spaces. (It was constructed in 1923 and consecrated the following year.) Staff numbers were increased once more and the office accounts also noted numerous overtime payments to his team. Baker now had 18 architects working on Delhi, and the lion's share of the work on the bank was yet to come. In Barton Street, Baker occupied the first-floor office overlooking the street, where as principal (as was the tradition), he worked alone. The practice was run on a strictly hierarchical basis, with Scott now clearly established as his number two and deputy when Baker was in India or France. In the context of the time, it was a friendly and sociable office with annual dinners, cricket matches and summer parties held for all at Owletts. The pay was above average, all the professional staff were salaried and there is nothing to suggest that Baker's team was anything but a loyal and relatively happy band.

While his team grappled with the production of detailed design for the legislative chamber, Baker was investing a considerable amount of personal effort in ensuring that

Baker's first-floor office in Barton Street with his perspective of "The Villa Arcadia" above the fireplace (courtesy Michael Baker).

the acoustics of the three debating chambers within it were perfect. Their semi-circular form was traditionally problematic in this context, and Baker drew on the research of Wallace Sabine of Harvard University, who had for the first time taken a scientific approach to the study of acoustics in his attempts to improve the acoustics of his university's Fogg Lecture Hall.[37] As Baker later recounted, "His principles I was able to apply to the Delhi Chambers. The panelling of the walls is convex-faceted and slopes forward, so that they reinforce the voice of the speaker instead of creating reverberations and echoes from above."[38] A governor of one of the Indian provinces later confirmed that Baker's design was so effective that, unfortunately, he could hear every word that was spoken in the chamber!

As the legislative chamber building began to rise from its foundations, there were increasing concerns being expressed regarding the architectural treatment of the building's exterior. Lutyens' great Classical colonnade was far removed from the synthesis of Western and Moghul architecture which had been the architects' aim in the other state buildings, and it was now being attacked as a symbol of British rule which completely failed to respond to Indian culture or architecture in any way. Baker, who already had his own concerns that the building's entrances in particular were completely dwarfed by the colonnade, gladly revised his design adding broad overhanging chajjas and topping each *porte cochere* with richly-carved chattris (as shown in Phillip Dalton Hepworth's perspective of 1924).

On the 1st of March 1923, the Court of Directors approved the appointment of Herbert Baker and Francis Troup as architects for the rebuilding of the Bank of England. Baker was to lead and Troup assist, providing his detailed knowledge of the operations of the bank, and later that year on Baker's recommendation, a young 36-year-old Oscar Faber whom Baker regarded very highly was appointed as their consulting engineer for this most complex of projects. In finally securing the Bank of England commission, Baker's position within his profession was assured, and to celebrate he took Florence to Italy on vacation that month for the first time.

While his strategy of retaining as much of Soane's work as possible had been approved by the Bank, there had been considerable concerns expressed by the Court of Directors that the building's operations should not be thus compromised and this was reinforced by the rebuilding committee who reminded Baker on several occasions that "the health of the staff and the suitability of the building for business purposes were important factors and must not be jeopardized by an excess of piety for Soane's work."[39] The year 1923 was therefore largely spent in convincing doubters, responding to their concerns and amending his plans accordingly. As a result, a number of minor modifications were made to the design, the most significant of which was the loss (once more) of Soane's intended entrance in the Tivoli Corner, for reasons of security. On the 1st of November the Court of Directors gave authority to the rebuilding committee to approve Mr. Baker's designs as submitted and amended and to instruct him to produce provisional contract drawings. Alex Scott was moved from leading the legislative chamber onto leading the bank with Dutchman Jan Hoogterp taking over the Indian work in London. By the end of 1923, Baker had 16 staff members working on Delhi under Hoogterp while 21 were now focused full-time on the bank under Scott. The 14 Barton Street office could no longer contain this enlarged team, and Baker was forced to rent further space in Thorneycroft House across Smith Square from Baker's own No. 2, where Hoogterp took his India team and from where India House in London was also later delivered.

Phillip Dalton's perspective of one of the *porte cocheres* of the Legislative Chamber (courtesy Michael Baker).

While construction of his cemeteries and memorials in France rolled on, in March 1923 Baker was asked to design a further memorial to commemorate the 4,843 troops of the Indian army who had fought in France and Belgium in defense of the empire. The site selected at Neuve Chapelle actually fell within Blomfield's district but, in deference to Baker's knowledge of Indian architecture, it was agreed that he should undertake this commission. The site selected for the memorial was the scene of the Indian Corps' great gallantry during the battle of Neuve Chapelle in March 1915. His design was a simple ring of stone, solid in one half to bear the names of the Indian soldiers and laborers who had served, and pierced on the other side. In the center of the pierced wall stood an Ashoka column guarded by carved stone lions, the two symmetrical entrances to the central space being via stone chattris and in its center the great War Stone. Unlike most of his other memorials, this one was completed in a single material and the consistent use of white Portland stone gives it a visual purity and sense of peace which is almost unique among all the First World War memorials. Approached from the road, the white Ashoka column is seen between two majestic weeping willows, the pierced screen then leads one on to the sacred space within, and entering through one of the chattri with a view of the other directly ahead, one is in no doubt as to the origin of the soldiers whom the memorial commemorates. As a result of a dispute over the purchase of the land for the site with a local farmer, the memorial was not completed until late in 1927.

Baker had been working with various sculptors since John Tweed had produced the large relief panel over the front entrance of Groote Schuur in the 1890s, but it was during this period when working on the various First World War memorials that he began to work almost exclusively with Charles Wheeler (1892–1974), who carved the two lions at Neuve Chapelle. Baker had designed a memorial to Rudyard Kipling's son in Kipling's local church in Burwash in Sussex and Wheeler had been commissioned to produce a bronze Madonna and child with which Baker was delighted. Since that first meeting, there had been a further commission for sculpture reliefs in the flint walls of the college memorial at Winchester and for a sculpture of St. Mary which was installed in the gable above the entrance to the cloister. In Baker's own words—"I formed the opinion that an architect should as far as possible work in close and continuous collaboration with the same artists and craftsmen. By working together year by year they may attain that full sympathy and understanding which is needed for any approach to perfection of thought, design and execution."[40]

Over the next 20 years, once again despite the generational divide, the two became close friends as well as regular collaborators. For Baker, Wheeler was a fellow artist with whom he could share his thoughts on art, poetry and literature, and being outside his profession, both offer a different perspective and be free from petty jealousies, conflicts or competition. While Baker still enjoyed close friendships with Nel Hichens, Lionel Curtis and Robert Brand among others, their interests lay elsewhere, and while he enjoyed their company and conversation, he missed the old Lutyens and their regular discussions on architecture. Encouraging and supporting Wheeler was also an opportunity for Baker to exercise a degree of artistic patronage himself, securing commissions for a fine young artist whom he regarded as having great potential, and with his own commission for the bank now secure, Baker set out to win the appointment as sculptor for the building for Wheeler.

Up to this point, Baker's dealings with the bank had been entirely with the rebuilding committee led by Cecil Lubbock, and it was Lubbock who reported their recommendations to the Court of Directors which was chaired by the governor of the Bank, Sir Montagu Norman. Following his appointment, Baker was invited to lunch with the governor himself during which Baker later recalled that there was no discussion of his commission but instead, they "talked of other things: of South Africa, where he had fought in the Boer War; of Kentish cricket, in which Normans are familiar names; and of his estate, St. Clair, which is not far from my home."[41] By the end of their meal there can have been little doubt in Norman's mind that they had chosen the right man.

Meanwhile Delhi rumbled on with another visit required that winter. The state buildings had just survived another financial inquisition led by Lord Inchcape, who, despite having previously described the move of the capital to Delhi as "a consummate blunder," now concluded that the project had gone too far with too much spent to be abandoned. Consequently, with its completion assured, work was finally accelerated on all the central buildings. Raisina Hill, at long last, became a hive of activity once more with thousands of workers again swarming over the site and its buildings. The stone yard increased its workforce to 3,000 men under master mason Cairns' direction, carving and sawing stone as their ancestors had done for conquering masters before. Baker had also gained the committee's approval to the involvement of master craftsman Joseph Armitage, who traveled to India several times to instruct the native workers in the carving of stone, plaster and wood. (The sourcing and transport of the stone was an epic tale in itself—one particular marble which came from the desert city of Jaisalmer having to be transported block by block by camel over the sand for the first 40 miles before reaching the nearest paved road.) With his dispute with Lutyens concluded (at least officially), and all the significant design decisions on both the Secretariat buildings and the legislative chamber now confirmed, it was largely architectural business as usual for Baker. Long days were spent on-site supervising the construction and setting and policing quality standards. The plain surfaces of the buff sandstone walls were now rising above the pink sandstone of the lower floors, while the columns of the great loggias were climbing sky-wards block by block in the baking heat of the strong Indian sun. Small windows were punched deep into the masonry where shadows kept the sun off their glass and soon teak shutters would be fitted to allow for cooling breezes, as in South Africa. The upper walls were double-skinned, again to help cope with the intense heat, and around the cool inner courtyards, the verandas, with their traditional Indian carved-stone screens, were nearing completion as was the "labyrinthine stage set of ingenious, vaulted staircases" whose "shadowy arches and massive masonry piers intersecting at various levels powerfully" evoked "Piranesi's emotive prison etchings."[42]

Baker spent much of his time that winter in India on the design and procurement of furniture and on the interior decoration of the Secretariat buildings. From the start of his work in Delhi (still imbued with the guild's belief in the unity of all the arts), he had promoted a number of initiatives to involve native craftsmen in the decoration of the Secretariat buildings. These included not just the production of chattris and continuous shading chujjas but also miles of the low carved-stone jaali balustrades so typical of Indian forts and temples. Stone elephants adorned the *porte cocheres* and elephant heads would soon surround his two great domes while stone balconies supported on richly carved brackets enlivened the elevations to the Great Place. Local artists were commissioned to provide mural paintings for several of the Secretariat's principal spaces and they executed their work with varying degrees of success, but for Baker their mere involvement had symbolic content. Before leaving for England it was arranged that Henry Medd would take over as Baker's resident architect from Walter George, who, of all the British architects to work on the creation of Imperial Delhi, was the only one to go on to establish his own practice in India (where he designed a number of fine churches and St. Stephen's College in Delhi).

Scott's team on the bank was now working flat out. Though still controversial, the portico had survived its initial criticism and Lubbock was now on board. A letter to *The Times* from Baker along with a supportive editorial the following day had gone a long way to convince almost everyone that it formed an appropriate link between the present and the past. Baker designed the upper floors of the new offices in a style which was likened (fairly accurately) to that of a palace or grand hotel, with the first two floors above Soane's wall rusticated with arched windows below two floors of smooth ashlar which terminated in a balustrade with two further floors of accommodation stepping back to conclude in a mansard roof. Only the pediment above the main entrance stepped forward above Soane's wall to form a new combined main entrance elevation with Soane's original main entrance doorway retained below. On Prince's Street a half-round bay broke the long elevation with a loggia to its top two floors, and behind Soane's Tivoli Corner a fine dome was raised above the new circular corner banking hall. Baker has been much criticized for also "tinkering" with Soane's external wall but as Christopher Hussey said of Lutyens' work to existing buildings, his "first care is to produce a united and homogenous whole" and he "is inclined in the process to alter the values of the original part,"[43] and this was the philosophy to which Baker also subscribed.

But the developing design and its public scrutiny was merely a part of Baker's challenge on Threadneedle Street. To add to his difficulties the bank wished to continue to operate on-site throughout its redevelopment and to also retain its stock of gold bullion there securely during construction. In the spring of 1924, the rebuilding committee considered and approved a phasing arrangement which had been developed by Alex Scott which allowed the construction work to be carried out in three phases with the bank (and their gold) staying on-site throughout the entire process. With this added level of complication, the retention of the Soane banking halls became even more difficult as excavations to three floors below street level would be required to accommodate the bank's full brief, to which had been added not only a further bullion yard but also a library and a 630-seat auditorium. Oscar Faber was desperately trying to find a structural solution which would allow the retention of the existing banking halls during the phased construction and the massive excavations that were required to provide temporary vaults. By May, he and Baker were convinced that the retention of the existing halls simply couldn't be achieved and as they were all finished in painted plaster, Baker proposed to the rebuilding committee that the originals would have to be demolished and that they should be reinstated in new plastered and painted concrete. Various alternatives were considered throughout the year but, short of the bank vacating the site, no practical alternative to demolition and reinstatement was found. Accordingly, in December 1924, "the committee again considered the question of the demolition of the Soane Halls and, after discussion, confirmed the decision made at the meeting held on the 11th instant that it would not be feasible to replace the existing stonework; Mr Baker was accordingly authorised to reconstruct these halls in concrete and plaster and, while preserving the spirit of Soane's work as far as possible, to effect such improvements in alignment, lighting &c. as may appear desirable."[44] Again, sensitive to potential public and professional criticism, in January, shortly before Baker's departure to India, the committee's minutes recorded, "Mr Baker was authorised to show the Model of the Bank at the next exhibition of the Royal Academy and the Committee agreed that it would then be necessary for them to be in a position to defend themselves against any criticism of the reconstruction of the Soane Halls; Mr Baker undertook to write an article on the subject and to arrange for photographs of the Model to be taken for publication with the article."[45]

In January 1925 (and in each subsequent year until the completion of their buildings), Baker and Lutyens set off for India *en famille*, with various children now accompanying them as well as their wives. The two groups often traveled on the same steamers with Lutyens continuing to refuse to speak to Baker throughout the journeys and also instructing his children not to speak to Baker's children. As Lutyens' daughter Mary recalled much later, "We were brought up to look on Baker as a villain who had ruined

Father's life's work. It is only now, in going into the subject, that I realise what a small matter the gradient really was and how little the loss of the level way detracts from the glory of Father's achievement."[46] In Delhi, work was now progressing apace with many decisions having to be made on the spot by the architects' local representatives to maintain progress and consequently much of Baker and Lutyens's time during these latter visits was spent providing tours of their partially completed buildings. The ultimate completion of the capital was now assured, all strategic issues were resolved and Lord Reading the Viceroy had more than enough to occupy him in dealing with the growing clamor for Indian independence. The autumn of 1924 had seen rioting throughout the country which continued into the new year with Mahatma Gandhi, the leader of the Congress Party, being released from prison in February, during their visit, after having served two years of a six-year sentence for sedition. Increased responsibilities for the day-to-day management of the new city were delegated to the Imperial Delhi Municipal Committee that spring, and in March a further milestone was reached with the retirement of Hugh Keeling, the chief engineer. He had been persuaded out of a previous retirement to undertake his role and it was agreed that as the ship that he had steered so effectively was now in calmer waters, he might be relieved of his command. His achievement had been exceptional and was recognized as such, then if not now, with the event being marked by a formal dinner hosted by the Viceroy, great bonfires being lit by the workers on-site and fireworks concluding the festivities. Finally, during this visit, the first staff moved into one wing of the northern Secretariat building to start what would be a long process of decanting from temporary accommodation to the new buildings, as completion was achieved in various phases over the next few years.

While still in Delhi, Baker learned that he had secured Charles Wheeler's appointment as sculptor for the bank and on his return to England in late March, informed Wheeler that, as Rhodes had done before for Baker, he intended to take his protégé on a tour of the Classical sites of Europe at his expense, before the two men started their work on the bank together. Baker, Florence, and their son Henry, who was now at Cambridge, set off for a vacation in Italy in April, where they were joined in Venice by Wheeler with whom Herbert and Henry continued to Greece, taking in Athens, Epidaurus, Corinth and Mycenae. Wheeler later recalled that Baker was greatly amused when he overheard an American tourist comment to his wife, *sotto voce*, "There goes an English Dean travelling with his two sons."[47]

T. E. Lawrence had now left Barton Street for the Tank Corps and Clouds Hill, his cottage in Dorset, from where he wrote, "I hope Italy was not a failure as a rest. You were looking very weary when you went, & weariness will mean failure with the Bank.... It's such a chance as few architects have ever had."[48] While their correspondence continued, Baker missed their evening walks in Westminster. On their return from Italy, in many ways, Wheeler stepped into that void too as he himself recalled—"The routine was to meet in the Victoria Gardens at 7.30, there to pace up and down under the great tower by the river discussing problems of the Arts with special reference to the Bank. Then we went in to his breakfast table to enjoy the delicious kedgeree or other equally nourishing and tasty dishes provided by his faithful Scottish housekeeper, Mrs Donat."[49] It was to be a relationship which would endure until the end of Baker's life.

That summer, construction work finally started on the bank, or to be more specific, demolition work commenced. There remained huge public interest in the rebuilding of this great British institution with the *London Illustrated News* carrying regular photographic updates on progress along with descriptions of archaeological finds, planned "electric walls" and dynamite-proof vaults. These were accompanied by editorials almost all of which continued to regret the loss of the Soane and Taylor banking halls while recognizing the bank's need to modernize and provide itself with a building which would allow it to maintain its global role in the 20th century.

There was certainly nothing in 1925 to even hint that Baker's rebuilding of the bank would eventually hang like an albatross about his neck and that he would be remembered not for what he saved, but for what was lost.

12

1925–1931

"Pageant of Empire"

The next few years were to represent the pinnacle of Baker's professional career. With the bank and his buildings in Delhi under construction, he now embarked on the design of a series of empire and church buildings in and around London, as well as a further group of buildings in Africa, which confirmed his position as one of the leading British architects of his generation. It was to be another of those intense periods of work and now in his mid-sixties, despite his extraordinary mental and physical stamina, on this occasion, it would take its toll.

Baker had hardly lifted a finger to win the bank commission and he was now to be offered another important opportunity with equally little effort. Cecil Rhodes had left the majority of his fortune to provide scholarships for young men of the empire and the USA to allow them the privilege of attending Oxford University, as he had briefly done himself. The scholarships had been overseen by the Rhodes Trust and administered by the Trust's general secretary. The scholars attended various Oxford colleges and except for an annual dinner (as prescribed by Rhodes) had little other contact during their time as undergraduates. The trust had offices in Oxford and in London from where it was administered, but otherwise, no significant meeting space or educational facilities of its own. In 1922, the trust founded its own library which was focused on the study of the British Empire and shortly after concluded that it should also have its own base in Oxford to accommodate the library, provide a venue for the annual dinner, some overnight accommodation for visitors and thus finally provide a natural focus for their scholars' life in Oxford, allowing them to meet more regularly, exchange ideas and better build the international network that Rhodes had envisaged. In 1925, the trust managed to buy two acres of garden (from cash-strapped Wadham College) on the corner of Parks and South Parks roads as its site. With Lord Milner chairman of the trustees and one of his protégés Phillip Kerr recently appointed as the trust's new general secretary, the choice of architect for their new building hardly merited discussion.

For Baker, Rhodes House, as it was to become, represented further confirmation of his position within his profession and allowed his name to be added to the long list of outstanding architects which included the great Sir Christopher Wren himself, who had built in Oxford, but there was also an intensely personal aspect to this particular commission too, which led him to write—"No work that fortune brought me gave me greater satisfaction than that of building the Oxford home of the spirit of my first patron and friend, Cecil Rhodes. When I was shown the proposed site amid the tall trees and old stone walls in the garden of Wadham College, I was very glad, as I knew that nothing would have been a greater solace to him than the thought that his ideas would be realized and live on enduringly so near the very heart of the old Oxford which he loved."[1]

Baker worked directly with Milner and Kerr once more, quickly developing a simple U-shaped plan with central double-height dining hall between two wings, one housing the library and the other the secretary's and guests' rooms—"something very simple and elemental such as Rhodes would like"[2]—but sadly their reunion lasted for only a few weeks as Milner died that summer. In his memory, the trustees proposed that the building should also now accommodate a room to serve as the great statesman's memorial. Baker revised his design accordingly, extending the wings of the U-shaped plan to form his familiar "H" with a circular memorial space now contained within the northern pair of wings and a new Ionic entrance portico serving it from South Parks Road. It was quickly agreed that the memorial space should be dedicated to both Rhodes and Milner, with scholars passing daily through it as they entered the building, as at Winchester and Harrow. The circular form was developed as a drum below a shallow dome with the cornice of the portico continued around it, while the remainder of the building was treated very much as an English country house executed in the rough local stone of the college's garden walls with dressed stone mullions and balustrades. In many ways it is a strange throwback to the start of his career, sharing numerous aspects of Ernest George's country houses such as nearby Shiplake Court, with its "H" plan and great double-height bay windows to the garden.

This combination of the Classical with the Vernacular was typical of Baker (and often Lutyens too, such as at Folly Farm) and detested as being stylistically confused by later critics, but it works well, both enlivening the rather dull South Parks Road with

Rhodes House from its garden (author's collection).

the graceful portico to the north while providing a relaxed series of internal and external spaces for meeting, study and discussion, to the south. The interior spaces of Rhodes House are particularly fine with (perhaps unsurprisingly given his clients) many echoes of Government House in Pretoria. Unfortunately, like so many of Baker's buildings, these beautiful spaces are rarely seen and thus unappreciated by the public, their wooden paneling, carved wooden Doric columns, great stone fire surrounds and leaded lights within stone mullions giving it something of the feeling of a last great Arts and Crafts country house, while in the domed rotunda "the marble cladding and the presence of engaged Doric columns at first floor level impart an appropriate air of sleek nobility."[3] It is loaded with symbols—carved Zimbabwe birds grace the stair's newel posts and one perches atop the dome, while inscriptions in Latin ring the rotunda, but nothing detracts from the sequence of one after another fine interior spaces. This is Baker at his best: calm, dignified and elegant; providing the perfect setting for a relaxed and civilized discussion of ideas; an idealized "Moothouse"; a building "of real imagination and merit which deserve(s) to be rescued from the condescension of posterity."[4] With money little object, work started quickly in 1926 and the building was officially opened in 1929.

Towards the end of 1925, Baker took up an invitation to visit Kenya from the Governor Sir Edward Grigg (himself co-editor of the *Round Table Journal* and secretary of the Rhodes Trust prior to Philip Kerr) to advise him on town planning and to potentially undertake the design of a number of public buildings. On his arrival, Baker was immediately plunged into a controversial debate between a European town planner who favored broad tree-lined avenues and the local government director of surveys who proposed traditional tall, closely-placed houses to provide shaded streets. Baker sided with local tradition with the fact that the director of surveys was Baker's younger brother Arthur being merely coincidental. By now Baker had a remarkable understanding of the challenges of designing for the harsh African climate—"What I learnt in South Africa was even more deeply impressed upon me in Kenya, in those higher latitudes under the vertical rays of the mid-day sun. The sun is the most powerful ally of the architect in designing for beauty; it is his priceless gift which costs the client nothing. He has only to model his plain wall surfaces and apportion his openings under wide overhanging cornices or eaves, and the kindly sun casts its deep cool shadows diffused with soft-toned reflected light on the bright warm whites and greys of the walls below."[5]

In addition to his advice on the planning of Nairobi, which included the provision of a new legislative chamber and Secretariat on a raised site in the center of the city (which he designed but were sadly never constructed), he designed and completed numerous public buildings in Kenya. These included his very fine and relatively little-known Law Courts in Nairobi which echo his design for Pretoria Railway Station with a rusticated base supporting two floors of office accommodation below a deeply overhanging tiled roof, but here entered through a crisply-detailed portico, which draws heavily on Wren's St. Paul's Church in Covent Garden. Interestingly, the comparison with his Pretoria Railway Station design of nearly twenty years previously shows just how far he has traveled from that early foray into Classicism to this example of his mature mastery of the language. Another elegant Government House was designed and soon under construction with a cool double-height colonnaded entrance enclosed by wings with first-floor loggias.

He advised on how the largest church in Nairobi could be converted into a cathedral, designed a model elementary school in the city, which included a sunken ground floor

Baker's Law Courts in Nairobi, Kenya (courtesy Michael Baker).

where the pupils could rest in the cool at midday (rather than walking home under the baking sun only to return a few hours later) and a similar but separate school for Indians in Nairobi—Nakuru School. Beyond Nairobi, he designed and built Kabete High School in which detached classrooms all enjoyed cross ventilation and were linked by connecting colonnades in which he "followed the excellent example set by President Jefferson in his beautiful University of Virginia"[6] and a further governor's residence in Mombasa which he described as "little more than a bungalow." What he created in Kenya was a new Classical colonial architectural language for the country, which through the use of the simplest of materials and finishes offered the example of a model for dignified public buildings. His trip that winter concluded with a journey on the governor's train, in which he "sat on the cow-catcher on a cold morning at sunrise with the expectation of seeing lions and leopards in the primeval forest, but they kept hid from the strange hissing monster advancing on the rails,"[7] before sailing from Mombasa to Bombay, where he joined his wife and eldest son Henry en route to Delhi once more.

As a business trip, his visit to Kenya had been an outstanding success, so much so that on his return to London he relieved Jan Hoogterp of his responsibilities for the Indian buildings and sent him to Nairobi to open a new office there. In January 1926 the two entered into a new contract under which Hoogterp would act as Baker's representative in Kenya, both overseeing the design development and construction of the projects that Baker had already won and also seeking further work. It was Hoogterp who oversaw the construction of the courts which were finally completed in 1932, the schools, both Government Houses and who continued to develop the detailed designs for the Secretariat and legislative chamber until they were later abandoned. Hoogterp built up a small practice in Nairobi operating largely independently before worsening economic conditions led to the conclusion of his work with Baker, his marriage to the socialite and former wife of Baron Blixen and a move to Johannesburg, where he set up and ran a very successful practice for many years.

In Delhi, as Baker had anticipated, the construction of the legislative chamber was overtaking that of the Secretariats and by the winter of 1925 the structure was largely complete. Its scale was overpowering and it made a strange symbol of devolved government with little on the exterior of the drum to either relieve the monotony of the 144 great sandstone pillars of the colonnade or to give any hint as to its purpose. Distant views of the central dome were quickly lost and without this indication of a meeting space within, its form resembles more a rather grand sports stadium or perhaps a bull-ring, rather than a legislative chamber, or in fact a series of chambers. In many ways it is the ultimate symbol of the breakdown of the architects' relationship, resulting in a compromising straightjacket, devoid of either symbolism or any expression of its purpose and a grossly inefficient building. As with the other central buildings, it rose from a red sandstone ground floor to the buff superstructure of sandstone colonnade and cornice. Its three entrances are marked only by the enclosure of three bays within the colonnade and a single-story *porte cochere* at ground level. While these offer a hint of Indian spice in their detailing, they are completely overpowered by the regiment of columns which form a defensive guard above.

The interior spaces of the three chambers are much more successful, striking a fine balance between an appropriate grandeur and an intimacy within the wooden paneling at ground level. In the Chamber of Princes, the paneling and benches are in blackwood while the columns which surround the space are in black and white marble with pink marble jaalis screening the balconies, which allow wives to watch and listen while maintaining purdah. The domed central library and reading room, which Baker designed to symbolize a united India, is a stunning space on a par with Lutyens' Durbar Hall on the hill above. Its coffered ceiling is based on that of the Pantheon and with its ring of great

Baker's three Legislative Chambers within Lutyens's encircling colonnade (courtesy Chris Belsten).

black marble columns (which would be reworked in the entrance to the bank), it provides the kind of rich symbolic gravitas which the exterior so lacks. Its detailing is flawless and like so many of Baker's excellent interior spaces, it is once more sadly, rarely seen by the public.

Perhaps only too well aware of the lack of symbolism in the building's exterior form, Baker went to town on the interior with numerous shields, heraldic emblems and coats of arms to represent the various provinces, regions and princes as well as offering inspiring carved inscriptions throughout the major spaces, all of which were carried out by Joseph Armitage. Apart from the architectural challenge of the overall design of the building, producing all the details required to support its accelerated construction was an incredible task for Baker and his office with literally thousands of drawings being sent by steamer from London to Delhi from the initial layouts of 1920 to the details of the interiors, complete with furniture, fittings, carved screens, floor tiling, ceiling decorations, paneling, doors, windows, mosaics, heating, lighting, color schemes, etc. throughout 1925 and '26. The result is a testament both to Baker's architectural and organizational abilities, which honed in Pretoria would now be required in Threadneedle Street.

Shortly after his return to London, he and Florence were off to France again with his memorials at Tyne Cot, Neuve Chapelle and Delville Wood all then under construction. With Hoogterp now in Kenya, Baker relied more and more on Alex Scott as his deputy when overseas and increasingly in the overall management of his practice. Vernon Helbing, who had worked with Scott in James Millar's office previously (and who would much later become Scott's partner), now took over the day-to-day management of the Indian projects, while Scott led the bank and covered for his principal.

On the 3rd of July 1926, Baker's knighthood was announced in the King's Birthday Honours list with a citation of "Knight Bachelor for his Services to Art" in recognition of both his architectural achievements and his encouragement of other artists' contributions to his buildings. Lawrence's congratulations were profuse—"Dear HB, Oh Lord! Sir HB! Gods! What a jest! I wish it had been a peerage…."[8] Shortly after, it was further announced that Sir Herbert Baker was to be the next recipient of the Royal Institute of British Architecture's Royal Gold Medal. Professionally, he had climbed from a sleepy little practice in Gravesend to the very peak of architecture's Mount Olympus. The only honor which now eluded him was to be elected as a Royal Academician, but that was being denied to him by Lutyens, who already elected, succeeded in blocking Baker's annual nomination.

Both architects were back in Delhi for the winter, but unaccompanied on this occasion, to be greeted shortly after their arrival by yet another Viceregal couple, Lord and Lady Irwin, who had arrived the previous April. They were to be the final clients for the architects and the first occupants of Lutyens' Government House and, despite being intensely involved in the continuing conflict over independence (which included several attempts on Irwin's life), both took a keen interest in the building projects with one or the other visiting the sites most days. For Lutyens, who was now involved largely in the decoration, furnishing and fitting out of Government House, they were the "country-house clients" he had longed for. He dealt directly with Lady Irwin in a relationship based on mutual admiration thus providing him with his happiest time in India. For Baker, the relationship was more distant as first, he was not involved in designing their home, and second unlike Lutyens, his work was nearing its end.

Lord Irwin presided over the official opening of the legislative chamber on the 18th of January 1927 with due pomp and ceremony—this was, after all, the first element of the new capital to be completed and the celebrations represented much more than just the opening of Baker's building. From their thrones under a scarlet pavilion, the Viceroy and Vicerene looked out on the pageant below them—"On the encircling banks were seated over 2,000 spectators, whose many-hued and flowing Indian robes, the brightly-coloured English sun shades and toilettes, and, at the right of the Throne, the gorgeous jewelled Durbar dress of the group of Ruling Princes, made a fascinatingly beautiful frame for the central arena."[9] Following speeches and the Viceroy's reading of a message from the King Emperor to the assembled throng, Sir Herbert Baker presented a golden key to the Viceroy with which to open the door to the building and guided the Viceroy's party around the chambers. Within 24 hours the Central Legislative Assembly was in session. The speed of the chamber's design, construction and occupation was in marked contrast to the other central buildings and must to many attending have symbolized the vigorous

Government Court and the great dome of Baker's Southern Secretariat building (courtesy Roddy Bray).

momentum of the independence movement, in comparison with the lumbering progress of their imperial masters on the hill above.

The emerging domes of the Secretariats now dominated Government Court while their completed towers could be seen from right across the new city at that time. That September, Henry Medd would represent Baker at the topping-out ceremony marking the completion of the dome of the north building and would also officiate on the south building some seven months later. Baker had managed to combine the Classical austerity of Wren's Greenwich with something of the majesty and romance of the Mughal forts and palaces which he had visited. His balance of Classical and Indian elements is finely judged and indeed so effective in linking this latest creation to the historic architecture of India that it somehow evokes the transience of one more conquering foreign empire, rather than the permanence of British rule. The strong horizontals seem to echo the great plains of the subcontinent and are further emphasized by the use of contrasting red and buff sandstone for the lower and upper floors. As in South Africa, Baker also understood and used the strong sunlight to full effect, creating dark shadows within his great porticos, in deeply-cut archways and below the angled blades of the mighty stone chujjas that project out several meters below his cornices. Each block of offices is once more terminated in great loggias as in Pretoria, but here overlooking the Great Place and beyond to the ancient Mughal city in the distance. They stand to attention on either side of the Processional Way like imperial guards protecting Government House beyond, which was now emerging in all its glory. It is powerful public architecture, which with a dash of the romance of Rajasthan is carried off with a confident imperial swagger.

Baker had now also successfully persuaded the governments of Canada, Australia, New Zealand and South Africa to contribute "Dominion Columns" to Government Court, an element of his overall design which he had included since the first perspectives. With Baker having finally secured their funding, Lutyens immediately proposed to Lord Irwin that they should be located in his Viceroy's Court but Baker prevailed in this dispute as well. As he wrote in his biography, the Dominion Columns "are similar in form to the columns which the Emperor Asoka set up throughout India, inscribed with the edicts of his united Empire, in size and unity equal only in India to the empires of Akbar and the British…. The columns are carved with the floral emblem of each Dominion, are surmounted by a full-rigged ship, symbol of the ocean-link of Empire, and on each is inscribed in English and three Indian languages; 'to India in token of their common loyalty to the King-Emperor.'"[10] For Baker, this last element of his grand design was now assured.

His achievements were marked with a major article on his work in *The Architects' Journal* on the 16th of February, commencing—"Until recently the average layman was said to be able to mention the name of one great architect only: Sir Christopher Wren. Of recent years, however, another has been added to the list, that of the designer of the Cenotaph; although as often as nought there is some difficulty over the pronunciation of his name. Now it is to be hoped that he will be able to mention Sir Herbert Baker, too, when tackled on the subject, although Baker himself would be the last person to wish it so," and continuing, "So often in Baker's work, is found strength and power combined with a grace, refinement, and simplicity which must please even the most casual observer; and when such a combination exists there is surely good design. It is probably true to say that Baker is, like his buildings, strong, even rugged, but simple. There is no nonsense, no sham about him, his work must last because there is this true mixture which makes a man loveable and his work understandable. Baker's work always gives the expression of being fit for purpose, well constructed, and decent to look at—probably the three main essentials of good building and good architecture," and concluding with a rather charming character sketch—"Baker's association with the Round Table is well known, but he is not a mixer, and not everyone's company: this is to his credit. He can be a conspicuous figure as he comes down Victoria Street in the morning, his Homburg hat the wrong way round, swinging a small basket full of vegetables picked from his country garden, one of the most beautiful in Kent (the work of Lady Baker), and striding along at six miles an hour," and finally concluding, "There is no fear that his work will be forgotten."[11]

Later in the summer, his RIBA Gold Medal was awarded at a banquet held in his honor on the evening of the 24th of June 1927. Baker was clearly affected by the significance of the award and in his speech referred to it as "this supreme occasion in an architect's life," and spoke further of how much he welcomed "this high testimony of your appreciation of my work."[12] For the "colonial architect" it represented both his acceptance in the capital of the empire and confirmed his new position as one of the leaders of his profession.

His war memorials were also all now reaching completion. His cloister at Winchester had been dedicated in 1924, the memorial at Harrow had been unveiled by old Harrovian and Prime Minster Stanley Baldwin in June 1926 and the completion of both the New Zealand Memorial at Tyne Cot and the Indian Memorial at Neuve Chapelle in 1927 brought much of his work for the Imperial War Graves Commission to a close. A few cemeteries remained to be completed, and it was not until the 31st of March 1928 that

Sir Herbert Baker at the unveiling of his memorial at Tyne Cot, France, 1927 (courtesy Michael Baker).

his appointment to the commission was concluded. They thanked him for his service, to which he responded, "It has all of course been a work of love and gratitude to those who fought for us."[13]

Any concerns that Baker may have had, that several major projects were concluding at the same time, were quickly assuaged by a flood of new commissions in 1928: two new banks back in South Africa, a church in central London for the Ninth Church of Christ Scientist and a further Indian building to provide a home in London for the Indian government.

During his winters in India, Baker had met and got to know Sir Atul Chatterjee who was then a senior member of the Indian Civil Service.[14] Chatterjee had a huge respect for Baker and his achievements in Delhi and also appreciated Baker's interest in Indian architecture. When he was appointed as High Commissioner for India in London with one of his first tasks being the procurement of a new London base for the Indian government, his choice of architect was straightforward and easily justifiable. A prominent site was procured on the Aldwych adjacent to the then recently completed Bush House, and Baker was commissioned to undertake the design work. His brief was to provide offices for the government as well as meeting rooms and a library, which were to be used to promote the study and understanding of India and its culture. It was to be the first of many subsequent buildings in which he acknowledged Scott's contribution to the design of the building rather than merely its execution, but while Scott certainly helped with the planning, its three-dimensional form is another finely-judged fusion of Indian and Classical architecture by Baker alone.

Its main elevation to the Aldwych is a stylish composition in which the grey granite of the *piano rustico* gives way to contrasting white Portland stone upper floors. Its focus is the black marble central entrance doorway, which is sheltered by a deep first-floor balcony supported on stone brackets with stone bell decorations. From this rise free-standing Ashoka columns with carved elephants at their base and capitols of crouching tigers. Between the columns a double-height arched window lights the principal circulation spaces within. These are a delight and instantly transport the visitor from a very busy, rather dusty London street into a Rajasthan palace which soars up through several levels of pierced and carved balustrades in red sandstone, past white marble jaalis to the beautifully painted murals of the top floor dome and final clerestory drum. As an evocation of the country, it is a stunning success. When it came to the detailing and decoration of the building, Baker was in his element: doorways with bell brackets; newel posts topped by crouching eagles; the heraldic arms of the twelve provinces of India carved both inside and on the exterior of the building; intricate glass and metal fretwork pendant lights and lotus flower friezes, yet despite the richness of the detailing, it is balanced by a cool background of smooth red sandstone and white-painted plaster ceilings and domes. This is interior design of the highest standard.

In the summer of 1927 Baker returned to South Africa for the first time since 1913. The then-chairman of Barclay's Bank, Frederick Goodenough, was keen to expand his bank overseas and had formed Barclay's Dominion Colonial and Overseas Bank in 1925 to do so. With Baker's ongoing work on the Bank of England and experience in South Africa, he was once more the natural choice to undertake their commissions in the new country. The Bank of England had also provided one of its senior employees, William Clegg, to undertake the role of first governor of the South African Reserve Bank and suggested to Clegg that Baker should also undertake any building work that he might also

The main entrance of India House with its carved Ashoka columns, bells, elephants and tigers (author's collection).

require. In 1927 both new clients commissioned Baker to design banks for them, and his visit was to both inspect the sites and make arrangements for the work to be supervised locally. Baker's partnership with Frank Fleming had been dissolved in 1918, but Fleming had continued to practice in the Transvaal and now stepped into the breach once more to act as Baker's local agent in the detailed design and supervision of the bank buildings. Baker again credited Scott with his assistance in the planning of both buildings, the first of which to be completed was the Reserve Bank on Church Square in Pretoria which was finished in 1928, and the second Barclay's Bank in Cape Town on central Adderley Street. Though relatively little known, the Reserve Bank is by far the more successful and offers an interesting parallel with Baker's contemporary work on the Bank of England. It provides a rusticated base of two floors to the square (much in the style of Soane's defensive wall) above which the office accommodation advances and retreats from the wall as in the upper floors of Baker's Bank of England. Two great loggias crown the flanking wings (as in Pretoria, Delhi, London, etc.) while the central section of accommodation is recessed with a linking colonnade. It has a lightness of touch, balance of solid and void and clarity of organization which is sadly lacking in Cape Town where his Barclay's Bank, completed in 1933, is very much a solid city block into which grand recessed porticos were carved in the upper levels. The detailing here is overworked and lacks the crucial balance between restraint and meaningful celebration which we have now come to expect of Baker's mature work. Before returning to England he visited Rhodesia, at the invitation of the Governor Sir John Chancellor, to advise on the planning of further government buildings and concluded his travels with a sentimental journey to visit Rhodes' grave in the Matoppo Hills.

Back in London, he immediately started work on his further new commission for a church and halls for the Ninth Church of Christ Scientist. This might have appeared to be an unusual commission for a devout Anglican such as Baker were it not for the presence of Phillip Kerr (soon to become Lord Lothian) on the building committee, along with Waldorf and Nancy Astor whose wealth ensured that funding was available to proceed from design to construction immediately. What Baker produced for them is an extraordinary building, largely hidden from public gaze behind a restrained brick Romanesque exterior. (The style of architecture was prescribed by his client with the original Mother Church in Boston being Romanesque.) Somehow accommodated within an irregular L-shaped site in Westminster is a vast first floor 1,000-seat circular auditorium along with a Sunday school, above classrooms and meeting rooms at ground level. The main space is divided horizontally with a base of timber paneling which accommodates bench seating that steps down towards the altar, and above which, encircling the entire space is a continuous series of arches supported on double Doric columns below a vast shallow dome, topped by a central clerestory rooflight. It is typically reverential Baker and an exemplar of how to naturally light a large city-center interior space. The committee demanded simplicity and their restraining hand restricted Baker to nothing more than sacred inscriptions. The secondary spaces are of a similarly high quality: the Sunday school in the form of a small Byzantine chapel while the entrance hall with its raw brick arches and vaults beneath a concrete dome is a return to an elemental Classicism unseen in his work since his South African monuments of nearly thirty years previously. It is yet another admirable sequence of almost unknown interior spaces.

Baker's working life in England had now settled into a steady pattern with his office at 14 Barton Street and his weekday home around the corner in beautiful Smith Square in the leafy shadows of Thomas Archer's baroque St. John's Church. He would occasionally allow himself weekdays off for test matches at Lords, but otherwise, his work schedule was as intense as ever. His evenings would be spent either working, relaxing with friends at 2 Smith Square or The Athenaeum Club, attending dinners or lectures at the Art Workers Guild, the Society for the Protection of Ancient Buildings, the Wren Society, the Royal Institute of British Architects, the Architecture Club, the London Society or the Royal Academy, where increasingly through the next few years he would be speaking from the podium rather than listening from below. Friday evenings would see him on the train to Sole Street Station in Cobham from where Owletts was a fast five-minute stride. At 66, he was established as a leader of his profession, a knight of the realm, a regular writer on the arts and friend to a group of individuals who now wielded real power across the empire. Conservative by nature, he looked back increasingly fondly, and his thoughts

The great encircling colonnade in the auditorium of the Ninth Church of Christ Scientist, London (author's collection).

and work constantly sought to connect with England's artistic heritage and glorious past. His correspondence continued to flow relentlessly to and from his Kindergarten friends as well as with Lawrence, Kipling, Jan Smuts, Monty Rendall and Charles Wheeler.

Most weekends were now spent in his garden, though village cricket, tennis on his own court and visiting friends and family nearby regularly intervened. Church on Sunday for the entire household was an institution followed by a family lunch in the paneled dining room of Owletts around the oak refectory table, which Baker had moved from the kitchen and restored. The eight walnut dining chairs, which had been carved by Joseph Armitage, he had designed himself, incorporating animals and children's heads representing the various family members, including a bear for Herbert. In the winter a wood fire burned in the grate. With his finances restored he had also been able to remodel and adapt Owletts, opening the old hall into the living room with a screen of two new Doric columns, where he installed a new plaster ceiling with a large wreath and two commemorative plaques, one with his and Florence's initials along with four stars—one for each of their children—and the other with symbols of the countries in which he had worked. In 1933, an Empire clock would be added over the fireplace, made by his eldest son Henry working with Robert Stewart and the indispensable Joseph Armitage, once more. With the bank commission alone, Owletts was once more secure and he would see to it that it would remain in his family for many years to come.

With so much traveling for work in which Florence could now afford to often join him, their vacations were generally spent in Britain "tramping the fells," either in the highlands and islands of Scotland, Wales or more often, in the Lake District. His son Henry had befriended Geoffrey Simpson, whose aunt, Eleanor Rawnsley, owned a large

The staff party at Owletts, 1925, with Baker in the front center, his daughter Ann on his right and partner Alex Scott on his left (courtesy Michael Baker).

house overlooking Grasmere which had once briefly been home to Wordsworth, where first Henry and soon his parents stayed on many occasions, with Herbert and later Florence maintaining a regular correspondence with this friend from the Lakes.[15]

Amidst this final greatest phase of his career, his family was growing up. They sat around the oak dining table for their Christmas dinner in 1928: Henry, 23, had graduated from New College Oxford that summer and was now an engineering apprentice with British Thomson Houston; Allaire, 20, had left Sherborne School and was serving his apprenticeship like his uncle as a fruit farmer; Alfred, 15, was still at Winchester and Ann, the youngest at 12, was being educated at home by a governess while indulging her passion for horses. Florence was a constant support to her husband and having successfully entertained in Johannesburg now ran the remaining 25 acres of the estate at Owletts with similar energy and enthusiasm. By 1928 she had three cherry orchards in full production and a herd of Guernsey milking cows as well as chickens and guinea fowl (a memory of her years in South Africa). She and Herbert shared their love of gardening and that year, with the assistance of their two gardeners, had just completed their new sunken garden to the north of Herbert's study and their wild garden in a former chalk quarry near the house. Opposite the garden doors from the living room, Herbert had placed a Corinthian capitol on axis, "saved" from the Bank of England, on which was inscribed in Latin *"Lately we were a sight for the bankers, now we are a pleasure for the birds: which is the better fate?"*

January 1929 brought another train, steamer and train journey to Delhi. With the structure of the Secretariats complete and the legislative chamber in use, Baker's focus that year was on the Secretariats' public spaces and the completion of the landscaping to Government Place. Communications with Lutyens remained ice cold with Lutyens reporting to his wife that "Baker has collared the emblems of the colonies for his babu court instead of my Great Place … again I am too late as Baker has been to all the Governors etc. for their consent. I suppose if I did no real work and only wire pulled I could do the same. It is a bore this selfishness with no thought of the scheme as a whole."[16] Despite the state of their relationship, Baker still recommended Lutyens to the RIBA as architect for their new headquarters in London later that year (along with a codicil that he must be appropriately controlled). Lutyens meanwhile was deeply involved with the detailed design of the interiors of Government House and its extensive (and stunning) gardens which, as instructed, he had based on the strict geometry of traditional Mughal gardens. While the architects were there, King George had decreed that Government House should be known as the Viceroy's House and that the legislative chamber (soon to become the Indian Parliament) should be known as the Council House. The change of the city's name from Imperial Delhi to simply New Delhi was a further sign of the times. As the complex neared completion, it attracted considerable interest back in Britain with *Country Life*, among other magazines and newspapers, providing an interim report in 1929—"Framed between the twin domes, a distant shadow, the climax of this stately composition, rises the vast dome of the Durbar Hall, resting like a crown upon the Viceroy's House. As we approach, its shape soars ever higher and higher in the air. The car passes through the Great Place, ascends the steep and short rise between Sir Herbert Baker's Secretariat buildings, and arrives on the summit, where the entire mass of the Viceroy's House jumps to the eye."[17] Interestingly, no criticism is made of the ramp and its effect on the long vista with the majority of commentators simply regarding the Viceroy's House's partial disappearance as a piece of picturesque theatrics. Lutyens' daughter Mary later spoke for most—"The approach to the palace has a pleasing mystery. Rising up to its full splendour as one gets close, it gives one a shock of delighted surprise which would be missing if it were fully revealed along the whole length of the avenue."[18] For Baker, his work in India was nearing its end in a mixture of pride, regret and relief.

In the autumn of that year on the 29th of October 1929, the New York Stock Exchange crashed, signaling a catastrophic economic correction that reverberated around the globe. Britain hadn't experienced the boom which had led to bust in the United States and in fact the British economist John Maynard Keynes's immediate reaction was, "There will be no serious direct consequences in London,"[19] but within days world trade began to contract. The impact on British manufacturing in particular was devastating. Within a year, British exports had reduced by half and unemployment had more than doubled from one million to two and a half million at a time when there was little or no unemployment benefit. Construction projects were among the first investments to be canceled. Baker's employers at the Bank of England were in the eye of the storm but for Baker and his team in London the Bank of England commission would see them through the worst economic depression of the 20th century. The modest first phase of the rebuilding adjacent to Bartholomew Lane (now the museum) had been completed and phase two was well under way which involved the construction of the new east wing of the building including the new portico. All demolitions and excavations were complete and for the first time the public would have witnessed the steel frame of the new bank rising above the old boundary wall. With half of their building now demolished, fortunately for everyone at Barton Street, by October 1929 the bank had no option but to proceed.

Despite the economic climate, Baker had rarely been busier with a number of commissions in addition to the South African banks, India House and the Ninth Church of Christ Scientist arriving shortly before the Wall Street crash. His new banking

Baker's familiar loggias terminating the wings of his northern Secretariat building (author's collection).

connections had brought him two private bank buildings, next door to each other in Lombard Street, just around the corner from the Bank of England. The first, Martins Bank, must have greatly appealed to him. Generally acknowledged as the oldest bank in England, it had traded for several centuries under the sign of a grasshopper, which Baker reinstated as a traditional hanging metal sign above the new main entrance door. The second, Glyn Mills, was much larger, for whom Baker produced a remarkable banking hall, inspired by his work around the corner at the Bank of England with arcaded side aisles under a large low dome with clerestory lighting. Both were completed in red brick with stone dressings above a stone, arched ground floor. They have a restrained if largely unremarkable elegance of which little remains today beyond their street elevations. More interesting was Baker's further new commission—a bridge over the river Thames at Chiswick.

London had expanded dramatically during the first decades of the 20th century, and by the 1920s the former villages of Chiswick and Mortlake had been subsumed within the advancing boundary of the city. As part of an ambitious scheme to relieve traffic congestion on the existing bridges in what had now become West London, it was proposed that two new bridges be constructed at Chiswick and Twickenham, with Baker being commissioned to design the bridge at Chiswick to replace a ferry which had been operating there since the 17th century. As in his approach to the design for the bank, Baker used the latest technology to produce what appeared to be traditional stone construction. Here, the bridge's cellular reinforced concrete superstructure is almost entirely clad with 3,400 tons of Portland stone with only the concrete below the arches exposed. Dignified and rather understated, it looks back to the great English stone medieval bridges, but thanks to its modern structure, crosses the mighty river Thames in three great strides.

In December 1929, Baker was invited to join two of his old friends, Jan Smuts and Phillip Kerr, on a tour of the United States. Both had been involved in the Paris Peace Conference which had spawned the League of Nations (a forerunner of the United Nations) to which they were both committed. Both Smuts and Kerr remained concerned that without the membership of the United States which had never officially joined, the League lacked international credibility (not to mention a significant stream of financial support) and that "the American people were unconscious of their responsibilities in a dangerous world"[20] (though with their economy in freefall following the Wall Street crash just two months earlier, it was probably not the best time to remind them of their international obligations). Baker justified his acceptance of their invitation as it would afford him an opportunity to examine the design of the new Federal Reserve Bank of New York at first hand. They sailed on the palatial *RMS Berengaria* which was then the premier ship of the Cunard line, but the winter Atlantic passage was a rough one. Baker was one of the few passengers who didn't succumb to seasickness by regularly pacing around the decks which, unsurprisingly, he recalled having "in the early morning much to myself"[21] before enjoying a similarly lonely Christmas lunch on board.

While he almost certainly shared their internationalist views and did indeed attend several of Smuts' lectures, his principal interest was architectural and as was the case with most Europeans at that time, he was utterly fascinated by the "skyscrapers" of New York— "They were a wonderment truly: they seemed the expression of boundless enterprise and of a spirit of adventure; and of very great beauty as seen through a sea-haze from the anchoring ship…. But when I saw them from nearer points of view in clear daylight I wished that such great skill, energy, and power could have achieved a greater harmony

Baker's perspective of Chiswick Bridge, London (courtesy Michael Baker).

of composition in the design of the city as a whole…. It seemed a giant city of a 'hundred towers' built by rival factions, like those of the Montagues and Capulets."[22] He was introduced to William Delano, a Classical architect whose work Baker greatly admired, and he acted as Baker's guide to New York's banks, apartment blocks and offices which they toured together before traveling out to Long Island where Baker stayed in Delano's house. Philip Sawyer, the architect of the Reserve Bank, provided a personal tour before Baker and his companions left for Washington. Here he attended dinner with the British Ambassador Esme Howard—the last ever dinner in the old British Embassy—with Howard providing him with a guided tour of Lutyens' recently completed new embassy the following day. Lunch with President Hoover at the White House was followed by a tour of the city to better understand L'Enfant's plan (the inspiration for New Delhi's), and the day concluded with a visit to Arlington Cemetery where the open-air amphitheater utterly captivated Baker. He then traveled from Washington to Virginia and Jefferson's works, Boston, Philadelphia, Harvard and Yale, and on north to Canada—Ottawa and Montreal—before finally returning to New York where the American Institute of Architects held a lunch in his honor and where he spoke briefly of his work. He was exhilarated once more by all that he saw, generally impressed by the public and domestic architecture though he found most towns "untidy." He felt a shared spirit with people whom he felt to be fellow colonials and understood only too well the challenges they had faced and overcome in building their new country. He grew much closer to Smuts too on the tour and journey home, and the former architect and client became close friends through their many discussions that ranged from botany, geology and fossils to religion, politics and the future of South Africa.

It cannot be a coincidence that shortly after his return passage with Smuts, Baker was commissioned to undertake the design of South Africa House, or the home of the South African Dominion as it then was, on Trafalgar Square. The High Commissioner for South Africa at the time was Charles Te Water, and though he had been a National Party politician and thus opponent of Smuts, he could have had little concern about Baker's appointment based on his work in South Africa and sizeable practice in London. The site for the building could hardly have been more prominent, taking up the entire east side of Trafalgar Square, in the shadow of William Wilkin's National Gallery, adjacent to James Gibb's Church of St. Martin in the Fields and facing Robert Smirke's Canada House. Baker's challenge was to respond to this historic setting while dealing with a full story-height change of level across the site, before it turned sharply into Northumberland Avenue. His solution was to provide a further central portico to his building which echoed that of Gibb's Church, nodded to Wilkin's on the National Gallery and addressed Smirke's directly across the square. As Baker explained, "According to a principle which Lutyens and I agreed to and acted on at Delhi, the new order should not be at a lower level to accord with the slope of the site, but should be raised to the same general level as the dominant buildings. Dignity would thus be gained by expressing the immutable order of the earth rather than the accident of the site."[23] His great Corinthian colonnade is therefore raised on a rusticated plinth whose deeply-cut arches provide the main entrance to the building.

The recently-formed Royal Fine Art Commission was unimpressed by Baker's logic and requested that the portico be lowered to ground level as in Smirke's Canada House across the square. Baker held his ground however, and the high commissioner appealed directly to Ramsey MacDonald, the prime minister, who acquiesced. Baker did, however,

The controversial portico of South Africa House from Trafalgar Square, London (author's collection).

concede his mansard roof to the commission's request for a flat roof thus matching the other buildings around the square. The great mass of the building was reduced by Baker's continuation of the cornice of the portico around the building with the two upper floors above this stepped back, while at the corner with Northumberland Avenue, the cornice continues above a further concave Corinthian portico which is played off against a convex wall plane behind, rather in the style of Soane's Tivoli Corner at the bank. Charles Wheeler assisted throughout and contributed the very fine winged golden springbok that leaps out from this prominent corner of the building (and which has subsequently provided a regular meeting place for South Africans in London ever since its completion). Above cornice level, further minor porticos (and a rather weak pediment above the main portico to the square) again reduce the mass of the office accommodation. As with the construction of the bank, Baker used the latest technology throughout the building and yet felt no need to express any of it externally or internally. As in the bank, the building structure is in welded steel infilled with reinforced concrete panels, all of which is faced with Portland stone above a granite base.

The ground floor housed the entrance hall, reading rooms and reception rooms, which included the recreated interior of a Cape Dutch farmhouse; the first floor was the high commissioner's suite with offices on the floors above, while the basement accommodated an exhibition space, billiard room and cinema. Internally, Baker lavished his usual care on the public spaces and state rooms in particular where timber paneling, beamed ceilings, marble flooring and stone fireplaces were all constructed from materials sourced from South Africa. The entrance hall contains two domes once more symbolizing the two South African races (English and Dutch) and as one would expect, the interior surfaces are adorned with heraldry, symbols and emblems of the country as well as tapestry maps, carved reliefs of scenes from South Africa, plaster and metal reliefs, carved wooden screens, busts of historic figures and a vast flock of Zimbabwe birds. English Heritage, in their listing of the building, accurately described these hidden interiors as "exceptional."

On Thursday the 22nd of June 1933, Baker could be found outside the main entrance awaiting the King and Queen, with a further golden key on a cushion to open its great front doors. "After the speeches Baker had taken the King and Queen through the building and out onto the balcony on the fifth floor, when once more cheering erupted from the huge crowd in the square below."[24] His new building was greeted with mixed reviews. The consensus among the critics was that its raised portico was overbearing and too assertive, with *Country Life* now particularly acerbic. Interestingly, their review of the building was followed by a letter from the prominent architect Basil Ionides the following week—"Having read your leading article on the new building in Trafalgar Square, I was induced to go and look at it, and I cannot understand why this building has been chosen for such adverse criticism. It has dignity and far from dwarfing St. Martin's Church, it rather frames it,"[25] which was then followed by a long response from the editor, renewing the attack.

The Birthday Honours of June 1930 brought Baker further glory with the award of "Knight Commander of the Most Eminent Order of the Indian Empire" in recognition of both his work in India and the completion of India House, which was opened the following month by the King-Emperor and Queen Empress. Their majesties were received at the entrance of the new building by the High Commissioner for India and presented with yet another golden key to unlock the door by the architect, Sir Herbert Baker, now KCIE ARA FRIBA. But this was to be nothing compared to that winter's events in New Delhi.

The architects arrived in early December with Florence accompanying Baker. Despite Lord and Lady Irwin having been living in the Viceroy's House for over a year, on the 23rd of December, their official occupation was due to be marked. As with Lord Hardinge's triumphal entry into Delhi almost twenty years earlier, the arrival of Irvin's train was greeted with a bomb attack. On this occasion no one was killed and the Viceroy and his party were uninjured, but their train almost derailed and the nationalists had made their point effectively once more. Following their procession down the King's Way through Government and the Viceroy's Court, Lutyens awaited them in his great portico at the top of the steps before the front doors were thrown open and the Viceregal couple officially entered their home. As Lutyens wrote home to Emily, "We left them alone and for the first time in 17 years the house closed on me."[26] It was his masterpiece, his palace and greatest country house, every proportion perfect and every detail crisp and beautifully refined. After his initial objections to Indian architecture, he had warmed to the decorative detail that it afforded him and even developed his own Delhi Order with pendant bells to grace the capitals of many of the columns while his Viceregal gardens were based purely on Moghul tradition but refreshed with his own brilliance and wit. Edward Hudson, the proprietor of *Country Life* and Lutyens' client and principal supporter, was euphoric—"Poor old Christopher Wren could never have done this," he told Lady Emily.[27] It was an architectural triumph but also a fascinating symbol of British rule with Lutyens' required reductions in accommodation resulting in much of the main façade to the Viceroy's Court now being no more than a single corridor deep. Behind the scenery, expectations of everlasting imperial rule were now replaced with vain hopes that India would become a self-governing dominion within the empire, but within less than twenty years it would be India's first president, Rajendra Prasad, who would occupy Lutyens' sumptuous state rooms.

The highlight of the inauguration of the new capital, much to Baker's delight, was to be the unveiling of the Dominion Columns in Government Court. As *The Times* reported on the 10th of February 1931, "Thirty-one guns thundered out a salute from the Ridge when Lord Irwin left the Viceroy's House at 11 this morning to perform what was virtually the inauguration ceremony of the Imperial Capital of the new India. The cold weather sunlight shone down on a brilliant spectacle staged between the north and south blocks of the twin Secretariats."[28] In front of a crowd of nearly five thousand guests including representatives of all the dominions and hundreds of civil servants looking down from the roofs of the Secretariats, Lord Irwin read out a message from the King Emperor which could have been written by Baker himself. The columns "are the gift of the four great dominions of the empire. For some they will commemorate the days when the Dominions fought shoulder to shoulder with India in the Great War; together they will tell of the long history of devotion and self-sacrifice which is our proud Imperial heritage; to all of us they enshrine the tradition of affection and loyalty to the person of the King-Emperor which is the strongest tie between the several members of our Imperial society. Devoutly let us pray that these four pillars of fellowship now given to India may forever symbolise such association—large in thought, and powerful under Providence to work for the service of mankind."[29] Having fought so hard and for so long to see these symbols of his beloved empire erected, it must have been a moment of intense pride for Baker to see them thus finally unveiled.

And so, Baker's great imperial adventure was over, at the cost of his friendship with Lutyens. Their buildings stand together on the Acropolis that Baker had proposed and while Lutyens' work receives most of the plaudits, there is nothing in the complex which comes close to the sheer drama of the view of Baker's Secretariats from below in the Great Place—the diagonals of the grand staircases, the stone chattris, the commanding towers and his great colonnades which look out over the plains of India brilliantly evoke his imperial vision—this is the Raj incarnate.

While the celebrations and commemorations were taking place, as Jane Ridley later wrote, "Ned was seeking revenge on Baker by manipulating publicity at home."[30] Robert Byron, a 26-year-old travel writer who was neither an architect nor an architectural historian, had been hired to review the Delhi buildings for both *Country Life* and *The Architectural Review*, and Edward Hudson ensured not only that it was Lutyens who briefed him but also that the reviews were written entirely from Lutyens' perspective. Thus the Viceroy's House was praised to the heavens while Baker's work was damned, vilified in a vitriolic attack which likened Baker's carved stone screens to "underwear hanging on a clothes line" and the domes of the Secretariats to "toreadors hats." The article in *The Architectural Review* was published while the Baker and Lutyens families were still in India, and Baker was understandably outraged, realizing immediately the damage that it would do to his reputation. Both families were booked to travel home together on the SS *Viceroy*, and Lady Emily suggested to her daughter that it "will be most uncomfortable."[31] Lutyens was unrepentant while Baker spent much of his time on the journey home shocked and shaken by the attack and writing a long memorandum setting out his entire involvement with New Delhi, in which his pain is obvious—"That there should have been any discussion or rivalry stimulated by a one-sided propaganda in our collaboration has and will ever cause me the deepest regret and a sense of failure. I know that I

One of Baker's majestic flights of steps leading up to the sacred plain of Raisina Hill (author's collection).

was appointed as one who might exercise a wholesome control over the wilful masterful-ness of a genius. But after this long and bitter experience I am convinced that there could be no successful midway between maintaining independence of view and becoming a puppet. I have realised throughout with the deepest regret how much harm our failure to collaborate has caused to the successful building of New Delhi and to the prestige of the architectural profession."[32] Little did he then know as he headed back to London that Lutyens was far from finished with him.

Byron's review was repeated and expanded over four issues of *Country Life*, which were published in May and June. The final issue concluded with a direct personal attack by Hudson and Lutyens on Baker. Under the title "Approach from the King's Way" (and accompanied by an inaccurate sectional drawing of the ramp), this final article ended with several paragraphs restating Lutyens' point of view on the issue, which as with most of his recollections on the subject was riddled with inaccuracies, such as "All went well until, in 1915–16, Sir Edwin learned that, contrary to the agreement, it had been decided to take the road between the Secretariats at the steepest gradient which traffic could conveniently negotiate," and, "Presumably it is too late … to construct the gradient as originally planned would now cost £80,000" (half of Keeling's actual estimate of £166,000). But worse was to come. The article concluded, "Sir Herbert Baker, it is known, opposed Lutyens' gradient and preferred, if he did not actually design, the present one…. Hitherto, Sir Herbert Baker has observed silence on this point. He cannot, unless his reason has failed, defend the present gradient now that it exists. Does Dignity prevent him from admitting a mistake, committed probably under the influence of a severe misapprehension? Dignity may be bought too dear. Either Sir Herbert must prove that the decision was not his, or he must admit his mistake and expound the sincerity of his misapprehension. If he does neither, his record in the archives of posterity will not be an enviable one."[33] For a magazine such as *Country Life*, which prided itself on the quality of its architectural coverage, it was a base and shameful attack. Lutyens could hardly contain his childish glee, as he wrote to his wife—"This morning's excitement was the C.L. number with Baker in it. So that closes the series. It wont help to make Baker amend his wrongs. In Africa when I was there he drew criticism from me & appeared grateful & keen to learn. He came to Delhi & he was most obstinate & did everything I warned him not to do. I have never been able to fathom out or connect the two faces."[34] Baker, meanwhile, went straight to his solicitor.

Drafts exist of responses to *Country Life,* but in the end, he was advised not to stoke further publicity either by demanding a retraction (which Hudson would certainly not have agreed to) or by suing the magazine. Lutyens, who was neither author nor publisher, was in the clear, and his attack was so successful that Baker's architectural reputation started on a slow and inexorable downward spiral from this point. The ramifications of his "long and bitter experience" of attempting to work as a partner with Lutyens were now being felt most personally and painfully.

13

1931–1946

"Through the Long Days" (Op. 16)

Whether judged by the moral standards of the 1920s or the 2020s, Lutyens' actions were contemptible. He had not merely sought to blame his partner for his own mistake but worse had quite callously set out to destroy his professional reputation. The *Country Life* article had accused Baker of "blundering" and being too proud to admit a mistake, and in finally concluding that he would not respond, Baker left those criticisms in its influential readers' minds. Architectural historian Roderick Gradidge was typically forthright—"I believe … that a great injustice has been done to the memory of the architecture of Herbert Baker and that Lutyens was largely responsible for that injustice."[1]

Baker's practice was fortunately unaffected by the Delhi reviews and indeed despite them and the economic depression which was now seriously affecting Lutyens and most other London architects, new work was still pouring in to Barton Street. Considering their existing commitments, it is astonishing that Baker and his loyal band of never more than three dozen staff could cope. Baker looked after them well, however, for example writing to Vernon Hellbing, who had been seriously ill the previous year—"This is by way of bonus for all the overtime you have put in and for all your dedicated service. I meant to pay your hospital bill but you have done it I believe! However I shall get the doctors,"[2] and in 1931 Scott's loyalty and commitment was finally publicly acknowledged as well with a change of practice name to Sir Herbert Baker and A.T. Scott. The new commissions included Assize Courts in Winchester (unbuilt), a church in Woldingham and another in Fairbridge, Australia, a new memorial hall and chapel for Haileybury School (where Lionel Curtis was an influential former pupil) and Baker's first contribution to the architecture of Cambridge—new residences for Downing College.

St. Paul's at Woldingham is a rather strange and, one has to conclude, unsuccessful attempt to design a traditional flint village church. The tower is largely detached from the body of the church which is capped with a heavy hipped roof giving it something of the character of a barn rather than a nave, while the interior is pure South Africa with exposed timber trusses and a circular apse. The contrast with his work at Haileybury could not be greater as we see here once more the contemporary influence of Soane and Taylor's work at the bank in the new dining hall in particular: a most unusual space which is almost entirely spanned with a great low shallow dome supported on four shallow-arched apses with a quotation from John Bunyan forming a golden ring around its base. Baker had made his views on functional memorials clear already and at Haileybury felt that "though I disliked the sentiment of a war memorial being used for such material purposes, that was no reason why it should not be beautiful in itself," but "as the spiritual memorial of the war I prefer to think of the Chapel."[3] Here he added a clergy chancel and an apsidal sanctuary beyond flanking Corinthian columns and for which he also designed the stone and marble altar. Haileybury had of course been the school which rejected Baker due to his lack of Classical scholarship 50 years previously, and he took this opportunity to exact his revenge with the help of his friend Monty Rendall (now Winchester College's former headmaster) who provided an inscription for the exterior of the new chapel apse in the most challenging Greek that he could devise.

His only building in Australia, Fairbridge Chapel in Pinjarra, was designed to serve the Fairbridge Farm School which had been founded by Kingsley Fairbridge in 1912 to provide agricultural and domestic education for impoverished children under various altruistically-inspired colonial migration programs. Fairbridge had been educated in Baker's buildings at St. Andrew's College in Grahamstown in the Cape and was later a Rhodes scholar, so yet again his choice of architect was fairly obvious and, with Baker expressing his admiration for Fairbridge's work in his autobiography, his design was provided as a gift. (Construction of the chapel was largely funded by Thomas Wall, of ice-cream fame.) Baker did not disappoint (despite not having visited the site prior to or during construction) with one of his finest small churches. The format is familiar with an offset Italianate campanile and tall buttressed brick nave under a steeply pitched tiled roof but there is a freshness and precision about Fairbridge Chapel which is very appealing.

Baker's only building in Australia—Fairbridge Chapel in South Western Australia (courtesy Mal Chatt).

Baker had hoped to build in Cambridge previously when his design for a new residence for Trinity College was approved in 1920, but unfortunately an outbreak of
death-watch beetle in the college's existing buildings had consumed the then-available
funding. When approached by Downing College, Baker was delighted to have the opportunity to fulfill his ambition of adding to the university's architectural heritage. As with
Haileybury, the original college buildings had been designed by the Neo-Classical architect William Wilkins. Unlike every other Oxbridge college, Wilkins had designed Downing as a series of Classical buildings arranged symmetrically within a park-like campus
approached through a Doric Propylaea from Downing Street. Regrettably, as with Baker's design for Trinity, the money had run out with only two elements of his grand plan,
the east and west ranges, actually constructed (between 1807 and 1821). The obvious solution to adding residential accommodation would have been to build Wilkins' missing
north range but this would have cut the great court off from the remainder of the college, and in any case would not have provided sufficient accommodation for the college's
current needs. Instead, Baker continued the lines of Wilkins' two ranges, thus extending
the central space, with two new L-shaped pavilions of accommodation whose porticos
addressed Wilkins' work and which effectively screened the sprawl of science buildings
which had built up at the back of the college's site. He further proposed that a new college chapel should be built linking his two new wings and addressing Wilkins' central
axis from Downing Street (which was later completed by Alex Scott after Baker's death).
As the opportunity to enter the college on axis directly from Downing Street had been
lost with the construction of a row of houses, Baker then proposed that a new entrance
to the college, with Classical gatehouse, should be constructed on Regent Street from
where a new cross-axis would bisect the site. It was a typically Baker approach: equally
sensitive both to the existing buildings and the needs of the college and his new blocks
are (despite the scale of their three-story accommodation) entirely consistent with the
spirit of Wilkins' original concept. By concluding each new wing with an Ionic portico,
Baker cleverly concealed the third floor of accommodation behind his pediments thus
reducing the apparent scale of his contribution while the two porticos directly address
Wilkins' gables, providing a series of frames along his new cross-axis. While this new
route has been reinforced in subsequent development, unfortunately Baker's gatehouse,
like Wilkins' before, was never constructed and this great classical composition is therefore sadly entered off-axis from the street. Despite the sneers of many critics, Baker's
intervention is extremely successful, his Ionic portico is quite the equal of Wilkins' versions across the green and he was able to provide the college with a vast amount of additional accommodation while respecting the unique spatial qualities of Downing College.

While his college buildings were under construction, Baker was awarded the commission for a further small building opposite the college entrance on Regent Street for
the Scott Polar Research Institute. For Baker, Captain Scott was another great hero of the
empire. Baker had personally contributed to Scott's expedition funds and he had maintained his friendship with Scott's widow after his death in Antarctica in 1912, so once
more his appointment for the museum and research facility was pretty much assured.
What he produced is a delightful little brick pavilion in which two large arched windows
face Regent Street symbolizing the two poles. On the keystone of one, Wheeler carved a
polar bear, while on the other, a king penguin. The hall behind is vaulted with two shallow domes behind the arches which are decorated with murals of maps of the Arctic and
Antarctic showing the routes of the famous navigators, while the columns flanking the

One of the porticos of Baker's residential buildings at Downing College, Cambridge (author's collection).

entrance to the museum have polar bear and penguin capitals. Completed in 1933, it is a charming tribute to Scott whose bust looks down from above the main entrance as well as being a building in which Baker's symbolic expression is finely judged.

That spring, Baker had been able to witness the completion of phase two of the Bank of England which included the new central portico, the re-created banking halls and everything to the right of center up to its towering slate mansard roof. If he had planned to deflect any criticism from his design of the new portico, he could not have done so more effectively than he did by securing Charles Wheeler's appointment as sculptor. Against the rusticated base below Baker's majestic Corinthian portico, Wheeler had produced six supporting sculptures—four male, representing guardianship, and two female, representing wealth. What shocked London, more than the rather avant-garde nature of Wheeler's designs on this most conservative of institutions, was the fact that the women were naked above the waist and the men entirely. *The London Illustrated News* was soon referring to them as Wheeler's "much-discussed sculptures"[4] and at the bank's annual General Court meeting that year, Mr. E. T. Hargreaves led the attack, referring to them as "very extraordinary monstrosities"[5] with good old Robert Brand countering that he very much admired the whole scheme.

As to the portico itself, it was a noble attempt to link the new with the old, with Soane's six Corinthian columns apparently extended as buttresses behind his wall to form the bases for Wheeler's statues which in turn supported Baker's six pairs of double Corinthian columns, with high above in the pediment a new "Lady of the Bank" by Wheeler. It was a genuine and thoughtful experiment in linking the two buildings which drew heavily on Wren's St. Paul's, but the scale of the new is simply crushing, particularly given the intricate detail of Soane's façade below. There is a distinct and intended horizontality to

The new main elevation of the Bank, with Baker's new portico above Soane's original entrance (author's collection).

Baker's pediment which works well with Soane's wall as you approach the entrance but from further back the essential verticality of the seven-story new building jars with the long horizontal of the old. There was never any doubt about the sincerity of Baker's effort to bring the old and new together in a single composition, nor actually the quality of his own work, but the reality is that architecturally his aim of combining the old and new in a single integrated whole was simply unachievable given the scale of the new.

Eventually in June 1932, just days before his 70th birthday and shortly after the unveiling of his new portico at the bank (and despite all Lutyens' efforts), Baker was elected to the Royal Academy. As Charles Wheeler recalled, "The story goes that when at long last Baker's candidature was successful, as members were leaving the Assembly, Derwent Wood, the sculptor, said to Lutyens who was going by: 'You've met your Baker-loo tonight, Lut.' In spite of this, which shows he had no heart in the quarrel, he strongly supported Lutyens candidature for P.R.A."[6] With phase two of the bank completed, the demolition of the existing buildings to the west of the portico commenced in 1933 and controversially, in March the pedimented attic of Soane's Tivoli Corner was removed. For Baker this was an entirely rational move as he saw the nature of Soane's wall having changed from a building seen against the sky whose silhouette therefore had significance to a mere rusticated base for his great new bank building which was to rise above it. What's more, he had designed a new domed and toplit circular banking hall behind the Tivoli Corner which he felt Soane's pediment largely obscured. At the same time as the pediment was removed, work commenced on the driving of the new pedestrian route through the Tivoli Corner at ground level to ease congestion on the pavements as the bank had agreed with the Corporation of London. While the new route proved to be an asset practically and aesthetically, the removal of the attic was unnecessary and ill-advised and the Soane Trustees were outraged as soon as the demolitions were reported.

Within a few months, their protests had attracted the support of the Royal Society, the Royal Academy, the Society of Antiquities of London and the Royal Society of Arts and resulted in just the kind of bad press that Baker and the bank had gone to such lengths previously to avoid. But, as with the Royal Fine Arts Commission's protests over South Africa House, Baker strongly resented their interference, viewing their protests as simply an artistic difference of opinion and as before convinced his client accordingly. Baker's proposal that a bust of Sir John Soane should be commissioned and placed in a new niche on the Lothbury façade along with the offer of several plaster casts to the Soane Museum cut little ice with the trustees or their supporters.

In part to counter the criticism, Baker arranged for his completed interiors and the new Garden Court to be photographed, and these were released to the press to universal acclaim. Charles H. Reilly, the contemporary architectural critic, spoke for many when he described the design of the exterior of the new bank as "a valiant attempt"[7] to blend the new with the old that was far surpassed by the quality of the new interiors where Baker had had a free hand. *The Times, The London Illustrated News* and *The Architectural Review* were consistently fulsome in their praise with the *Daily Herald* describing the interiors as "breathlessly beautiful poems of delicate architecture"[8] while the public reaction was one

The main staircase of the Bank of England (courtesy the Bank of England Archive, reference 15A13/1/1/59/9).

of great enthusiasm for this great national phoenix which was now rising from the dust of the demolitions. For the first time those outside the bank and project team were able to see the new double-height entrance behind Soane's modest arch with its elegant black marble Corinthian columns; its inner vestibule which opened up through the building to the beautiful stone vaults above and looked down to the depths below, thus giving a sense of the scale of the new building; the recreated toplit banking halls (which would one day surprise even Pevsner by their quality); the staircases, vestibules and ante rooms; the recreated Court Room and the elegant new Garden Court with four mulberry trees and two new lime saplings that Baker had grafted from the old trees of its predecessor. The nation was absolutely delighted with their new bank.

While the photographs gave some understanding of the scale of the task which Baker's team was undertaking, few outside ever really understood the complexity of the building project in which almost half the new accommodation lay below the level of the London streets, the building had to be occupied by the bank throughout construction and such minor matters as the secure transfer of £161 million in gold bullion from the old vaults to the new during the phasing. A scan of a single contemporary minute of the rebuilding committee from the 1930s gives just a flavor of the day-to-day matters which Baker, Scott, Troup and Faber had to address—sourcing teak, railings, mosaic floor, sectional handovers, phased demolition, temporary entrances, Latin inscriptions, air inlet ducts, wood block flooring, desks, swing doors, strong-room doors, counters, flagstaff, refrigeration, phased vacation, curtains and blinds, clocks, bronze gates, letter boxes,

Baker's new Garden Court of the Bank of England (courtesy the Bank of England Archive, reference 15A13/1/1/68/41).

statues, bookcases, sanitation, windows, temporary heating and hot water supply, elevators, fuel, wall treatment, lighting, kitchens, desk lamps, fire precautions, bullion yard hoist, drinking water, weighing machines, sculpture, paintings, roof tiles, carpets, cases, underpinning, stone cleaning, archaeological finds and the allocation of offices.

If their task was not already complex enough, Charles Lubbock's successor as chairman of the rebuilding committee, George Booth, informed the team that summer in 1933 that substantial savings would now have to be made on the outstanding work and the program extended to reduce the building's overall cost from £5 million to £4 million in response to the impact of the Depression on the bank's own resources. Unlike many abortive schemes to reduce costs on projects that were already under construction (such as in New Delhi), the bank through Booth drove down the final cost of the project substantially and succeeded entirely. Savings were sought and achieved—all polished steel columns were omitted, coves and fillets omitted to vaults, linoleum in offices in lieu of wood block, bronze doors omitted, teak skirtings omitted, teak paneling omitted—the list went on and on. For the design team under Baker's leadership, it created a vast amount of additional work, identifying potential savings, costing and gaining approval to the proposals, revising drawings and specifications and worst of all this had to be done in the context of a percentage fee which would, under the terms of their professional appointment, be reduced as well by 20 percent. Baker immediately flagged this issue but, as in India, in the new circumstances in which his clients found themselves, his request for reasonable additional compensation to deal with the changes was initially balked at, and once more necessitated further time-consuming justification. He finally submitted his detailed claim for additional fees on the 3rd of November 1933.

With his numerous other projects to also deal with in addition to this further work and worry on the bank, the pressure on Baker had become unsustainable and shortly after Christmas in 1933 it took its toll when the now 71-year-old architect suffered a massive stroke. Initially confined to bed in Cobham, he received best wishes from around the globe. His speech slowly returned but he was severely paralyzed on the right side of his body and had to teach himself to write and draw with his left hand—a tragic blow for such a fine draftsman, artist and prolific letter writer. His movement was similarly compromised, and he had to learn to walk once more with a cane which he required for the rest of his life. With the force of character, drive and determination that had brought him his professional success, he now focused on his recovery. By February he could walk unaided and by March made his first journey back to Barton Street to see Scott and their team. Scott had already been leading on the bank and had now also had to instantly assume the role of sole partner for the busiest practice in London. From this point on, Baker's correspondence is either in his shaky left-hand writing or, increasingly, typed (rather badly, with one finger of his left hand), but he managed to resume his correspondence, replying to many of the kind letters that he and Florence had received. To General Smuts in March he wrote, "I am soon going back to light work; then, if, in danger of getting into the thick of it, I shall want an escape, South Africa would be the place for me,"[9] and to Rudyard Kipling, "I've been one day in town, none the worse."[10] With typical self-discipline, in an effort to both divert himself and continue to drive his recuperation (as well as to counter what had become increasing criticism of Rhodes), he now embarked upon writing a biography of Rhodes, *Cecil Rhodes: By His Architect,* which was published the following year. It was a largely uncritical and fairly often adulatory account of Rhodes, their relationship and their many discussions which was apparently much appreciated by those who knew the man. But learning to write and walk once more was a long way short of getting back to where he had been before, as Charles Wheeler recalled in his memoirs—"After he had had a stroke, he would struggle down to my studio in Kensington from his office in Westminster, bring his sandwiches, I would make coffee and we would lunch together by a large open wood fire or, in the summer, beneath the old mulberry tree in my garden. He always spoke of art and poetry."[11] It was going to be a long, and in the end never fully completed, road back.

With more time to think, he must have begun to realize that while he, Lutyens and Blomfield had once led the development of British architecture and in many ways still dominated it, a radical new architectural wind of change was blowing strongly across the Channel from Germany. Baker had always been more willing than Lutyens and many others to adopt and use new technological advances but contrary to the emerging cult of Modernism, he had no wish to give expression to them. A steel frame to Baker was simply that—a skeleton which should then be appropriately clothed—not exposed to public gaze. While the new generation of young architects were encouraged by Gropius, Le Corbusier and the other heroes of the early Modern Movement to reject the past, Baker and Lutyens still wished only to connect with it and by doing so to add to the long and distinguished history of their art and the architectural heritage of their country. Where others increasingly sought clean lines, minimal decoration and industrialization, Baker in particular still reveled in rich detail, fine natural materials, the apparently endless possibilities of the Classical language, symbolism, heraldry and traditional craftsmanship.[12]

His beloved empire, far from continuing to grow, was becoming a commonwealth of independent nations whose only link was soon to be allegiance to the British Crown, and Baker was politically conservative at a time when organized labor was beginning to demand radical change and power. In 1934 his views and attitudes to life and his art were still in the majority, but they would not survive the war that was to come.

As he had suggested he might in his letter to Smuts, he took a vacation in South Africa

Sir Herbert on an early excursion after his stroke (courtesy Michael Baker).

in August to aid his recuperation, accompanied this time by Florence, Henry and Allaire. They visited the Cape, Pretoria and Johannesburg, and Baker was able to show his sons his work and also meet up with old friends such as Sir Patrick Duncan (by then a cabinet minister) and his wife, and of course, the general himself. While the visit was largely social, Baker was nevertheless disturbed by the many changes since his last visit, including the development of Muizenburg where his little cottage (which now sat on Baker Street) had been subsumed within a seaside resort, and in Johannesburg where so many of his houses had new owners, or even in some cases new uses, such as Florence Phillips' magnificent Villa Arcadia, which was now a children's orphanage.

Meanwhile, Scott somehow held the fort while Baker recovered and after his vacation he returned to Barton Street on a more regular basis, reassuring his clients that all was well and even seeking new opportunities for Baker & Scott. Frederick Goodenough, Baker's client for the Barclay's Bank building in Cape Town, was stepping down as chairman of the bank and now wished to establish a hostel in London for post-graduate students from around the empire who were coming to study there. Reassured that Baker was able to undertake the work, he commissioned him to design what was to be the first phase of London House (now Goodenough College) on Mecklenburgh Square in Bloomsbury. Construction started the following year comprising the main triple-arched entrance which would eventually lead to a central courtyard and two wings of accommodation including the main hall which was approached by a rather grand staircase which rises and turns in the corner of the L-shaped block. On the inside of the courtyard a continuous attached vaulted colonnade (echoing Wren's Chelsea Hospital) provides ground-floor circulation and a very attractive and still popular first-floor external terrace. The language here is Harrow School with brickwork and stone facings above a flint base, which

London House from the courtyard (courtesy Cate Buxton).

Baker described simply as "a novelty in London."[13] His increasing use of flint in central London was somewhat idiosyncratic as there is no real architectural precedent for it (certainly after medieval times), and its selection can only have been on symbolic grounds as being for Baker an essentially English building material. (The further phases, that completed the inner court, were later carried out by Scott.)

More interesting in many ways was his next commission for a further empire building—the new headquarters for the Royal Empire Society, just around the corner from South Africa House on Northumberland Avenue. With Baker's background, experience and continuing contacts within the Round Table, his appointment was once more assured. On what was a very tight site, Baker and Scott were able to squeeze in an assembly hall, a large dining room, a substantial library and various other offices and smaller meeting rooms. He himself acknowledged that the entrance hall was insufficient to cope with the capacity of the assembly hall, but as he explained to his client there was little more that could be done on their constricted site without omitting other elements of accommodation. The public rooms, particularly the library and the lounge, had a relaxed elegance evoking a 20th-century London club (with more than a whiff of Art Deco for the first time) while all the main spaces enjoyed a combination of marble Doric columns and wooden paneling of various types, gifted by the dominions. Its greatest success however is its sheer Portland stone elevation to Northumberland Avenue whose dignified restraint is contrasted with two of Charles Wheeler's finest figures supporting the entrance canopy and embodying, in Baker's words, "The Spirit of Thought and Action, the characteristics of the men who have made the Empire."[14] The foundation stone was laid by the Prince of Wales on the 3rd of June 1935, and the completed building was opened by his brother, the Duke of York, on the 12th of November 1936, who would be King a month later following the abdication crisis.

Baker's circle of friends was now being depleted year by year but nothing prepared him for the news, in May 1935, that Lawrence was dead. The hero of the Arab Revolt had been killed in a motorcycle accident on a sleepy Dorset lane. They had remained good friends after Lawrence vacated Barton Street with Lawrence even suggesting at one point that he would value the tranquility, if Baker could secure him a position as night watchman on the Bank of England building site. Baker recalled that he had been "full of sound and fury, such as I had never heard before, against the agents of Publicity, who disturbed the peace of his country cottage. I am sorry that he was angry, as it was the last time I saw him…. Whom the Gods love die young before their work is done, it may seem to us who remain."[15] Baker had always hoped that Lawrence's heroic work was not yet complete and, like many of his friends, was unable to contemplate the true nature of his character as Lionel Curtis confided to Baker in response to the press coverage of Lawrence's death— "If it is of course possible he found that he had that temptation as a boy, I am sure he set himself to conquer it, just as he set himself to conquer the hereditary temptation to drink of total abstinence…. That L. indulged animal appetites of any kind is to me just inconceivable."[16] Tragic as his death was, it was to be but the first of many losses for Baker. Rudyard Kipling, with whom Baker had corresponded to the end, died in January 1936, and it would now seem that every winter would claim another friend. With all work in India concluded, nothing further to draw him back to Africa and his own health now compromised, Baker's travel was now much constrained and his vacations were limited to late summer or autumn breaks, often staying at Allan Bank in Grasmere and walking the surrounding Lakeland fells.

The Royal Empire Society building on Northumberland Avenue, London, with Wheeler's sculptures supporting the balcony (author's collection).

Scott now bore the burden of the daily management of the bank and the practice, allowing Baker to immerse himself in the detailed design of the interiors and their decoration. Working once more with his friends Charles Wheeler and Joseph Armitage, David Cameron and his band of mural painters, Lawrence Turner who carved plaques and metalwork, and Boris Anrep who produced the mosaics, he designed friezes, murals, carved

Third floor vestibule of the Bank of England (courtesy the Bank of England Archive, reference 15A13/1/1/59/10).

keystones, wrought balustrades, suspended light fittings, and decorative plaster ceilings as well as inscriptions and suitable heraldic devices. George Booth, the chairman of the committee, was much involved, and Baker recalled the many occasions when he "came with me to see some model in the clay or the more finished plaster that Wheeler had made for his criticisms," with Baker seeing in Booth a man of "unique gifts, a combination of quick insight and the understanding of complicated plans and practical problems, as well as sympathy for the artist … a personality of great charm, responsiveness, and kindness which endeared him to all who collaborated with him."[17] Baker and Wheeler incorporated several touches of humor at the bank—with alternate lions and eagles representing the pound and the dollar, chasing each other around a circular bronze pendant light fitting, while the carved head of Pythagoras on a keystone was surrounded by a mist of numbers and one permanent director's room received a winged Pegasus plaque reflecting his exploits as a steeplechase rider. The bank was thus one of the last great public or institutional buildings in London to receive such extraordinary care and investment and provided one final fading echo of Arts Workers Guild collaboration.

By 1936, Baker was also finally able to start work on what he saw as his "crowning work done for my Church"[18]—Church House in Westminster, the central administrative building for the Church of England and the meeting place of the Church Assembly (now the General Synod). His building, which was just a few hundred yards from Barton Street, was to replace the earlier and smaller one on the same site which had been designed by Sir Arthur Blomfield. The creation of the new site in central Westminster had been a long and tortuous process involving various acquisitions and demolitions, negotiations with Westminster Abbey and School, the rebuilding of one of the school houses, a long legal dispute and finally an Act of Parliament. In Baker's own words—"The Church House comprises the Assembly Hall (which seating six hundred, is larger than the House of Commons) and connected by the circular ambulatory round it, a House of Laymen for four hundred, a Clergy Convocation Hall for two hundred, a chapel with presbytery stalls for fifty bishops and a large hall for general purposes overlooking Dean's Yard and the Abbey. Thus it may be compared to a Parliament House of several 'houses' with close inter-communication one with another."[19] To all this was added the need to

CHURCH HOUSE

PLAN OF FIRST FLOOR

Church House first floor plan. Key: A Entrance Hall, B Assembly Hall, C Hoare Memorial Hall, D Chapel, E House of Convocation, F Offices (from *Architecture and Personalities*).

include commercial accommodation around part of its perimeter to provide a source of future funding. For a devout Anglican like Baker, his appointment was a great and greatly appreciated honor—"This opportunity in perhaps my last great work of expressing in the fabric of the building some little of the story and ideals, as I conceived them, of the Church of England."[20]

It was an extremely demanding architectural problem, inserting this vast amount of accommodation within a complex and highly irregular site while doing justice to his church and faith. His design is organized around the vast circular Assembly Hall, itself in many ways a reworking of his Ninth Church of Christ Scientist in nearby Marsham Street but here with an upper-level balcony below the shallow dome. The remainder of the accommodation is then distributed around the perimeter of the site with the spaces between the circular and rectilinear geometries cleverly used to provide courtyards and thus natural light and air to the Assembly Hall. The Memorial Hall is located on Great Smith Street and marked by a great first-floor bay window; the House of Convocation is slotted in above Tufton Street while the chapel occupies a first- and second-floor space above a new arched entrance to Dean's Yard from Great College Street. The new building spans and entirely completes the south side of Dean's Yard with the main entrance to the building marked by an arched balcony (strangely reminiscent of Pretoria Station) below a rather subtle dropped pediment between what appear to be two palatial wings. As Peter Davey noted of Church House, Baker "never quite forgot the lessons of Pugin and sometimes attempted to fit the bulk of his huge commissions quietly into context."[21]

The architectural language is Harrow School via London House with more than a hint of Chelsea Hospital in the brick Corinthian pilasters and pediment to Dean's Yard.

The exterior of Church House with the great bay window of the Memorial Hall above Great Smith Street (author's collection).

The elevations to the surrounding streets are equally restrained in similar red brick with stone dressings topped off with a stone balustrade and supported once more on a strong flint base. Whereas on London House in Bloomsbury the flint struck a discordant note, here in the ancient lanes and courts of Westminster it seems appropriate. Baker took a great deal of care with his flintwork and on this occasion was pleased to accommodate flint from Owletts and Nurstead Court as well as from various churchyards in Kent in this, his church's most important London building. While the Assembly Hall is a fine space which evokes (though rarely observes) a church united, the architectural highlight of the building is the delightful Presbytery Chapel. This is entered centrally and with its two apsidal ends and vault of a similar radius has a geometric purity with which even Wren would have been content. The entire complex forms both a catalog of Baker's previous buildings and a masterclass on urban intervention and design. As one would anticipate, almost every surface is subjected to coats of arms, emblems of saints, plaques and inscriptions so dear to Baker, but here excessive.

The foundation stone was laid by Queen Mary on the 26th of June 1937, and in November Baker found himself standing next to the Archbishop of Canterbury, Cosmo Lang, as they awaited the King and Queen at the opening of the Royal Empire Society building. The Archbishop confessed to being rather overwhelmed by the responsibility of building Church House and inquired if Baker could recommend a suitable man of business to assist him. Baker suggested someone like Lionel Hichens his best friend, who was then chairman of Cammell Lairds shipbuilders, and the Archbishop looked no further, eventually persuading Hichens to add membership of the rebuilding committee of Church House to his many other responsibilities. For Baker it was a delight to work with Hichens again and he wrote, "As soon as he came to help us the work lightened for all concerned…. He would join us at our simple lunches in my little house in Smith Square, and our discussions cleared and raised our thought and strengthened and quickened consequent action. He had, moreover, interest in and sympathy with the ideas which I wished to express in the building, and, when he agreed, explained and supported them to the busy members of the Committee, or directly to the Council over which the Archbishop presided."[22] It was to be as happy and congenial a project as perhaps only the Winchester Memorial had been so many years before when Baker worked with Hichens and their friend Monty Rendall.

The year of 1938 saw the final scaffolding coming down on the bank to reveal Baker's completed building to London for the first time. On Prince's Street, a great semi-circular colonnade stepped forward to break up the long elevation, and on Lothbury Street the two great wings of offices swept forward to the very parapet of Soane's wall, with their great loggias proving the last occasion that Baker would employ this favorite motif. At either end, two new domes turned the corners, with the one to Tivoli Corner surmounted by a gilt bronze figure of Ariel as a symbol of trust. The rear elevation to Lothbury Street, despite Baker's slate mansard roof, is more palatial than domestic with its great swooping concave corners, venetian windows, urns and sculptures whereas the final elevation to Threadneedle Street is much more well behaved. It was likened to "a palace of banking" or "a deluxe hotel" but perhaps the best architectural analogy is a Parisian "hotel" or town house, in which the obvious wealth of the owners is projected from behind a defensive enclosing wall. It portrayed the bank as being above the direct commercialism of the activities that surround it, reserved, independent, and offering a historical continuity in which a gentlemanly capitalism is preserved. Architecturally, despite his

The main entrance to Church House on Dean's Yard (author's collection).

"tinkering" with Soane's details and the cleaning of his screen, it still fails to achieve his aim of an integrated whole. Soane's wall continues its historic function as a secure perimeter while Baker's palace rises within—aloof—and only offering the public access at the single point where Soane's and Baker's work are joined in its grand entrance. Baker had delivered what the bank had aspired to: a state-of-the-art facility for an historic institution which effectively communicated the bank's mythic identity. The interiors remain one of his greatest achievements including his very successful Garden Court, and they are still hugely appreciated by all who have the privilege of working in them as well as by their many visitors from around the globe. Work on the interiors continued for several years with the rebuilding committee issuing its final report in February 1941 and the final workmen leaving the site the following year.

With the final occupation of the bank, the slowing of new commissions and the growing threat of a further war, at 76, Baker began a process of putting his affairs in order. Scott was already running the practice and though he had neither Baker's ability as a designer nor his exceptional network to draw upon, he was quite capable of completing the current projects and winning further work (as he successfully did in partnership with Vernon Helbing). The future of Owletts was a different matter, and Baker was only too well aware both that its remaining 25 acres could not support it and also how close the family had come to losing it on his father's death. His friend Phillip Kerr, now Lord Lothian, faced a similar dilemma with his rather larger Blickling Hall in Norfolk and was also well aware of further important country houses that had an uncertain and threatened future. As a result, Kerr promoted and achieved the passing of the National Trust Act of 1937 under which families would be allowed to pass their homes to the National

The final appearance of Baker's Imperial loggia on the rear of the Bank of England, above Soane's encircling wall (author's collection).

Trust for safekeeping along with their contents and land thus escaping inheritance tax and with the added benefit that they would be allowed to remain in their homes under a variety of financial arrangements while opening them to the public for viewing. In 1938 Baker offered Owletts to the Trust as an example of a small Kentish Squire's home and it was accepted, thus securing its future, and by deed of the gift the family would have (and still enjoy) the first right to the lease in the normal order of succession. Baker had also bought and restored a number of historic timber-framed cottages on Sole Street in Cobham and these too he gifted to the nation. Like many other tenants of National Trust properties, Florence was equally delighted by the security which this new arrangement offered and appalled by the visitors to her home. In 1942 James Lees-Milne, the Historic Buildings Secretary of the National Trust, recorded in his diary a visit to the aging Sir Herbert and his wife at the house. Sir Herbert was "kind, Christian-like, and cultivated" and Lady Baker "no less delightful than her husband." He noted, "They call themselves with justifiable pride, yeomen of Kent; but they are more than that."[23]

Another significant loose end for Baker was his relationship with Lutyens. The two had barely spoken for years and (astonishingly) it still bothered Baker. He was well aware of Lutyens' role in *Country Life's* attack on him and that he continued to deprecate him and his work whenever the opportunity arose, and yet as Charles Wheeler recorded, "The quarrel caused Baker much pain and he very often referred to it in considerable sadness. He was far more generous to Lutyens than he to him…. Baker always spoke of Lutyens as being a pre-eminent architect and said he 'did things right by instinct.'"[24] As a Christian gentleman, admirer of his extraordinary architectural ability and former friend, Baker felt obliged to heal the wound and believed that it was now or never. Hearing late in 1938 that Lutyens was planning to stand for the presidency of the Royal Academy, he offered him one final olive branch—"I should like to vote for you, if you want to stand, for the sake of our old friendship which I enjoyed and valued so much; and forget all the soreness and the harm. As one must in the assurance and peace of old age."[25] To which Lutyens responded positively the following day—"Many thanks for your charming and friendly letter."[26] And so, after all the ill-feeling, the hurt and damage, they recommenced their correspondence, at one point both writing more than a letter a day to each other. Topics ranged from

Sir Herbert in his office in Barton Street, London in late 1930 (courtesy Michael Baker).

the affairs of the Royal Academy and the Royal Institute of British Architects to Modern Architecture (both violently opposed) and occasionally to events from their earlier friendship. While Lutyens often slipped back into rancor—"The first blow you gave me was your perspective of the Delhi building, when you showed the domes within the towers instead of designed with the towers inside the domes"[27]—Baker soon smoothed the waters once more. His aim was to rebuild an old friendship that he valued and to that end he succeeded in what most people would not have attempted. No doubt Lutyens saw it as a sign of weakness, or more likely as a sign of Baker's guilt over the ramp, but the opposite in both instances was the case. Baker had for one last time used all his powers of diplomacy and tenacity to successfully achieve his goal.

Although limited work continued on the bank, Baker's Empire Houses were all complete and Church House had become the focus for his practice along with the continual flotsam and jetsam of alterations and extensions that occupy most architects. While Lutyens grappled with the complex geometry of what would have been his greatest building, the new Roman Catholic Cathedral for Liverpool, Baker, equally characteristically, was deep "in research into Church history to find authentic arms or emblems of saints, or, if there had been none assigned to them by medieval heralds, historical facts of their lives for the invention of appropriate symbols"[28] for Church House.

The clouds of war were gathering once more and with memories of the slaughter in what Baker and his contemporaries had hoped would be "the war to end all wars" still fresh, most of Baker's Round Table friends were now part of Nancy Astor's Cliveden Set and strongly for appeasement. By 1938, Phillip Kerr had already met Hitler on several occasions in an attempt to find a peaceful resolution to the growing tensions in Europe. By the summer of 1939, it seemed however that war was once more inevitable and following Germany's invasion of Poland on the 1st of September, on the 3rd of September 1939, Britain and France declared war on Germany. For those like Baker who had witnessed the carnage on the western front two decades before, it was a bitter blow. As in the First World War, there was little work for architects as the country switched to war production. The construction of Church House continued despite restrictions and delays caused by the war and was officially opened by King George VI and Queen Elizabeth on the 10th of June, with its 78-year-old architect there to be presented to his monarch for the last time.

By that summer of 1940, the German bombing campaign of London had commenced in anticipation of an invasion of Britain, and in the early evening of October the 14th, a high explosive bomb fell upon the Dean's Yard façade of newly completed Church House, smashing through the fifth and fourth floors and exploding on the third, blasting a gap thirty yards wide in its front elevation. The hall itself survived but, in Baker's words—"All the panelling and sculpture … were hurled like driftwood across the floor … and, together with the band of architects and artists who worked so loyally with me," lost, "the work on which we had laboured so long and devotedly."[29] Three hundred people had been sheltering from the air raid in the basement of the building and all had survived, but six who had been in the building itself were killed, including to Baker's horror, his best friend Lionel Hichens.

Rhodes, Milner, Kipling, Lawrence, John Buchan earlier that year, and now Hichens—all now gone, and in December 1940, the name of Phillip Kerr, then British Ambassador to the United States, was added to this lengthening list. To conclude a desperate year, a bomb fell near Barton Street and the office had to be evacuated while Baker's house around the corner in Smith Square was also badly damaged. His old partner

John Buchan's grave in the village churchyard in Elsfield, England, designed by his friend Sir Herbert Baker (author's collection).

Frank Fleming sympathized from Cape Town—"It is hard lines to be evicted from one's own office … but you seem to take it very cheerfully … altho' you say the damage was not very noticeable…. It is sad about Lionel Hichens & also Lord Lothian—both of whom you will miss as personal friends as well as for their splendid work."[30] Scott had no option but to split their team with those still working on Church House accommodated there and the remainder in an office at the bank. Worse was to come on the night of the 16th of April 1941 when the Royal Empire Society building on Northumberland Avenue was struck by a two-ton bomb. Seventy-four people were there at the time, one member was killed and another injured and two members of the staff badly hurt. The building caught fire and many of the unique contents of its library, including 35,000 books that had been collected over the previous 70 years, were lost. The building was badly damaged but the main façade and most of the main rooms survived. Unfortunately, on the night of the 10th of May, the worst night of the Blitz, it was hit by a further bomb which destroyed the dining room, what remained of the library and most of the rooms on the front of the building. The assembly hall and the bedroom wing survived and the society continued to operate from there throughout the rest of the war while the remainder of their building stood as a blackened shell.

Though he continued to work on it, Lutyens' great Liverpool Cathedral was doomed—its ever-increasing cost could never be met by the working-class Catholic poor of the city and even his fees were unpaid. As president of the Royal Academy, he was invited to chair a committee on the rebuilding of London. He invited Baker to join him, but he declined, writing, "I don't feel that I can put full weight of time and energy into all the complicated issues involved to justify any half-service on the committee; and half-service is mutually of small value."[31] He offered Scott in his place, whom Lutyens accepted.[32] While there was little architectural work for Baker, his energy remained astonishing and he still spent most of the week in London, often visiting Wheeler in his studio, entertaining as far as rations permitted at Smith Square and attending the Royal Academy and his club. He and Lutyens had moved on from their correspondence and were now lunching occasionally and regularly attending the academy together.

Sir Patrick Duncan died, like the other two great Scots in Baker's life, Kerr and Buchan, in office, as Governor-General of South Africa in July 1943, and Fleming attended his funeral as Baker's representative, writing after of "the simple beauty of the service … it all forms a wonderful demonstration of heartfelt appreciation of his great qualities and personality."[33] Though Baker had been "Grandpapa" to the Kindergarten, he was to outlive most of them. His autobiography *Architecture and Personalities* was well underway, and he was sharing drafts with friends while attempting to find a publisher against a backdrop of wartime paper shortages.[34] He maintained his regular correspondence with family and friends around the globe, though sadly, many were now letters of condolence. There were still Lionel Curtis, Geoffrey Dawson, Dick Feetham, Hugh Wyndham and Robert Brand from the Kindergarten, Frank Fleming and Jan Smuts in South Africa; from Indian days—Lords Hardinge and Crewe and William Marris; fellow-artists, Charles Wheeler and Alfred Nicholson and fellow-gardener Harold Compton, the director of the National Botanic Gardens at Kirstenbosch. Letters to his offspring (which included honorary son, Charles Wheeler—the "sapling" to his "parent oak") were now generally typed with carbon copies for all, while vacations were restricted to his beloved Grasmere, Wordsworth's old home in the Lakes. He was actively involved in raising funding for new memorials and continued to be a regular contributor to the letters page of *The Times* voicing his opinions on everything from Imperial Architecture to his opposition to the retention of bomb-damaged London churches as ruins. Modern Architecture he condemned on principle for its rejection of the past, referring on several occasions to its "ugly contortions," and proposing instead, "a golden mean between heritage and invention."[35]

A message, early on New Year's Day 1944, informed him of Lutyens' death. He had been suffering from lung cancer for several years—the price for his ubiquitous pipe. Baker was saddened but also relieved that he had rescued their old friendship before the end. Their lives and careers had been intertwined for over 50 years and few would have thought in 1887, the year that they first met, that either the ill-educated Lutyens or the somber senior assistant would scale the heights of their profession together as the most prolific and successful architects of their generation. Their disagreement in India had led to a bitter dispute, which though not of his making, Baker deeply regretted, but he had finally succeeded in rekindling their fellowship in the end. He paid a suitable tribute to him in *The Times*—"In sunshine and storm I have watched with admiration the flame of his great talents … become fiercer and stronger as it fired his passion for the monumental, the Grand Manner of the Great Masters; the Olympian attitude," though he added, "careless of mankind."[36] His burial, as befitted one of England's greatest architects, was at Westminster Abbey, and Baker read one of the lessons from Ecclesiasticus—"But they will maintain the state of the world and *all* their desire is in the work of their craft."

Baker's autobiography was published later that year. It is a curious book, weaving his life together with those whom he knew and worked with, and one can't help feeling that it would have been so much better had it been written by another. It comes across as self-congratulatory, with the recollections of his famous friends akin to name-dropping, and yet these were genuine friendships which were valued by both parties. In lieu of architectural criticism or at least independent validation, he quotes letters from his friends praising his buildings, and the many literary quotes with which it is liberally sprinkled (which he could have quoted verbatim, with source) simply add to a general air of pretentiousness. Perhaps, like his book on Rhodes, he already felt the need to respond to criticisms of his work, but sadly its main impact has been to gain him a reputation for self-congratulation. He was much better, much more capable, honorable and genuine than the book suggests. Nevertheless, its epilogue gives a helpful insight into his last days.

> As the journey of life draws to an end we must think of an inn for a resting place; a roof to shelter one for the time when the dark hours begin. Retirement is a difficult thought to face for one who loves to work, and who feels that he may still have much to give. But when England became the besieged outpost in the world war for civilisation, retirement was for an architect inevitable and enforced; the call to me to cease work was sounded with the declaration of war…. My feelings are perhaps common to all who reach old age with the retention of an active and not unadventurous mind…. But we know within ourselves that it is right and in the interest of ultimate progress that old age should retire from the strife and leave the path open to youth…. So the old fox returns to the burrow where he was born and bred. The life of the country has always been a vital part of my being, the deeper part … the supreme glory is seen in April, when Owletts with its red-brick walls is an island in a sea of white cherry blossom, scenting all the air.[37]

He lived to see the end of that second great war and the landslide election of a Socialist government—"It is a shock such a swing to the Labour; remembering the Khaki election, as it was called in like circumstances after the last war. I am most devoutly sorry for Churchill who has saved us really from destruction … the worst is that Labour can try experiments now with such a big majority and the majority is so big that it will last my time,"[38] and as a staunch conservative and landowner, he soon even feared for his home— "No one here and I am afraid the Socialist govt will say there is a half-vacant house."[39] Christmas 1945 was spent at Owletts with children and grandchildren (Florence counted 17) when after lunch, Sir Herbert announced that as this would be his last Christmas, they were all going to plant a tree in the garden! Outside, the family found a hole already prepared by the gardeners, into which was planted a cedar of Lebanon by Sir Herbert and his youngest grandchild Charles, which now shades the tennis court.

His last badly typed letter to his children was sent on Thursday the 31st of January 1946—"Dear Offspring…. I want to see Scott who went to Harrow on Monday and saw the H. Master they discussed what was tio be donw for the memorial—well done one up on sluggish Winchester who have begun to think—they wont do very much as the building is all there merely cut the 300 names—so far—and inscription and some piece of sculpture I think an I have got to work on that! In my mind; its refreshing to have a job however small in being."[40] He died on the following Monday the 4th of February of another stroke, asleep in his bed at Owletts.

Charles Wheeler can take up the tale of his burial in Westminster Abbey—

> His ashes are interned beneath the nave because the Dean, Bishop de Labilliere, told me, he considered him to be "the greatest architect of the Commonwealth." He said to Henry Baker, the eldest son, who went to the Abbey with the sad news: "We would love to have him here." Custom required an outside backing. Therefore the Dean asked me if the Academy would present a plea to him for a burial in the Abbey of one of its most distinguished members. To my astonishment the Academy would not do this. When I spoke to Walter Lamb, the Secretary,

about it, he received the proposal coldly and muttered something about "creating a precedent." This seemed to me to be unreasonable when the initiative had come from the Dean himself. I had rather ashamedly to confess my failure to Dean de Labilliere who then asked if I myself would write him a letter and get it signed by half-a-dozen men of importance. This I was able to do. It was necessarily a hasty business. I secured Smutts signature by cable. Vincent Massey and Lord Salisbury signed willingly, so did Giles Gilbert Scott, but I had difficulty with Munnings, the PRA. He reluctantly agreed and then only if Scott would do so. By agitated telephoning I eventually reached him, got his consent to sign on his behalf, then raced to the Deanery with the letter, arriving a few minutes before 6 p.m.—zero hour. Had I needed a spur to this business it would have been provided by a recollection I had of an incident during the war. It was during the first days of the bombing of London. Baker and I were walking together in Westminster. The warning sounded. He said: "Shall we go into this shelter or walk on to the Abbey?" He walked on after a moment's pause, saying: "I'd rather die in the Abbey than in an underground dug-out."[41]

The service took place on the 13th of February, commencing with "I Vow to Thee, My Country" and concluding with "Jerusalem." Dorothy Ward, who attended, described the proceedings to Eleanor Rawnsley, Baker's great friend in Grasmere—"There was a wonderful atmosphere of affection and esteem in the big congregation and the Lesson was most beautifully read. The whole thing went with extraordinary reverence and love. The grave of the little casket is in the Nave, rather on the left as you stand facing the entrance to the Choir. Lady Baker walked just behind the coffin when they went in procession from the Lantern to the graveside, her daughter with her, the 3 sons and their wives just behind.... Well there is another good and great man gone!"[42]

Epilogue

"Fate's Discourtesy"

Sir Herbert Baker was, as *The Times* put it so well, "supremely happy in his generation." His guiding beliefs were commonly held during his lifetime: the superiority of the British and the benign influence of their great global empire; the supremacy of Western art, springing as it did from the ancient wells of Classical Greece and Rome; the duty of Christians to propagate their religion among heathens; the power of architecture to project political thought and ideals; architecture's role in connecting our present with our past, and perhaps most of all, the moral code demanded of a Victorian Christian gentleman. They reflect a very different world from the one we now live in.

His architecture too has for much of the last century been seen as entirely irrelevant by contemporary practitioners. Prior to the Second World War the exponents of Modern Architecture in Britain were few and worked for a small, wealthy, avant-garde elite, but in the decades after, the cult of Modernism held sway throughout the Western world. It was, in the words of historian David Watkins, "a morally, socially, politically, and artistically cohesive package from which no one must be at liberty to abstain."[1] From social housing through schools and universities to hospitals, offices and town halls (as with the previous century's Gothic revival), for contemporary architects there could be "but one true style" for all new buildings.

Nikolaus Pevsner, perhaps the last great arbiter of British taste, was in the vanguard of Modernism's promotion in Britain. For him, Classical buildings were "inexpressive of the Zeitgeist" and perhaps unsurprisingly, he bitterly detested Baker and his work. He thought his architecture showed "the same astonishing self-assurance which appears so naively in his memoirs,"[2] and Baker building after Baker building received excoriating reviews in his guide books. He described the destruction of Soane's work at the bank by Baker as "the greatest architectural crime, in the City of London, of the twentieth century"[3]—a phrase that is still regularly repeated, even today.

Despite the damage which Modernism has wrought upon our towns and cities now being generally acknowledged, Sir Edwin Lutyens' work now once more being appreciated and outstanding contemporary Classicists such as Demetri Porphyrios and Craig Hamilton finding themselves much in demand, Baker's reputation has yet to recover from almost a century of sustained attack. Fortunately, most of his buildings survive and, interestingly, are both still in use and held in great affection by their users.

Sir Herbert Baker himself (largely seen through Lutyens' eyes) has been consistently portrayed as "a dull committee man." He was certainly reserved, he took himself and his work seriously, he left no witty one-liners, but under what often appeared as a rather severe exterior, his many friends found a strong, thoughtful, cultured, talented, warm and highly intelligent man. Like so much of his architecture, a cool public persona concealed a depth and richness within which was only experienced by those who were allowed beyond the threshold. Both the man and his work are now long overdue for reassessment.

Chapter Notes

Chapter 1

1. Herbert Baker, *Architecture and Personalities* (London: Country Life, 1944), p. 9. (Carl Jung in fact did not describe "introversion" in his "Psychological Types" until 1921).

2. Herbert Baker, *Architecture and Personalities* (London: Country Life, 1944), p. 6.

3. John Ruskin, *Lectures on Art* (London: G. Allan, 1905), p. 36.

4. Herbert Baker, *Architecture and Personalities* (London: Country Life, 1944), p. 13.

5. Haileybury School had originally been founded by the East India Company as a training college and became a public school in 1862 following the dissolution of the company after the Indian Mutiny of 1857.

6. Herbert Baker, *Architecture and Personalities* (London: Country Life, 1944), p. 13.

7. For those who haven't played the game, cricket appears to be some arcane ritual which is almost impossible to fathom, but for anyone who has walked out to bat leaving one's team behind in the pavilion and then finding oneself surrounded by the enemy, it immediately appears as a strangely appropriate preparation for Imperial service.

8. Robert Graves, *Goodbye to All That* (London: The Folio Society, 1981), p. 49.

9. Letter from J. A. Babbington to Mrs. Baker, August 29, 1877, Collection of Michael Baker (MB).

10. As Baker spent much of his life in male company, it seems necessary to confirm that there was no hint of homosexuality in any correspondence relating to this or any of his other male relationships; indeed Baker later commented to his best friend Lionel Curtis in private correspondence regarding T. E. Lawrence that, "It is an almost invariable symptom of a pervert that he believes that everyone else is subject to the same perversion." Letter from Herbert Baker to Lionel Curtis, May 24, 1935, Royal Institute of British Architects (RIBA) Archive.

11. Odette Keun, *I Discover the English* (London: John Lane, 1934), p. 151.

12. Herbert Baker's diary, 1886, RIBA.

13. F. H. Crossley, *English Church Design* (London: B. T. Batsford, 1945), p. 7.

14. Herbert Baker, *Architecture and Personalities* (London: Country Life, 1944), pp. 14, 15. The South Kensington Museum became the Victoria and Albert Museum in 1899, when Queen Victoria made her last public appearance to lay the foundation stone of the new Aston Webb building.

15. Herbert Baker's diary, 1886, RIBA.

16. Michael Keith, *Architecture and Idealism 1892–1913, The South African Years* (Gibraltar: Ashanti Publishing, 1978), p. 11.

17. Jane Ridley, *Edwin Lutyens, His Life, His Wife, His Work* (London: Pimlico, 2003), p. 49.

18. Osbert Lancaster is also credited with "Mock Tudor."

19. Margaret Richardson, *Architects of the Arts and Crafts Movement* (London: Trefoil Books, 1983), p. 59.

20. Darcy Braddell, "Architectural Reminiscences…Fugaces Anni," *The Builder*, December 15, 1922, pp. 900–903.

21. Herbert Baker, *Architecture and Personalities* (London: Country Life, 1944), p. 15.

22. Henri Jean Louis Marie Joseph Massé, *The Art Workers Guild 1884–1984* (Stratford-on-Avon: Shakespeare Head Press, 1934), p. 8.

23. Gavin Stamp, "A Hundred Years of the Art Workers' Guild," Artworkersguild.org.

24. William Blake, "Jerusalem." https://www.poetryfoundation.org/poems/54684/jerusalem-and-did-those-feet-in-ancient-time.

25. John Ruskin, *The Stones of Venice*, Volumes I and II (London: George Routledge and Sons, 1907), p. 181.

26. Peter Davey, *Arts and Crafts Architecture* (London: Phaidon, 1995), p. 19.

27. Reginald Blomfield, *Memoirs of an Architect* (London: Macmillan, 1932), p. 15.

28. Herbert Baker, *Architecture and Personalities* (London: Country Life, 1944), p. 15.

29. Christopher Hussey, *The Life of Sir Edwin Lutyens* (London: Country Life, 1950), p. 182.

30. Herbert Baker, *Architecture and Personalities* (London: Country Life, 1944), p. 15.

31. *Architectural Association Journal* 36 (1920): p. 55.

32. Herbert Baker, *Architecture and Personalities* (London: Country Life, 1944), p. 17.

33. Baker/Lutyens Letters, January 28, 1942, RIBA.

34. Herbert Baker, *Architecture and Personalities* (London: Country Life, 1944), p. 17.

35. Herbert Baker, *Architecture and Personalities* (London: Country Life, 1944), pp. 15–16.

36. Nigel Worden, Elizabeth Van Heyningen, and Vivian Bickford-Smith, *Cape Town: The Making of a City* (Cape Town: New Africa Books, 2004).

37. Rudyard Kipling, *Something of Myself and Other Autobiographical Writings* (Cambridge: Cambridge University Press, 1991), p. 57.

38. Herbert Baker, *Architecture and Personalities* (London: Country Life, 1944), p. 19.

39. Bruce Rosen, "Income vs Expenditure in Working-Class Victorian England," http://vichist. blogspot.com/2014/05/income-vs-expenditure-in-working-class.html, June 19, 2014.

40. Doreen E Greig, *Herbert Baker in South Africa* (Cape Town: Purnell, 1970), p. 37.

Chapter 2

1. Quoted in Richard Faber, *The Vision and the Need: Late Victorian Imperialist Aims* (London: Faber, 1963), p. 64.

2. Edward Linley Sambourne, *Punch*, December 10, 1892.

3. John Flint, *Cecil Rhodes* (London: Hutcheson, 1976), pp. 248–249.

4. Such extreme colonial attitudes were by no means confined to the British, as Niall Ferguson related in his book on Western Civilization: "A century ago hardly anyone in the West doubted that white men were superior to black....In German South-West Africa, blacks were forbidden to ride horses, had to salute whites, could not walk on the footpaths, could not own bicycles." Niall Ferguson, *Civilization: The West and the Rest* (London: Allen Lane, 2011), p. 177.

5. Letter from Herbert Baker to Percy Baker, June 9, 1892, Rondebosch, MB.

6. Herbert Baker, *Cecil Rhodes by His Architect* (Oxford: Oxford University Press), 1934, pp. 19–20.

7. Letter from Herbert Baker to Percy Baker, June 9, 1892, Rondebosch, MB.

8. Herbert Baker, *Architecture and Personalities* (London: Country Life, 1944), p. 30.

9. Strange as this may seem, it was and still is not unusual for a fully qualified 30-year-old architect to not have designed a building. Most architects, like Baker, serve an extended period as an assistant in an existing practice after qualification during which they generally work on more experienced architects' projects. Sadly, many architects thus actually complete their career having designed very few, if any, buildings themselves.

10. Letter from Herbert Baker to Percy Baker, Rouwkoop, Rondebosch, October 31, 1892, MB.

11. Letter from Herbert Baker to Percy Baker, January 15, 1893, MB.

12. Herbert Baker, *Architecture and Personalities* (London: Country Life, 1944), p. 23.

13. Herbert Baker, *Architecture and Personalities* (London: Country Life, 1944), p. 24.

14. Letter from Herbert Baker to Percy Baker, South African Chambers, Cape Town, April 20, 1893, MB.

15. Mary Cook, *Africana Notes and News*, March 4, 1947, p. 170.

16. Herbert Baker, *Architecture and Personalities* (London: Country Life, 1944), p. 30.

17. As with the East India Company, the preferred method of expansion of the British South Africa Company was by treaty with the existing tribal rulers, but where this failed, force was regularly used in their conquests throughout Africa. The first Matabele War which Rhodes had left Baker to direct, was the first occasion on which the new "Maxim Gun," the world's first machine gun (invented by Hiram Stevens Maxim in 1884), was used. It was said to have mown down the Matabele warriors, "literally like grass."

18. Herbert Baker, *Cecil Rhodes by His Architect* (Oxford: Oxford University Press, 1934), p. 22.

19. Herbert Baker, *Cecil Rhodes by His Architect* (Oxford: Oxford University Press, 1934), p. 26.

20. Herbert Baker, *Architecture and Personalities* (London: Country Life, 1944), p. 30.

21. Letter from Herbert Baker to Percy Baker, 18 SA Chambers, St. George's Street, March 6, 1894, MB.

22. Letter from Herbert Baker to Percy Baker, January 5, 1895, MB.

23. Letter from Herbert Baker to Percy Baker, February 4, 1895, MB.

24. Chris Ash, *The If Man: Dr Leander Starr Jameson, the Inspiration for Kipling's Masterpiece* (West Midlands, England: Helion, 2012).

25. Letter from Herbert Baker to Percy Baker, March 2, 1895, MB.

26. The First Boer War was also the last time that the British fought in their famous "redcoats," with the introduction of the khaki uniform following their defeat.

27. Herbert Baker to his mother, Rondelbosch with Lionel, May 5, 1896, MB.

28. Letter from Herbert Baker to Percy Baker, July 19, 1896, MB.

29. Donald and Ruth Fassler papers, 1933–1945, Purdue University Libraries, Archives and Special Collections.

30. Herbert Baker, *Architecture and Personalities* (London: Country Life, 1944), p. 31.

31. J. G. Macdonald, *Rhodes: A Life* (London: Philip Allan, 1952), p. 218.

32. Herbert Baker, *Architecture and Personalities* (London: Country Life, 1944), p. 31.

Chapter 3

1. James Bryce, *Impressions of South Africa* (London: Macmillan, 1897), p. 490.

2. Charles Wheeler, *High Relief—The Autobiography of Sir Charles Wheeler Sculptor* (London: Country Life, 1968), p. 58.

3. John E. Flint, *Cecil Rhodes* (London: Little Brown, 1974), pp. 248–249.

4. John Buchan, *Memory Hold the Door* (London: Hodder and Stoughton, 1941), p. 113.

5. Doreen E Greig, *Herbert Baker in South Africa* (Cape Town: Purnell, 1970).

6. Herbert Baker, *Architecture and Personalities* (London: Country Life, 1944), pp. 27, 32.

7. Doreen E Greig, *Herbert Baker in South Africa* (Cape Town: Purnell, 1970), p. 48.

8. Jane Ridley, *Edwin Lutyens, His Life, His Wife, His Work* (London: Pimlico, 2003), p. 156.

9. Letter from Edwin Lutyens to Herbert Baker, March 30, 1901, RIBA, BaH/1/1/1.

10. Jagger Library Manuscripts Archive, University of Cape Town Libraries.

11. Frank Kendall to Pearse, December 6, 1945, copy in collection of Human Sciences Research Council (HSRC), Pretoria.

12. Letter from Frank Kendall to Pearse, January 16, 1946, copy in collection of HSRC, Pretoria.

13. Letter from Cecil Rhodes to Herbert Baker, Baker Archive, RIBA, BaH/5/1. These were such rare documents that Baker had them framed; they always hung in his own office.

14. Herbert Baker, *Architecture and Personalities* (London: Country Life, 1944), p. 31.

15. Baker's search for furnishings for *Groote Schuur* is covered in one of his letters to Rhodes on December 26, 1900: "With regard to old furniture and china I have never charged anything & I will willingly agree to do so still for china or anything for Groote Schuur, but for other houses which I have had or may still have to furnish, I think I ought to charge 10% in future as it involves a considerable amount of time."

16. Letter from Herbert Baker to Percy Baker, June 3, 1897, MB.

17. Herbert Baker to Archbishop of Cape Town, September 28, 1897, Jagger Library Manuscripts Archive (JLMA), University of Cape Town Library, BC 206.

18. *Ibid.*

19. Doreen E. Greig, *Herbert Baker in South Africa* (Cape Town: Purnell, 1970), p. 54.

20. Letter from Frank Kendall to Professor Pearse, September 9, 1925, JLMA.

21. Drawings Collection, University of Witwatersrand, Johannesburg.

22. Herbert Baker, *Architecture and Personalities* (London: Country Life, 1944), pp. 32–34.

23. Sir Reginald Blomfield, *History of Renaissance Architecture in England 1500–1800* (London: G. Bell and Sons, 1897).

24. Thomas Pakenham, *The Boer War* (London: Abacus, 1979).

25. Robert Baden-Powell (1857–1941) was an almost exact contemporary of Herbert Baker and his guide to the Boy Scouts, *Scouting for Boys*, first published in 1908, draws on many of his own experiences in South Africa. As in Baker's own education and upbringing, the Knights of the Round Table feature prominently.

26. Letter from Herbert Baker to Percy Baker, Lionel's Farm, January 14, 1900, MB.

27. Herbert Baker, *Cecil Rhodes by His Architect* (Oxford: Oxford University Press, 1934), p. 15.

28. Letter from Herbert Baker to Percy Baker, March 6, 1900, MB.

29. Herbert Baker, *Architecture and Personalities* (London: Country Life, 1944), p. 36.

30. Letter from Herbert Baker to Frances Baker, Grand Continental Hotel, Cairo, April 24, 1900, MB.

31. Letter from Herbert Baker to Frances Baker, Athens, April 30, 1900, MB.

32. Herbert Baker, *Architecture and Personalities* (London: Country Life, 1944), p. 36. Baker's response was in stark contrast to Lutyens' first visit to the Acropolis over 30 years later, when he described it as, "The most tragic spot I ever visited… The Parthenon has no relation to its site…. I looked at it long, and the more I looked the more depressed I became." Christopher Hussey, *The Life of Sir Edwin Lutyens* (London: Country Life, 1950), pp. 538–539.

33. Letter from Herbert Baker to Frances Baker, Grand Hotel des Palmes, Palermo, May 29–30, 1900, MB.

34. Letter from Herbert Baker to Frances Baker, Hotel D'Angleterre, Rome, June 6, 1900, MB.

35. Herbert Baker, *Architecture and Personalities* (London: Country Life, 1944), p. 36.

36. Frank Kendall, "Appreciation—Herbert Baker," September 9, 1925, JLMA.

37. Herbert Baker, *Architecture and Personalities* (London: Country Life, 1944), pp. 38, 39.

38. Roderick Gradidge, *Edwin Lutyens Architect Laureate* (London: George, Allen and Unwin, 1981), p. 77.

39. Herbert Baker, *Architecture and Personalities* (London: Country Life, 1944), pp. 34, 35.

40. Rudyard Kipling, *Something of Myself* (London: Macmillan, 1937), p. 166.

41. Alan Crawford, *C. R. Ashbee; Architect, Designer and Romantic Socialist* (London: Yale University Press, 2005), p. 119.

42. Lionel Curtis, *With Milner in South Africa* (Oxford: Blackwell, 1931), p. 250.

43. *Sir Herbert Baker: In Memoriam*, South African Architectural Record, July 31, 1946, pp. 168–171.

44. As the Commissioner, Alfred Milner wrote to Chamberlain the Prime Minister: "The black spot—the only very black spot—in the picture is the frightful mortality in the Concentration Camps…. The whole thing I think now, has been a mistake." By the end of the war 27,927 people had died in the camps—mostly children under 16.

45. Herbert Baker, *Architecture and Personalities* (London: Country Life, 1944), pp. 47–48.

Chapter 4

1. John Buchan, *Memory Hold the Door* (London: Hodder and Stoughton, 1941), pp. 102–103.

2. Herbert Baker, *Architecture and Personalities* (London: Country Life, 1944), p. 49.

3. Almost all the members of *The Kindergarten* went on to achieve positions of considerable eminence and influence across the Empire. Of those Buchan mentioned, Alfred Milner (New College,

Oxford) became first Baron and then Lord Milner and Chairman of Rio Tinto Zinc, before joining Lloyd George's five-man First World War Cabinet and assisting in the negotiations of the Treaty of Versailles to which he was a signatory. Patrick Duncan (Balliol), later Sir Patrick Duncan, became Minister of the Interior, Education, Public Health and Mines to the South African Government and Governor General of South Africa 1937–43. Major William Lambton of the Coldstream Guards (Sandhurst) was appointed commanding officer of the Coldstream Guards in 1912 and General Officer commanding the 4th Division of the British Army during World War I. Lord Brooke (Eton) became Brigadier General during World War I and Earl of Warwick in 1924. Lord Henry Seymour commanded the 1st Company of the British Army in World War I; Geoffrey Dawson (Magdalen) later became Editor of *The Times*; Lord Basil Blackwood (Balliol) became a barrister, Colonial Secretary of Barbados and private secretary to the Lord Lieutenant of Ireland; Hugh Wyndham (New College) later became Baron Leconfield; Gerard Craig Sellar (Balliol) was a career diplomat with the Foreign Office before inheriting a large and wealthy Highland Estate; Lionel Curtis (New College) founded *The Round Table* and the Royal Institute of International Affairs (Chatham House); Robert H. Brand (New College), later Baron Brand, became Managing Director of Lazard Brothers, Chairman of the North British and Mercantile Insurance Company and Director of Lloyds; Lionel Hichens (New College) because Chairman of Cammell Laird and Philip Kerr (New College), later Lord Kerr, Marquess of Lothian, became private secretary to Lloyd George and British Ambassador to the United States 1939–40. And of course, John Buchan himself (Brasenose), now best known as an author, but was also a publisher and eventually Baron Tweedsmuir, Governor General of Canada 1935–1940. Baker would certainly have added his host Peter Perry (New College), John Dove (New College) later Editor of *The Round Table*, Dougal Malcolm (New College) later Sir Dougal, Richard Feetham (New College), Fabian Ware (University of Paris), later Major General Sir Fabian Ware and founder of the Imperial War Graves Commission.

4. Michael Keath, *Herbert Baker: Architecture and Idealism 1892–1913: The South African Years* (Gibralter: Ashanti Publishing, 1993), p. 89.

5. Herbert Baker, *Architecture and Personalities* (London: Country Life, 1944), p. 48.

6. Letter from Herbert Baker to Frances Baker, Government House, Bloemfontein, May 3, 1901, MB.

7. Herbert Baker, *Architecture and Personalities* (London: Country Life, 1944), p. 48.

8. Herbert Baker, *Architecture and Personalities* (London: Country Life, 1944), p. 48.

9. Andrew M. Reid and Paul J. Lane, *African Historical Archaeologies* (Springer: Switzerland, 2004), p. 347.

10. Dale Lace's wife Josephine was a famous beauty, a mistress of Edward VII and rumored to be the only woman whom Cecil Rhodes ever asked to marry.

11. Herbert Baker, *Architecture and Personalities* (London: Country Life, 1944), p. 53.

12. Sir George Farrar had been one of Jameson's accomplices in *The Raid* and was also responsible for successfully addressing the labor shortage in the mines by importing poorly paid Chinese laborers—a total of 60,000 arriving between 1904 and 1907.

13. Letter from Herbert Baker to Sir George Farrar, March 12, 1902, Strange Collection, Museum Africa, Johannesburg Public Library.

14. John Flint, *Cecil Rhodes* (London: Hutcheson, 1976), p. 224.

15. J. G. Lockhart and C. M. Woodhouse, *Rhodes* (London: Hodder and Stoughton, 1963), p. 478.

16. Herbert Baker, *Cecil Rhodes by His Architect* (Oxford: Oxford University Press, 1934), pp. 123–124.

17. Jane Ridley, *Edwin Lutyens, His Life, His Wife, His Work* (London: Pimlico, 2003), p. 145.

18. W. G. Bull, *Gippsland Mercury*, Bulawayo, April 21, 1902.

19. Herbert Baker, *Architecture and Personalities* (London: Country Life, 1944), p. 41.

20. John Flint, *Cecil Rhodes* (London: Hutcheson, 1976), p. 217.

21. Herbert Baker, *Architecture and Personalities* (London: Country Life, 1944), p. 39.

22. Letter from Franklin Kendall to Pearse, December 6, 1945, Human Sciences Research Council Collection, Pretoria.

23. Herbert Baker, *Architecture and Personalities* (London: Country Life, 1944), p. 33.

24. Interestingly, John Buchan's hero, South African mining engineer Richard Hannay, finally married and settled down in the Cotswolds at 40, from where his adventures continued.

25. Letter from Herbert Baker to Florence Baker, The Rand Club, Johannesburg, September 27, 1902, MB.

26. Herbert Baker, *Architecture and Personalities* (London: Country Life, 1944), p. 49.

27. Herbert Baker, *Architecture and Personalities* (London: Country Life, 1944), p. 48.

28. Alan Crawford, *C. R. Ashbee; Architect, Designer and Romantic Socialist* (London: Yale University Press, 2005), p. 120.

29. Herbert Baker, *Architecture and Personalities* (London: Country Life, 1944), p. 48.

30. Letter from Edwin Lutyens to Herbert Baker, February 15, 1903, RIBA, BaH 1/1/2.

31. Roderick Gradidge, *Edwin Lutyens Architect Laureate* (London: George, Allen and Unwin, 1981), p. 153.

32. "It has been estimated that between 1815 and 1914, 22.6 m people left the shores of Britain to settle somewhere abroad…. Migration … was an absolute essential pre-requisite of a successful empire. The creation and maintenance of the British Empire was arguably the greatest achievement of the British and the migration of its people to conquer, administer, maintain control, farm and develop the colonies

was essential to its success." britishempire.me.uk. Various "assisted passage" programs continued from Britain to many of its former colonies up until the 1970s.

33. Letter from Ernest Wilmott Sloper to Herbert Baker November 3, 1904, Collection of Michael Keath.

34. Letter from Herbert Baker to Pearse, November 22, 1925, Human Sciences Research Council archive, Pretoria.

35. Letter from Herbert Baker to Florence Baker, on train to Cape Town, October 24, 1903, MB.

36. Letter from Herbert Baker to Florence Baker, Stonehouse, November 17, 1903, MB.

37. Graham Viney, *Colonial Houses of South Africa* (Johannesburg: Struik Publishers, 1987), p. 214.

Chapter 5

1. Letter from Lionel Curtis to Herbert Baker, Pretoria, April 19, 1904, RIBA.

2. Letter from Herbert Baker to Florence Baker, Owletts, May 27, 1904, MB.

3. Letter from Lionel Curtis to Herbert Baker, Pretoria, June 19, 1904, RIBA.

4. Letter from Lionel Hichens to Herbert Baker, Pretoria, June 19, 1904, RIBA.

5. Letter from Lionel Baker to Herbert Baker, June 20, 1904, MB.

6. Letter from Herbert Baker to Frank Fleming, August 16, 1904, Strange Collection, Museum Africa, Johannesburg.

7. Herbert Baker, *Cecil Rhodes by His Architect* (Oxford: Oxford University Press, 1934), pp. 52–53.

8. Letter from Herbert Baker to Frank Fleming, September 12, 1904, Strange Collection, Museum Africa, Johannesburg.

9. Letter from Edwin Lutyens to Herbert Baker, December 26, 1904, RIBA.

10. Letter from Frank Kendall to Herbert Baker, January 9, 1905, Collection of Michael Keath.

11. Letter from Edward Lowther Baker (fellow executor) to Herbert Baker, Delce Grange, Rochester (black edged) October 5, 1904, MB.

12. *Cape Times*, August 1905, cutting in JLMA, UCTL.

13. Letter from Herbert Baker to Florence Baker from Stonehouse, September 20, 1905, MB.

14. Angus Wilson, *The Strange Ride of Rudyard Kipling: His Life and Works* (London: Martin Secker and Warburg, 1977), p. 224.

15. Letter from Francis Masey to Herbert Baker, August 28, 1905, Collection of Michael Keath.

16. Letter from Herbert Baker to Col. J. W. Bell, December 12, 1905, letter books of Baker and Fleming, Strange Collection, Museum Africa, Johannesburg.

17. Doreen E. Greig, *Herbert Baker in South Africa* (Cape Town: Purnell, 1970), p. 112.

18. Letter from Herbert Baker to Harold Spicer, January 15, 1906, letter books of Baker and Fleming, Strange Collection, Museum Africa, Pretoria.

19. Letter from Herbert Baker to the Reverend H. Hammersley, July 30, 1906, letter books of Baker and Fleming, Strange Collection, Museum Africa, Pretoria.

20. Herbert Baker, *Architecture and Personalities* (London: Country Life, 1944), p. 51.

21. Elizabeth Hutchings, *Discovering the Sculptures of George Frederick Watts, O.M., R.A.* (Newport, UK: Hunnyhill Publishers, 1994).

22. Herbert Baker, *Architecture and Personalities* (London: Country Life, 1944), p. 165.

23. Baker's report to the Rhodes Memorial, June 13, 1907, University of Cape Town (UCT) Library.

24. Herbert Baker, *Architecture and Personalities* (London: Country Life, 1944), p. 165.

25. Letter from Herbert Baker to Percy Baker, January 5, 1895, MB.

26. Report from Herbert Baker to W.K. Whittaker, January 15, 1908, letter books of Baker and Fleming, Strange Collection, Museum Africa, Pretoria.

27. Letter from Herbert Baker to Francis Masey, January 3, 1908, Jagger Library, UCT.

28. Letter from Herbert Baker to Francis Masey, January 10, 1908, Jagger Library, UCT.

29. Letter from Herbert Baker to Francis Masey, January 16, 1908, Jagger Library, UCT.

30. Private and Confidential letter from Edwin Lutyens to Herbert Baker, May 10, 1908, RIBA BaH/1/1/5.

31. Clayre Percy and Jane Ridley, eds., *The Letters of Edwin Lutyens to His Wife, Lady Emily* (London: Collins, 1985), p. 163.

32. Christopher Hussey, *The Life of Sir Edwin Lutyens* (London: Country Life, 1950), p. 180. (Baker's reference is to Captain Dobbin in William Thackeray's *Vanity Fair*.)

33. Christopher Hussey, *The Life of Sir Edwin Lutyens* (London: Country Life, 1950), p. 182.

34. Jane Ridley, *Edwin Lutyens, His Life, His Wife, His Work* (London: Pimlico, 2003), p. 179.

35. At that precise moment, John Buchan was writing *Prester John*, which he would dedicate to Lionel Phillips.

36. Doreen E Greig, *Herbert Baker in South Africa* (Cape Town: Purnell, 1970), p. 218.

37. Letter from Lionel Baker to Herbert Baker, February 25, 1909, MB.

38. Letter from Herbert Baker to Florence Baker from Stonehouse, March 6, 1909, MB.

39. Letter from Herbert Baker to Florence Baker from Stonehouse, March 8, 1909, MB.

40. Letter from Herbert Baker to Francis Masey, March 18, 1909, letter books of Baker and Fleming, Strange Collection, Museum Africa, Pretoria.

Chapter 6

1. Herbert Baker, *Architecture and Personalities* (London: Country Life, 1944), pp. 53, 54.

2. Dorothea Fairbridge, *Gardens of South Africa* (London: A&C Black, 1924), pp. 31–33. Like so many of the beautiful gardens on the ridge, Mrs.

Phillips and Baker's garden was almost entirely destroyed by the construction of the 6-lane M1 De Villiers Graff motorway in 1962.

3. Roy Digby Thomas, *Two Generals: Buller and Botha in the Boer War* (London: AuthorHouse, 2012), p. 254.

4. Letter from Herbert Baker to Florence Baker from Stonehouse, March 16, 1909, MB.

5. Letter from Herbert Baker to Florence Baker from Stonehouse, April 9, 1909, MB.

6. Letter from Herbert Baker to Florence Baker from Stonehouse, March 24, 1909, MB.

7. Robert Henry Brand, *The Union of South Africa* (Oxford: Clarendon Press, 1909).

8. *Ibid.*, p. 41.

9. *Ibid.*, p. 10.

10. *Ibid.*, p. 57.

11. *Ibid.*, p. 62.

12. *Ibid.*, pp. 61–62.

13. *Ibid.*, p. 86.

14. *Ibid.*, p. 98.

15. *Ibid.*, p. 85.

16. Letter from Herbert Baker to Edward Solomon, June 3, 1909, letter books of Baker and Fleming, Strange Collection, Museum Africa, Pretoria.

17. Herbert Baker, *Architecture and Personalities* (London: Country Life, 1944), p. 58.

18. Herbert Baker, *Architecture and Personalities* (London: Country Life, 1944), pp. 59, 60.

19. Letter from Edwin Lutyens to Herbert Baker, February 1, 1910, RIBA.

20. Letter from Herbert Baker to B.P. Wall, Chief Engineer, Central South African Railways, June 9, 1909, letter books of Baker and Fleming, Strange Collection, Museum Africa, Pretoria.

21. Letter from Herbert Baker to Francis Masey, November 2, 1909, letter books of Baker and Fleming, Strange Collection, Museum Africa, Pretoria.

22. Herbert Baker, *Architecture and Personalities* (London: Country Life, 1944), p. 59.

23. Letter from Richard Feetham to Florence Baker, December 1, 1909, MB.

24. Marcus Binney, *Attributes of the Eternal: Sir Herbert Baker's Union Buildings, Pretoria* (London: Country Life, 1982), p. 468.

25. Herbert Baker, *Architecture and Personalities* (London: Country Life, 1944), pp. 61–62.

26. Letter from Herbert Baker to Florence Baker, May 28, 1909, MB.

27. Letter from Herbert Baker to Francis Masey, August 14, 1909, letter books of Baker and Fleming, Strange Collection, Museum Africa, Pretoria.

28. Letter from Florence Baker to Henry Edmeades, May 29, 1910, MB.

29. Jane Brown, *Lutyens and the Edwardians* (New York: Viking/Penguin Books Limited, 1996), p. 146.

30. Letter from Herbert Baker to Florence Baker from Rust en Vrede, Cape Town, October 4, 1909.

31. Jane Ridley, *Edwin Lutyens, His Life, His Wife, His Work* (London: Pimlico, 2003), p. 198.

32. Letter from Edwin Lutyens to Herbert Baker, July 15, 1909, RIBA.

33. Christopher Hussey, *The Life of Sir Edwin Lutyens* (London: Country Life, 1950), p. 203.

34. Christopher Hussey, *The Life of Sir Edwin Lutyens* (London: Country Life, 1950), p. 205. The term "Brer Bear" was taken from Rudyard Kipling's "Jungle Book" and Baker was often alternately known as "the Brer" or after Kipling's character—"Baloo"—almost certainly with reference to his towering frame.

35. Letter from Edwin Lutyens to Emily Lutyens, December 12, 1910, RIBA.

36. Letter from Florence Baker to Henry Edmeades, December 18, 1910, MB.

37. Jane Ridley, *Edwin Lutyens, His Life, His Wife, His Work* (London: Pimlico, 2003), p. 199.

38. As Ridley continued, "There was something slightly desperate about Ned's clowning. Being a balding forty-two-year-old who refused to grow up wasn't easy. Never Never Land was not a comfortable place to live." Jane Ridley, *Edwin Lutyens, His Life, His Wife, His Work* (London: Pimlico, 2003), pp. 199–200.

39. Jane Brown, *Lutyens and the Edwardians* (New York: Viking/Penguin Books Limited, 1996), p. 154.

40. *Memorandum of my Relations with Lutyens*, March 1931. Baker Papers, RIBA.

41. Letter from Herbert Baker to E.A. von Hirschberg, May 10, 1911, letter books of Baker and Fleming, Strange Collection, Museum Africa, Pretoria.

42. Parliamentary Papers, *Announcements by and on Behalf of His Majesty the King-Emperor*, no. 3, p. 6.

43. Christopher Hussey, *The Life of Sir Edwin Lutyens* (London: Country Life, 1950), p. 246.

44. Letter from Edwin Lutyens to Herbert Baker, March 15, 1912, RIBA.

45. Christopher Hussey, *The Life of Sir Edwin Lutyens* (London: Country Life, 1950), p. 247.

46. Herbert Baker, *Architecture and Personalities* (London: Country Life, 1944), p. 40.

47. The poem was included in a letter from Rudyard Kipling to Herbert Baker, 9th February, 1905.

48. Roderick Gradidge, *Edwin Lutyens Architect Laureate* (London: George, Allen and Unwin, 1981), p. 155.

Chapter 7

1. Letter from Edwin Lutyens to Emily Lutyens, June 9, 1912, in Clayre Percy and Jane Ridley, eds., *The Letters of Edwin Lutyens to His Wife, Lady Emily* (London: Collins, 1985), p. 252.

2. Christopher Hussey, *The Life of Sir Edwin Lutyens* (London: Country Life, 1950), p. 270.

3. Sir Reginald Blomfield, *Memoirs of an Architect* (London: Macmillan, 1932), pp. 148–149.

4. Sir Lionel Earle, *Turn Over the Page* (London: Hutchinson, 1935), p. 87.

5. Letter from Edwin Lutyens to Emily Lutyens, September 16, 1912, in Clayre Percy and Jane Ridley, eds., *The Letters of Edwin Lutyens to His Wife, Lady Emily* (London: Collins, 1985), p. 265.

6. Herbert Baker, *Architecture and Personalities* (London: Country Life, 1944), pp. 218–222.

7. Letter from Edwin Lutyens to Herbert Baker, October 14, 1912, RIBA.

8. Letter from George Swinton to Charles Hardinge, October 3, 1912.

9. Robert Grant Irving, *Indian Summer* (London: Yale University Press, 1981), p. 97.

10. Roderick Gradidge, *Edwin Lutyens Architect Laureate* (London: George, Allen and Unwin, 1981), p. 158.

11. Letter from Florence Baker to Henry Edmeades, Stonehouse, November 4, 1912, MB.

12. Letter from Herbert Baker to Florence Baker, on board S.S. *Kenilworth*, December 8, 1912, MB.

13. Sir Reginald Blomfield, *Memoirs of an Architect* (London: Macmillan, 1932), pp. 148–149.

14. Letter from Herbert Baker to Florence Baker, from Owletts, December 16, 1912, MB.

15. Wife of Robert Falcon Scott of Antarctica fame.

16. Letter from Herbert Baker to Florence Baker, from 25 Wilton Place, London, December 1, 1912, MB.

17. Letter from Edwin Lutyens to Emily Lutyens, Delhi, December 26, 1912, RIBA.

18. Letter from Edwin Lutyens to Emily Lutyens, Delhi, January 21, 1913, RIBA.

19. Letter from Herbert Baker to Florence Baker, from Owletts, December 26, 1912, MB.

20. Letter from Herbert Baker to Florence Baker, Gare de Lyon, in sleeping car, January 4, 1913, MB.

21. Letter from Herbert Baker to Florence Baker, Palace Hotel, Rome, January 7, 1913, MB.

22. Letter from Herbert Baker to Florence Baker, Palace Hotel, Rome, January 14, 1913, MB.

23. Letter from Herbert Baker to Florence Baker, London, January 18, 1913, MB.

24. Letter from Herbert Baker to Florence Baker, train, January 21, 1913, MB.

25. Letter from Herbert Baker to Florence Baker, train in Italy, January 25, 1913, MB.

26. Letter from Herbert Baker to Florence Baker, on board S.S. *Egypt* in the Red Sea, January 30, 1913, MB.

27. Letter from Herbert Baker to Florence Baker, on board S.S. *Egypt*, February 4, 1913, MB.

28. Letter from Herbert Baker to Florence Baker, on train with Lutyens, February 5, 1913, MB.

29. Letter from Herbert Baker to Florence Baker, on train with Lutyens. February 8, 1913, MB.

30. This was the death of Captain Scott, whose wife Baker had met a few weeks previously in London, with the news of his death the previous year having only just reached Delhi via New Zealand and London. Despite being beaten to the Pole by Norwegian Roald Amundsen his demise while attempting to reach it confirmed him in the public's eyes as another great hero of the Empire. Baker certainly regarded him in this light having himself contributed to the fund-raising for the British Antarctic Expedition in 1910 and he would go on to design the Scott Polar Research Institute in Cambridge many years later, in 1933.

31. Letter from Herbert Baker to Florence Baker, Delhi, February 16, 1913, MB.

32. Letter from Edwin Lutyens to Emily Lutyens, Delhi, February 18, 1913, RIBA.

33. Letter from Fleetwood Wilson to Hardinge, February 17, 1913, Fleetwood Wilson Collection.

34. Edwin Montagu Indian Diary, vol. III, ff 32–4. Jane Ridley, *Edwin Lutyens, His Life, His Wife, His Work* (London: Pimlico, 2003), p. 226.

35. Herbert Baker, *Architecture and Personalities* (London: Country Life, 1944), p. 64.

36. Jane Ridley, *Edwin Lutyens, His Life, His Wife, His Work* (London: Pimlico, 2003), pp. 224–225.

37. Herbert Baker, *Architecture and Personalities* (London: Country Life, 1944), pp. 77–80.

38. Letter from Herbert Baker to Florence Baker, Architects Office, Raisina, February 19, 1913, MB.

39. Letter from Herbert Baker to Florence Baker, Delhi, February 20, 1913, MB.

40. Letter from Herbert Baker to Florence Baker, Delhi, February 21, 1913, MB.

41. Letter from Herbert Baker to Florence Baker, Delhi, February 22, 1913, MB.

42. Herbert Baker, *Architecture and Personalities* (London: Country Life, 1944), pp. 72–73.

43. Letter from Herbert Baker to Florence Baker, Delhi, March 13, 1913, MB.

44. Edwin Lutyens site plan, RIBA.

45. Letter from Herbert Baker to Florence Baker, Delhi, March 14, 1913, MB.

46. Letter from Herbert Baker to Florence Baker, one day off Bombay, March 23, 1913, MB.

47. Letter from Herbert Baker to Florence Baker, nearing Aden, March 25, 1913, MB.

48. Letter from Florence Baker to Henry Edmeades, Sandhills, April 30, 1913, MB.

49. "Proceedings of the One Hundred and First Meeting of the Imperial Delhi Committee," February 25, 1916.

Chapter 8

1. Letter from Florence Baker to Henry Edmeades, February 24, 1913, MB.

2. Letter from Florence Baker to Henry Edmeades April 30, 1913, MB.

3. Baker's letter of January 30, 1913, refers to his revising the design of the terraces while in the Red Sea en route to Bombay.

4. Doreen E Greig, *Herbert Baker in South Africa* (Cape Town: Purnell, 1970), p. 181.

5. Doreen E Greig, *Herbert Baker in South Africa* (Cape Town: Purnell, 1970), p. 186.

6. Herbert Baker, *Architecture and Personalities* (London: Country Life, 1944), p. 60.

7. Letter from Herbert Baker to Sir David P. de V. Graff, September 26, 1911, L.H. Fleming collection.

8. *The Transvaal Leader*, July 1, 1910.

9. Letter from Herbert Baker to Percy Baker, January 5, 1895, MB.

10. Christopher Hussey, *The Life of Sir Edwin Lutyens* (London: Country Life, 1950), p. 296.

11. George Farrar had lent Lutyens the mews

house at 7 Apple Tree Yard, behind his house in St James' Square, which Lutyens had designed for him. Farrar was also Lutyens' client for "The Salutation" in Kent.

12. Christopher Hussey, *The Life of Sir Edwin Lutyens* (London: Country Life, 1950), p. 323.

13. Jane Ridley, *Edwin Lutyens, His Life, His Wife, His Work* (London: Pimlico, 2003), p. 237.

14. Letter from George Swinton to Charles Hardinge, November 13, 1913.

15. Herbert Baker's diary, 1913, RIBA.

16. Baker later wrote in his "Memorandum of New Delhi" of 1931 (RIBA Collection) that the clause, as revised, had eventually actually worked in his favor rather than Lutyens', "owing to the long delay over Government House during the last few years of the prolonged contract" and that, "the advantage which should thus have accrued to me, I renounced in the final settlement made in the end of 1930, thus reverting to my original proposal of mutual equality."

17. Letter from Herbert Baker to Florence Baker, nearing Suez, November 19, 1913, MB.

18. Letter from Herbert Baker to Florence Baker, Delhi, December 16, 1913, MB.

19. Letter from Edwin Lutyens to Emily Lutyens, Delhi, December 28, 1913.

20. Letter from Herbert Baker to Florence Baker, Delhi, December 25, 1913, MB.

21. Letter from Herbert Baker to Florence Baker, Delhi, January 14, 1914, MB.

22. Letter from Herbert Baker to Florence Baker, Delhi, January 18, 1914, MB.

23. Jane Ridley, *Edwin Lutyens, His Life, His Wife, His Work* (London: Pimlico, 2003), p. 262.

24. Christopher Hussey, *The Life of Sir Edwin Lutyens* (London: Country Life, 1950), p. 323.

25. Letter from Herbert Baker to Florence Baker, Delhi, January 26, 1914, MB.

26. Clayre Percy and Jane Ridley, eds., *The Letters of Edwin Lutyens to His Wife, Lady Emily* (London: Collins, 1985), pp. 294–295.

27. Letter from Herbert Baker to Florence Baker, Delhi, February 3, 1914, MB.

28. Letter from Herbert Baker to Florence Baker, Delhi, March 4, 1914, MB.

29. Letter from Herbert Baker to Florence Baker, Delhi, March 8, 1914, MB.

30. Herbert Baker diary, January 1, 1914, RIBA.

31. Letter from Herbert Baker to Florence Baker, Delhi, March 9, 1914.

32. Walgate Papers, University of Cape Town.

33. Catalogue of the 1914 Summer Exhibition, p. 54.

34. Letter from Emily Lutyens to Edwin Lutyens, September 11, 1914 in Clayre Percy and Jane Ridley, eds., *The Letters of Edwin Lutyens to his Wife, Lady Emily* (London: Collins, 1985).

35. Letter from Edwin Lutyens to Emily Lutyens, September 14, 1914 in Clayre Percy and Jane Ridley, eds., *The Letters of Edwin Lutyens to his Wife, Lady Emily* (London: Collins, 1985).

36. Aubrey Herbert had already been wounded at the Battle of Mons, captured, escaped and then declared unfit for further service and went on to be the model for John Buchan's mystical hero Sandy Arbuthnot in *Greenmantle* and a number of his other works.

37. Margaret Fitzherbert, *The Man Who Was Greenmantle* (London: John Murray, 1983), p. 145.

38. Herbert Baker, *Architecture and Personalities* (London: Country Life, 1944), pp. 82, 83.

39. Letter from Edwin Lutyens to Emily Lutyens, March 18, 1915 in Clayre Percy and Jane Ridley, eds., *The Letters of Edwin Lutyens to His Wife, Lady Emily* (London: Collins, 1985), p. 311.

40. Letter from Edwin Lutyens to Emily Lutyens. January 17, 1915 in Clayre Percy and Jane Ridley, eds., *The Letters of Edwin Lutyens to His Wife, Lady Emily* (London: Collins, 1985), p. 309.

41. A short glossary of Indian architectural terms may be of use from this point onwards:
Chattri—an elevated dome-topped pavilion
Chajja or *Chujja*—a sloping stone projection to protect a window, door or wall from sun and rain
Jaali—a perforated carved stone screen.

42. Letter from Herbert Baker to Florence Baker, January 3, 1915, MB.

43. Letter from Edwin Lutyens to Emily Lutyens, March 18, 1915 in Clayre Percy and Jane Ridley, eds., *The Letters of Edwin Lutyens to His Wife, Lady Emily* (London: Collins, 1985), p. 311.

44. Herbert Baker, *Architecture and Personalities* (London: Country Life, 1944), p. 77.

45. Letter from Herbert Baker to Florence Baker, Delhi, March 11, 1915, MB.

Chapter 9

1. Letter from Phillip Sassoon to Herbert Baker, HQ IV Corps France, July 24, 1915, RIBA.

2. Letter from Herbert Baker to Florence Baker, Eaton Place, Summer 1915. The outbreak of the First World War had brought to an end a period of industrial turmoil led by the Trades Union Congress in which miners, dockers and railwaymen had either struck for improved wages and working conditions or to avoid them being even further reduced which, in Herbert's view, threatened to bring the mother country of the Empire to its knees.

3. Letter from Edwin Lutyens to Emily Lutyens, on train to Rome, July 2, 1915, in Clayre Percy and Jane Ridley, eds., *The Letters of Edwin Lutyens to His Wife, Lady Emily* (London: Collins, 1985), p. 312.

4. Letter from Edwin Lutyens to Emily Lutyens, on train to Rome, November 16, 1915, in Clayre Percy and Jane Ridley, eds., *The Letters of Edwin Lutyens to His Wife, Lady Emily* (London: Collins, 1985), pp. 321–322.

5. Letter from Herbert Baker to Florence Baker, Raisina, December 31, 1915, MB.

6. Letter from Edwin Lutyens to Emily Lutyens, Delhi, January 3, 1915, in Clayre Percy and Jane Ridley, eds., *The Letters of Edwin Lutyens to His Wife, Lady Emily* (London: Collins, 1985), pp. 325–326.

7. Letter from Herbert Baker to Florence Baker,

Viceroy's Lodge, Delhi, January 9, 1916. This letter also contains the Viceroy's amusing after dinner tale of Lord Buxton, a member of the cabinet, who visiting friends in Kent had decided to walk back to the train station, resting on the way on what turned out to be an ants' nest. When he got on his train, "he took off & shook his trousers out of the window when a passing train whipped them off." He then got off at the next station and tried to borrow a pair but the stationmaster, who "thought him mad."

8. Letter from Herbert Baker to Florence Baker, Viceroy's Lodge, Delhi, January 3, 1916, MB. This was William Sinclair Marris, friend, barrister, Indian Civil Servant and fellow member of the Round Table.

9. Letter from Herbert Baker to Florence Baker, Raisina, Delhi, January 16, 1916, MB.

10. Letter from Edwin Lutyens to Emily Lutyens, Delhi, January 19, 1915, in Clayre Percy and Jane Ridley, eds., *The Letters of Edwin Lutyens to His Wife, Lady Emily* (London: Collins, 1985), p. 329.

11. Letter from Edwin Lutyens to Emily Lutyens, Delhi, January 27, 1915, in Clayre Percy and Jane Ridley, eds., *The Letters of Edwin Lutyens to His Wife, Lady Emily* (London: Collins, 1985), p. 330.

12. Christopher Hussey, *The Life of Sir Edwin Lutyens* (London: Country Life, 1950), p. 244.

13. With the exception of those interested in the architecture of Lutyens or Baker or in the history of New Delhi, the controversy has largely now faded into the distant past. Indeed on my first visit to Raisina Hill I was driven down the Processional Way towards the ramp with my local Indian guide advising me to "watch the Dome" as it disappeared and reappeared, at which point he exclaimed, "See, this is the brilliance of Lutyens!"

14. Mary Lutyens, *Edwin Lutyens: By His Daughter* (London: Black Swan, 1991), p. 149.

15. Letter from Edwin Lutyens to Herbert Baker, January 27, 1916, RIBA.

16. Letter from Herbert Baker to Florence Baker, Raisina, Delhi, January 26, 1916, MB.

17. Letter from Hugh Keeling to Herbert Baker, March 29, 1916, RIBA.

18. Extract from the minutes of the 101st Meeting of the Imperial Delhi Committee, February 18, 1916.

19. Letter from Herbert Baker to Florence Baker, Raisina, Delhi, undated, MB.

20. Note on Interview with Lutyens, Charles Hardinge to Malcolm Hailey, March 13, 1916, Charles Hardinge Papers, Cambridge University Library.

21. "Confidential Notes on My Interview with Viceroy," Herbert Baker, March 14, 1916, MB; Letter from Herbert Baker to Florence Baker, Raisina, March 15, 1916, MB.

22. Jane Ridley, *Edwin Lutyens, His Life, His Wife, His Work* (London: Pimlico, 2003), pp. 321–322.

23. Letter from Herbert Baker to Sir Malcolm Hailey, March 18, 1916, RIBA.

24. Herbert Baker's diary, Sunday March 26, 1916, RIBA.

25. Telegram from Sir Claude Hill to Herbert Baker, May 13, 1916, RIBA.

26. Letter from Sir Claude Hill to Herbert Baker, May 18, 1916, RIBA.

27. Letter from Edwin Lutyens to Lord Cunliffe, July 14, 1916, Bank of England Archive.

28. Letter from Herbert Baker to Florence Baker, Aden, December 14, 1916, MB.

29. Letter from Herbert Baker to Florence Baker, Delhi, December 25/27, 1916, MB.

30. Letter from Herbert Baker to Florence Baker, Delhi, January 3, 1917, MB.

31. Letter from Edwin Lutyens to Emily Lutyens, on train to Rome, January 15, 1917. Clayre Percy and Jane Ridley, eds., *The Letters of Edwin Lutyens to His Wife, Lady Emily* (London: Collins, 1985), p. 340.

32. Letter from Edwin Lutyens to Emily Lutyens, on train to Rome, February 21, 1917. Clayre Percy and Jane Ridley, eds., *The Letters of Edwin Lutyens to His Wife, Lady Emily* (London: Collins, 1985), pp. 341–342.

33. Letter from Herbert Baker to Florence Baker, Delhi, March 9, 1917, MB.

34. Letter from Herbert Baker to Florence Baker, Delhi, March 19, 1917, MB.

35. Herbert Baker, *Architecture and Personalities* (London: Country Life, 1944), p. 88.

36. Letter from Herbert Baker to Florence Baker, near Montreuil, France, July 9, 1917, MB.

37. Letter from Edwin Lutyens to Emily Lutyens, France, July 12, 1917, in Clayre Percy and Jane Ridley, eds., *The Letters of Edwin Lutyens to His Wife, Lady Emily* (London: Collins, 1985), p. 349.

38. Letter from Herbert Baker to Florence Baker, "On Active Service," France, July 11, 1917, MB.

39. Letter from Herbert Baker to Florence Baker, "On Active Service," France, July 12, 1917, MB.

40. Letters from Herbert Baker to Florence Baker, "On Active Service," France, July 14/16, 1917, MB.

41. Tim Skelton and Gerald Gliddon, *Lutyens and the Great War* (London: Frances Lincoln, 2008), p. 26.

42. Letter from Edwin Lutyens to Fabian Ware, May 27, 1917, CWGC Archives.

43. Charles Aitken's undated comments on "Minutes of the Working Party Committee Meeting," July 14, 1917, CWGC Archives.

44. Letter from Lord Hardinge to Herbert Baker, South Park, Penshurst, Kent, May 1, 1917, MB.

45. Letter from Edwin Lutyens to Fabian Ware, August 20, 1917, CWGC Archive.

Chapter 10

1. Mary Lutyens, *Edwin Lutyens: By His Daughter* (London: Black Swan, 1991), p. 184.

2. Mary Lutyens, *Edwin Lutyens: By His Daughter* (London: Black Swan, 1991), p. 178.

3. Tim Skelton, in his excellent book *Lutyens and the Great War,* recounts the tale of one of the AIF's, Wilfred von Berg, which was shared in a letter

to Gavin Stamp: "I was awaiting demobilisation and wondering rather grimly what were likely to be my prospects of re-entering the profession in England when a notice arrived in the Orderly Room stating that architects were invited to apply for positions in the Imperial War Graves Commission. Without a moment's hesitation I saddled my horse, galloped off to a neighbouring town, was interviewed and accepted." August 13, 1977.

4. David Gilmore, *The Long Recessional: The Imperial Life of Rudyard Kipling* (London: Pimlico, 2003), p. 279. The IWGC's stance that there should also be no repatriation of bodies was under constant challenge with 90 letters a week requesting repatriation being received during 1918.

5. Letter from Herbert Baker to Florence Baker, New College, Oxford, November 17–18, 1918, MB.

6. Letter from Herbert Baker to Florence Baker, London, November 25, 1918, MB.

7. Letter from Herbert Baker to Florence Baker, Hesdin, November 28, 1918, MB.

8. Herbert Baker, *Architecture and Personalities* (London: Country Life, 1944), p. 96.

9. Herbert Baker, *Architecture and Personalities* (London: Country Life, 1944), p. 97.

10. Herbert Baker, *Architecture and Personalities* (London: Country Life, 1944), p. 96.

11. Herbert Baker, *Architecture and Personalities* (London: Country Life, 1944), p. 99.

12. Baker's seconder was Viscount Milner.

13. Herbert Baker, *Architecture and Personalities* (London: Country Life, 1944), p. 206.

14. While in Bombay, Lutyens had been introduced to Tommy Lascelles who would later serve as Private Secretary first tot King Edward VIII and then to King George the VI through the abdication crisis. Lascelles found Lutyens amusing but concluded that, "a little of him goes a long way. He makes a facetious curtsey to Blanche (Lady Lloyd) when he meets her in Bombay—that's his genre of humour." Duff Hart-Davis, *End of an Era: Letters and Journals of Sir Alan Lascelles 1887–1920* (London: Hamish Hamilton, 1988).

15. Herbert Baker's diary, January 17, 1919, RIBA.

16. Letter from Herbert Baker to Florence Baker, December 20, 1919, MB.

17. Letter from Emily Lutyens to Edwin Lutyens, January 13, 1920, in Clayre Percy and Jane Ridley, eds., *The Letters of Edwin Lutyens to his Wife, Lady Emily* (London: Collins, 1985), p. 378.

18. Herbert Baker, *Architecture and Personalities* (London: Country Life, 1944), p. 75.

19. Herbert Baker's diary, January 31, 1920, RIBA.

20. Letter from William Marris to Herbert Baker, Delhi, February 22, 1920, RIBA.

21. Herbert Baker's diary, February 20, 1920, RIBA.

22. Herbert Baker's diary, February 21, 1920, RIBA.

23. Herbert Baker's diary, February 23, 1920, RIBA.

24. Herbert Baker's diary, March 23, 1920, RIBA.

25. Herbert Baker's diary, March 24, 1919, RIBA.

26. Letter from Edwin Lutyens to Emily Lutyens, Delhi, March 20, 1920, RIBA.

27. Paper presented by Herbert Baker to a symposium on the life of Lawrence of Arabia, *By His Friends*, July 24, 1935, RIBA.

28. Charles Wheeler, *High Relief—The Autobiography of Sir Charles Wheeler Sculptor* (London: Country Life, 1968), p. 58.

29. Letter from Thomas Edward Lawrence to Herbert Baker, Clouds Hill, Dorset, May 1925, RIBA.

30. Walgate Papers, CAD.

31. Herbert Baker, *Architecture and Personalities* (London: Country Life, 1944), p. 89.

32. Herbert Baker, *Architecture and Personalities* (London: Country Life, 1944), pp. 90, 91.

33. Herbert Baker, *Architecture and Personalities* (London: Country Life, 1944), p. 90.

34. Herbert Baker, *Architecture and Personalities* (London: Country Life, 1944), p. 92.

35. Letter from Herbert Baker to Edwin Lutyens, London, May 28, 1920, RIBA.

36. Letter from Edwin Lutyens to Herbert Baker, London. May 29, 1920, RIBA.

37. Letter from Herbert Baker to Edwin Lutyens, London, June 30, 1920, RIBA.

38. Robert Grant Irving, *Indian Summer* (London: Yale University Press, 1981), p. 125.

39. Letter from Herbert Baker to Florence Baker, Delhi, February 22, 1921, RIBA.

40. Letter from Herbert Baker to Florence Baker, Delhi, March 6, 1921, RIBA.

41. Herbert Baker, *Architecture and Personalities* (London: Country Life, 1944), p. 122.

Chapter 11

1. Daniel M. Abramson, *Building the Bank of England: Money, Architecture, Society, 1694–1942* (London: Yale University, 2005), p. 207.

2. Daniel M. Abramson, *Building the Bank of England: Money, Architecture, Society, 1694–1942* (London: Yale University, 2005), p. 208.

3. "Report of the Rebuilding Committee of the Bank of England to the Court of Directors," March 3, 1921, Bank of England Archive.

4. "Minutes of the Court of Directors of the Bank of England," March 3, 1921, Bank of England Archive, 5A162/1.

5. Jane Ridley, *Edwin Lutyens, His Life, His Wife, His Work* (London: Pimlico, 2003), p. 306.

6. Daniel M. Abramson, *Building the Bank of England: Money, Architecture, Society, 1694–1942* (London: Yale University, 2005), p. 211.

7. Letter from Charles Lubbock to Herbert Baker, March 30, 1921, RIBA.

8. Letter from William Stantiall, Under Secretary of State for India, to Herbert Baker and Edwin Lutyens, June 16, 1921, RIBA.

9. Jane Ridley, *Edwin Lutyens, His Life, His Wife, His Work* (London: Pimlico, 2003), p. 306.

10. Letter from Herbert Baker to Cecil Lubbock, July 7, 1921, Bank of England Archive.

11. Letter from William Lethaby to Herbert Baker, June 23, 1921, Bank of England Archive.

12. Herbert Baker, *Architecture and Personalities* (London: Country Life, 1944), p. 89.

13. Letter from Herbert Baker to Cecil Lubbock, December 12, 1921, Bank of England Archive.

14. Alex von Tunzelman, *Indian Summer: The Secret History of the End of an Empire* (New York: Simon & Schuster, 2007), p. 65.

15. Herbert Baker's diary, February 19, 1922, RIBA.

16. Clayre Percy and Jane Ridley, eds., *The Letters of Edwin Lutyens to His Wife, Lady Emily* (London: Collins, 1985), p. 398.

17. Clayre Percy and Jane Ridley, eds., *The Letters of Edwin Lutyens to His Wife, Lady Emily* (London: Collins, 1985), p. 399.

18. Herbert Baker's diary, March 9, 1922, RIBA.

19. Letter from Paul Waterhouse to C. Lubbock, March 1922, Bank of England Archive.

20. Letter from Hugh Keeling to Herbert Baker and Edwin Lutyens, June 16, 1922, RIBA.

21. Letter from Herbert Baker to Edwin Lutyens, June 22, 1922, RIBA.

22. Letter from Edwin Lutyens to Herbert Baker, July 4, 1922, RIBA.

23. Letter from Herbert Baker to Edwin Lutyens, July 14, 1922, RIBA.

24. Letter from Edwin Lutyens to Herbert Baker, July 20, 1922, RIBA.

25. *The Daily Telegraph*, July 28, 1922.

26. *The Spectator*, August 19, 1922.

27. *The Daily News*, August 22, 1922.

28. *Country Life*, July 29, 1922.

29. *The Architect*, July 28, 1922.

30. *The Architect's Journal*, August 9, 1922.

31. Letter to *The Times*, July 25, 1922, from Aston Webb, Reginald Blomfield, Paul Waterhouse and Edwin Freshfield as trustees of the Soane Museum.

32. *The Daily Mail*, July 28, 1922.

33. Herbert Baker's diary, October 23, 1922, RIBA.

34. Letter from Cecil Lubbock to George Booth, October 16, 1922, Bank of England Archive.

35. Letter from Cecil Lubbock to Herbert Baker, November 14, 1922, Bank of England Archive.

36. Letter from Herbert Baker to Cecil Lubbock, December 21, 1922, Bank of England Archive.

37. The unit of sound absorption, the Sabin, was named in his honor.

38. Herbert Baker, *Architecture and Personalities* (London: Country Life, 1944), p. 76.

39. Memorandum of the Meeting of the Rebuilding Committee, April 16, 1924. Bank of England Archive.

40. Herbert Baker, *Architecture and Personalities* (London: Country Life, 1944), p. 167.

41. Herbert Baker, *Architecture and Personalities* (London: Country Life, 1944), p. 129.

42. Robert Grant Irving, *Indian Summer* (London: Yale University Press, 1981), p. 286.

43. Christopher Hussey, *The Work of Sir Robert Lorimer* (London: *Country Life*, 1931), p. 44.

44. "Memorandum of the Meeting of the Rebuilding Committee," December 19, 1924, Bank of England Archive.

45. "Memorandum of the Meeting of the Rebuilding Committee," January 23, 1924, Bank of England Archive.

46. Mary Lutyens, *Edwin Lutyens: By His Daughter* (London: Black Swan, 1991), p. 216.

47. Charles Wheeler, *High Relief—The Autobiography of Sir Charles Wheeler Sculptor* (London: Country Life, 1968), p. 59.

48. Letter from Thomas Edward Lawrence to Herbert Baker, May 1925, RIBA.

49. Charles Wheeler, *High Relief—The Autobiography of Sir Charles Wheeler Sculptor* (London: Country Life, 1968), p. 55.

Chapter 12

1. Herbert Baker, *Architecture and Personalities* (London: Country Life, 1944), p. 136.

2. Herbert Baker, *Architecture and Personalities* (London: Country Life, 1944), p. 22.

3. Geoffrey Tyack, *Baker and Lutyens in Oxford: The Building of Rhodes House and Campion Hall* (Oxford: Oxoniensia, 1997), p. 7.

4. Geoffrey Tyack, *Baker and Lutyens in Oxford: The Building of Rhodes House and Campion Hall* (Oxford: Oxoniensia, 1997), p. 1.

5. Herbert Baker, *Architecture and Personalities* (London: Country Life, 1944), p. 110.

6. Herbert Baker, *Architecture and Personalities* (London: Country Life, 1944), p. 109.

7. Herbert Baker, *Architecture and Personalities* (London: Country Life, 1944), p. 112.

8. Letter from T. E. Lawrence to Herbert Baker, July 5, 1926, RIBA.

9. *The Times*, January 19, 1927.

10. Herbert Baker, *Architecture and Personalities* (London: Country Life, 1944), pp. 74–75.

11. *The Architects' Journal*, February 16, 1927.

12. Gold medal acceptance speech by Herbert Baker, June 24, 1927, RIBA.

13. Commonwealth War Graves Commission.

14. Atul Chatterjee is a fascinating example of Anglo-Indian integration. Born in Calcutta, he won a scholarship to Cambridge where he sat for and passed the entrance examination for the Indian Civil Service. Returning to India, he enjoyed a very successful career with the ICS. In 1924, following the death of his Indian wife Vina Mookerjee, he married barrister Gladys Mary Broughton and later that year accepted the position as High Commissioner to London, which he held until 1931, after which he served on the Council of India for five years before acting as advisor to the Secretary of State for India.

15. Wordsworth had in fact only leased Allan Bank for three years from 1808. It was bought by Canon Rawnsley who was one of the co-founders of the National Trust in 1915 and he moved into it on his retirement in 1917, shortly after the death of his first wife. He then married his secretary, Eleanor

Foster Simpson, before dying himself on the 28th of May, 1920, leaving Allan Bank to the National Trust, having secured a lifetime's tenancy for his widow Eleanor. She remained there until her death in 1959, during which time she often hosted and maintained her regular correspondence with the Bakers.

16. Clayre Percy and Jane Ridley, eds., *The Letters of Edwin Lutyens to His Wife, Lady Emily* (London: Collins, 1985), p. 412.

17. *Country Life*, November 30, 1929.

18. Mary Lutyens, *Edwin Lutyens: By His Daughter* (London: Black Swan, 1991), p. 167.

19. Richard Overy, *The Twilight Years: The Paradox of Britain Between the Wars* (London: Penguin, 2010), p. 96.

20. Herbert Baker, *Architecture and Personalities* (London: Country Life, 1944), p. 114.

21. Herbert Baker, *Architecture and Personalities* (London: Country Life, 1944), p. 114.

22. Herbert Baker, *Architecture and Personalities* (London: Country Life, 1944), p. 115.

23. Herbert Baker, *Architecture and Personalities* (London: Country Life, 1944), p. 131.

24. Roy Macnab, *The Story of South Africa House: South Africa in Britain—The Changing Pattern* (Johannesburg: Jonathan Ball Publishers, 1983), p. 10.

25. Letter from Basil Ionides to *Country Life*, November 26, 1932.

26. Clayre Percy and Jane Ridley, eds., *The Letters of Edwin Lutyens to His Wife, Lady Emily* (London: Collins, 1985), p. 420.

27. Jane Ridley, *Edwin Lutyens, His Life, His Wife, His Work* (London: Pimlico, 2003), p. 376.

28. *The Times*, February 11, 1931.

29. *The Empire Mail*, February 1931.

30. Jane Ridley, *Edwin Lutyens, His Life, His Wife, His Work* (London: Pimlico, 2003), p. 358.

31. Jane Ridley, *Edwin Lutyens, His Life, His Wife, His Work* (London: Pimlico, 2003), p. 380.

32. Memorandum by Herbert Baker on New Delhi, S.S. *Viceroy*, March 1931, RIBA.

33. *Country Life*, June 27, 1931.

34. Letter from Edwin Lutyens to Emily Lutyens, July 3, 1931, RIBA.

Chapter 13

1. Roderick Gradidge in Andrew Hopkins and Gavin Stamp, eds., *Lutyens Abroad: The Work of Sir Edwin Lutyens Outside the British Isles* (London: The British School at Rome, 2002).

2. Letter from Herbert Baker to Vernon Hellbing, December 24, 1930, RIBA.

3. Herbert Baker, *Architecture and Personalities* (London: Country Life, 1944), p. 100.

4. *The London Illustrated News*, March 7, 1931.

5. Minutes of the Bank of England's General Court Meeting, March 19, 1931, Bank of England Archive.

6. Charles Wheeler, *High Relief—The Autobiography of Sir Charles Wheeler Sculptor* (London: Country Life, 1968), p. 63.

7. Charles H. Reilly, *The Banker*, August 1933.

8. *The Daily Herald*, February 2, 1931.

9. Letter from Herbert Baker to General Smuts, March 22, 1934, RIBA.

10. Letter from Herbert Baker to Rudyard Kipling, March 26, 1934, RIBA.

11. Charles Wheeler, *High Relief—The Autobiography of Sir Charles Wheeler Sculptor* (London: Country Life, 1968), p. 61.

12. The previous year, in 1933, a young German architectural historian, Nikolaus Pevsner, had sought refuge in England, only to be appalled that Modernism there was regarded as a subject only suitable for cartoons in *Punch*. He concluded that this rejection of the *Zeitgeist* must be symptomatic of a diseased society.

13. Herbert Baker, *Architecture and Personalities* (London: Country Life, 1944), p. 135.

14. Herbert Baker, *Architecture and Personalities* (London: Country Life, 1944), p. 135.

15. "Lawrence of Arabia," Baker's chapter for a symposium, *By His Friends,* July 24, 1935, RIBA.

16. Letter from Lionel Curtis to Herbert Baker, May 24, 1935, RIBA.

17. Herbert Baker, *Architecture and Personalities* (London: Country Life, 1944), p. 129.

18. Herbert Baker, *Architecture and Personalities* (London: Country Life, 1944), p. 154.

19. Herbert Baker, *Architecture and Personalities* (London: Country Life, 1944), p. 154.

20. Herbert Baker, *Architecture and Personalities* (London: Country Life, 1944), p. 156.

21. Peter Davey, *Arts and Crafts Architecture* (London: Phaidon, 1995), p. 141.

22. Herbert Baker, *Architecture and Personalities* (London: Country Life, 1944), p. 160.

23. James Lees-Milne, *Ancestral Voices 1942–43* (London: Chatto and Windus, 1975).

24. Charles Wheeler, *High Relief—The Autobiography of Sir Charles Wheeler Sculptor* (London: Country Life, 1968), p. 63.

25. Letter from Herbert Baker to Edwin Lutyens, October 7, 1938, RIBA. In fact, it was Baker's one vote that won Lutyens the Presidency at the second ballot.

26. Letter from Edwin Lutyens to Herbert Baker, October 8, 1938, RIBA.

27. Letter from Edwin Lutyens to Herbert Baker, January 28, 1942, RIBA.

28. Herbert Baker, *Architecture and Personalities* (London: Country Life, 1944), p. 156.

29. Herbert Baker, *Architecture and Personalities* (London: Country Life, 1944), p. 160.

30. Letter from Frank Fleming to Herbert Baker, January 1, 1941, RIBA.

31. Letter from Herbert Baker to Edwin Lutyens, February 14, 1941.

32. Lutyens' plan for London was greeted with derision on its publication as it demolished much of what had survived the blitz to create a series of grand Parisian avenues which were ruthlessly driven through what remained of the capital.

33. Letter from Frank Fleming to Herbert Baker, July 22, 1943, RIBA.

34. Ironically, after their duplicity in Lutyens'

attack on Baker, it was *Country Life* who eventually published his autobiography in 1944.

35. Letter from Herbert Baker to William Marris, September 5–6, 1942.

36. Herbert Baker, *Architecture and Personalities* (London: Country Life, 1944), pp. 207–208.

37. Herbert Baker, *Architecture and Personalities* (London: Country Life, 1944), pp. 209–210.

38. Circular letter to his children, July 27, 1945, RIBA.

39. Circular letter to his children, November 5, 1945, RIBA.

40. Circular letter to his children, January 31, 1946, RIBA.

41. Charles Wheeler, *High Relief—The Autobiography of Sir Charles Wheeler Sculptor* (London: Country Life, 1968), p. 57.

42. Letter from Dorothy Ward to Eleanor Rawnsley, February 14, 1946, MB.

Epilogue

1. David Watkin, *Morality and Architecture* (Oxford: Clarendon Press, 1977), p. 95.

2. Nikolaus Pevsner, *Buildings of England: Cambridgeshire* (London: Penguin, 1954), pp. 86–87.

3. Nikolaus Pevsner, *Buildings of England: The City of London* (London: Penguin, 1957), pp. 276.

Bibliography

The principal archives which have been consulted are those of the Royal Institute of British Architects, which holds the majority of Herbert Baker's documents as well as an extensive collection of his drawings; the Bank of England, which has a significant collection of documentation covering the rebuilding of the Bank; the University of Cape Town's Special Collections and Museum Africa in Johannesburg, both of which hold both documents and drawings covering Herbert Baker's work in South Africa; and the considerable private collection of letters, documents, photographs and drawings of Michael Baker, Herbert Baker's eldest grandson.

Abramson, Daniel M. *Building the Bank of England: Money: Architecture: Society: 1694–1942.* Yale University Press, 2005.

Ash, Chris. *The If Man: Dr. Leander Starr Jameson, the Inspiration for Kipling's Masterpiece.* Warwick: Helion, 2012.

Baden-Powell, Robert. *Scouting for Boys.* London: C. Arthur Pearson, 1955.

Baker, Herbert. *Architecture and Personalities.* London: Country Life, 1944.

Baker, Herbert. *Cecil Rhodes by His Architect.* Oxford: Oxford University Press, 1934.

Baker, Michael. *Travels of a Tin Trunk.* Bristol: published by Michael Baker, 2016.

Basdeo, Stephen. "The Public School Ethos and Late Nineteenth Century Juvenile Literature." *PublisHistory Blog*, 2002.

Blomfield, Sir Reginald. *History of Renaissance Architecture in England 1500–1800.* London: Bell, 1897.

Blomfield, Sir Reginald. *Memoirs of an Architect.* London: Macmillan, 1932.

Brand, Robert Henry. *The Union of South Africa.* Oxford: Clarendon Press, 1909.

Bremner, G.A., ed. *Architecture and Urbanism in the British Empire.* Oxford: Oxford University Press, 2016.

Brookner, Anita. *An Iconography of Cecil Rhodes.* London: Rhodes Trust, 1956.

Brown, Jane. *Lutyens and the Edwardians.* London: Viking (Penguin Books Limited), 1996.

Buchan, John. *Memory Hold the Door.* London: Hodder and Stoughton, 1941.

Butler, JRM. *Lord Lothian, Philip Kerr 1882–1940.* London: Macmillan, 1960.

Crawford, Alan. *C.R. Ashbee; Architect, Designer and Romantic Socialist,* Yale University Press, 2005.

Curtis, Lionel. *With Milner in South Africa.* Oxford: Basil Blackwell, 1931.

Davey, Peter. *Arts and Crafts Architecture.* London: Phaidon, 1995.

Draper, Peter, ed. *Reassessing Nikolaus Pevsner.* Farnham: Ashgate Publishing, 2004.

Earle, Sir Lionel. *Turn Over the Page.* London: Hutchinson, 1935.

Fairbridge, Dorothea. *Gardens of South Africa.* London: A&C Black, 1924.

Ferguson, Niall. *Civilization: The West and the Rest.* London: Allen Lane, 2011.

Flint, John. *Cecil Rhodes.* London: Hutcheson, 1976.

Games, Stephen. *Pevsner—The Early Life: Germany and Art.* London: Continuum International, 2010.

Gilmore, David. *The Long Recessional: The Imperial Life of Rudyard Kipling.* London: Pimlico, 2003.

Gilmour, Ian. *Inside Right: A Study of Conservatism.* London: Hutchinson, 1977.

Gradidge, Roderick. *Edwin Lutyens Architect Laureate.* London: George, Allen and Unwin, 1981.

Graves, Robert. *Goodbye to All That.* London: The Folio Society, 1981.

Greig, Doreen E. *Herbert Baker in South Africa.* Cape Town: Purnell, 1970.

Hardinge, Charles. *My Indian Years: 1910–1916, The Reminiscences of Lord Hardinge of Penshurst.* London: John Murray, 1948.

257

Harries, Susie. *Nikolaus Pevsner: The Life.* London: Chatto and Windus, 2011.

Hart-Davis, Duff. *End of an Era: Letters and Journals of Sir Alan Lascelles 1887–1920.* London: Hamish Hamilton, 1988.

Hartoonian, Gevork. *The Mental Life of the Architectural Historian.* Cambridge: Cambridge Scholars Publishing, 1911

Hope, E. *Stanley and Africa.* London: Walter Scott Press, 1902.

Hope, E. *The Life of General Gordon.* Edinburgh: W. P. Nimmo, 1888.

Hopkins, Andrew, and Gavin Stamp, eds. *Lutyens Abroad.* London: The British School at Rome, 2002.

Hussey, Christopher. *The Life of Sir Edwin Lutyens.* London: Country Life, 1950.

Hussey, Christopher. *The Work of Sir Robert Lorimer.* London: Country Life, 1931.

Huxley, Elizabeth. *A White Man's Country, Vol II.* London: Chatto and Windus, 1956.

Irving, Robert Grant. *Indian Summer.* Yale University Press, 1981.

Jackson, Neil. *F. W. Troup. Architect 1859–1941.* London: Building Centre Trust, 1985.

Keath, Michael. *Herbert Baker: Architecture and Idealism 1892–1913: The South African Years.* Gibralter: Ashanti Publishing, 1993.

Keun, Odette. *I Discover the English.* London: John Lane, 1934.

Kipling, Rudyard. *Something of Myself and Other Autobiographical Writings.* Cambridge: Cambridge University Press, 19, 91.

Lawrence, James. *The Rise and Fall of the British Empire.* London: Abacus, 1994.

Lockhart, J. G., and C. M. Woodhouse. *Rhodes.* London: Hodder and Stoughton, 1963.

Longworth, Philip. *The Unending Vigil.* London: Leo Cooper, 2003.

Lutyens, Mary. *Edwin Lutyens: By His Daughter.* London: Black Swan, 1991.

McDonald, J. G. *Rhodes: A Life.* London: Philip Allan and Company, 1952.

Macnab, Roy. *The Story of South Africa House: South Africa in Britain—The Changing Pattern.* Johannesburg: Jonathan Ball Publishers, 1983.

Mangan, J. A., and C. Hickey. "Missing Middle-Class Dimensions: Elementary Schools, Imperialism and Athleticism." *European Sports History Review* 4, 2002, pp.73–90.

Metcalf, Thomas R. *An Imperial Vision: Indian Architecture and Britain's Raj.* London: Faber & Faber, 1989.

Middleton, Robin, and David Watkin. *Neoclassical and 19th Century Architecture.* London: Faber & Faber, 1987.

O'Neill, Daniel. *Sir Edwin Lutyens Country Houses.* London: Lund Humphries, 1980.

Overy, Richard. *The Twilight Years: The Paradox of Britain Between the Wars.* London: Penguin, 2010.

Pakenham, Thomas. *The Boer War.* London: Abacus, 1979.

Paxman, Jeremy. *The English.* London: Penguin Books, 1999.

Percy, Clayre, and Jane Ridley, eds. *The Letters of Edwin Lutyens to His Wife, Lady Emily.* London: Collins, 1985.

Pevsner, Nikolaus. and Bridget Cherry. *London 1, The Cities of London and Westminster,* 3rd Edition. New York: Penguin, 1973.

Plomer, William. *Cecil Rhodes.* London: P. Davies Limited, 1933.

Quennell, Peter. *John Ruskin.* London: Collins, 1949.

Reid, Andrew M., and Paul J. Lane. *African Historical Archaeologies.* Boston: Springer, 2004.

Ridley, Jane. *Edwin Lutyens, His Life, His Wife, His Work.* London: Pimlico, 2003.

Searle, G. R. *A New England? England 1886–1918.* Oxford: Oxford University Press, 2004.

Skelton, Tim, and Gerald Gliddon. *Lutyens and the Great War.* London: Frances Lincoln, 2008.

Smyth, Fiona. *Science, Music, and Architectural Acoustics in Britain (1901–1951).* London: Architectural History, volume 62, 2019

Taine, Hippolyte. *Notes on England.* London: Thames and Hudson, 1958.

Thomas, Roy Digby. *Two Generals: Buller and Botha in the Boer War.* London: Author House, 2012.

Tunzelman, Alex von. *Indian Summer: The Secret History of the End of an Empire.* New York: Simon & Schuster, 2007.

Watkin, David. *A History of Western Architecture,* Third Edition. London: Lawrence King, 2000.

Watkin, David. *Morality and Architecture.* Oxford: Clarendon Press, 1977.

Wheeler, Charles. *High Relief—The Autobiography of Sir Charles Wheeler Sculptor.* London: Country Life, 1968.

Williams, Alpheus. *Some Dreams Come True.* Capetown: Rustica Press, 1947.

Williams, Basil. *Botha, Smuts and South Africa.* London: Hodder and Stoughton, 1946.

Index

Numbers in **bold italics** indicate pages with illustrations

Acropolis 44–45, 74, 89, 113, 118, 140, 141, 214
Agrigentum 43
Aitken, Charles 148, 150–151
Architectural Association 10, 14
Armitage, Joseph 190, 228
Art Workers Guild 15, 177, 230
Arts and Crafts 16, 25, 36–37, 42, 49, 54, 60, 63, 97, 101, 118, 137
Ashbee, Charles Robert 49, 60
Athenaeum Club 159, 205
Athens 43, 44, 46–47

Baden-Powell, Robert 43
Bailey, Abe 58, 91, 94
Baker, Alfred Patrick Edmeades 124, 207
Baker, Allaire (Henry Edmeades) 81, 93, 207, 226
Baker, Ann Mildred Frazer 143, 146, 207
Baker, Arthur 9, 196
Baker, Edward (Ned) 27, 131
Baker, Florence (nee Edmeades) 59, **60**, 65, 67, 77–79, 86, 92–94, 98, 106–110, 112, 114, 116, 123, 127, 134–135, 138, 140–143, 146–149, 153, 151, 162, 178, 180, 182, 187, 207, 213, 224, 226, 235, 239, 240
Baker, Frances Georgiana 5, 146
Baker, Henry 72, 79, 108, 112, **117**, 192, 197, 206, 226
Baker, Lionel 18, 23, 42, 66, 72, 82
Baker, Percy 21, 23, 25, 27, 36, 43, 78
Baker, Thomas Henry 5
Bank of England 2, 3, 5, 144, 171–172, **173**, 174–178, **179**, 180, 183, 185, 192, 186, 187, 194, 204–205, 207–209, 220, **221**, **222**, **223**, 227, **229**, 232–233, **234**
Bannerman, Campbell 77

Barclay's Bank, Cape Town 204, 226
Bedford Court 54
Beit, Alfred 73
Belcaire, Port Lympne 101, 126, 137, **138**
The Big House, Bloemfontein 63, 84
Black, Neil 25
Blackmoor War Memorial Cloister, Hampshire 155
Bloemfontein 62, 67, 70–71, 77, 88
Blomfield, Reginald 16, 42, 100, 104, 109, 152–154, 166, 172, 174, 185, 225
Boer War, First 28
Boer War, Second 50
Bolton, Arthur 185
Booth, George 173, 185, 224, 229
Boschendal 36
Botha, Louis 77, 86–89, 91–96, 101, 168
Braddell, Darcy 14
Brand, Robert Henry 51, 61, 82, 86, 87–88, 174–175, 220, 238
British East India Company 99
British Empire 2, 5, 7, 18, 21, 42–43, 45, 54, 83, 139, 153
British South Africa Company 20, 24, 29, 43, 46, 74
Brodie, John A. 99, 106
Buchan, John 3, 33, 51, 236–238
Burghersdorp 40
Burne Jones, Edward 26
Byron, Robert 214–215

Cairo 44, 139
Cambridge 47
Cape Dutch 23, 39, 41–42, 49, 54, 57, 70, 101, 137, 212
Cape Institute of Architects 50
Cape Town 2, 18, 21, 25, 27, 29, 34, 43, 45, 49, 50–53, 56–58, 62, 64, 72, 74, 80, 83, 88, 94,

98–99, 106, 116, 119, 124, 226, 237
Cape Town Cathedral, St George 37, 75, **76**, 80, 83
Cape Town University 75
Capitoline Hill 45, 113, 118, 140–141
Castle Line Shipping Company 36
Chamberlain, Austin 145
Chaplin, Drummond 68, 92, 154
Chaplin, Marguerite 68, 71
Charles, Ethel Mary 14
Charterhouse School 9
Chelmsford, Lady (Frances Charlotte Guest) 146
Chelmsford, Lord (John Napier Thesiger, Viscount, Viceroy 1916–21) 139, 142–144, 146, 147, 153, 160, 163–165, 171
Chilham Castle 154
Chiswick Bridge 209, **210**
Church House, Westminster 230, **231**, **233**, 236–237
City Club, Cape Town 29, 30, **35**, 36, 45
Cobham 5, 8, 54, 155, 165, 205, 224
Cockerell, Charles 172, 175–176
Collingham Gardens 10, **13**, 14
Connaught, Duke of (Prince Arthur) 94, 99, 157
County of Kent Memorial, Canterbury 155
Crewe, Lord (Robert Offley Ashburton Crewe-Milnes, Marquess of Crewe) 100, 104–107, 115, 150, 238
Cunliffe, Lord (Walter, Baron) 144, 172
Curtis, Lionel 49, 51–52, 54, 57, 61, 67, 77, 86, 107, 164, 189, 217, 227, 238
Curzon, Lord (George Natahniel Curzon, Marquess of Kedleston) 99, 130, 133

Dale Lace, John 54, 70, 72
Dalrymple, William 92, 97
Davis, Sir Edmund 154
Dawber, Guy 12, 14
Dawson, Geoffrey 51, 61, 238
Deanery Garden 55
Delville Wood 149, 166–167, *168*, 199
Donnat, Mrs. 159, 192
Dove, John 53, 61
Downing College, Cambridge 217, 219, *220*
Duncan, Patrick 51, 61, 124, 226, 238
Dunn and Watson Architects 36

Earl of Reading (Rufus Isaacs, Marquess) 176, 181, 192
Elizabeth (Queen; Elizabeth Angela Marguerite Bowes-Lyon) 236
empire clock 77

Faber, Oscar 191, 223
Fairbridge Chapel, Pinjarra 217, *218*
Farrar, George 54, 67
Feetham, Richard 53, 65, 91, 238
Fleming, Frank 67, 70, 92–94, 122–124, 127, 129, 131, 204, 237, 238

Gass, John Bradshaw 14
Geddes, Patrick 99, 160
George V (King; George Frederick Ernest Albert) 99, 113, 127, 133–134, 143, 145, 208, 213
George VI (King, Arthur Frederick Arthur George Windsor, previously Duke of York) 227, 236
George, Ernest 12–14, 16, 23, 39, 43, 81, 137, 145, 195
George, Walter Sykes 132, 134, 142, 182, 190
George Findlay and Company offices 40
Gladstone, Lord Herbert (Viscount) 93, 96, 106, 109
Glenshiel 92, 97, *98*
Glyn Mills Bank 209
Goodenough, Frederick 203, 226
Government House, Nairobi 196
Government House, New Delhi (Viceroy's House) 100, 103–104, 109–110, 113, 124, 127–128, 130–131, 140–142, 144–145, 150, 160, 162, 169, 181, 199, 201, 208
Government House, Pretoria 57, 63, 68, *69*, 75, 77, 88, 106, 121, 175, 196

Gradidge, Roderick 62, 102, 106, 217
Graves, Robert 9
Greenwich Hospital 89, 122, 201
Greig, Doreen 33, 37–38, 57, 75, 118, 123
Grey College, Bloemfontein 62, 71
Groot Drakenstein 36, 72, *73*
Groote Schuur 23, 24–5, 27, 29, 30, 32, 36, 38, *39*, 40, 47, 49, 54, 56, 69, 71, 84, 94–95, 121, 189
Grosvenor, Lord (Hugh Richard Arthur, Duke of Westminster) 63, 67
The Grotto 27, *28*, 33, 43, 45, 60
Guardian Assurance Company Offices 37

Hailey, William Malcolm (Baron) 129, *130*, 141–142, 146–147
Haileybury School 8, 217, 218
Hampshire and Isle of Wight Memorial, Winchester 155
Hardinge, Lady (Winifred Sturt) 112, 128, 130–131, 134, 142
Hardinge, Lord Charles (Baron Hardinge of Penshurst, Viceroy 1910–16) 99, 103–105, 107–108, 113–114, 127–129, 131, 133, 135, 139, 142–143, 145, 147, 150–151, 238
Harrow School War Memorial 157, *158*, 195, 202, 226, 231, 239
Hartley Manor 143
Hastings, Warren 29, 109
Hellbing, Vernon 217, 234
Hichens, Lionel (Nel) 51, 61, 65–66, 69, 108, 175, 189, 232, 236, 237
Hill, Arthur 148, 149
Hill, Claude 144, 163, 169
Holderness, Sir Thomas 106, 109, 150
Hoogterp, Jan 187, 197
Hoover, Pres. Herbert 211
Hudson, Edward 34, 55, 109, 183, 213–214, 216
Hussey, Christopher 16, 81, 95, 126, 128, 140, 191

Imperial Delhi Committee 114, 132, 141, 144, 162
Imperial War Graves Commission 148, 150, 202
Inanda 54
India House (High Commission for India) 203, *204*, 208, 213
Indian Parliament (Council House/Legislative Chamber) 5, 160, 162–3, 178, 181, 187, *188*, *198*, 199, 200, 208

Innes, James Rose 22, 27, 54, 67
Irving, Robert Grant 106
Irwin, Lord (Edward Frederick Lindley Wood, Earl of Halifax, Viceroy 1925–31) 199–200, 201, 213–214

Jacob, Samuel Swinton 105, 109–110, 114
Jameson, Leander Starr 27, 28, 54, 85
Jameson Raid (The Raid) 29, 42–43
Jekyll, Gertrude 17, 40
Johannesburg 18, 29, 50–51, 53, 56–57, 60, 63, 67, 70–72, 75, 77, 92–94, 98–99, 107, 124, 132, 154, 155, 207, 226
Johannesburg Art Gallery 96
Johannesburg Cathedral, St. Mary's 95

Kabete High School, Nairobi 197
Keath, Michael 51
Keeling, Hugh 129, *130*, 131, 139, 141–142, 144, 160, 163, 170–171, 181–182, 185, 192, 216
Kendall, Franklin Kaye 29, 31, 34, 40, 45, 56, 58, 62, 67, 71, 77, 91, 94, 101, 106, 124
Kensington Museum 10, 11
Kenyon, Sir Frederick 151–152
Kerr, Philip (Lord Lothian) 51, 61, 128, 194–196, 205, 210, 234, 237, 238
Kimberley 20, 42, 43, 62
The Kimberley Honoured Dead Memorial *46*, 47, 51, 74, 121
Kipling, Rudyard 2, 18, 27, 47–48, 62, 72, 78, 101, 126, 153, 189, 206, 224, 227, 236
Kruger, Paul 43, 58

Ladysmith 43
Lanchester, Henry Vaughan 99, 103
Lane, Hugh 94–96
Lang, Cosmo Gordon (Archbishop of Canterbury) 232
Languedoc 36
Law Courts, Nairobi 196, *197*
Lawley, Arthur 57
Lawrence, Thomas Edward (of Arabia) 3, 133, 153–154, 164–165, 192, 199, 206, 227, 236
Lethaby, William Richard 15, 26, 177–178
Lloyd George, David 145
London House (Goodenough College) 226, 231–232
Lord's Cricket Ground 159
Lubbock, Cecil 171–175, 177–

178, 180, 182, 185, 189, 190, 224

Lutyens, Edwin 2, 3, 12, 15, 16, 22, 34, 40, 42, 47, 54, 55, 61–62, 78, 80–82, 90, 94–95, 100, 102–114, *115*, 123–124, 126–129, 131–135, 138–139, 141–142, 144–147, 149, 150–154, 159–163, 169, 171, 174, 176, 180–183, 185, 187, 190, 195, 199, 201, 208, 211, 213–217, 225, 235–238, 241

Lutyens, Emily (Lytton) 55, 81, 128, 133, 139, 146, 151, 162, 181, 213–214

Lutyens, Mary 191–192

Mafeking 43
Manchip, Herbert J. 164
Marienhof 68, 70, 92, 154
Marks, Samuel 58
The Marks Building 58, 62, 67, 71
Marshcourt 55
Martins Bank 209
Mary (Queen; Victoria Mary Augusta Louise Olga Pauline Claudine Agnes) 145, 147, 150, 213, 232
Masey, Francis Edward 30, 31, 34, 36–37, 40, 42, 45, 49, 50, 56, 58, 62–64, 67, 70, 72, 75, 77, 80, 83, 91–93, 96
Medd, Henry 190, 201
Medical Research Institute, Johannesburg *122*
Memorial Baths 45
Meopham 7, 155
Merriman, Agnes 21
Merriman, John 21, 85, 93
Milner, Lord Alfred (Viscount) 29, 50–54, 57, 61, 67, 70, 77–78, 83, 105, 145, 147, 194–195, 236
Moffat, J.B. 22
Montagu, Edwin 111, 153, 171, 176
Morris, William 15
Muizenberg 41, 49, 53, 54, 58, 62, 82, 93, 107, 151, 226
Murray, Charles 92, 122

Nakuru School, Nairobi 197
National Mutual Life of Australasia Company building 40, 72, 75
Ness, George 25
Neuve Chappele 166, 188, 199, 202
New Delhi (Imperial Delhi) 2, 3, 5, 47, 81, 100, 103–108, 110, 116, 121–123, 128, 131–133, 137, 139–141, 144–146, 149, 160, 166, 169–171, 180, 185–186, 189, 190, 192, 194, 198, 207–208, 214–217, 224, 236, 238

Nicholls, Henry 115, 128
Nicholson, William 133
Nicholson, Rear Admiral 21, 31
Ninth Church of the Christ Scientist 203, 205, *206*, 208, 231
Nooitgedacht, Stellenbosch 42
Noordhoek 154
Norman, Montague 172, 176, 189
Northwards 54, 67, 72
Nurstead Court 7, 54, 59–60, 65–66, 98, 123, 126, 128, 232

Orange Free State 28, 43, 57, 62, 77
Owletts 5, 17, 43–44, 65–66, 71, 78, 98, 123, 128, 131, 139, 143, 146–147, 151, 169, 175, 185–186, 205–207, 232, 235, 239
Oxford University 20, 33, 47, 56, 194

Paestum 43, 44, 45
Palermo 44
Pantheon 45
Perry, J.F. (Peter) 52
Peto, Harold Ainsworth 12–13
Pevsner, Nikolaus 2, 60, 223, 241
Phillips, Florence 82, 84–85, 94–95, 116, 226
Phillips, Lionel 82, 95
Pickstone, Harry 21, 23
Plas Mar, Conwy 12
Pretoria 47, 50, 57–58, 75, 89, 99–100, 116, 135, 201, 226
Pretoria Railway Station 85, *87*, 89, 91, 105, 174
Prince of Wales (Edward Albert Christian George Andrew Patrick David Windsor, later King Edward VIII) 138, 181, 227
Prior, Edward Schroeder 26
Processional Way (King's Way) 113, 115, 124, 128, 134–135, 140, 161, 164, 169, 171, 181–182, 213, 215
Pugin, Augustus Welby 15

Rand Regiment Memorial 95–96
Rawnsley, Eleanor 206, 240
Read, Herbert 14
Rees-Poole, Vernon 30, 49
Rendall, Montague 155, 206, 218, 232
Reserve Bank, Pretoria 204
The Retreat, Government House 49, 52
Rhodes, Cecil 2, 20, 23–5, 28–29, 31–34, 36, 38–39, 42–45, 47–48, 50, 54, 56, 58, 63, 71, 74–75, 78, 81, 98, 100, 102, 118,

154, 194–196, 218, 224, 236, 239
The Rhodes Building 43, 45, *48*, 49, 51, 67, 123
Rhodes College 94
Rhodes House 194
The Rhodes Memorial 71- 73, *74*, 77, 83, 94, 101, *102*
Rhodesia 28, 49, 83, 88, 91–92, 96
Ridley, Jane 14, 34, 81, 94, 127, 128, 175
Rochester Memorial 155
Roedean School, Johannesburg 67
Rose Innes, James 22
The Round Table 105, 139, 227, 236
Royal Academy 10, 17, 152, 191, 205, 221, 222, 235–238
Royal Empire Society 227, *228*, 232, 237
Royal Institute of British Architects (RIBA) 2, 10, 17, 43, 82, 97, 99, 144, 172, 202, 205, 208, 236
Rust en Vrede 58, *59*, 68, 91, 94

St. Alban Cathedral, Pretoria 80
St. Andrew's, Great Ilford 186
St. Andrew's, Newlands 25, *26*, 27, 36, 45
St. Barnabas, Tamboerskloof 29, 36
St. Boniface, Germiston 80
St. Faith's Church Memorial, Overbury 155
St. George's, Cullinan 67
St. John the Baptist, Mafeking 49
St. John the Divine, Randfontein 67
St. Michael and All Angels, Observatory 38
St. Michael and All Angels, Pretoria 80, 92
St. Padern, Llanberis 11, 25
St. Paul's, Woldingham 217
St. Philips, Woodstock 38, 45
Salisbury Cathedral, Rhodesia 96, 97
Sandhills 41, 42, 54, 62, 67, 72, 87, 124
Sassoon, Philip Albert Gustave David (Baronet) 101, 108, 132, 137, 139, 151, 154
Sauer, Hans 23, 85
Schultz, Robert Weir 14
Scott, Alexander Thomson 132, 159, 164, 166, 186, 190–191, 199, 203–204, 217, 219, 223, 224, 226–228, 234, 237, 239
Scott, George Gilbert 10

Scott Polar Research Institute 219
The Secretariats (Indian Government Buildings) 5, 104, 121–122, 125, 128, 130, 162, 169, *170*, 178, 181, 184, 190, *200*, 201, 207, *209*, 214, *215*
Segesta 44, 75
Selbourne, Lady (Maud Gascoyne-Cecil) 77, 88–89, 93, 155
Selbourne, Lord (William Waldegrave Palmer) 77, 88, 155, 175
The Shangani Memorial 43, 46–47, 56
Shaw, Richard Norman 10, 15, 16, 37, 54, 105
Sloper, Ernest Willmott 55, 57, 62–63, 67, 70, 72, 75
Smuts, Gen. Jan 2, 77, 86, 88, 95–96, 109, 116, 143, 206, 210, 211, 224–225, 238, 240
Soane, John 2, 3, 174–177, 179, 180, 183–184, 187, 190–191, 193, 204, 212, 217, 220–222, 232–233
Solomon, Edward Phillip 87, 88
Solomon, Joseph M. 75, 95
South Africa House 211, *212*, 227
South African Association Headquarters 40
South African Institute of Medical Research 101
South African Republic 28, 43

South African Society of Architects 49–50
Stellenbosch 21
Stent, Sydney 29, 40
Stokesay Castle 17
Stonehouse 53, 57, 60, *61*, *62*, 67, 79, 92, 124
Streuben, H.W. 27, 40–41
Swan, John 78, 101
Swinton, George 99, 106, 112, 127
Syracuse 44–45

Taylor, Robert 173, 175–176, 184, 193, 217
Thebes 43
Tokai 22
Tonbridge School 8–9
Transvaal 28, 54, 57, 63, 71, 77, 86, 91, 100, 122, 204
Transvaal Institute of Architects 75
Troup, Francis William 173, 176, 183, 187, 223
Tweed, John 39, 46, 189
Tyne Cot 166–167, *167*, 199, 202

Uitlanders 28
Union Buildings (South African government buildings) 5, 89, 92, *93*, 94, 97–99, 105, 109, 116–117, *118*, *120*, *121*, 123, 157, 174–175, 178, 184
Union Club, Johannesburg 101, 123
Union Parliament 91

Villa Arcadia 82, 84, *85*, 86, 92, 94–95, 97, 226
Villa D'Este, Tivoli 12, 45, 75, 109
Vintcent, Lewis 21

Walcot, William 126, 140
Walgate, Charles Percival 126, 131–132, 134, 144, 166
Ware, Fabian 147–148, 150–154
Waterhouse, Paul 185
Webb, Aston 185
Welgelegen Manor 42, 100, *101*
Westminster Abbey 5, 159
Wheeler, Charles 31, 165, 189, 192, 206, 212, 219, 220–221, 225, 227–229, 235, 238–239
The White House 57
Whitmell, Charles 9
Williams, Alpheus 33
Wilson and Miller Department Store 40
Winchester Assize Courts 217
Winchester College 108–109, 155, 218
Winchester College War Memorial 155, *156*, 195, 202, 239
The Woolsack 43, *47*, 48, 51, 78, 95
Wordsworth, William 9
Wren, Christopher 42
Wynberg Boys High School 22
Wyndam, Hugh 51, 238

The Yarrows 135, *136*